Fort Robinson and the American West, 1874–1899

The namesake of Fort Robinson, Lt. Levi H. Robinson, Fourteenth Infantry, was killed near Laramie Peak on February 9, 1874. Unless otherwise noted, all photographs are from the Nebraska State Historical Society.

Fort Robinson and the American West, 1874–1899

by Thomas R. Buecker

For Mark —
Enjoy this tale of old
Fort Robinson —
Tom Buecker
10-17-00

Nebraska State Historical Society

Portions of chapters 4 and 7 appeared in "'Can You Send Us Immediate Relief?': Army Expeditions to the Northern Black Hills, 1877–1878," *South Dakota History* (Summer 1995): 97–115, and "The 1887 Expansion of Fort Robinson," *Nebraska History* 68 (Summer 1987): 83–93.

Library of Congress Catalog Card Number: 98-68787
ISBN 0-933307-26-8

This book is printed on acid-free paper.
Find more books at www.nebraskahistory.org

Publication of this book was made possible by The Ronald K. and Judith M. Stolz Parks Publishing Fund established at the Nebraska State Historical Society Foundation, and use of this Fund for this purpose is made in memory of Wayne Kemper Parks (1909–1995) and Hazel Viriginia Hill Parks (1911–1991), lifelong Nebraskans who were born on Madison County farms, were married on March 19, 1930, and were farmers in Madison and Pierce counties.

Contents

Illustrations

Figures

frontispiece
Lt. Levi H. Robinson

following page 76
Red Cloud Agency, 1876
John J. Saville
Frank Appleton
Red Cloud
Col. John E. Smith
Sketch of the first Camp Robinson
Capt. William H. Jordan
Lt. Jesse M. Lee
Camp Sheridan
Earliest known photograph of Camp Robinson, 1875
West barracks
Capt. Emmet Crawford
Red Dog's village
Post trader's store
Struggling through a blizzard
Gen. George Crook
Col. Ranald S. Mackenzie
Ninth Infantry camp
Camp Custer
Crowd scene at Red Cloud Agency, Oct. 24, 1876
Lakota records of historic events
Arapaho tribal leaders, 1877
Surrender of Crazy Horse's band
Lakota Sun Dance
Touch the Clouds
Little Big Man

following page 148
Officers at Camp Robinson, 1877
Colonel Bradley's quarters
Stabbing of Crazy Horse
Crazy Horse's first grave
Angeline Johnson
Little Wolf and Dull Knife

Fort Robinson, 1878
"The Latest Illustration of Our Humane Indian Policy"
Cheyenne Outbreak, Jan. 9, 1879
Antelope Creek fight by Frederic Remington
Freight train at Fort Robinson depot
Construction of the new officers' row
1887 barracks interior
Field ordnance at Fort Robinson
Lt. John H. Alexander
Lt. Charles Young
Col. Edward Hatch
Troop K, Ninth Cavalry
Portraits of Fort Robinson soldiers
Ninth Cavalry noncommissioned officers
Ninth Cavalry drill
"The Pursuit" by Frederic Remington
Guard and prisoner detail
Main post, 1893
Old buildings on original parade ground

Maps

Preface and Acknowledgments

Fort Robinson played a vital part in the story of the American West. One of the most important military posts of the Indian wars, Fort Robinson, Nebraska, "survived" after the peace because of its advantageous location on the railroad. The United States Army used the fort longer, from 1874 to 1948, than any other Indian wars post on the upper Plains, with one exception.*

Notwithstanding its important role, no complete history of Fort Robinson has been written, a somewhat surprising omission. Early histories of other notable army forts, such as those for Fort Laramie, Wyoming, and Fort Sill, Oklahoma, and more recent works on Fort Meade, South Dakota, and Fort D. A. Russell, Wyoming, have appeared, placing those posts in their proper context in Western history.

In its early years Fort Robinson continually received prominent mention in the contemporary press, a dateline where important events occurred. The press steadily reported the significant events that took place there in the 1870s, such as the surrenders of the northern Lakota bands, the death of Crazy Horse, and the Cheyenne Outbreak. After the wars ended, Fort Robinson was portrayed as one of the largest and most notable of America's military establishments, "a famous Nebraska post."

Because of the dramatic and sometimes tragic events that the fort witnessed, general histories of the Indian wars invariably mention it as a key location. Early historians, including George Bird Grinnell and E. A. Brininstool, and writers, such as Howard Fast, Mari Sandoz, and Dee Brown, chronicled specific historical episodes. In some early works, however, both misconception and misinformation often appeared, unfortu-

---

*Fort D. A. Russell (est. 1867), at Cheyenne, Wyoming, was renamed Fort Francis E. Warren in 1930. In 1948, the year the army left Fort Robinson, the post was transferred from the army to the fledgling United States Air Force. Today as Francis E. Warren Air Force Base the old post remains an active military installation.

nately to be repeated by subsequent uncritical use of those sources.

Fort Robinson has also been the topic of several academic theses, including one by this author. But again, those works have treated only specific and restricted periods in the fort's history. A recent study, originally a Ph.D. dissertation by historian Frank N. Schubert, gives an excellent portrayal of the years when the Ninth and Tenth Cavalry regiments were stationed there. Fort Robinson frequently appears in scholarly journals and publications as modern researchers and historians attempt to fill the gaps of Western history. Such works merely provide vignettes from Fort Robinson's long history. Although the fort is well-documented, and its historical significance clearly known, Fort Robinson's history has thus far failed to receive full-length, comprehensive treatment. This is half of that undertaking, the first of a two-volume history of Fort Robinson, and it covers the nineteenth century.

The creation of the Fort Robinson Museum by the Nebraska State Historical Society provided the eventual vehicle for such an undertaking. The establishment of this facility served as an impetus to gather materials and create a repository to store information on all aspects of the post's colorful and exciting history. After years of this kind of effort the time has come to put pen to paper and place the post in its proper context within the western experience and America's military past. This book is the result.

A project of this magnitude succeeds only after numerous contacts with a multitude of helpful historians, fellow workers, and friends. To all of them I am indebted. They assisted in gathering useful information and suggested how to present it. Without their help this story of Fort Robinson would have been impossible to craft.

First, I would like to express my appreciation to Larry Sommer, director of the Nebraska State Historical Society, and Lynne Ireland, museum director, for their support and interest in my work. Likewise, Brent Carmack, head of the Historical Society branch museums and my immediate supervisor, was always extremely supportive and understanding as I pursued this undertaking. The collective members of the Society staff constantly stood ready to provide reference materials and photographs in the course of my research. Patiently answering the call were our archivists and librarians, particularly Cynthia Monroe and Marty Miller. Deb Brownson designed and layed out the book, Steve Ryan designed the dust jacket, Dell Darling drew the maps, and Pat Gaster put together the index.

Two long-time colleagues warrant special mention. Eli Paul, senior research historian and my good friend, has always been of key assistance and counsel to my various projects over the past two decades. And for the same period, James Potter, editor of *Nebraska History*, was always ready to contribute information and constructive criticism that invariably improved my work. To Eli and Jim, thanks, good fellows.

Staff of various federal and military archives are most certainly deserving of my salute for their patience and assistance while working with their collections. At the National Archives, Michael Musick, Michael Meier, and William Lind, who opened a plethora of original fort documents and records, helped make the long-distance trips to Washington worthwhile. Additionally the staffs of the United States Military Academy Library at West Point and the U.S. Army Military History Institute at Carlisle Barracks provided copies of valuable research papers in their respective collections. At Fort Laramie National Historic Site, the "founding father" of Fort Robinson, Steve Fullmer and Sandra Lowry were always most helpful.

Thanks are also due to key historical organizations and libraries, primarily the South Dakota State Historical Society in Pierre, the Wyoming State Division of Cultural Resources and Archives in Cheyenne, the Denver Public Library, and the Nebraska Library Commission in Lincoln.

A number of individual historians of the frontier army were very supportive of this work from the onset. From the National Park Service, professional associates and close friends Jerome Greene, Paul Hedren, and Douglas McChristian freely provided advice and continual encouragement. John D. "Jack" McDermott of Sheridan, Wyoming, was always willing to provide information and materials as well as good fellowship. Robert Utley, whose knowledge and work we have all admired, kindly offered valuable suggestions.

Many historian friends have graciously shared information and sources used in this book, including: Robert Lee, Sturgis, South Dakota; the late Charles Hanson, The Museum of the Fur Trade, Chadron, Nebraska; Chris Nelson, Annandale, Virginia; Gerald Adams, Cheyenne, Wyoming; Carol Breuer, Fort Collins, Colorado; Ramon Powers, Kansas State Historical Society, Topeka, Kansas; Pamela Robinson, Downers Grove, Illinois; and Dr. James Wengert, Omaha, Nebraska. Ephriam Dickson, Houston, Texas, a former seasonal employee at the Fort Robinson Museum, provided key information on the last days of Crazy Horse. Joining this fine group is Frank Schubert, historian with the Office of the Chairman of the Joint Chiefs of Staff in the Pentagon. "Mick" taught us what we know about the "buffalo soldiers" and willingly shared his knowledge of their service at Robinson.

James Hanson, while he was director of the Nebraska State Historical Society, urged me to write the history of Fort Robinson and got me started. Thanks, Jim, for both friendship and faith—you know what I mean. Because part of this project originated as my Master's thesis at Chadron

State College, it is fitting to recognize the members of my committee: Richard Loosbrock, Thomas Detwiller, and Rolland Dewing, who was also my advisor. Edwin Bieganski of Chadron, himself a veteran of service at Fort Robinson, read the original draft. Over the years several personal associates were especially encouraging in this project and shared my interest in Fort Robinson: Robert McCaffree, Sterling, Colorado; Harry Burk, Hermosa, South Dakota; Loren Pospisil, Bayard, Nebraska; Doug Scott, Lincoln, Nebraska; and Roye Lindsay, Fort Hartsuff State Historical Park at Burwell, Nebraska. And I thank them for that.

Private individuals providing photos include Eleanor Roubique, Arvada, Colorado, who donated to the Society the earliest known photograph of Camp Robinson, and Jack Ringwalt of San Francisco, California, for use of items from his private collection.

In the long course of research, preparation, and writing, thanks are overdue to my fellow workers at the Fort Robinson Museum—Rebecca Serres, Steven Scoggan, and Terry Steinacher—for support, assistance, patience, and cooperation, which I greatly appreciate.

A very special thanks goes to Ron and Judy Parks, whose interest in the work of the Nebraska State Historical Society and generosity has made publication of this history possible.

On a personal note, to Kay, Michael, and Anne, thank you for understanding and accepting the time lost to you while I was working on this project.

Finally, I wish to dedicate this book to Rev. John Steffenson (1897–1978), who first interested me in history.

Thomas R. Buecker
Fort Robinson, Nebraska

and then became the commanding general of the Department of the Missouri, a subdivision of the Division of the Missouri, which then included Missouri, Kansas, Indian Territory, Colorado Territory, and New Mexico Territory. As a brigadier general, he led successful winter campaigns, most notably the Washita Campaign of 1868–69, against hostile groups and compiled an enviable record as an Indian fighter.

Although Sheridan thought acculturation was the answer to the growing "Indian problem," he also believed the army should police the Indians and severely punish crimes or acts of war against the whites. More important Sheridan held a philosophy of total war—bringing the horrors of war to a civilian population—a brutal concept that eventually proved successful in the military subjugation of the Plains Indian.

In 1869 President Grant appointed Sheridan lieutenant general in command of the Division of the Missouri. Its principal department and the one important to this story was the Department of the Platte, consisting of Iowa, Nebraska, and the territories of Wyoming and Utah. With a large measure of autonomy, ample access to knowledge of local conditions, and strategically headquartered in Omaha, the department commander was considered the key link in the frontier army chain of command. In 1874 that link was Edward O. C. Ord, an 1839 graduate of West Point who had risen to the rank of major general of volunteers in the Civil War. He received the permanent rank of brigadier general in 1866 and commanded the Department of California before moving to the Platte late in 1871. Characterized as honest while impulsive, he was described by Sherman as a "rough diamond, always at work in the most distant frontier." Although Ord worked through his subordinates on campaign planning, he remained secretive and used what some thought devious methods to achieve his ends. According to frontier military historian Robert M. Utley, Ord's relations with division commander Sheridan "varied between frigidity and hostility."

In 1874 Ord's department contained fourteen army posts garrisoning a total of 4,762 officers and enlisted men, divided into twenty cavalry and fifty infantry companies. The nearest troop stations to northwestern Nebraska were Forts Laramie and Fetterman on the North Platte River. South along the Union Pacific, soldiers were located at Sidney Barracks at Sidney, Nebraska, and at North Platte Station and Fort McPherson near the forks of the Platte River. One hundred miles west of Sidney on the railroad sat the large post of Fort D. A. Russell at Cheyenne, Wyoming Territory. Additional troops at other posts on the railroad, mainly Omaha Barracks, Nebraska, Forts Sanders and Fred Steele, Wyoming, and Camp Douglas, Utah, could be rapidly sent to trouble areas via the Union

Pacific. Soldiers also manned posts along the Missouri River, but were several hundred miles distant by overland march from the western Sioux range. Fort Laramie was ultimately the nearest military post to the White River country and the logical point from which troops could be dispatched should the need arise.

Meanwhile the long-running controversy over which government entity, military or civil, should have control over the Plains Indian remained a heated debate. Until 1849 the War Department had complete charge of all Indian affairs. Control was then transferred to the newly created Bureau of Indian Affairs in the Department of the Interior. The bureau became responsible for negotiating treaties, distributing annuity goods, and mediating between whites and Indians, all in an attempt to influence the tribes to accept and conform to government policies. Always opposed to the "mailed fist" of the military in its Indian dealings, eastern humanitarians welcomed the change.

As settlement continued apace in western regions, however, it became evident that the government lacked any clear Indian policy, one that satisfied all parties involved. The inability to draw distinctions between peaceful and warring elements of the same tribal groups created more difficulties. With no central control by any single Indian leader, and rabid expansionism urged by westerners, government policies or treaties often proved worthless. Both western settlers and government officials grew frustrated. By 1874 Grant's administration was wracked with charges of fraud and corruption and found itself unable to formulate or enforce a policy protecting the Plains Indian way of life. The failure to arrive at a civilian consensus on a policy fair to the Indian side ultimately resulted in a long-term military presence in northwestern Nebraska.

After the first turbulent years of Camp Robinson, the post evolved to reflect other important themes of frontier military history and of the army's changing role in the late nineteenth century. Camp Robinson, eventually to become Fort Robinson, serves well as a microcosm. The fort's role changed from agency protector to reservation guardian after the Oglalas, Cheyennes, and Arapahos left the immediate area in 1877.

Ironically, as Sioux reservation lands shrank in the following years, Fort Robinson's importance as a military troop station grew. Undoubtedly this new role was due to the arrival of the railroad in the mid-1880s and coincided with the army's evolution from a purely military force used against the Plains Indian to a domestic police force. No longer solely defending the frontier, troops boarded the train to protect property during labor strikes and other civil unrest. The soldiers certainly did not desire this type of duty, but performed with obedience, a characteristic of the Old Army.

Additionally, a landmark breakthrough in racial equality came with the garrisoning of African Americans to posts such as Fort Robinson. For sixteen years the majority of its troops were the "buffalo soldiers" of the Ninth and Tenth Cavalry.

As the end of the nineteenth century neared, and although the army's mission had changed considerably, the basics of "soldiering," the customs and the daily routine, remained remarkably similar for soldiers at posts across the country. The regular army officers and enlisted men, some of whom had served since the Civil War, were yet present when the closing shots in the long conflict on the Plains were fired in 1890–91.

The end of the frontier army came with the sinking of the battleship *Maine* in 1898. Our little, domestic army became a large, imperial force, with overseas duty during the Spanish-American War and in our newly-gained foreign possessions. As the twentieth century dawned, Fort Robinson reflected the effects of the closing of an old frontier and the opening of a new one .

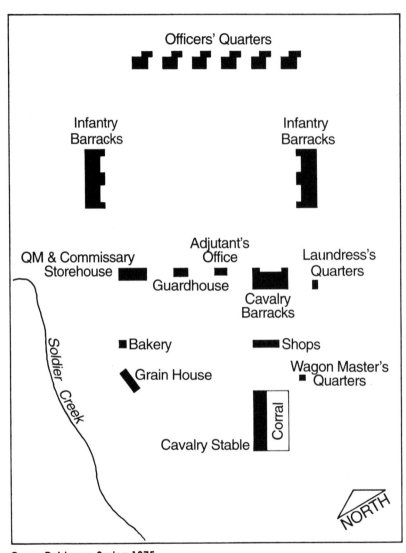

Camp Robinson, Spring 1875

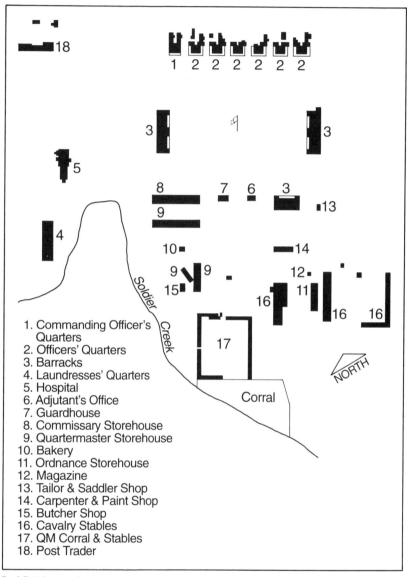

1. Commanding Officer's
   Quarters
2. Officers' Quarters
3. Barracks
4. Laundresses' Quarters
5. Hospital
6. Adjutant's Office
7. Guardhouse
8. Commissary Storehouse
9. Quartermaster Storehouse
10. Bakery
11. Ordnance Storehouse
12. Magazine
13. Tailor & Saddler Shop
14. Carpenter & Paint Shop
15. Butcher Shop
16. Cavalry Stables
17. QM Corral & Stables
18. Post Trader

Fort Robinson, September 1879

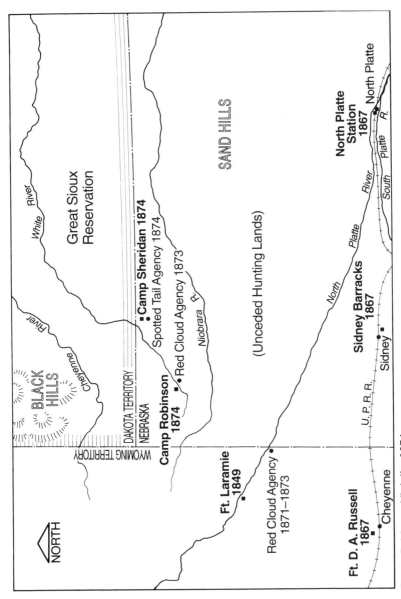

Camp Robinson Vicinity, 1874

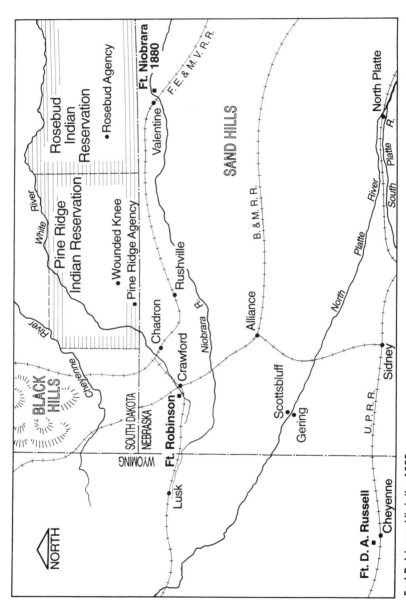

Fort Robinson Vicinity, 1899

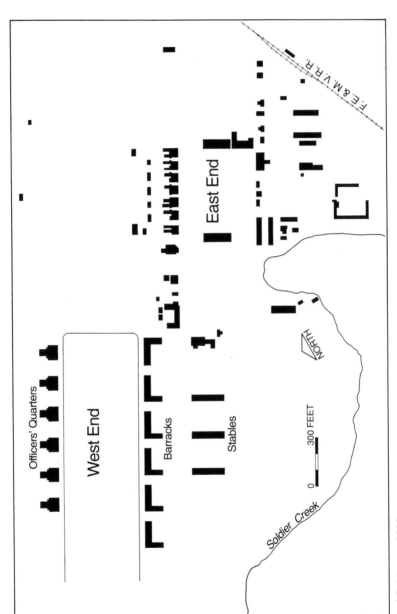

Fort Robinson, 1888

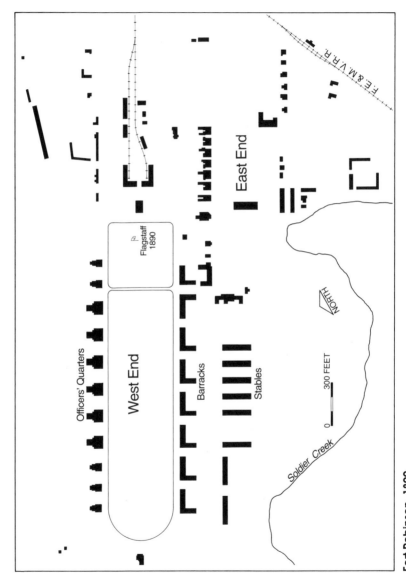

Fort Robinson, 1899

Chapter 1

The Soldiers Come

The Fort Laramie Treaty of 1868 begat the Red Cloud Agency, and Red Cloud Agency begat Camp Robinson. The treaty optimistically declared, "From this day forward all war between the parties to this agreement shall forever cease."[1] Besides bringing an uneasy peace to the northern Plains, the treaty created the Great Sioux Reservation and its associated agencies for the Indian people who signed, including the defiant Oglala Lakotas. In fact, one of the agreement's main objectives had been to secure peace with the Oglalas, who had proved worthy adversaries to westward expansion.

The purpose of any agency was as an administrative center for a particular tribe under the supervision of an appointed Indian agent. It also served as the distribution point for government-issued rations and annuity goods guaranteed by the treaty. Eventually the agents inaugurated schools to educate the young and to provide a program of agricultural training for adult men. They hoped the process would gradually transform the hunters and warriors into productive farmers, following the white man's way of life.

The agencies were supposed to be located along the Missouri River, where navigation eased the problem of transporting the vast amounts of subsistence and material goods necessary to placate the often belligerent Sioux.[2] In addition, the forts along the river kept the Indians under close military observation. Although all of this sounded good in theory, the Oglala and Brulé Sioux did not want to move to the river; they preferred inland agency sites in traditional hunting areas. Locating agencies proved a continual point of contention between the Indians and whites.[3]

Because of the failure of previous Indian policies to bring peaceful coexistence, many reformers and politicians were ready for a change of approach in Indian–white relations. Violent military actions, such as the attack on a Cheyenne village along the Washita in 1868 and another against the Piegan tribe in northwest Montana, led to dissatisfaction among Indian sympathizers. In the latter incident several Piegan Indians had been accused of committing depredations against white settlers. In retaliation in January 1870 a strong cavalry and mounted infantry force commanded by Maj. Eugene M. Baker, Second Cavalry, attacked and destroyed a Piegan village on the Marias River. In the resulting slaughter, 173 Piegans were killed. Humanitarians saw the affair simply as a massacre of peaceful Indians. Although Baker had been cited for "zeal and energy" in previous actions against hostile bands, the senseless carnage on the Marias tarnished his image.[4]

Some months earlier, a group of Quaker leaders had called on President Ulysses S. Grant and offered a possible solution to the Indian problem. Grant possessed no firm Indian policy and exhibited an open-mindedness to remedy a difficult political situation for his administration. The plan the Quakers proposed became known as the "Peace Policy." There was really nothing new in their approach. Its basic tenet was to concentrate Indian tribes on reservations and "civilize" them through education and agricultural self-support. What the Friends really wanted was to have religious denominations nominate the agents and thereby inject a dose of Christian influence into the process. They proposed the creation of a board of Indian commissioners, also church appointed, to oversee Indian administration and to help in the decision-making. An act of Congress created the board on April 10, 1869. Composed of prominent citizens who served without pay, the board began supervision of Indian affairs.[5]

Although the new Quaker policy held promise, some whites wanted control over the Indians to remain with the U.S. Army. Disillusionment with the army as the enforcer of Indian policy, though, grew particularly vocal after the Baker Massacre, and it appeared the army would henceforth play a minor role during the new peace policy era.

The selection of church groups to appoint agents and to supervise agency affairs began. The Episcopalians were given charge of the largest and most powerful group of Lakotas, the Oglalas. Led by the militarily accomplished and politically astute Red Cloud, the Oglalas proved one of the largest and most difficult obstacles to the peace policy's success. The Episcopal agents in charge of Red Cloud's agency soon became aware of this fact.[6]

After the Fort Laramie Treaty the Oglalas, along with the Brulés under Spotted Tail, and other tribes, gathered at the post to receive their annuity goods, but too many whites lived nearby or passed through the area to establish an agency at that point. Officials concluded that the new treaty agency had to be located farther from the fort. The Brulés moved away first to the White River country far to the north and east. As early as 1871 some considered also moving Red Cloud's Oglalas to the White River.[7]

The Oglalas were reluctant to leave the Fort Laramie area. They believed all the land around the post was theirs. Red Cloud himself had declared, "The bones of Oglalas are there all around that fort."[8] Moreover, at the 1868 treaty signing, the Oglalas had been led to believe they would be allowed to trade at Laramie. In 1871 their agency was moved some thirty miles below Fort Laramie on the North Platte River, and Dr. Jared M. Daniels arrived in March 1872 as the new agent. Daniels, described as a "good sensible Christian man," had previously served as Indian agent at Lake Traverse, Minnesota. Soon after his arrival the necessary agency buildings were constructed, but the river site proved unsatisfactory; the North Platte Valley offered an inadequate source of fuel—firewood—for the thousands of Sioux gathered at the new agency. Raids and depredations against white targets in the vicinity brought renewed pressure to relocate the Oglala agency in a less settled area. Daniels began negotiations with Red Cloud and other tribal leaders to do just that.

In April 1872 Daniels convinced the Oglala hierarchy to move the agency to White River and traveled with a delegation, which included Red Dog, leader of the strongest group of northern Oglalas, to select a new site. Later that summer Red Cloud went to Washington, where in the presence of President Grant and Secretary of the Interior Columbus Delano he agreed to the move. The secretary warned Red Cloud, however, that an agency on White River might be in Nebraska and not on his reservation lands, in which case the agency eventually would have to be moved again. Delano added that he would try to keep the Indians at the White River location as long as possible, but in September Red Cloud reversed his position and refused to move away from the Platte. In response the Indian bureau threatened to cut off subsistence rations until the Oglalas moved.

After months of haggling, Commissioner of Indian Affairs Edward P. Smith appointed a special commission to persuade the Oglalas to relocate. The commission succeeded in its efforts. The Oglalas agreed to move to White River, as did the Arapahos and Cheyennes who received rations and goods near Fort Laramie. Although the agency was for Red Cloud's people, the latter two tribes were allowed treaty privileges. After nearly two years of frustrated dealings with the Oglalas, however, Daniels resigned. His last official activity was telegraphing Commissioner Smith on August 2, "Agency has gone to place selected."[9]

On August 13, 1873, the new Episcopal appointee, Dr. John J. Saville of Sioux City, Iowa, arrived to take charge of the agency. Saville, originally from Indiana, received his medical training at the University of Michigan before moving to Sioux City in 1856. In 1859 he saw opportunities in Colorado Territory and migrated to Denver. During the Civil War he served as a surgeon with the Second Colorado Infantry. After the war he worked as a government contract surgeon in New Orleans, then returned in 1870 to Sioux City and resumed a medical practice there. On July 7, 1873, he was nominated for an Indian agent's position with the Interior Department. The executive committee of the Indian Commission of the Episcopal Church noted on his nomination, "Dr. Saville's testimonials are very satisfactory."[10]

His military and government service notwithstanding, Saville apparently had nothing in his background that supported his appointment as an Indian agent—particularly at an agency with a reputation for difficulty. Agent selection, the appointment of well-intentioned but inept men, often proved disastrous, a major failing of the Quaker peace policy. Saville admitted that he (and the Indian bureau for that matter) was ill prepared for the trying task ahead:

> Inexperienced in this business myself, and having no one familiar with the forms of business, and without papers, books, or instructions for guides, I was left in a sufficiently embarrassing position to undertake so complicated a business.[11]

But his immediate problem was to move his employees, government property, and a large amount of issue supplies to White River and immediately commence the construction of agency facilities.

The new agency sat near the confluence of Soldier Creek and White River. Offices, a warehouse, stables, and other wooden buildings needed for agency functions were arranged in a two hundred by four hundred foot compound on a bluff above and south of the river. The site possessed water, timber, and bottomland considered sufficient for Indian farming. Daniels declared that no better site was to be found on the Sioux reservation.[12]

The great variations in populations of nearby Indians marked these years of the agency's existence. Together with the assigned Oglalas, Arapahos, and Cheyennes, thousands of non-agency Lakotas came in yearly, particularly during the winter months, to draw free rations. Sans Arcs, Hunkpapas, and Minneconjous, whose proper agencies at that time were located along the Missouri River, often appeared and raised discord among the agency Sioux. At Red Cloud they made demands on Saville and exhibited, as he termed it, "vicious and insolent" behavior.[13] These northern Indians came to the agency expecting to be fed, and the agent was in no position to refuse them. Consequently, for the situation at the agency to remain peaceful, adequate stocks of food and issue supplies needed to be on hand at all times. Before issue goods could be ordered, the agent needed a hard count of the Indians, which led to the call for a census. A myriad of troubles for the novice agent soon ensued.[14]

In November 1873 Saville decided to enumerate the agency Indians, but many Sioux bitterly opposed any type of government counting. Saville ran into immediate obstacles. Once while attempting to count their lodges, he was "arrested" by three hundred of "these wild fellows" and taken to the agency for trial by the angry Indians.[15] Little Wound, a prominent Oglala leader, and Red Cloud rode to Saville's rescue with a large number of armed followers, undoubtedly saving his life. Although Red Cloud extricated Saville from harm's way, he too opposed the census. After this incident agency whites rarely ventured to the camps without an escort of Indian allies.

Saville reported his difficulties to Commissioner Smith; he also warned the commissioner that at any time he might have to call for military assistance. Twice during the month of December the harried agent advised the Indian bureau that soldiers might be needed.[16] In January 1874 Saville finally requested an army post be established at the agency. The Indian bureau agreed because it seemed impossible to conduct a census or to control the agencies without the army's support; however, Lt. Gen. Philip H. Sheridan, commanding general of the Division of the Missouri, opposed military intervention. Along with other high-ranking officers, he thought the Oglala and Brulé agencies should be moved to the Missouri River away from the White River country. He had always maintained that the new White River agency sites were not on the Sioux reservation, but in the state of Nebraska. Besides being stipulated by treaty, he also believed Missouri River locations were more economical to supply, declaring "the expense of supporting the agencies would be much less."[17] Sheridan also thought sending soldiers to Red Cloud Agency would result in hostilities, not to mention the difficulty in moving a large force during the harsh winter season. He promised to consider sending troops in April or May when the weather improved.[18]

The situation at the agencies deteriorated further. Northern Indians, particularly the Minneconjous, were bent on causing trouble for the agents. They were disgusted with the cooperation of the friendly agency Indians and decided to raid south along the Platte Valley. On February 6 several hundred mounted and armed warriors rode to the unfinished agency stockade singing war songs, and the employees scurried into their buildings and barred the doors. The Indians rode around the buildings, shooting out windows and according to one white witness, "whipping themselves into a wild frenzy."[19] The whites dared not shoot back at the Indians, who then defiantly left the agency and headed south. Later that day Edward Gray, a teamster hauling freight from Fort Laramie, was stopped and killed on the Niobrara River, probably by the same parties that terrorized the agencies.

Hostile demonstrations by northern Indians were not limited to the Oglala agency. On February 4 Agent Edwin A. Howard reported to Col. John Smith, commanding officer at Fort Laramie, that a group of Minneconjous had disrupted the beef issue at Spotted Tail. While the agency herders were issuing beef on the hoof, the Minneconjous drove them off and conducted their own issue. One Indian man attempted to shoot Howard, but was prevented from doing so by another. Howard also concluded military force was necessary to maintain control over the agencies. He wrote to Smith at Fort Laramie, "As I may be compelled to call upon you at short notice for military protection, I trust you will be prepared to aid me."[20]

On February 8 Howard reported to Smith that war parties from Red Cloud were out raiding, with agency cattle grazing near the Niobrara River suffering one attack. Saville went that day to Spotted Tail to confer with Howard about a joint call for troops to protect and restore order at the agencies. Downplaying his own recent problems, Saville wrote to Smith, "Knowing that Major Howard was in trouble with these parties, I rode to his agency to see if I could render him any assistance."[21] Before leaving Red Cloud Agency, he delegated his chief clerk (and nephew) Frank Appleton, as acting agent in his absence. Earlier Saville had arranged for several family members, including Appleton, to work at the agency.[22] The die was cast for a dramatic series of events that would bring Camp Robinson into existence.

Dr. Saville had been warned that at least four different Indians had threatened to kill him; after taking over as acting agent, Appleton received a similar warning. An Indian friend told him not to respond if anybody called on him during the night, but Appleton apparently disregarded the warning. Staying as usual in his uncle's residence, a two-story frame structure that stood in the center of the agency compound, Appleton, Dr. Eugene A. Grove, the agency physician, and B. F. Walters, agency trader, retired by 11 P.M. on the evening of February 8. All were asleep in the front room.[23]

Meanwhile a young Minneconjou warrior, bent on revenge, had evidently decided to shoot the agent and found an opportunity. During the day, carpenters had been shingling the warehouse in the southeast corner of the agency stockade. When they quit work, they carelessly left a ladder standing outside the stockade. Although the stockade gates were locked and a watchman was on duty, about 2:00 A.M. on February 9 the intruder climbed the ladder, crossed the wall, and passed the sleeping agency watchman. He unlocked the gate and then crossed the compound to the agent's residence. The noise of the Indian man pressing against the window awakened Walters, who asked what he wanted. The Indian replied that he wanted the agent and beat on the door with his rifle. Appleton, now awake, went to the door and inquired the reason for the disturbance. He faced the Indian for several moments and then called out for the sleeping watchman. When Appleton turned and took one or two steps, the attacker raised his rifle and fired, then ran through the unlocked front gate.

Appleton was hit but did not initially realize how seriously he was wounded. He described his assailant as a Minneconjou man belonging to Lone Horn's band.[24] By 3:50 A.M., though, Appleton had died of his wound, and an Oglala named Afraid of the Eagle was quickly dispatched to Spotted Tail for Saville.

For several days the watchman suffered enormous remorse over his negligence and finally fled the agency. Appleton's corpse was cleaned and shaved, wrapped in a blanket, placed in a pine coffin, and shipped to his hometown of Sioux City for burial. Dr. Grove escorted the remains to Fort Laramie, vowing on arrival "that he will not return to be made a target of."[25]

Before leaving Spotted Tail, Saville and Howard agreed to call in the military. Howard telegraphed the commissioner of Indian affairs and asked for soldiers. When Saville returned to Red Cloud, he found his employees in a state of panic over the killing and sent a quick message to inform Fort Laramie of the murder, but confidently added that he anticipated no more trouble. For the next several weeks Oglala allies provided guards for the agency buildings and employees. In return Saville agreed to Red Cloud's suggestion that the government pay the guards for their services. Saville took the opportunity to inform the Indians that the government would be sending soldiers to their agency.[26]

Another critical event occurred later on February 9 and involved 1st Lt. Levi H. Robinson, Fourteenth Infantry, and Cpl. John C. Coleman, Company K, Second Cavalry. Robinson had been assigned to escort wood and supply trains moving between Fort Laramie and its woodcutting camp near Laramie Peak, some forty miles to the west. At daylight the escorted train left the wood reserve sawmill to return with a load of firewood to the post. Two hours later Lieutenant Robinson, Corporal Coleman, and Pvt. Frank Noll, Company A, Fourteenth Infantry, left the train in order to hunt deer on a different return route. The trio rode about twelve miles when they were suddenly surrounded and attacked by forty to fifty Indians. Noll quickly dismounted and returned their fire; he saw the last of Robinson and Coleman riding away, chased by the main body of warriors. Noll mounted his horse and sped off in the direction of the train, pursued by four or five riders, who continued their pursuit to within half a mile of the wood train. Concerned for the safety of the missing men, the soldiers halted their wagons and made camp. A messenger reported the attack to the fort and requested help.[27]

The next morning Capt. James Egan and his Second Cavalry company searched for the missing men. Led by Private Noll, they eventually found the bodies of Robinson and Coleman about half a mile apart. The bodies were badly shot up, and three arrows were sticking in each, but were not otherwise mutilated. Their deaths were attributed to one of the war parties that had recently left Red Cloud Agency.

At Fort Laramie Robinson's widow prepared to return home to Connecticut with his body. Robinson was eulogized in general orders issued February 19, "[W]e tender our most heartfelt sympathy, in token of which the officers of the regiment will wear the usual badge of mourning for thirty days."[28] Several days later Mrs. Robinson, with her husband's remains, departed for the East. The officers at Fort Laramie were assessed, according to rank, a total of $163.24 in order "to ease the burden to Mrs. Robinson in transporting his body home."[29]

Although Saville anticipated no further trouble at his agency, considerable fear and frustration existed among his employees. The whites, who feared assassination, dared not venture out after dark. John W. Dear, one of the two licensed traders at Red Cloud, thought the Indians, incensed by word that troops had been called, would burn the agency and slaughter all the whites.[30] Several days after the Appleton shooting, he had angry words with Saville, declaring that instead of punishing the Indians, Saville "licks their moccasins for peace policy."[31] Fearing an impending disaster, Dear shipped out the hides and furs he had received in trade and halted the restocking of his store.

Dear's friends at Fort Laramie also became alarmed at the deteriorating state of affairs at Red Cloud. They expected to receive word at any time of a general uprising and the death of every white man at the agency.[32] At Red Cloud the ever-optimistic Saville nevertheless took steps to protect the agency. He moved all employees into the agency compound, issued them arms, and pushed work to completion on the still unfinished stockade. On February 26 he reported to the commissioner that he had attempted to unite the cooperative Oglalas and Brulés against the northern Indians. A force of Indian allies, commanded by the Oglala Pumpkin Seed, guarded the agency day and night. In addition the agency mule herd was gathered together for protection and the steam sawmill moved inside the stockade.[33]

Contrary to his previous insistence that no danger existed, Saville now realized his predicament and wrote to Colonel Smith on several occasions to urge haste in the troop deployment. He informed Smith that conditions at the agency were "unsettled" and far from peaceful.[34] Events at Red Cloud had reached a critical juncture for the Indian bureau, the agency Indians, and soon, the military.

Critics of the peace policy saw the calling of troops to the agencies as a blatant admission of its failure. The call also reinforced the army's contention that the Indian bureau could not control the agencies. While peace policy proponents had anxiously awaited transformation of the Plains Indian into "productive" members of society, the Sioux rejected all attempts to alter their traditional way of life. White westerners in particular considered military force necessary and welcomed peace policy failure. After reporting the tragic series of events at Red Cloud Agency, an Omaha paper sarcastically remarked, "The Quaker Indian policy is bearing fruit."[35] Another editor encouraged the call for soldiers:

> A vigorous Indian campaign after the style peculiar to Sheridan, at this stage of the game, would do more towards settling the Indian question than the theories of peace commissioners, which have thus far signally failed, and it begins to look as the Government could begin to see it.[36]

The army now became the main player. On February 12 Commissioner Smith received Howard's telegram asking for military protection and replied that application had been made to the War Department to send troops. The same day while in New York, General Sheridan contacted William T. Sherman, commanding general of the army, regarding the agency situation. Trouble at the agencies had reached the point where military intervention was mandatory, Sheridan advised. "I will go home tomorrow to superintend any action that may be necessary."[37] He then returned to division headquarters to begin preparations, which on February 18 meant sending instructions to Department of the Platte

Commanding General Ord in Omaha. Ord was to dispatch Colonel Smith with a sufficient force to establish order at the agencies and to "protect the agent, employees and public property of the Indian Bureau."

Smith had commanded Fort Laramie for several years and had experience in dealing with the Oglalas, including once serving as acting agent at the North Platte River agency before Daniels arrived. He was instructed to use Red Cloud Agency as his headquarters until further orders, and in case of attack he was authorized to fight back. If necessary he could strike the first blow, "always saving women and children." Finally, Smith was to hold no official council with the agency Indians, only to inform them that the soldiers were there to make the country safe for the whites.[38]

To some westerners this prolonged process of Indian bureau application for troop protection and methodical military preparation appeared a time-consuming farce. Why didn't the agents simply call on Smith for Fort Laramie troops and be done with it? Instead the channels of civil and military authority had to be properly followed, a delay that seemed to outsiders as a foolish waste of time. Westerners had grown tired of "peace policy" administration and called for the Indian bureau to be returned to military control.[39]

The generals warned that sending soldiers to the agencies could bring the country an Indian war. Sheridan was convinced the Sioux had been preparing for war for several years through purchasing arms from agency traders and stockpiling ammunition. Thus, being well armed, they were "growing more insolent and exacting" in their demands on the government.[40] Sherman advised Sheridan to gather as many troops as available in his division to march on the agencies. Colonel Smith also feared a general war if troops were sent in.

The potential for war also alarmed Nebraska's citizens and its leaders. Governor Robert W. Furnas quickly applied to the federal government for arms to issue to vulnerable settlers. One congressman expressed fear that an Indian war could "compel the depopulation of northern Nebraska."[41]

The Department of Interior, which administered Indian affairs, was well aware of the chances for war. A concerned Secretary Delano warned Secretary of War William W. Belknap, "I shall exceedingly regret the occurrence of hostilities with the Sioux, and if they do occur I trust that your department will be able to show clearly that they did not result from this effort to protect Red Cloud's and Spotted Tail's agency."[42] President Grant, who was also well aware of the difficult situation, endorsed the letter. Ominous warnings in hand, the army continued with its preparations.

Colonel Smith at Fort Laramie commanded the troop movement. Fearing war, Smith was also not particularly enthusiastic about sending soldiers to the field during severe winter weather; no facilities were available at the agencies for quartering or subsisting troops. His other concern was the high winter expense of hauling forage for cavalry mounts.[43]

On February 19 General Ord sent Smith instructions regarding operations against the agency Indians and demanded extra precautions. The soldiers were not to take any liquor, except that approved for medical purposes. Officers, field officers in particular, were forbidden under threat of court-martial to carry or use liquor on the expedition. Smith must write Saville and Howard ordering that no liquor of any kind be allowed at their agencies. Also, Ord wanted no information to leak out on the army's plans. The soldiers must arrive unannounced at the agencies in order to prevent organized Indian resistance. The general, secretive in the extreme, encouraged Smith to be the same:

> To ensure success of any move it should not be communicated to any agent, officer or employee—either of that [Indian] Dept. or of the army. . . . [H]ence I never say even to my own staff what my intended moves are.[44]

Sheridan ordered Ord to detail troops to both Red Cloud and Spotted Tail agencies, although it compounded the logistics. Spotted Tail's Brulés seemed more peaceful towards the whites, but northern Indians at that agency kept things stirred up. They had openly talked of war among the agency young men, and it was generally perceived that Spotted Tail could not control them.

Because of insufficient troop strength at Fort Laramie, soldiers had to be gathered from other points for the coming expedition. On February 16–17, five companies of cavalry (two companies from Omaha Barracks and one each from Fort Fred Steele, Fort McPherson, and Fort Sanders) and three of infantry (two from Steele and one from Sanders) arrived by train at Fort D. A. Russell near Cheyenne. They joined five companies of the Eighth Infantry and one of the Third Cavalry that were detached from Russell's regular garrison. The concentrated force numbered nearly one thousand soldiers divided into fourteen companies.[45] Because of a wood shortage along the route north, the force was divided into two columns. On February 22 half the cavalry and infantry companies left Fort Russell under the command of Capt. Henry M. Lazelle; two days later the remaining troops, under command of Maj. Eugene Baker (the same officer who led the 1870 attack on the Piegans), left for Fort Laramie. Moving large numbers of troops during winter weather was not a pleasurable experience, as 1st Lt. James Fornance later recalled: "The weather was terrible cold several days on the march being as low as 33 below zero one night but no one was frozen."[46] Lazelle's column made the ninety-three-mile march to Fort Laramie in four days; Baker's troops subsequently arrived on February 27.

Meanwhile a council of war had been held at Smith's headquarters. On February 21, Generals Ord and Sheridan arrived at Fort Russell and quickly headed north. Meeting with Smith at Fort Laramie, final arrangements were completed. All were confident that enough men were being sent to protect both agencies. But the problem of sending the men an additional hundred miles, the distance from Fort Laramie to Red Cloud Agency, through bitter winter conditions still concerned them. Regardless of winter, military operations remained in motion. Smith was given overall control of the combined forces, suitably designated the "Sioux Expedition."

While army forces underwent consolidation, Saville anxiously awaited the arrival of military protection. Realizing his imperiled situation, the worried agent sent suggestions to Smith regarding the troop movement. If the troops could leave in the evening and ride without delay, the agency Indians could be taken by surprise. If the soldiers left Fort Laramie by the lower North Platte River ford, the column would be less likely to encounter Indians passing between Red Cloud and the fort. Saville also warned against sending too small a force. He feared several thousand warriors soon could be concentrated at his agency and added helpfully, "A regiment, inside of this stockade, could defend it against any force," but he also recognized "the difficulty is to get here."[47]

Just before the troops left for the agencies, Smith gave detailed orders to his field commanders, Lazelle to command the infantry column and Baker the cavalry. One army surgeon and three civilian contract surgeons served the troops. Each infantryman had two hundred rounds of ammunition, five days' rations, and the necessary camp equipment for field service, all to be carried by two wagons per company. Second Lt. Patrick H. Ray, Eighth Infantry, detailed as quartermaster officer for the expedition, oversaw the supply train and beef cattle herd that accompanied the troops. The reliable civilian scout Baptiste "Big Bat" Pourier was hired as guide and interpreter. A .50-caliber Gatling gun traveled with Lazelle's column. The various staff officers at Fort Laramie were ordered to assist with the preparations for departure.[48]

Major Baker's instructions for the cavalry column were similar. Along with the allotted ammunition, each cavalryman carried ten days' rations and five days' forage for his horse. Sabers were left at Fort Laramie. Each cavalry company was allowed four, six-mule wagons to haul camp supplies and forage. A second Gatling gun accompanied this column. Baker's command was slated to leave Fort Laramie first and push on to Red Cloud, with Lazelle's to follow and to protect the large wagon train.

While on the march, Lazelle, a West Point graduate and veteran of thirteen years with the Eighth Infantry, was instructed to take every precaution to prevent an attack on the supply train. He was to assign a sufficient front and rear guard daily and march the remainder of the companies on the train's flanks. Smith had warned that soldiers straggling behind the column would be in extreme danger. The column commanders were directed to have no communication with Indians encountered on the march and to maintain a vigilant guard against treachery. Surprise was critical to the success of the Sioux Expedition.

Baker received additional orders. Although the expedition's objective was to establish protective camps, and Smith hoped this would be accomplished without hostilities, he told Baker "in case that any hostile demonstration is made you will hold your command in readiness to strike as hard as possible." Parroting Ord's prohibitions, Baker's column was forbidden any intoxicating liquor while at the agency. Ord worried about the drinking habits of Baker and another officer and told Smith, "[I]f either of them get under the influence of liquor while under your command place them in arrest at once and send me the charges," adding "I will sign them or direct them signed here [at department headquarters]."[49] Colonel Smith accompanied the cavalry column to observe personally the Indians' reaction to the soldiers' arrival.

On March 2 the six companies of the Second Cavalry and two of the Third under Baker's command left Fort Laramie; the following day Lazelle's infantry column and the supply train headed north. As the soldiers toiled through the snow-covered landscape, Saville appeared to have changed his mind on the need for soldiers at the agencies! On March 5 he wrote the commissioner and described the difficulties he had experienced in reconciling the agency Indians to the coming of the soldiers. Although he was the person most responsible for calling for troops, Saville tried to shift the responsibility of military intervention to Colonel Smith. "Whether Gen. Smith has done his duty in thus coming to the relief of the agency, I leave to his own conscience to determine."[50] From this apparent hypocrisy, it is understandable why the army mistrusted him. Saville now told Commissioner Smith that he could maintain agency control by using friendly Indians to provide security. He boasted, "By perseverance and constant work I have gained an influence over the [Indian] soldiers and united them in favor of carrying out my desires."[51] Meanwhile the Sioux Expedition continued its march.

Smith took Ord's advice, kept troop strengths and disposition confidential, and prevented any leaks to the press. He feared that educated mixed-bloods would read the newspapers and pass on the information to relatives at the agencies. Smith, who disapproved of the way the press covered agency matters, later reassured Ord that he would volunteer no information to correspondents.[52]

After a relatively routine march, the cavalry column arrived at Red Cloud on March 5; however, the infantry column and supply train encountered much more difficulty. The route to the agency followed the old Fort Laramie–Fort Pierre trail, fairly easy going for the wagons until they reached the headwaters of the White River. Difficulties came when the wagons descended into the river valley. The White meandered considerably, and the soldiers had to make thirteen aggravating crossings in the last fifteen miles of the march. At one point it took the tired soldiers, who labored to make the way passable, twenty-one hours to move the wagons only seven miles. As the column neared the agency, it fully expected to be attacked, and Lazelle ordered out skirmishers for the last several miles.[53] The infantry and supply train arrived at Red Cloud late on the morning of March 8, three days after Colonel Smith and the cavalry column.

The earlier appearance of the cavalry had totally surprised the agency Indians, who hurriedly gathered to verbally spar with the soldiers. The cavalry troops camped along the river just north of the agency stockade. Occasionally over the next few days angry warriors fired arrows and bullets across the cavalry camp. Smith authorized his sentry to fire on any Indian in sight if a member of the command was hit by hostile fire.[54]

Soon after the cavalry column arrived, Smith informed Saville to gather Red Cloud and other agency leaders for a talk. Saville suggested that he say something "sweet and soft to them" to help reconcile them to the soldiers' presence. Smith took an opposing view; he would advise the Indians of the consequences if further shooting demonstrations continued.[55]

Red Cloud and about a dozen headmen met with Colonel Smith at the agency, who informed them he was there to make the Indians behave. They should help him keep order and help the army control the northern Indians. But if any Indians fired into the army camp, or took any army stock, his soldiers would attack their villages. Because the agency Indians had failed to follow previous instructions, soldiers had been sent for, and more soldiers could come if necessary.

During the conference Red Cloud seemed sullen and said nothing. After Smith reiterated the ban on shooting at his camp, an Oglala headman named Blue Horse stated that the Indians sometimes fired guns in their camps during the night. Did Smith object to that? Smith had no objection, and with that the Indians left, and the conference ended.

Smith had made his point, and the shooting ceased. Although Sheridan had ordered that no official councils be held, Smith felt he had been within his bounds. The soldiers had been ordered to the agency, and as their commander he could determine what steps were necessary for their protection. He received support for his hard-line stand. The Cheyenne newspaper wrote:

> This is plain language and easily understood by the treacherous savages. They know that Gen. Smith means exactly what he says and that he will not hesitate to let loose his "boys in blue" if the "boys in red" give him the slightest provocation.[56]

Emitting its usual mixed signals, the Indian bureau requested the soldiers to "display forbearance" while at the agency.[57] Interior Secretary Delano saw the army's job as protecting the agencies and preserving friendly relations. On March 7 he wrote Belknap to express the hope that the army would maintain the peace and continue its cooperation with the Indian bureau. Bureaucratic mutterings aside, the rapid appearance and overwhelming numbers of the army at Red Cloud truly saved the day. An officer with the infantry column best assessed the operation: "[O]ur force was probably to[o] large and came to[o] suddenly to allow them [the Indians] to act."[58]

After all the infantry and wagons arrived at Red Cloud, Smith prepared to move troops to Spotted Tail. On March 8 he issued orders for troop assignments: one surgeon to remain at Red Cloud to take care of sick members of the expedition, the other doctors to proceed to Spotted Tail. The first garrison at Red Cloud was Company F, Eighth Infantry, Companies B and K of the Thirteenth Infantry, and Company F of the Fourteenth Infantry, with Company G, Third Cavalry, as the camp's single cavalry company. Capt. James Van Horn, Eighth Infantry, commanded the camp, and Smith ordered him to exercise a vigilant guard against surprise attack and to prohibit the enlisted men from visiting Indian camps or "having intercourse with them in any way." Also, Van Horn must prevent any Indians from entering the military camp.[59]

Smith was dissatisfied with having his soldiers right at the agency. With numerous Indians camped in its immediate vicinity, the soldiers might encounter trouble, even while gathering firewood. Also, no grazing was available for his animals. He asked Saville whether the agency would be safe if the army camp sat five or six miles away, but before receiving a reply, on March 9 Smith left for the Brulé agency.[60]

The next day the soldiers reached the Spotted Tail Agency and established another camp. Surprisingly the Indians seemed glad to see them.[61] The army camp was laid out atop a low bluff south of the agency buildings, and regardless of the apparent friendliness, incorporated defensive measures in its arrangement. The soldiers dug redoubts at points along the bluff edge and rifle pits behind the tent area.[62]

Here Smith was satisfied with the situation. He assigned the four companies of the Eighth Infantry and Company B, Third Cavalry, under Lazelle's command to remain and guard the agency. On March 11 Smith and Baker's cavalry column left for the return trip to Red Cloud, where they arrived the next day.

At the Red Cloud camp, the perceived trouble spot, Smith, according to orders, established his headquarters. More orders followed, specifically ones sending Baker and the Second Cavalry companies back to Laramie. With the agencies peacefully occupied, the extra force was not needed, nor was there enough forage to sustain their horses.

Initially caught off balance, northern Indians at both agencies quickly recovered, broke camp, and fled to the north. Army observers noted the brooding attitude of those who stayed behind. The young warriors and malcontents usually avoided the soldiers, but when near did not disguise their hostility. Reluctantly, and gradually, the Indians became accustomed to the soldier presence.[63] Saville reported that, with the excitement of the Indians having subsided, they were much more cooperative. He was able to complete his census with "little or no difficulty, as they readily comply with almost any request I make."[64]

The problem of jurisdiction over the soldiers at the agencies remained to be resolved. The military authorities wanted to maintain full control over their troops; the civilian authorities disagreed. To the army the soldiers protected the agencies; they were not the agent's personal police force. Smith complained of Saville and Howard's demands and discourtesies toward him and his officers.[65] As an example, Saville wanted the soldiers to arrest the Minneconjou man who killed Frank Appleton. The officer in charge refused; his troops were there to guard the agency only. General Ord stepped in and supported his officers, and Colonel Smith received specific orders that "the troops of the United States will not be used as a police force, on request of Indian agents, to arrest either citizens or Indians."[66] The soldiers were to prevent an outbreak and to protect lives and government property.

On the other hand, at times the camp officers clearly interfered in agency affairs. For instance, in the late spring Lazelle directed the agent at Spotted Tail to halt the sale of arms and ammunition by its Indian trader. Smith promptly informed Lazelle that he had no authority to interfere with agents acting under instructions from their department, but he could continue to report through military channels any matters "inconsistent with the interests of the government, that may come under his observation."[67]

As a result of this jurisdictional conflict, astute Indian leaders attempted to play one government entity against the other.[68] Red Cloud once wanted to travel to Washington and applied to the military for the trip, even though he knew Saville opposed it. Routinely agency chiefs made social calls on officers at their camp, which aroused the suspicious agent who thought the military was unnecessarily influencing the Indians. Spotted Tail also played one side against the other, especially when the time came to pick a new site for his agency. The crafty politician wanted the army, not the chosen Indian commissioners, to select the new location. It was this charged atmosphere of interdepartmental jockeying, and a somewhat peaceful coexistence between the U.S. Army and Indian bureau, that characterized the initial years at Red Cloud Agency and Camp Robinson.

Chapter 2

The Establishment
of Camp Robinson

Members of the Board of Indian Commissioners, which included eminent
civilians who served without pay, were disturbed that they had not been
consulted before their agents had called in troops. The board hastily
decided to send a special commission to the agencies to investigate the
matter. Within two weeks of the arrival of the Sioux Expedition, a four-
member team, headed by Episcopal Bishop William H. Hare from Santee
Agency, arrived at Red Cloud.

One issue to resolve was the constant bickering between Saville and
Colonel Smith. The agent, so often contradictory in his desire for military
assistance, did not want to lose control over his agency. Adding fuel to the
fire, Red Cloud complained to the commission of Smith's rough talk to the
Indian leaders at their recent conference. The commission members
asked the Interior department to decide which authority, the agent or the
officer, was superior. Secretary Delano later came down firmly in the
middle. He replied that President Grant had told him that "the duties of the
military authority and of the agent are distinct and independent;" in other
words, neither was subordinate to the other.[1] Hereafter, their differences
were to be referred directly to the president for settlement.

The commissioners spent several weeks at the agencies, conferring
with the agents, counselling with the chiefs, and awaiting Delano's reply.
They often found the Indians angry and threatening; a cavalry company
escorted the commissioners during their travels away from the agencies.
Bishop Hare recounted years later that he believed his life was in more
danger during that visit than at any other time.[2]

What the commissioners heard and saw convinced them that the presence of troops was warranted and the only means by which order could be maintained, and so read their report. Colonel Smith supported their views, but remained typically critical of agency management:

> There can be no question of the good effect of the presence of the troops upon the Indians at these agencies. The Indians will "bully" when they can do so with impunity[.] [O]f their peculiarities or of their general management I do not deem it necessary to touch upon for obvious reasons—but with firmness and justice may be accomplished.[3]

The army command, however, was upset by the Hare Commission's ultimate failure. It had failed to recommend a permanent location for the agencies. What the commissioners favored was the creation of a new agency for the northern Indians farther north on the Sioux reservation. This would remove a potential threat to the more peaceful operation of the Nebraska agencies.

But there was a more convincing reason for agency removal—the Treaty of 1868. Article Two specified that the reservation lands would lie north of Nebraska's northern boundary. Although the army was reasonably sure both agencies now sat in Nebraska and not on the reservation, the Indian bureau apparently was not. Article Four stipulated that the government would construct agency buildings on the Sioux Reservation at some point along the Missouri River. In the eyes of the army the present agency sites were poorly located in relation to transporting supplies and moving troops. Spotted Tail Agency sat in a particularly poor location to maintain a military camp; the water was bad, the terrain was exposed, and it was far from timber. The relocation issue would irritate the army for the next several months.

While the Hare Commission met at the agencies, department headquarters arranged for the camps' continuation. On March 24, 1874, orders came that officially transferred the companies stationed at the agencies from their previously assigned posts, a decision that resulted in several months of separation from loved ones. Officers' families were allowed to retain quarters at those posts "until provisions can be made for them at the stations at which they are now serving."[4]

The soldier camp at Red Cloud was at first designated simply "Camp at Red Cloud Agency," but Colonel Smith soon decided on a new and more fitting name. On March 29 he issued the following order:

Headquarters, Sioux Expedition
Camp Robinson
March 29, 1874

General Orders No. 4

To honor the memory of the late 1st Lieut. Levi Robinson,
14th Inf., killed by Indians near Laramie Peak, W. T. Feb.9,
'74, the camp at Red Cloud Agency will hereafter be known
as Camp Robinson.

By order of Colonel Smith, 14th Inf.

The new camp was, thus, officially named, and logically so.[5] Levi
Robinson had been the most recent army officer to be killed in the line of
duty, and the army traditionally named new posts in this manner.[6]
Additionally, Robinson and Smith were members of the same regiment—
both officers were undoubtedly well acquainted—and the unfortunate
lieutenant lost his life in the midst of the same round of Indian troubles
during which the camp was established.

Colonel John E. Smith, so instrumental in the establishment of Camp
Robinson, can be considered one of the best field commanders of the
Indian wars. Described by his men as "strict but just," Smith entered the
army at the outbreak of the Civil War as the colonel of the Forty-fifth
Illinois Infantry. A year later he was promoted to brigadier general and
was cited for actions in the siege of Vicksburg and the capture of
Savannah. As a result of his sterling war service he was appointed colonel
of the Twenty-seventh U.S. Infantry in July 1866.[7]

In the aftermath of the 1866 Fetterman fight, Smith and the Twenty-
seventh regiment were sent to the Bozeman Trail country. There he
assumed command of the Mountain District, his headquarters at Fort Phil
Kearny. In this difficult area of operations Smith "did his job, coolly,
efficiently, and well."[8] After the army reorganization of 1869, he was
unassigned until taking charge of the Fourteenth Infantry, usually as
commander of Fort Laramie.

Colonel Smith, as overall commander of the Sioux Expedition, held
the responsibility of assigning officers as camp commanders. He placed
Captain Van Horn in command of the companies at Red Cloud; however,
the first real post commander of Camp Robinson was Capt. Arthur
MacArthur, father of Gen. Douglas MacArthur. Later awarded the Medal
of Honor for bravery in the Civil War, the senior MacArthur served as a
major general during the Philippine Insurrection. MacArthur, who led

Company K, Thirteenth Infantry, when the expedition arrived, received command of the camp about April 14, when Van Horn left on detached duty. He was the first to sign a post return (April 30, 1874) as the camp's commanding officer.[9]

Post returns, the official statistical compilation of troop strength at all army posts and forts, needed to be filled out at month's end. The units at the camps had been dropped from the returns of their original stations on March 24. Normally this would have required a return from Camp Robinson on March 31. But department headquarters was far from the wilds of northwest Nebraska, and orders that would have required this monthly report did not arrive until April 12.

The first garrison at Red Cloud comprised basically the same units that Smith assigned in March. The total number of men generally ranged between 300 and 350, although as many as half were absent on detached duties. Four of the five companies were infantry.[10] Because of the lack of forage, Smith realized grain and hay needed to be shipped in, an additional and considerable transportation expense. As a result only one cavalry troop was kept at each agency, used mostly to escort the supply trains.

The soldiers were armed with .50/70 Springfield breech-loading rifles, replaced later that year with the improved .45/70 rifle. Twenty-five .50-caliber Sharps carbines were kept on hand to arm civilians, if necessary. The two .50-caliber Gatling guns brought along were assigned one to each camp. Later that summer Smith added to the firepower by sending a twelve-pounder mountain howitzer and all its necessary "appendages" to Camp Robinson.[11]

The infantrymen pitched their tents just outside the east stockade wall of the agency and the first tent, nearest the corner bastion where Indian annuities were issued, was Smith's. Company G, Third Cavalry, under command of 1st Lt. Emmet Crawford, made its camp in the river bottom, just across White River and north from the agency.[12]

At this location difficulties arose when the soldiers went to cut firewood. The Sioux objected to the soldiers cutting wood—just as they did when civilians cut it for the agency—on what they considered their reservation. The threat to the woodcutters concerned the soldiers. One officer recalled, "It was necessary to send out the wagon train daily under a heavy guard, and with the memory of the Fetterman massacre in the minds of everyone, those in camp habitually kept near their arms during the absence of the wood cutting party."[13] The Indians imposed a dead line to prevent agency employees from cutting wood on the north side of White River, so it came from the ridges six or seven miles to the south. The soldiers disregarded this demarcation and took wood from the north, and considerably closer, side of the river. By late spring civilian contractors provided the camp's firewood.

The supply line for the agency camps ran from Fort Laramie. Freighters hauled military goods by wagon from the quartermaster depot at Cheyenne to Fort Laramie, then north to Red Cloud. Smith recommended at least a sixty-day supply be maintained at Red Cloud, where shelter was available. He wanted only a thirty-day stock on hand for the Spotted Tail troops because of the uncertainty of its continued location. The wagon trains hauling supplies used over three hundred mules, which in turn required large amounts of forage to be shipped to Red Cloud. Sixty days of forage amounted to eighty-seven tons of oats, forty-three of corn, and two hundred of hay.[14] All of this forage, plus food, clothing, ordnance, and the other countless items needed to support the troops, had to be regularly forwarded. Troop transfers often were arranged so departing companies served as escorts. Expedition quartermaster Lieutenant Ray organized and personally traveled with supply trains to keep the forces in the field adequately supplied.

Along with this supply route, regular mail delivery had to be organized. Mail left the camps once a week with the agency courier to Fort Laramie; the army was charged fifty dollars per month for this service. Mail coming from Fort Laramie had to wait for someone going to Red Cloud, but this arrangement was disrupted when contractors took over and carried the Indian bureau mail from Cheyenne north via the old North Platte River site of the first Red Cloud Agency. This route bypassed Fort Laramie and halted the army's weekly delivery schedule. Smith complained to headquarters that he could find no one to carry mail between Fort Laramie and Red Cloud for the same rate the agency charged. It would be better, he reasoned, if the new route from Cheyenne passed through Fort Laramie. The new route served only three ranches, whose mail volume did not exceed fifty letters per year. Smith's complaints brought no change to the route; however, in December the army let a contract to carry its mail between Camp Robinson and Sidney, a substantially shorter distance than the regular route via Cheyenne—and a glimpse into the future, regarding transportation lines. Civilian carriers later reestablished direct mail service between Fort Laramie and the agencies.[15]

Confusion still reigned about the exact locations of the two White River agencies. First Lt. James Fornance could not clarify matters when he wrote, "We are about 70 miles from Fort Laramie, either in Dakota, Nebraska or Wyoming no one knows which [,] this portion of the country never having been surveyed."[16] The first inspector general to visit the camp thought that Red Cloud was in Nebraska, but Spotted Tail fell just north in Dakota Territory. General Sheridan doubted that both were on the reservation, and to resolve the issue he dispatched an engineer officer to determine the latitude of the agencies. The officer found both agencies to be in Nebraska. In the summer of 1874 a party of civilian surveyors ran the northern boundary line of Nebraska and also verified Sheridan's geographical assumption.

Now the question arose whether to keep camps at each agency or to build one for both. Smith preferred one large post on the Niobrara River that would have easy access to both agencies. It would be much easier to build and maintain one post than two. But if Spotted Tail Agency was moved farther north, as the commissioners wanted, this would increase the distance from military oversight. Sheridan expressed the same concern: "If these agencies are left up in their present location, they can both be governed by a single military post." He added, "If they are to be more widely separated, it will require two military establishments."[17] Smith changed his views, realizing that the agents would not consider their lives or agency property secure if soldiers were not nearby. The plan of keeping a post at each agency proceeded.

The Indian bureau's indecision concerning permanent locations for the agencies continued to irritate the army. If troops were to guard the agencies, their locations should be firmly decided. The army was still under the impression that the Oglala and Brulé agencies belonged on the Missouri River, not in northern Nebraska. Nevertheless, if they were to remain on the White River, plans needed to be made to shelter the troops. Sheridan pressured the Indian bureau to decide, and in March wrote General Sherman in Washington:

> The Indians at these agencies cannot be governed except by the presence of troops, and some understanding should at once be had with the Indian Bureau which will determine the permanent location of the agencies. There is no time to lose on this matter. May I therefore ask you to push it to a solution?[18]

The logistical problems of garrisoning troops in this wild country were considerable, especially when the Indian bureau seemed to lack any desire to aid the planning. If posts were destined to be built, an appropriation for construction needed to be promptly secured. While the bureaucratic wrangling continued, the soldiers at Red Cloud settled into a regular military routine.

The soldier's daily schedule involved camp fatigue work, drill, guard detail, and escort duties. Keeping the camp next to the agency proved unwise because it unduly restricted soldier activity, besides the friction of daily contact between the soldiers and the Indians. Thousands of Indian horses grazed nearby, leaving no grass for the army animals. When warm weather arrived, the closeness to the Indian camps proved somewhat distressing. The Indians slaughtered their issued beef just southeast of the agency, and the result was a large amount of scattered, rotting refuse. Warm weather made the stench of the cattle remains, as one observer understated, "difficult to bear." The camp surgeon criticized the sanitation of the nearby Indian camps; the soldiers were "surrounded by dirty filthy Indians with all their attendant cats and dogs." It would be "impossible to observe a proper system of police which the approach of summer would soon require."[19] The arguments for moving the camp were bolstered.

After surveying the nearby country Colonel Smith and Captain MacArthur selected a new camp site on the north side of White River, about a mile and a half above the agency. Here they found a level bench just north of where Soldier Creek emptied into the river. Army horses and mules would no longer compete with the Indian ponies for grazing, there was a good source of water and wood nearby, and most important the camp was some distance away from the Indians but near enough to provide rapid assistance if the need arose (which later proved true).

On May 6 Smith ordered Camp Robinson moved to the new site. Lieutenant Ray, aided by 2nd Lt. William H. Carter, Eighth Infantry, paced out the new camp and staked out the tent rows, with greater spacing than the old camp. The infantry companies tented on the higher ground, and the cavalry company set up camp nearer Soldier Creek to the south. Cleanliness became a priority, and orders were posted regulating camp sanitation. The officer of the day made daily inspections and reports. The company tents, kitchens, and space around them were to be policed and put in order immediately after reveille.[20] At least one visitor failed to be impressed with the new camp, describing its location as being "on White River, where mosquitoes are so thick only a part of them can find anchorage at a time."[21] Camp Robinson now occupied the site where it would remain for the rest of its history.

Smith realized that many Indians remained hostile to the soldiers' presence. Therefore, he restricted military visits to the agency, and eventually the enlisted men could not go more than a mile from camp unless on duty. Soldiers going to the agency required written permission of company officers, approved by the camp commanding officer, and then only in parties of at least three men, fully armed.[22]

The uneasy state of affairs mandated constant vigilance. A daily guard of fifteen men was posted at the camp, and a sentinel was placed on the high hill between the camp and agency, a picket post manned for some months afterward.[23]

The temporary nature of the agency camps gradually changed to reflect more "permanence." Before the move the camps drew supplies from the Fort Laramie quartermaster. On May 15 Smith learned that both camps were now on equal footing with other garrisons in the department in regard to procurement. Henceforth Camp Robinson and Spotted Tail ordered supplies directly through regular quartermaster channels.[24]

The problem of putting up an adequate supply of hay, or long forage, to sustain supply train animals demanded immediate attention. To continually haul hay from Fort Laramie was not feasible. Because of the hungry Indian ponies, hay was impossible to obtain along the White River. Lieutenant Ray reported in April that the agency had turned to the Niobrara River, some twenty miles to the south, for its hay supply. The army contracted with Indian trader J. W. Dear and another party to cut 475 tons of hay at $20 per ton, with delivery due over the summer months. Dear feared that the Indians would burn his haystacks if left unattended, so the hay was delivered from the Niobrara Valley to the camp as soon as it was cut.[25]

Soon after the camp's relocation, a phenomenon of nature nearly disrupted the uneasy peace at Red Cloud. In the fall of 1873 *Harper's Weekly*, a national newspaper, had commissioned two French artists to sketch for publication scenes from across the United States. In early June, Jules Tavernier and Paul Frenzeny arrived at Camp Robinson to draw scenes at Red Cloud Agency.[26] Meanwhile the Oglalas were preparing for their annual Sun Dance, and several Brulés from Spotted Tail came to attend the ceremony. As interested army officers commonly observed Indian ceremonies and dances held at the agency, Lieutenant Carter and Tavernier were permitted to watch. On the ceremony's third day, a violent storm came up and lightning struck the dance pole. According to Carter, the Indians took this as a bad omen, a sign of displeasure at the white men's presence. Carter and the Frenchman were warned to leave the dance area quickly. The Brulés immediately struck camp and returned to their agency. After their visit Tavernier and Frenzeny collaborated to make one of the earliest illustrations of the Sioux Sun Dance.[27]

During an unrelated incident a week later, the army's arrest of Toussaint Kenssler, an actual attack occurred. It further illustrated the value of keeping soldiers at Red Cloud. Kenssler, a mixed-blood man, had been arrested some months previous on a charge of murder by Capt. James Egan and 2nd Lt. James Allison of the Second Cavalry. In spring 1874 he escaped from jail in Cheyenne and took refuge with his kinsmen Oglalas at Red Cloud. Kenssler, a rough character, threatened the lives of agency employees, including Saville and Captain Egan, and also forcibly detained the agency mail carrier. Agency Indians ignored Saville's repeated demands to turn Kenssler over to the authorities. Officers at Camp Robinson heard rumors that Kenssler was planning his revenge on Egan and Allison when they returned from escorting the Spotted Tail supply train.[28]

On Sunday, June 14, Lieutenants Crawford and Ray, who had driven to the agency trader's store in a hospital ambulance, heard that Kenssler had just passed the door, heading for the rear of the agency buildings that overlooked White River. Ray borrowed a Winchester rifle from the trader and ordered several soldiers, who were at the store on pass, to help the officers apprehend the fugitive. The soldiers went behind the agency and spotted Kenssler sitting on the edge of the river talking to an Indian woman. He saw the soldiers and attempted to escape by jumping into the river. Ray shot him in the legs, and the soldiers captured and carried the wounded prisoner to the ambulance. The Kenssler shooting alarmed some of the agency Indians, who tried to surround the ambulance but failed to prevent its return to camp.

Meanwhile at Camp Robinson the sentries saw the impending danger when they noticed figures rushing about and the Indian horse herds being gathered. After the ambulance arrived, Kenssler was taken to the hospital tent and his wounds treated; then he was shackled and placed under heavy guard. Other than the hurried gathering of horses, the soldiers apparently noticed no other suspicious activity on the part of the Indians.

About midnight several angry Indians retaliated by firing on the camp. The soldiers, somewhat prepared for this, left their tents in the darkness. Lieutenant Carter recalled with some humor the ensuing confusion:

> Upon leaving my tent the commanding officer called to me in the dark to take command of the first company which was without officers. As I started towards it with pistol in hand, I suddenly found myself astride a man crawling on the grass, and I was admittedly very much shocked, I cocked my pistol when I recognized the voice of our Irish soldier cook Finnerity, who said "Don't shoot—its Finnerity." I don't know which of us was most scared, but I was always prompt to admit that I did not like being astride an Indian in the dark. Finnerity had

put [on] his belt upside down, running to join his company, and spilled his cartridges in the grass, and had turned to pick them up when I encountered him.[29]

A skirmish line was formed and moved toward the flashes of the Indian guns. As the soldiers moved forward, the firing gradually died down. Captain MacArthur feared the warriors would rush camp and ordered the command to cease firing and return. Most of the soldiers stayed under arms the rest of the night. In the morning it was discovered that during the shooting raiders had torn down a temporary corral and scattered the soldier beef herd. Lieutenant Crawford's company recovered most of the cattle, which had drifted along the river bottom.

The consternation created by Kenssler's arrest soon subsided. Crawford and a detachment escorted the fugitive to Cheyenne, where he was turned over to the civil authorities. On November 19 Kenssler was hung for the murder of Adolph Peno, bringing "general rejoicing . . . that the law vindicated itself in this instance."[30] In addition to this crime some evidence hints that Kenssler had led the war party that killed Lieutenant Robinson and Corporal Coleman the previous February.[31] The affair fully demonstrated that the agency Indians would not intimidate the soldiers.

———

By necessity the army's attention had to turn to more pressing, if more mundane, matters. Whether or not the agencies remained at their present locations, the construction of shelters to house and support the solders topped the agenda. The multitude of logistical, design, and construction problems experienced in Camp Robinson's establishment largely mirrored those faced at other new posts in the American West. More likely than not, decisions on structure size, construction techniques, and building arrangement fell to officers in the field. At those frontier army posts that evolved into large, permanent installations, the early, often crude structures, were usually demolished and eventually replaced with improved quarters and facilities. Little physical evidence remained of what once had been.

The early construction histories of frontier forts often can be pieced together. The surviving historical records of how a post was built are surprisingly and exceptionally rich in detail. Vast amounts of quartermaster paperwork, reports, estimates, and plans, an oftentimes neglected resource, show how key decisions were made and implemented. The documents sometimes point out the strained relationship between headquarters and distant posts, as well as structural details. This type of information is particularly important where the historic site is also its research center. Fortunately the story of the building of Camp Robinson can likewise be reconstructed from the countless pages of reports and correspondence sent to headquarters by post officers.

By the spring of 1874 Bishop Hare and his commissioners had agreed that soldiers were needed to protect the agencies. Decisions by the field commissioners needed approval by Commissioner of Indian Affairs Edward P. Smith and then by the Interior Department, which administered all Indian policy. Decisions moving up and down the various levels of bureaucracy took time. After several months of indecision and persistent inquiry by army officials, the Indian bureau made several decisions regarding the disposition of troops at the agencies. On May 25 Acting Commissioner H. R. Clum officially reported to the Interior Department that it was "necessary to have troops stationed in the vicinity of these agencies for the purpose of keeping order."[32] The next day the secretary of the Interior officially informed Secretary of War Belknap: Red Cloud Agency would not be moved. A location for Spotted Tail, however, was not firmly fixed. By now the army was convinced the best site for that agency was south and east on Beaver Creek. With the move yet undecided, the post at Spotted Tail remained in limbo. Nevertheless, preparations proceeded for construction at Camp Robinson.

The next step involved securing funding. The Department of the Platte staff officers in Omaha estimated at least $30,000 was needed to construct cantonments at both agencies. The figure remained the magic number on which all paperwork for the next fiscal year's expenditures for construction was based.

In mid-June General Ord traveled to Washington to confer with General of the Army Sherman regarding the posts. Sherman told his department commander that he had no money for him in the army's remaining appropriation. Furthermore, he and other officers remained perturbed at recent Indian bureau actions and its policy in general; they particularly resented that the Indian bureau had waited until winter before calling for troops. Soldiers should have been sent when the agencies first moved to the White River, and then the February trouble could have been avoided.

But the posts needed to be built, so Sherman sent Ord to Secretary of the Interior Delano to apply for funding. Ord told Delano that his troops would be withdrawn from the agencies when winter set in again—unless the department furnished money for shelter. Delano called in Commissioner Smith for a conference with Ord and him. Smith reiterated the necessity of soldiers for agency protection. He thought the needed $30,000 could be taken from Indian bureau funds.[33]

Secretary Delano objected to Smith's idea. His department, as with the army, neared the end of its fiscal year pressed for funds. The next stop for both Smith and Ord was Capitol Hill and the Senate Committee on Indian Affairs, where they requested the needed amount. The committee apparently concurred, and thus came the funds to build Camp Robinson. By June 26 the press announced that appropriations had been made for building posts at the northern Nebraska agencies.[34] The army, impatient with the administrative delays, stood poised to begin construction.

In July the infantry units at the camp were rotated. Company H, Eighth Infantry, and Company F, Fourteenth Infantry, left the post, and on July 12 two companies of the Ninth Infantry arrived from Omaha Barracks. In charge of the detachment was Capt. William H. Jordan, who assumed command of the camp. Jordan, an Ohio native, graduated from West Point in 1860 as an infantry officer. In February 1861 he was assigned to the Ninth Infantry, becoming a captain with that regiment in 1862. Cited for "gallantry and meritorious service" at Gaines Mill in the Seven Days Battle, he was promoted to major with the Eighth California Volunteer Infantry. After the war he returned to the Ninth Infantry and served for years as an unheralded yet efficient frontier army officer.[35]

Before leaving Omaha, Ord instructed Jordan to "build shelter at this post according to [Jordan's] own plan."[36] Several weeks later he received a package of building plans and instructions from the department quartermaster's office. Although the Omaha headquarters designed Camp Robinson's first buildings, Captain Jordan was certainly responsible for the post's layout.

Camp Robinson was intended to be a temporary cantonment. The army was confident that the northern Nebraska agencies would be moved the next year to the Missouri River. Building appropriations were first requested for "winter quarters" at the agencies.

The architectural plans were accepted as general guidelines for the structures, barracks, officers' quarters, and storehouse and were not precisely followed in the field. For example, Jordan and 1st Lt. Jesse M. Lee, post quartermaster when building commenced in fall 1874, took certain liberties regarding window and door placement and log construction technique. The plans Ord approved called for quarters to house a garrison of four companies. Six sets of officers' quarters were planned at a cost of $6,500. Barracks for the enlisted men were estimated at $2,400, plus mess halls for $1,200. Completing the original plan was one storehouse. This brought the total estimated cost for building Camp Robinson to $10,700, the same amount intended for Spotted Tail.[37]

The builders raised the question of whether to build barracks or huts to house the enlisted men. Maj. Alexander J. Perry, department quartermaster, submitted plans for twelve-man huts as an alternative to barracks-type housing. Twenty-eight huts could house four companies and would cost an additional $1,800. But he recommended adopting barracks housing, and the hut idea for Camp Robinson was subsequently dropped. The building estimates, forwarded to the division level, came with a request for early approval.[38]

On July 14 General Sheridan received Perry's spending plan for both agencies. Sheridan approved the plans as recommended "with the condition that not one cent more than the sum estimated for ($21,400) be expended on these two camps."[39] He believed money spent at Spotted Tail was a waste since the agency would eventually be moved, but felt the soldiers needed protection until the final site was selected. Four days later the plans moved on to the secretary of war. Upon examination Quartermaster General Montgomery C. Meigs pointed out a sticky detail: there was nothing in the Sundry Civil Service Bill on the actual appropriation, although the *Congressional Record* indicated both houses had adopted a report on the matter. Meigs thought more investigation was required to determine if funding really existed, but after raising the necessary caution flag, he approved the expenditure. The submitted estimates were basically for building hardware, doors, and windows and for labor; he saw no figure for lumber. Meigs assumed, as did the subordinate quartermaster officers, that logs would be cut and prepared on site. He also cautioned that if timber for military use was harvested on the Indian reserve, the agent would probably bill the War Department for the loss.[40]

On July 24 Secretary of War Belknap approved the plans and ordered the construction of barracks and quarters at Camp Robinson to begin immediately. Those at Spotted Tail were to be built after a permanent location for the agency was fixed. An application for funds to cover the work was "made in due form."

It seemed eminently practical to the army to use soldier labor for construction. Perry's estimates originally submitted on July 7 were for buildings "to be erected by the labor of the troops."[41] If the agency had quieted down, enough men could be spared from military duties to build the post.

Considering the limited nature of the funding, locally available building materials had to be used. In the hills west and north of the camp along Soldier Creek, pine timber was readily available. The best trees averaged between fifteen and twenty inches in diameter and could yield good building logs about twenty feet long. Some officers were critical of the local pines, claiming they were brittle and would rapidly decay. Once cut and trimmed, the logs would have to be hauled three to seven miles to the camp.

The soldiers found good quality stone for foundations about two miles south of the camp, also sand and gravel, but no adequate source of limestone for lime. Needed building materials could come by rail from Omaha to Cheyenne Depot, then be hauled north.

A portion of the building appropriation could go to civilian workers with carpentry and masonry skills. "Master" civilian employees served as foremen–supervisors for soldiers and other laborers. On July 15 1st Lt. William Auman, post quartermaster, hired a mason and a carpenter at $125 each a month. On July 16 he requested four work oxen, the necessary bows and yokes, and log chains for hauling logs. With ox teams unavailable at Fort Laramie, Perry authorized Auman to hire locally, which he did through John S. Collins, the post trader at Fort Laramie, who also served in the same capacity for Camp Robinson.[42]

An essential asset to building the new post proved to be the steam-powered, Indian agency sawmill. In early August 1874 Captain Jordan arranged with Dr. Saville to use the mill to cut lumber for rafters, joists, posts, and studding for $8 a day, a sum that paid for the agency sawyer and engineer. With the available logs, Jordan figured some twenty thousand feet of lumber could be cut in seven days at $4 per thousand feet. The estimate included reimbursing agency employees and twenty enlisted men to get out the logs. Colonel Smith at Fort Laramie approved this plan.[43]

Meanwhile in Omaha, Perry was officially informed to expend funds from the appropriation for Camp Robinson only. On August 6 he wrote Jordan that the building plans and specifications were on the way. Jordan was charged with building the structures according to plans and procuring lumber and stone immediately. He was authorized to take five additional teams from the Fort Laramie supply train to use in the project.

But Jordan had already had several weeks' start on the project. Two days after assuming command of the post (July 14) he had issued orders to start cutting lumber. A detail of one first sergeant and twenty-seven privates, under command of 2nd Lt. John H. H. Peshine, Thirteenth Infantry, began felling tree in the forested area west of the post. They received camp supplies and forty rounds of ammunition with a thousand round reserve for protection. Jordan also had the post quartermaster requisition additional carpentry and masonry tools on July 21.[44]

Major Perry requested the construction of additional necessary buildings not included in the initial planning or funding. Original plans for quarters for four companies totaled $10,700. Perry wanted the remainder of the $15,000 appropriation for Camp Robinson work to go for a blacksmith shop, bakery, guardhouse, three sets of laundresses' quarters, and a barracks and stable for a cavalry company. General Ord immediately approved the additions and forwarded the request to division headquarters. Perry's additional estimates totaled $3,798.24, well within the allotted appropriation, and division commander Sheridan approved the additional expense. On August 21 Perry forwarded his proposal to the chief quartermaster in Washington. Ten days later Quartermaster General Meigs informed the division quartermaster that the additional funds had been transferred to his account.

What was to be the first major layout plan for Camp Robinson soon evolved. Typical of military post designs of the era, its planners arranged the buildings around an open parade ground, in this case, 160 yards square. The officers' row ran on its north side and the company barracks on the east and west sides, somewhat of a departure from the usual plan (enlisted men's barracks usually sat opposite officer housing). On the south a headquarters building, guardhouse, cavalry barracks, and storehouse were subsequently built. Other utility post buildings, including corrals and stables, were added later to the south side closer to Soldier Creek.

On August 8—two days after his official authorization—Jordan made his first progress report. Nine hundred logs had been cut and five hundred hauled to the site. A supply of stone had been accumulated at the camp. Workers had prepared enough framing lumber for the company barracks and dug their foundations. The barracks were built of log in panels fifteen feet long. Square posts, each grooved on two sides, were set in the ground at fifteen-foot intervals. Logs cut that length were then placed between the posts, secured by spikes driven into the upright posts and the cleated ends of the logs. Spaces were allowed for door and window openings, and chinking was then packed between the logs. This construction method was used on the barracks and other log buildings.[45]

The two infantry barracks were 150 x 24 feet, divided in the middle to accommodate two companies. Sawed lumber was used for rafters for a single-gabled roof covered with wood shingles. The interiors were floored, but the initial construction did not allow for ceilings. On the front (parade ground) side, a company storeroom and first sergeant's room, each fifteen feet square, projected outward on each company half of the building. On the back a twelve-foot-wide shed was added, running the full length of the building. This shed housed kitchens, mess rooms, and washrooms for each company. The squad bays allowed 685 cubic feet of air space per man, the acceptable standard for barracks, but had no provision for roof ventilation. Single, iron, "composite" bunks sat on the floor. With the mess hall additions running the full length, no windows could appear in the back wall. The dormitory areas were undoubtedly dark and poorly ventilated.[46]

Six sets of officers' quarters were authorized for the post, five for company officers and a single house for the commanding officer. The plans called for them to be built of adobe bricks set on stone foundations, with plastered interior walls and board ceilings. The main part of adobe was 38 x 32 feet, divided into four rooms, with a four-foot-wide hallway down the center. On the rear of each building a two-room frame addition for a dining room and kitchen adjoined the east half, each room thirteen feet square.

The buildings provided decent, but cramped shelter for their occupants. Each set was intended to house three officers, the number normally assigned each company; the captain would have two rooms on one side, and his two lieutenants were to share the other half. Evidently all three were to jointly use the kitchen and dining facilities.[47] Obviously no provision was made for the men's dependents.

Adobe brick was used extensively in military construction on the northern Plains. Adobe had appeared as early as 1849 at Fort Kearny in present Nebraska and 1850 at Fort Laramie, and by the 1870s the army used it to reduce costs at other posts in Nebraska, Wyoming, Montana, and the Dakotas. The department quartermaster's office approved it for Robinson, where clay was available, and in August an adobe yard was set up.

Jordan thought he would attempt to build one set of officers' quarters from adobe before continuing with the others. This delayed their completion until the next spring. The disadvantage of adobe was that its unprotected exterior walls would "melt" with exposure to the elements. Preventive measures—wood siding and porches—were eventually taken with the adobe buildings.[48]

Additional arrangements were made for hauling logs. Five more teams were transferred from the supply train, keeping fifteen teams busy hauling logs out of the Soldier Creek hills. Colonel Smith at Fort Laramie had thought ox teams unnecessary; the mule teams on hand would suffice.

On August 12 Smith wrote Perry that he had informed the commanding officer at Spotted Tail that "under no circumstances should a post be built where the camp was."[49] Smith wanted the agency ten miles south on Beaver Creek. Even with funds for this other post secured, Smith wanted to concentrate on Camp Robinson.

By summer's end the Third Cavalry company was designated for retention as part of the permanent garrison at Camp Robinson. Now an additional set of barracks was needed. Perry requested permission to add the new barracks to his second authorized set of buildings. Because of the generally larger size of cavalry versus infantry companies, he asked for a longer, wider building (30 x 100 feet versus 25 x 75). His estimated cost was $712.25. By August 12 work on the cavalry barracks had already commenced. Jordan picked a site on the southeast corner of the parade ground, sixty-six feet east of the post headquarters, or adjutant's office.[50]

Difficulties in timely communication between department headquarters and the distant post led to confusion concerning this barracks's construction. Jordan started work on a barracks seventy-five feet long, the same length as the infantry quarters. On August 31 he conferred with the cavalry company commander and decided the structure needed to be lengthened, so work proceeded on a building *ninety* feet long. When 1st Lt. Jesse M. Lee replaced Auman as post quartermaster in September, he immediately ran into the complications that continually plagued the new post. On September 5 he received directions from Perry to build a barracks one hundred feet long. Lee and Jordan replied that they could not comply. Work was well underway, with the foundations in and frame up for a ninety foot building. It was too late in the season to rebuild. Jordan had to justify in writing his decision. Fortunately, since he had been given leeway to carry out the construction as he saw fit, General Ord formally approved the change after-the-fact on September 23.

Other than a greater length and width, the cavalry barracks appeared the same as the infantry models. The squad bay was thirty by ninety feet. A storeroom and first sergeant's room were on the parade (north) side. The mess hall, kitchen, and washroom were identical to the other barracks.[51]

Due to its isolated location, Camp Robinson was also cursed with problems in receiving its supplies. Quartermaster, subsistence, ordnance, and building supplies were requisitioned through department headquarters in Omaha. Sent via the Union Pacific Railroad to the quartermaster depot at Cheyenne, then shipped north by wagon, the time of arrival naturally depended on weather conditions. Lieutenant Auman foresaw order and delivery problems and requested that he be allowed to order supplies eleven months in advance, not the usual three months. Lieutenant Lee later made a similar request; he doubted the post could subsist over the winter with a three month supply.[52]

Other needs arose. Supplying the post kept many quartermaster teams and wagons busy, so in August funds for corrals were requested. Critical construction tools and materials needed to be forwarded without delay.

There was even an acute shortage of stationery. Lee reported that he had borrowed from Saville and the agency traders until he hesitated to ask for more. He had no forms for company, post, or board reports and urgently requested—probably on borrowed stationery—department headquarters to send each item.[53]

As large quantities of supplies for Camp Robinson were unexpectedly transferred to the post at Spotted Tail Agency, a shortage of subsistence supplies occurred in October. The commissary officer at Fort Laramie had to transfer ten thousand rations of coffee, sugar, soap, and candles to Robinson; other needs of both Robinson and Spotted Tail were supplied from North Platte Station, a post near the forks of the Platte River at present North Platte, Nebraska.[54]

Construction continued into the fall. On September 28 Lee requested permission from Jordan to continue the number of men on extra duty construction work. He believed good weather could not continue much longer. Although twenty-six men were authorized, forty-six were on extra duty. Soldier laborers assisted the mason, hauled logs, attended lime kilns, and quarried rock; ten soldiers worked the adobe yard; the others regularly worked as carpenters. Perry recommended that extra duty men over the authorized number be placed on "daily duty." The decision saved money in the budget because the army was not required to provide extra pay to daily duty men.[55]

Meanwhile Spotted Tail Agency moved to the Beaver Creek site. With that matter finally settled, building shelter for the troops there was pushed forward. The number of extra duty men at the new Spotted Tail post, suitably named Camp Sheridan, was doubled.

The additional buildings at Camp Robinson meant the demand for more lumber. On October 15 Lee requested hiring the agency sawmill for sixty days at a rate of $393 per month. Since Saville did not want inexperienced men to operate his mill, the army again had to hire agency employees. Although Perry approved the additional expense, General Ord preferred making the payment in kind with bartered lumber rather than from declining quartermaster funds.[56]

In October Lt. Col. Cuvier Grover, Third Cavalry, the department inspector general, visited the new post. He reported that construction work involved every available man and recommended all items that Lee requisitioned be sent as soon as possible. He also pointed out a potential hazard to the new post:

> It is stated that thunder and lightning storms are very frequent in the season and very severe here. Would it not be

well to send lightning rods not in use at other posts near here to this post for the protection of as many buildings as might be covered in this way?

Perry replied that lighting rods for the buildings could be purchased when funds were available, but they could wait until spring.[57]

Construction of Camp Robinson could have ground to a halt when "lightning" nearly struck at Red Cloud Agency, and the "rod" was nothing more than a seemingly innocent flagpole. In late October Agent Saville decided to erect a flagpole at the agency. As with the Kenssler affair, open war nearly broke out between the non-agency Sioux and the soldiers.[58]

Saville's motivation sounded reasonable. Indians came to the agency every day of the week; they did not observe Sunday as a day of rest. Raising a flag on Sundays would indicate that no business would be conducted at the agency. One agency resident employee claimed its real use was as a signal to the soldiers in case of trouble. Another later said the reason was more mundane, simply the patriotic ceremony of displaying the flag at public institutions. Whatever the reason, Saville's flagpole nearly ignited a conflagration.

On October 22, 1874, Saville sent men up Soldier Creek to cut several tall pines to make the pole and to haul them inside the agency stockade. Some Indians noticed them, asked their purpose, then spread word of the proposed flagstaff through the camps near the agency. Many Sioux strongly objected to Saville's planned use of the flag; they heatedly claimed that he was making a military post out of the agency, reasoning that only soldiers flew the American flag. They demanded it not be flown at their agency. More strident objections came from Minneconjou warriors who happened to be at the agency. They saw the erection of a flagpole as a declaration of war by the whites.

On October 23 a group of about two hundred angry men, mostly non-agency northern Indians and Brulés, entered the agency. They attempted to carry off the prepared logs, still on the ground, but found them too heavy. They then proceeded to chop the flagpole to pieces with hatchets. At that moment both Red Cloud and Red Dog, the latter the Oglala leader instrumental in the agency move to White River, were inside the stockade conferring with Saville; they did not—or could not—stop the actions of their angry comrades. Saville, after ordering the vandals to desist, sent a runner to the soldier camp for help.

About 1 P.M. Captain Jordan received Saville's request to send a company of men to the agency; the note did not state why. Somewhat at a loss, he decided to send "as much cavalry as I could spare." He later recalled, "[M]y force [at the camp] was the weakest that it had been up to that time (only 140 men) and it was not the time to try any experiment with Indians, especially such as would excite them to war."[59] He dispatched Lt. Emmet Crawford and twenty-six men of his company to ride out and explore the problem.

At Red Cloud more and more Indians assembled, incensed by the news that soldiers had been sent for. When Crawford's detachment arrived near the stockade, over five hundred mounted warriors had massed, with more arriving all the time. Crawford recalled the Indians were "all mounted and stripped, and when they saw me coming over the hill they commenced putting cartridges in their guns and cock them."[60] Many warriors raced back and forth to give their horses a second wind preparatory to battle. The situation looked ugly.

At that critical moment yet another large body of Sioux men came charging up, Oglalas under Young Man Afraid of His Horses and Sitting Bull, the nephew of Little Wound. Sitting Bull, a noted warrior of the Oglala often confused with the Hunkpapa leader of the same name, swung a great swath with his renowned, three-bladed war club. He quickly forced an opening in the hostile crowd, which enabled Crawford and his men to reach the protection of the agency stockade. The actions of the friendly chiefs averted an attack on Crawford's detachment. One shot fired could have "opened the ball," as one eyewitness put it.[61]

A general riot ensued between the two rival groups. The opposing factions fought in deadly earnest with whips, war clubs, and gun butts, knocking one another from their horses. Old Man Afraid of His Horses and Red Dog harangued the crowd, which finally heeded their words and broke up. About 4 P.M. Crawford was able to send a message back to camp to warn Jordan. Sitting Bull told Saville that if the soldiers were dismissed, his people would guard the agency. About an hour later the detachment set off for Camp Robinson, although Crawford saw Indians prepared to burn the agency and heard threats against the soldiers.

The agency Indians told their defiant northern cousins that they would tolerate no more trouble at *their* agency. The northern warriors expressed their disgust with this apparent desertion of the agency bands to the side of the whites. By morning the northern camps had disappeared from the vicinity.

Saville, understandably shaken, decided against erecting his flagpole for which the military greatly criticized him. He had placed Crawford and his men in grave jeopardy, and his failure to now raise the pole showed weakness. Lieutenant Crawford, whose cool behavior served to extricate him and his men from a dangerous position, commented later, "I think it is the only way to deal with the Indians; that he [Saville] ought not have given in to those Indians the way he did."[62] To the Indian allies went much of the credit for preventing a disaster.

Some placed the blame on the Wazhazhas, a troublesome Brulé band under Red Leaf that seemingly found fault with everything. One of the firebrands that day was Conquering Bear, the son of old Chief Conquering Bear, who had been killed by Lt. John Grattan's men near Fort Laramie in 1854. Saville, thankful for the support he received, declared the unruly warriors to be Minneconjous, who undoubtedly made up many of their number.[63]

The flagpole incident was important enough to the Sioux that their historians recorded it as a "winter count" event for the year. For the whites it reinforced how factionalized the Sioux people were, and how difficult it was to deal with them. To the Sioux it pointed out the division between the non-agency, northern Indians and the agency Sioux, whose leadership frequently supported the white agent. To agency personnel, it was simply "some for the agent & others against." Luckily for the whites, Sitting Bull supported Saville and desired order at the agency. President Grant later personally presented a Winchester rifle to Sitting Bull in appreciation for the courage he showed that day.[64]

The flagpole incident did not slow the post's construction. The first buildings occupied by mid-October were the enlisted men's barracks. On October 19 Company G occupied the cavalry barracks. All that remained to be done in the other infantry barracks was installing baseboard, doors, and windows in the mess halls. By November all the camp's enlisted component were under roofs.[65]

Now the quartermaster officers realized that they were running out of funds to pay their civilian workers. By November 19 all civilian employees had to be discharged, except for the master mason and carpenter. Lieutenant Lee estimated that he had enough money in his account to keep them on until year's end.[66]

The problem of housing for the company laundresses had to be addressed next. According to policy, army washerwomen were authorized quarters at their assigned troop stations, usually some sort of shelter near the parade ground. Lieutenant Lee pointed out that the eight sets the department quartermaster authorized were insufficient; he had fifteen laundresses at Camp Robinson. Lee was allowed to build the extra quarters if any money remained after paying for civilian labor. This delayed construction of the laundresses' quarters, and unfortunately the women and any spouses and dependents remained in tents through the winter of 1874–75.

A post hospital was another building not included in the initial plan. Accommodations for the sick consisted of four, framed hospital tents: one tent was used as a dispensary and steward's quarters; two served as sick wards of seven beds each; and one provided for hospital stores and "meager quarters for the post surgeon."[67] This crude facility was grouped above Soldier Creek west of the parade ground. Nearby, the soldiers excavated a dugout into the creek bank for a hospital kitchen and sleeping quarters for its cook. Work on a permanent hospital building did not begin until the next fiscal year.

As the building season tapered off, so did work on the officers' quarters. By the end of October two sets were nearly completed, but lack of adobe brick delayed work on the rest. The post surgeon reported, "[T]he season for making them [adobe bricks] has nearly expired, the chances for most of the officers remaining in tents all winter seems more than probable."[68]

With cold weather approaching, the garrison became painfully aware of the complete absence of stoves, both for heating and cooking. Large-sized stoves were needed in barracks dormitory areas and mess halls, smaller ones for officers' and laundresses' quarters and in other offices. By November only two stoves could be found at the post. Requisitions for seventy-three stoves had been forwarded to Omaha in August, but apparently never acted on. Requests were made to nearby posts in the Department of the Platte for their extra stoves, but none materialized. Post Surgeon John F. Randolph lamented:

> In the matter of stoves there has been criminal neglect somewhere. . . . It will be mid winter before they will probably get here, and there must be great suffering for the thermometer already ranges nightly considerably below the twenties![69]

Subsequent requisitions and pleas finally met with success. On November 23 Lieutenant Lee dutifully reported that fifty-three stoves had been received from Cheyenne Depot. Although one of the wagons had overturned on the road from Fort Laramie, wrecking four of the Imperial box heating stoves and one Charter Oak No. 5 cooking stove, the survivors were hurriedly installed and replacements reordered. The troops settled in for the winter.[70]

With as many men as possible assigned to building projects, Captain Jordan became particularly annoyed when district headquarters at Fort Laramie ordered him to detail a company to improve the wagon road and crossings of the White River. The drain on his manpower would delay the hauling of logs. The laundresses and one officer were still living in tents; other officers were forced to live in the dining rooms of the completed officers' quarters. No shelter was up for his cavalry and quartermaster animals. Jordan argued that escorts returning with the supply trains could do the road repair work; his soldiers needed to complete Camp Robinson. Late in December the repair order was revoked, and work pushed forward.[71]

By the end of the year most of the initial $15,000 had been expended. Lieutenant Lee reported that, after buying materials and paying civilian labor (less their daily rations), only $381.91 remained. This sum was applied to the laundresses' quarters, but only the foundations for this long building, 144 x 26 feet, and divided into twelve, two-room apartments, were completed.

During Camp Robinson's first winter the "log barricade" came into being. Private contractors generally cut and delivered firewood for army posts, and Camp Robinson was no exception. In May 1874 the post quartermaster reported that 2,250 cords of wood would be needed during the fiscal year. With the post's defense in mind, Jordan had the cordwood stacked to form a barricade around the main post area. The waist-high wall ran a short distance to the rear of the entire building perimeter, with "bastions" laid out in the corners nearest the Red Cloud Agency. A later visitor to the post savaged this defensive measure:

> If therefore the Indians were on the war-path and disposed to crawl upon the garrison and attack the fort, as they would probably do in such a case, this excellent barricade would belong to them and not to the garrison, for the Indians would get to it first. . . . [T]wo or three men could crawl up to the cordwood in a dark, windy night, and start fires and clear out. Others at a distance would cover the fires with their rifles till sufficient headway was obtained, and soon the whole place would be surrounded by a circle of flame from which every building would catch fire and the post and its contents be utterly consumed.[72]

Such derision aside, the cordwood barricade did give Camp Robinson an air of the log palisade that so many visitors then and now expect to see at western forts.

As weather permitted, construction continued, and Camp Robinson took on a more permanent appearance. Lumber, stone, and hardware were stockpiled, and Lee managed to siphon off enough money from the department quartermaster's office to finish the desired additions. By spring 1875 the first major building phase of Camp Robinson had ended.

On the south side of the parade ground stood two structures that would play a significant role in Camp Robinson's history. West of the cavalry barracks was the adjutant's office, or post headquarters, a small log structure divided into two offices for the adjutant and post commander. Both offices had doors that opened onto the parade ground. In line with the adjutant's office to the west was the guardhouse, also built of logs, boards, and iron grating for windows. It too was evenly divided into two rooms, one a guardroom, the other a general prison. Spacing between each building on the south side of the parade—cavalry barracks, adjutant's office, guardhouse, and warehouse—was exactly sixty-six feet.[73]

South of the cavalry barracks in late spring was added a troop stable, 150 x 30 feet. It contained thirty-four stalls for sixty-eight horses. A corral for the horses ran along the stable on its east side.

Behind the storehouse, a temporary frame building with a canvas roof, 60 x 25 feet, stored grain or "short forage." For some time, other quartermaster supplies had to be kept in three hospital tents. Near the storehouse, soldiers dug a root cellar.[74]

By mid-March the long laundresses' quarters dormitory was occupied and provided cramped, but seemingly adequate housing. Its cost totaled $1,000. The four infantry companies required three laundresses each, accounting for the twelve-unit quarters built on the creek. That spring a single set of quarters was built east of the cavalry barracks. This small log building housed washerwomen for the troopers.

Behind the cavalry barracks, quarters for a wagonmaster was built. This 14 x 14 foot hut was the only quarters built on the post strictly for a civilian employee. Next to it were the shops for the soldier blacksmith, carpenter, and saddler, housed in a single, long building. The last building completed during the fiscal year 1874–75 was the bakery, south of the warehouse, which replaced the post baker's inadequate field ovens. Now his log and board structure contained a brick oven with a bread-making capacity for six companies.

Although the buildings at Robinson were crude by any standard, they surpassed the small huts of its sister post at Spotted Tail in which the men lived their first year. A newspaper correspondent, who saw both posts, wrote of Camp Robinson's "neatly constructed adobe brick quarters and log barracks" that "give it an air of permanence and comfort that is not possessed by the primitive earth covered cantonments at Camp Sheridan."[75]

On July 29, 1875, Lieutenant Lee reported to Perry that the buildings were officially completed. He had spent $14,801.36. Lee also commented, "[T]he labor of enlisted men has contributed greatly to the construction of the buildings," but since they were all paid from the quartermaster "incidental" expense accounts for extra duty pay, he conveniently did not include that expense in his final figures.[76]

Although having moved out of their tents, some officers criticized their new housing, complaining that their quarters still lacked kitchens and dining rooms. Most hated the common hallway dividing the quarters. They faulted the lack of porches and the small size of the dormitories in the barracks. The barracks needed separate mess halls and company kitchens.[77] Finally, no provision for quarters for the post surgeon had been allowed. During the next fiscal year, his quarters and a regular post hospital were built. Complaints notwithstanding, by the summer of 1875 Camp Robinson looked like a frontier post, an appearance that would endure until the great expansion of 1887.

Chapter 3

Life and Death at Camp Robinson

Until the fall of 1876 Ninth Infantry and Second and Third cavalry units continued to garrison Camp Robinson. Occasionally companies from the same regiments were rotated with units from other posts in the sprawling Department of the Platte. Although troop strength normally numbered around two hundred men, for most of 1875 some 350 officers and enlisted men were assigned to the post. This was generally found to be an adequate force to keep order at the agency. At times troop strength dropped below levels acceptable to camp officers. For instance, in June 1876 Capt. William Jordan complained when two companies were ordered from the camp to scout toward the Black Hills. Their departure left fewer than one hundred men at the post, "a force insufficient . . . to properly protect this post and Red Cloud Agency in case of outbreak."[1]

Good reasons explained the larger proportion of infantry compared to cavalry at Camp Robinson. The garrison was supposed to guard a fixed point, Red Cloud Agency, and infantry troops were better suited for that type of deployment. Infantry soldiers were easier to maintain in the field, with fewer horses and lesser forage needs. Also the long-range infantry rifles posed more of a danger to an attacking foe than the carbines of the cavalry. Some cavalry troops came in handy, though, for scouting and rapid pursuit, so a cavalry company remained a part of the garrison.

The garrison at Camp Robinson fortunately had capable officers who provided able leadership during the critical early years. All were either West Point graduates or veterans of the Civil War; they had some expertise in Plains warfare. One such officer, Captain Jordan, built the post and served as its commanding officer for several years. Also among this group was Capt. Guy V. Henry, Third Cavalry, an 1861 West Point graduate and an artillery and infantry officer during the war. In 1870 he transferred to the cavalry and was stationed at Camp Robinson in 1874–75 and again in

1877. Henry eventually returned for a third tour in the early 1890s as a Ninth Cavalry major.[2]

Another exceptionally capable officer at the camp was 1st Lt. Emmet Crawford, also of the Third Cavalry. Crawford, from Pennsylvania, served through most of the Civil War as a noncommissioned officer in a Pennsylvania infantry regiment; in 1864 he was commissioned as a lieutenant in one of the black volunteer infantry regiments. After the war he continued with black regular troops until transferring to the Third Cavalry, eventually becoming a captain in 1879. In the 1880s Crawford saw duty in the Southwest and actively campaigned in the Apache wars. In January 1886, while leading a detachment across the border into Mexico in pursuit of Apaches, Crawford suffered a mortal wound in a sharp engagement with Mexican nationals.[3] Afterward the town of Crawford, neighbor to Fort Robinson, was named in his honor. Crawford, Henry, and Jordan were typical of the professional officers who led the American army through the difficulties of the Plains Indian wars.

With a large number of Indians living nearby, Red Cloud Agency was described by some historians as a dangerous "powder keg."[4] Doubtless the close proximity of soldiers to the agency deterred hostile demonstrations. Obviously the soldiers gave additional weight to the agent's authority, their "assistance" in census-taking being a good example. Never did the agents and Indian bureau authorities request the removal of the soldiers during the White River years.

Nevertheless, with this ever-present potential for violence, troop duties at Camp Robinson—and at all army posts—could be divided into two broad categories, either field service or garrison duty. Field service for the Camp Robinson garrison included scouting and escort duty, pursuit of raiding bands, and occasionally assisting with law enforcement on the agency.

Although initially opposed to using soldiers as an agency police force, the military's attitude shifted coincidentally about the same time Dr. Saville was replaced as agent. In November 1875 the Interior secretary requested military assistance to the new agent at Red Cloud, who intended to withhold rations until the Indians turned over an accused party. Indian bureau officials feared trouble, requested support, and Secretary of War Belknap informed them that soldiers from Camp Robinson were ready to help enforce the agent's orders. In another matter the agent arrested several individuals on suspicion of murder. Commander Jordan allowed the suspects, including famed scout Moses "California Joe" Milner, to be held in the camp guardhouse until they were cleared and released.[5]

Both the army and Indian bureau stood as one on the issue of the illegal sale of whiskey at the agency. In the fall of 1875 several Mexicans worked for the government wood contractor, and one was arrested for "introducing liquor within the limits of the Indian reservation." Jordan also had his men arrest two other individuals for selling liquor to soldiers at the post. The parties were destined for Cheyenne for trial before a civil court. Concerning the accused Mexican, the agent could not prove that the individual had actually sold whiskey, so he was released from confinement and told to leave the area.[6]

In January 1876 the new agent, James S. Hastings, reported that "a set of idle, worthless vagabonds with no means of support" had persisted in remaining at the agency, and he requested military assistance to remove them.[7] Since this case apparently did not involve the illegal whiskey trade, Jordan replied that he had no authority to act. Several days later department headquarters told Jordan to assist with the evictions, but only after the agent put the request in writing. The next month the department judge advocate ruled that post commanders should be informed in writing of probable cause before making arrests. The agent should plainly set forth the complaint so the party or parties charged could be properly informed of the accusation. The army could assist the agent, but its soldiers could not place the rights of private citizens in jeopardy by making unsubstantiated and unnecessary arrests.[8]

In the spring of 1876 Camp Robinson soldiers arrested several other whiskey peddlers; other undesirables were "removed beyond the limits of the reservation." The post and agency sat not on the reservation, but in what the government considered "Indian country." In May General Sherman stated that the army should assist the Indian bureau in civil matters. Sheridan remained skeptical of military involvement and remarked that care should be taken to prevent conflict with civil authority.[9]

When the army was given control of the agencies, it possessed the authority to enforce measures against civilian lawbreakers both at the agencies and in Indian country. In the winter of 1876–77 a number of undesirables were arrested for stealing horses and money from agency Indians and sent to Omaha for prosecution. Soldiers seized two men for "building and keeping a ranch for selling whiskey on the reservation without the proper authority." Also that spring, "Sage Brush Bill" Underwood and "Black Doc" Porgood were arrested for persistently returning to the agency after having been evicted several times.[10] Regardless of conflicting views over jurisdiction, Camp Robinson soldiers played a conspicuous role in maintaining civil control at the agencies.

The influx of miners illegally into the Black Hills in 1874 brought additional field duty for the Camp Robinson garrison. In that year Lt. Col. George A. Custer's expedition explored the mysterious Hills, and word quickly spread that gold had been discovered. Although the Black Hills lay in Indian territory, and white incursions were prohibited by the 1868 treaty, small parties of miners sneaked in. The difficult and unpopular task of keeping out the whites fell to the army.[11] With the nation in the grip of a financial depression, gold in the Hills was seen as a welcomed economic boost, but at surrounding army posts the troops prepared for their onerous assignment. The winter march of Capt. Guy Henry's Third Cavalry company typified the hardship and futility incurred in this duty.

On December 24 a dispatch from Fort Laramie ordered Henry's company to search for and remove a party of twenty miners reportedly seen on Elk Creek on the eastern slope of the Hills. Captain Jordan also sent along 1st Lt. William L. Carpenter and twelve Ninth infantrymen, making the detachment fifty men strong. Together with twelve wagons carrying tents, Sibley stoves, blanket covers for the horses, and thirty days' rations and forage, Henry's command left the post the day after Christmas.[12]

Two days later the "expedition to the Black Hills" reached Camp Sheridan, where Henry expected to pick up an Indian guide. Due to the extreme cold—the winter of 1874–75 was thought the coldest on record—the guide, who had also reported the miners on Elk Creek, refused to join the troops. After securing the services of a local resident familiar with the country, Henry marched north toward the Dakota Badlands, and five days later the party reached Elk Creek. With the thermometer having dropped to forty degrees below zero, the march was hell on men and horses. After finding no sign of the trespassers, Henry wisely decided to return to Camp Robinson. Later it was learned the miners entered the Hills farther to the north, not by way of Elk Creek.

Luckily for the suffering command the wind was slight for much of the return trip. On the last day's march, January 8, the troops broke camp "in gay spirits" as they thought evening would find them back at the post. As the troops moved out, the cavalry rode ahead and soon became separated from their wagons. At 7 A.M. a fierce blast of Arctic wind, commonly called a "norther" on the Plains, hit the cavalrymen with full force. Producing subzero windchills, the norther also brought blinding snow, high drifts, and disorientation to the hard-pressed travelers.[13]

Now unable to return to the previous campsite or search for the wagons, Henry ordered his men to dismount and lead their horses. Their struggle through the storm became a fight for life, as some of the frozen, exhausted men had to be strapped in their saddles or beaten to force them to keep on. By afternoon their plight was desperate, their only hope to reach Camp Robinson or some other shelter from the deadly wind. In a last bid for survival Henry had his men mount and trust the natural instincts of their horses to find shelter. Miraculously the horses brought the command to a solitary ranch cabin located in a bend on White River. After corralling their horses, the men tumbled inside to thaw out. The rancher, a man named Bridgeman, informed Captain Henry that Camp Robinson still lay fifteen miles beyond. Aware that shelter at the ranch was only a temporary respite for his men, Henry and three of the stronger men set out for the post.[14]

Later that evening Henry's party staggered into Camp Robinson. The next morning Jordan sent wagons to bring in the remainder. Meanwhile Lieutenant Carpenter and the expedition's wagon train had also stumbled on Bridgeman's cabin. The harrowing ordeal of Henry's winter march had ended.

As a result of their exposure forty-five of the fifty men on the expedition suffered frostbite—but not a man was lost. Captain Henry, who it was reported suffered the most, later remarked, "Entering my own quarters, I was not recognized owing to my black and swollen face."[15] He also lost a portion of one frostbitten finger. But his recovery was brightened later when a son, Guy V. Henry, Jr., was born on January 28, the first recorded birth at Camp Robinson. The other casualties were hospitalized for several weeks, which seriously depleted the cavalry force at the post. Although the wisdom of deploying troops to the virtually unknown Black Hills in winter was rightly questioned, Henry later stoically declared a la Rudyard Kipling, "[I]t was not ours to question why."[16]

Although Henry had failed to enlist an Indian guide for his mission, the army continued to seek Indian help to locate trespassing miners and to augment its limited manpower. Commanding officers at both agency camps used the agents to recruit competent and discreet Indians to discover miner camps, but warned them not to molest the miners themselves. Three months later further orders called for the enlistment of fifty Indians to serve as scouts. Such military surveillance by soldier and ally, however limited, continued through 1875.[17]

Because of its inherent mobility, the main occupation of the cavalry company remained scouting and pursuit. The Second and Third cavalrymen often spent many days, even weeks, scouting for signs of purported Indian raiders. In May 1875 Captain Egan's company hunted for a party of Southern Cheyennes reportedly moving north. The company covered 120 miles in two days, but found no sign of the Cheyennes. In June Company K twice searched for Indian raiders who had taken horses from whites and also from the Pawnee Indian reservation in central Nebraska. And weather continued to interfere with scouting missions. In December 1875 Company K, Third Cavalry, set forth to find a party of Indians who had run off forty-seven horses near Antelope Station (now Kimball, Nebraska). A sudden snowstorm came up, obliterated the raider trail, and forced the troops to return to Camp Robinson.[18]

Another mission brought no results. On December 27, 1876, 2nd Lt. James F. Simpson and Company B left to hunt Indians who had attacked a party of whites *en route* from Hat Creek Station to Camp Robinson; two men were reported killed and two wounded in the fight. A civilian, confident he could lead Simpson to the spot where the Indians had attacked, guided the soldiers. Simpson soon found out that the civilian had no idea of where the attack took place and in fact knew nothing about the surrounding country. In disgust the troops returned to the post.[19]

Occasionally the troops achieved limited success in the field. On September 19, 1876, a Fourth Cavalry company rushed out in pursuit of a hostile band. Six days later the men returned, having covered 250 miles. Although they did not capture the warriors, they managed to sight their quarry and capture ten of their ponies.[20]

Desertion was a serious problem in the frontier army, and one deterrent was swift pursuit and sure punishment. Soldiers were quickly dispatched to hunt down and apprehend deserters. Lieutenant Crawford seems to have been particularly adept in capturing fugitives. In October 1874 he was commended in orders for pursuing and capturing three deserters, who were mounted and had a twelve-hour head start. "This is the third time Lieut. Crawford has been detailed on such duty and he has succeeded in apprehending every deserter that he had been sent after, making in all 17 that he has apprehended since the 22nd day of May."[21]

Others met with less success. In October 1876 two soldiers held for desertion and horse stealing escaped from the post guardhouse. Although cavalrymen searched the Sidney and Fort Laramie roads, the logical escape routes, the deserters made good their escape.[22]

Due to the continual Indian threat, armed escorts were mandatory for travel to and from the agencies. Even the sympathetic commissioners sent to reason with and coerce the Oglalas and Brulés dared not travel without military protection. In the summer of 1875 Captain Egan's company spent nearly a month escorting the Sioux Commission from Robinson to the Cheyenne River Agency in Dakota Territory and back, a total of 594 miles.

Troops, both infantry and cavalry, escorted the supply trains moving between the agencies and Fort Laramie. Colonel Smith favored the use of mounted troops, figuring that traveling with the slow moving wagons would not injure his horses. Infantrymen commonly guarded supply trains and occasionally rode on the loaded wagons, but this practice proved more dangerous to the stores than to any marauders. Orders followed in October 1874 that prohibited the men from riding atop wagons with perishable loads.[23] Stepped up military operations resulted in more escorts accompanying supply trains, which further depleted post manpower. Conversely, as the threat of hostilities waned, so did the number of men attached to the trains. By 1878 small details of one noncommissioned officer and three privates normally supplied a train escort.

Soldier escorts served a variety of groups. Senior officers required escorts from the garrison. In September 1876 Fourth cavalrymen escorted Col. Ranald S. Mackenzie between the post and Fort Laramie. Gen. George Crook, who replaced Ord as department commander, criss-crossed the area with his escort from the post. At the other end of the social scale, during the fall of 1876 small details escorted from Cheyenne groups of recruits assigned to the regiments then massed at Camp Robinson. Prisoners destined to Cheyenne (civilian offenders) and to Forts Laramie or D. A. Russell (soldiers) for confinement and trial also required guards. Once, soldiers escorted laundresses and another time remount horses from the railroad at Sidney to the post.[24]

When Red Cloud Agency was moved to a new home in Dakota Territory in 1877, Camp Robinson provided escorts for the slow-moving body of Indians and their vast amounts of subsistence supplies. Later the soldiers guarded the numerous shipments of goods to the new agency.

Civilian lawbreakers, especially horse thieves, continued to demand the attention of the Camp Robinson troops. In March 1877 a cavalry company and twenty-two Indian scouts left the post in pursuit of thieves and returned two weeks later after covering 340 miles and apprehending three men. The soldiers also recovered two army horses, one mule, sixty-eight Indian ponies, one government carbine, two revolvers, and two army saddles. The next year a small detail set off after thieves who had stolen three horses from the army beef contractor. The contractor was temporarily furnished one public horse and saddle "in order to enable him to assist in the pursuit and capture of the thieves."[25]

In September 1877 troops were hurriedly dispatched to hunt for the desperadoes who had robbed a Union Pacific train near Big Springs, Nebraska. They joined troops from other posts in the region in the hopes of quickly nabbing the robbers. The Camp Robinson troops returned after fruitlessly searching for four days south along the Sidney–Black Hills Trail.

Other forms of field duty were more mundane, yet controversial in their own right. During the initial construction of the post, Captain Jordan became incensed when Lt. Col. Luther P. Bradley ordered a sizeable part of his work force into the field to do road repair. Jordan's soldiers worked to bridge the crossings of the White River east of the post. After three weeks the troops were finally allowed to return to camp. In 1876 a large detachment of recruits marching to Camp Robinson were likewise required to work their way on this same road to their first post.[26]

The building of the telegraph line to Camp Robinson in 1877 brought additional field service for the soldiers. Prior to 1876 mounted couriers had to carry telegraphic dispatches between Camp Robinson and the nearest station, located at Fort Laramie. With the construction of the main line from Fort Laramie north to Deadwood in mid-1876, the station at Hat Creek, fifty-three miles west of Camp Robinson, became the closest access to the telegraph. In March and April 1877 the soldiers built a line to Hat Creek Station, finally giving Camp Robinson direct telegraphic connections. After completion troop details frequently went out to repair or improve the line.

Regardless of the variety of field duties Camp Robinson soldiers performed, they spent the majority of their time on regular garrison duty. Garrison duty consisted of a daily, almost relentless, routine that maintained the post as a military operation. Regular routine helped instill discipline in the soldiers. Don Rickey, a noted historian of the frontier army, best described discipline as "the foundation of military authority, . . . essential to the efficient functioning of any military unit, and for maintaining order." He added, "Discipline refers to the training of soldiers to comport themselves in a prescribed manner."[27] Discipline regulated garrison life and was maintained by the rigid schedule of the post.

Every military post—and Camp Robinson was no exception— announced its hourly schedule by service calls. On July 14, 1874, the first schedule was published in general orders. Unless specified otherwise in orders, the calls remained the same each and every day. Times of specific calls had to be adjusted to season, with hours advanced as winter approached and set back as spring turned into summer. Musicians assigned to the guard made the calls on drum and/or bugle.

The routine of garrison duty may best be appreciated by following the series of calls that governed the soldier's day. The day actually began with the gathering of buglers and field musicians at 5 A.M. At 5:10 they sounded reveille, the signal for the soldiers to rise and for the sentries to cease challenging. Five minutes later, a drum or bugle sounded assembly. According to regulations at least three roll calls were required each day, with the first just after reveille.[28] After reveille the soldiers put the barracks area in order.

In 1875 two stable calls, one in the morning and one in the afternoon, were incorporated into the post schedule for the cavalry troops. Morning stables was sounded immediately after assembly, when the mounted troops went to feed their horses and police the stable.

At 6 A.M. the soldiers hurried to their barracks mess halls after hearing breakfast call. Company cooks, who had risen much earlier, prepared the meal. Sick call came just after breakfast. Ailing men were allowed to see the post surgeon at his hospital for treatment.

The real workday came with the sounding of fatigue call at 6:30 A.M. Fatigue was defined as the labor of soldiers distinct from the use of arms, in other words, any type of work demanded around the post. Soldiers were assigned various fatigue chores, along with special instructions, at company formations. The general police of the post occupied many of the morning hours during which details cleaned buildings and grounds, disposed of garbage, and removed night soil. Regular fatigue work included hauling and distributing water from the creek by water wagon to barrels at each building. The company gardens, located southeast of the post, had to be tended in season. During the winter months ice was cut and stored. Regular fatigue also included stable police work and kitchen detail.

Much of the work generally required short terms of special service for enlisted men and was classified "daily" duty. If necessary, individuals could be assigned for longer periods on "special" duty. These men performed tasks essential to the post's operation but not necessarily considered military. Special duty men included cooks, hospital attendants, mechanics, and company clerks. In between calls or when not on duty, the men lounged around the barracks or post area, pretty much on their own as long as they remained within bugle call.[29]

Fatigue was a continual source of discontent among soldiers, who often felt like cheap laborers for the army. Fatigue work, though, was essential for the maintenance of any military post, and at distant posts such as Camp Robinson soldiers were the only available work force from which to draw.

Compensation in addition to their regular pay came when men were assigned to "extra" duty. Extra duty was the continuous special duty of enlisted men at a specific task. If men were so employed at a certain job for more than ten consecutive days, they were entitled to receive twenty-five cents a day in extra pay. Men with previous experience as carpenters, stone masons, or mechanics qualified for thirty-five cents extra pay. Extra duty men were required to work a full day and therefore were excused from drill and firing practice. During construction periods as many as thirty-six men were on extra duty at the post. Quartermaster officers argued that it was more economical to use extra duty men than to hire civilian labor "at the high rates which rule this section."[30] Extra duty men cut logs, quarried rock, made adobe bricks, and worked as carpenters and plasterers.

The most important event of the daily routine was guard mount, which occurred each day promptly at 9 A.M. Guard mount was "the act of going on guard, the military ceremony of marching on guard."[31] Changing the post guard began at 8:50 with the assembly of buglers and drummers, who provided the martial marches heard during this ceremony. Assembly was at 8:55, when the soldiers designated for the new guard gathered in front of their barracks and marched to the guardhouse.

Adjutant's call sounded at 9 A.M. The new and old guards formed before the guardhouse for inspection by the post adjutant, usually a lieutenant. The highlight of guard mount was the daily selection of the orderly of the day. The adjutant chose the neatest and most soldierly-looking private of the new guard as the commanding officer's orderly.[32] Companies in garrison competed for the honor of having one of their own selected. The new guard was then divided into platoons for reliefs, and charge of the guard passed to the new officer of the day, who was responsible for all camp police, safety, and order. The officer of the day also enforced all post regulations, took charge of prisoners, and inspected the barracks. The new guard received any special instructions and then was posted for the next twenty-four-hour period. The old guard was dismissed, its members excused from fatigue and police duty for the rest of the day.

Army regulations called for a camp or post guard to be detailed daily. To the army, guard duty was one of the most important jobs of a soldier, and most training and drill prepared him for that function. Through the guard a military post was always secure and alert to any emergency or surprise by an enemy. Besides protecting the camp from theft and attack, the post guards watched for fire and raised and lowered the national flag.[33]

The guard came under the immediate command of the officer of the day, a position rotated among officers, sometimes coming once every five days. The officer of the guard visited the guardhouse at roll calls and made rounds of the sentry posts once each night at any time between 11 P.M. and reveille. The daily guard detail had two noncommissioned officers, assigned as sergeant and corporal of the guard, and one duty bugler who made all the daily calls and could alert the garrison during night hours. Eleven to fifteen privates made up the bulk of the guard. Extra guards, called supernumeraries, could be added specifically to guard prisoners during working hours. Guardhouse prisoners usually performed some type of useful work during daylight hours. The supernumeraries, dismissed after retreat, returned to their barracks for the night. The regular guard remained in the guardhouse when not on relief.[34]

Camp Robinson guards manned four sentry posts. Post number one was directly in front of the guardhouse; number two was at the quartermaster storehouse; number three watched over the hay yard and quartermaster corrals; and number four guarded the cavalry stable and ordnance storehouse. All watched for deserters. The men at the stable protected the army horses from theft. Guards for the four posts were divided into reliefs posted for two-hour periods beginning just after guard mount. Soldiers coming off their sentry posts could rest in the guard room for four hours, then went back on post for two hours, were off again for four, for a full twenty-four-hour cycle. Guards spent eight hours on post and sixteen off post, but were constantly available for call in the guardhouse during their tour.[35]

Men awaiting charges, trial, or sentencing were held in the guardhouse. Soldiers sentenced to the military prison at Fort Leavenworth, Kansas, were held in confinement, sometimes for months, until available transportation. Sentences for confinement varied from ten days to six months, generally at hard labor. An assortment of axes, saws, shovels, brooms, and rakes were kept on hand for prisoner details to cut wood, dig privy vaults, and clean stables. An 1876 inspector found,

> The guard house is suitable and clean. The prisoners number four, of whom two are awaiting sentence, one undergoing sentence and one awaiting trial. They are properly treated.[36]

Civilians often joined soldiers in the post guardhouse. They were usually confined for shorter periods, with longer stays for serious offenders awaiting transportation to Cheyenne. One "citizen prisoner" was confined from January 26 until his departure to Cheyenne on May 27. In October 1876 the sergeant of the guard was court-martialed for neglecting his duty; he had permitted a female prisoner to leave the guardhouse without a sentinel. The sergeant was admonished to be more careful in the future.[37] In an October 1876 incident the post guard failed to be as vigilant, for the record shows that two industrious prisoners escaped at night by cutting out a log from the wall of the prison room.

The guards also maintained order on the post, and an order issued in 1876 gave them additional instructions. For a logical reason General Order No. 59 forbade the discharge of firearms in the immediate vicinity of the post except when absolutely necessary. The order also prohibited livestock from roaming the garrison limits. Any horses or colts running loose on the post were to be caught by the guard, kept for three days, and then offered for sale at auction. Enlisted men who let their private animals run were thereafter not permitted to have private stock without special permission.[38]

After the end of the Great Sioux War and the removal of Red Cloud Agency in 1877, the number of men on guard duty was reduced considerably. By 1878 only six privates manned two guard posts, number one at the guardhouse and the other at the stable.

After guard mount water call sounded at 10 A.M. The cavalry troops assembled to take their horses to the river for water. Before the call became a regular event of the daily schedule, the cavalrymen were released from fatigue duty at 10 A.M. to water the horses. The troops remained on fatigue until "recall from fatigue" was sounded at 11:30, when they went to the barracks washrooms to clean up.

Dinner call came at noon, and the men had an hour to eat and relax. First sergeants' call came at 12:45 P.M., when the first sergeants of every company gathered at the adjutant's office to receive orders or information. The sergeants were required to bring pencils or "means to copy in their company order books" all orders and memorandums relating to their individual companies. Such intelligence was then passed on to the troops at company formations.[39]

Individual and company drills helped instill discipline and refine good obedience and reaction in the soldiers. When the commanding officer deemed it necessary, service training fell during the fatigue period, usually for an hour before the noon meal and sometimes for an additional hour in the afternoon. Times for drill and the troops required to attend were published in post general orders; however, this function was often suspended during periods of construction activity.

After the arrival of new enlistees, basic recruit drill was held two hours a day, Monday through Friday. The new men were sometimes consolidated into one squad and instructed by an officer who was detailed each day for the task. Basic instructions included the school of the company, manual of arms, and skirmish drill. In addition, the cavalry rookies had to master a regimen of mounted exercises and saber practices. Practice eventually paid off; as one observer remarked, "[T]his service training is having a very marked effect upon the psysigne [sic] of the recruits."[40]

Winter weather frequently dictated the amount of military training the soldiers received. The mild winter of 1876–77 permitted considerable drill and instruction to the Camp Robinson veterans and the recently arrived recruits. Even on the frontier, soldiers were expected to maintain a high degree of military bearing exacted through drill practice. Although drill competed with the demands of construction work, an inspector general visiting the post in October 1876 managed to give the troops a passing mark:

> The only instruction in military exercises and duties which has been possible has been a weekly dress parade and a daily guard mounting—still their appearance under arms was reasonably good—and certainly all that could be expected.[41]

Other specialized training periods were occasionally added to the post schedule. With one piece of field ordnance assigned to the camp, an artillery detachment was organized and ordered to hold artillery drill for one hour on Saturday afternoons. In 1875 signal practice for the troops took place from 11 A.M. to noon on Fridays.

Unless required to attend drill, the soldiers returned to work details when fatigue call was resounded at 1 P.M. For several hours they continued work that had begun in the morning. When weather permitted, target practice was held on Monday afternoons during the normal fatigue period. For the cavalry an afternoon water and stable call sent them back to the stables at 4 P.M. The cavalrymen again took the horses to drink and then groomed their mounts with brushes and currycombs. Recall from fatigue sounded at 5:00. In the longer daylight months the soldiers would clean up, have supper, and lounge around before being called to evening retreat. During the winter the daily retreat preceded supper.

First call for retreat was sounded at ten minutes before sunset, when the whole garrison prepared for evening parade. In army jargon, "parade" meant to assemble troops in a uniform manner for the purpose of regular muster, exercise, and inspection, as opposed to a "review," where the troops actually marched in formation.[42] At five minutes before sundown the companies assembled in front of their barracks for the second roll call of the day, preparatory to the retreat ceremony. Army regulations stipulated that the troops were to parade once a day, usually at retreat, unless dispensed with because of urgent or extraordinary cause or occasion.

At retreat parade the cavalry company formed first in the center of the designated assembly line. Then the four infantry companies marched into place, two companies to the right and two to the left of the cavalry company. The guard detail and its military prisoners marched out of the guardhouse, but stood at parade rest. Once the troops were properly aligned, the first sergeants of each company made a report of the evening roll call to their company commanders, who in return reported to the post adjutant the number present or accounted for. After all companies had reported, the adjutant "published" or read the new general orders relating to the post for all to hear. Then, the ranks opened, and the adjutant executed a short drill, "adding such exercises as he may think proper." With the troops all accounted for and new orders published, the retreat formation was dismissed. The soldiers returned to their barracks.[43]

Although evening parade was supposed to be a full dress formation, the Camp Robinson garrison frequently appeared in "undress", particularly during construction periods. Occasionally, parades were held without arms in order to dispense with time-consuming inspections, a practice more common in winter to reduce the men's exposure to the cold. The lack of dress uniforms was sometimes the reason parades were held in undress. For several months the infantry companies had the new, Model 1872 dress uniform, but the cavalry had not received theirs, and full dress appearance was dispensed with.[44]

After their dismissal from retreat the soldiers enjoyed another period of free time. At 8:50 P.M. the trumpeters and field musicians assembled, and at 8:55 they sounded "tattoo," the traditional signal that the soldiers should be in their quarters. Five minutes later assembly was called and the third roll call taken. About 9:15 taps was played; all lights in the soldiers' quarters were to be extinguished, and the men retired for the night. This was the daily schedule of Camp Robinson; it rarely varied.

Special parades commemorated public figures or holidays. In observance of the Fourth of July 1876 a special parade was held at 9 A.M., after which the troops received the day off. In August 1875 the troops had a special parade where President Grant's order was read relative to the death of former President Andrew Johnson. In December of that same year the troops staged a similar mourning parade in full dress to honor Henry Wilson, the recently deceased vice president.[45]

A double commemoration was observed on Washington's birthday in 1876. To honor the "anniversary of immortal Washington," all labor except necessary fatigue was suspended for the day. This occasion was also the first time the national flag was raised at Camp Robinson. After nearly two years of existence without displaying the colors, a flagstaff was erected February 21. At daylight the next day Sgt. John Kailey, Company

I, Ninth Infantry, hoisted the national flag. Kailey was given the honor because of his twenty-seven years of military service, longer than any other man on the post. From that day on, the post guard raised the flag at reveille and lowered it at retreat.[46]

In the spring of 1875 target practice became a permanent training activity at the post. Range practice was held on Mondays, at 1 P.M. in the spring and fall and at 7 A.M.. during the hot, summer months. All the troops were required to attend except the post guard, the sick, the bakers, and one cook from each company. Men on extra duty were also excused, but they could be ordered to participate if their duties were not pressing.

The infantrymen shot at targets seventy-two by twenty-two inches in size, placed at two hundred yards, with their long-range, .45/70-caliber rifles, that had replaced the earlier, .50-caliber models. The cavalrymen used .45/55 carbines and shot at wider targets 150 yards away. With limited allowances of ammunition allotted for target practice, each soldier fired a miserly ten rounds per month, alternating three shots one week and two the next. A typical consolidated report of target practice recorded that in September 1875 the Camp Robinson garrison fired a total of 1,570 shots. Only 652, forty-two per cent, hit the target board.[47]

Company commanders divided their men into two classes of marksmen. The first class were the better shots, who then fired at longer range; the second class had to fire at short range, with their targets no more than thirty yards away. Primitive as it was when compared with modern standards, target practice in the frontier army sincerely sought to better prepare the men for their roles as soldiers.

Inspection and pay muster occurred bimonthly. In proper military definition, "muster" was "a review of troops under arms fully equipped, in order to take an account of their numbers, inspect their arms and accouterments, and examine their condition."[48] The soldiers and the camp withstood a "minute and careful" inspection by their post commander or his designee. Inspecting officers reported on the condition of quartermaster and subsistence stores, fuel, public animals, means of transportation, and ordnance stores. Several times muster began at 7:30 A.M. in fatigue uniform, especially during the post's building period, instead of the usual 9 A.M. so the men could continue with construction. At one muster during the Indian difficulties, the cavalry troops were assembled mounted and fully equipped for field service. Muster was also a convenient time to read pertinent articles of war to the command.[49]

The garrison was subjected to two other types of inspections, one regularly, the other much less so. One of the most disliked institutions of the Old Army was the Sunday morning inspection. This weekly chore was a full dress, white glove inspection of men and quarters, done each and every Sunday at 9 A.M. Less frequently, the department inspector general made visits, sometimes unannounced.

More popular was pay muster. Base pay for the frontier soldier started at thirteen dollars a month for privates, with upward increments for promotion and longevity. The department paymasters were sent the last week of every second month to distribute funds in order for the posts to have pay muster on the last day of the pay month. Post commanders furnished escorts when the paymaster traveled in their vicinity.

Pay muster brought a sudden influx of cash to the military community, also a rush of unscrupulous civilians to lighten the pockets of the flush soldiers. In February 1877 1st Lt. John G. Bourke, aide to General Crook, described the scene after both the soldiers and Indian scouts at Camp Robinson had been paid:

> The harpies and vultures attracted by such occasions began flocking to the agency; gamblers, whores and horse thieves. Major [Capt. Daniel W.] Burke, post commander, had his hands full to arrest and confine all unauthorized people found within reservation limits. The guard house was packed and not till ready to escort them to the boundary of the agency would the commanding officer allow a single one of those bummers and dead beats to leave the calaboose.[50]

The officers of the frontier army provided the leadership and the military knowledge necessary for unit and post operation. Line officers administered a specific military organization, for example, a company, within the cavalry or infantry arm assigned to a particular duty station. A company was composed of forty or fifty enlisted men, commanded by a captain who was assisted by first and second lieutenants. With officers often absent on detached service or leave, company commanders relied heavily on ranking noncommissioned officers to assist in management.

Line officers often developed certain loyalties or dislikes toward their field-grade superiors. For example, in 1875 several Ninth Infantry officers tried to arrange the transfer of their units from Fort Laramie, a regimental headquarters, to the relative isolation of Camp Robinson. Officers jealously guarded their commands and resented any interference of colleagues from other units. One cavalry captain, particularly annoyed after Captain Jordan ordered part of his company on escort duty, argued that his company was at Camp Robinson on detached duty solely to scout the

Sidney road; none of his troops were available for other duty.[51]

Besides company duty, selected officers were assigned special administrative duties. Usually the senior ranking officer present served as post commanding officer. The commanding officer appointed an efficient junior lieutenant to serve as post adjutant. The adjutant assisted in the execution of all details of post operation and administration and channeled communication between headquarters and the other officers. He prepared reports, kept charge of records, and wrote all orders issued to the command. A senior noncommissioned officer, known as the sergeant major, assisted him.

One of the most demanding jobs was post quartermaster. In Camp Robinson's early years the quartermaster oversaw the supply trains that continually hauled necessities to the agency camps. Second Lt. Patrick Henry Ray performed particularly well, and his superior, Colonel Smith, complimented him:

> I cannot let the opportunity pass of expressing my entire satisfaction with you, both officially and socially during your connection with these headquarters. The zeal and intelligence you have evidenced at all times, whether upon the march, or in camp, gave me reassurance that in your future in the army you will obtain the appreciation and rank to which your qualities entitle you.[52]

During the post's initial construction phase Quartermaster Jesse Lee held this extremely important post. Besides being responsible for all construction, Lee requisitioned all building materials, assigned work, prepared reports and official correspondence, and managed the construction account. He ordered and issued all supplies and equipment needed by the garrison and let bids for hay and wood contracts. Many times the quartermaster also served as commissary officer in charge of all subsistence stores; the two closely related jobs required efficiency and constant attention.

Other jobs required officer assignment. The post ordnance officer supervised the receipt and preservation of arms, ammunition, and accouterments; he maintained an adequate supply of ordnance stores and issued them as needed. The engineer officer, usually a junior officer, was "saddled" with the duties of a qualified engineer; he was generally involved with construction projects and removal of manure and post garbage. At times the post had a signal officer, who trained the soldiers in sending messages by flag.

In addition to their company and post duties, officers served on various committees, such as boards of survey, which were usually called to investigate damages or losses and to affix blame. In 1878 three survey officers investigated a fire that damaged one of the officers' quarters. Boards of survey also were convened to deal with late delivery of public stores by contractors and to examine subsistence supplies, such as beef and commissary stores reportedly unfit for issue. They could assign responsibility for the loss of equipment and supplies while troops were in the field. In 1877 a board even met to determine the cost of articles taken by a Fourth Cavalry deserter.[53]

Other boards included the post council of administration, a council of two or three officers convened periodically to audit the accounts of the post treasurer, who was also in charge of the post bakery. The council of administration also discussed and regulated the prices the post trader charged in his store. In January 1878 a council administered the effects of the late James Caraley, a Third Cavalry private who had died of remittent fever. Boards of survey and councils of administration brought a degree of oversight to post operations.[54]

Officers sat on garrison and general court-martials, with three officers required to hear the cases. Several cases were usually heard before each court session, and case loads could be time-consuming, as indicated by a 1878 convening order that stated, "The court will sit without regard to hours."[55] The number of court-martials increased when larger numbers of soldiers lived at the post. The year 1877 was a particularly busy one for garrison court. At one session in March 1877 six cases were tried at the post and nine others in the adjoining cavalry camp; in that year alone a total of 228 court-martials were held at the post and in the adjacent cavalry camp. In other years the court averaged about twenty-five cases.[56]

After October 1877 the garrisons at Camp Robinson were considerably reduced, and the various post jobs fell to a much smaller officer staff. For instance, during 1878 2nd Lt. Bainbridge Reynolds served as post adjutant, treasurer, signal officer, and engineer officer. Other officers found themselves serving on countless boards, councils, and court-martials in addition to their regular company duties. Shortages of officers due to absences found officers from one arm commanding troops of another. Such was the case on May 28, 1878, when 1st Lt. Charles A. Johnson of the Fourteenth Infantry temporarily commanded Company C, Third Cavalry. He was relieved of this duty when Lt. James F. Simpson, one of the company's assigned junior officers, returned to the post on June 8; on June 12 Johnson was back in command of Company C while Simpson was on court-martial duty. On June 16 Simpson returned to company duty when Johnson had to go to Cheyenne to appear before a civil court. By June 30 Johnson had returned to Camp Robinson, but had to leave that day for Camp Sheridan on Indian bureau business.[57]

Along with being absent from the post on official duties, officers frequently took personal or sick leave. Leaves of absence could be applied for and granted for varying periods, depending upon the amount of activity in the department. Officers could apply for extensions, too. Sometimes officers going on leave performed useful tasks on their way to "civilization." After several months of duty with the Sioux Expedition, Captain Lazelle went on leave and on his way to Cheyenne to catch the train was placed in charge of an escort taking three prisoners to Fort D. A. Russell. Health problems, coupled with regular leave, could deplete the officer staff and can be traced in the post records. One sickly cavalry officer, for example, was absent on sick leave for most of October 1876, then took regular leave from November to July 1877, and was back on sick leave in August. On duty from August 18 to September 19, he was allowed nevertheless to remain sick in quarters. Out again on leave in October, finally the officer—and his problems—were transferred to Fort Laramie.[58]

Detached service was a persistent drain on the officer corps of frontier army posts. Such service included general recruiting service in eastern cities and escorting drafts of recruits to the West. When the army arrested civilians near the agency or post, officers had to appear in civilian court as witnesses. Some officers taught military science and tactics at eastern colleges and universities. Second Lt. Edgar Z. Steever, Third Cavalry, joined the post in October 1876, after being on detached service for two years with the Palestine Exploration Society. Conversely, some men on detached service voluntarily returned to their units from eastern assignment, as was the case when 2nd Lt. Harrison G. Otis, Fourth Cavalry, requested to be relieved from duty at the Fortress Monroe, Virginia, artillery school to join his regiment for the 1876 winter campaign.[59]

With many military personnel and dependents at the post the services of the post surgeon were always in demand. Military surgeons at Camp Robinson fell into two categories: regular army doctors, or "assistant surgeons," who held the rank of first lieutenant, and civilian doctors, or "acting assistant surgeons," who were appointed and contracted to serve for one-year periods. Along with the obvious medical obligations to the garrison, the post surgeon was responsible for the proper condition and operation of the post hospital. In this undertaking two or three enlisted men were detailed as stewards and cooks to assist him. He also administered the hospital fund, filed sanitary reports, and kept meteorological records.[60]

The surgeon daily attended to ailing soldiers, who were either already in the hospital or had reported at early morning sick call. A wide assortment of other needs and emergencies awaited his attention. In October 1877 the Black Hills stage overturned and Acting Asst. Surg. Valentine T. McGillycuddy was dispatched to the scene. Lt. Col. William B. Royall and the driver were seriously injured and brought to the post for treatment. Also riding in the coach was General Crook, who was "not much hurt." Earlier in January the surgeon was called to Yates's trading post at the agency to tend to a civilian shot by soldiers. The next month the surgeon was called on to perform a post mortem on a deceased soldier. When deaths invariably occurred, surgeons also served as morticians, preparing bodies for burial in the post cemetery. Once Dr. McGillycuddy had to open the casket of noted geologist Henry Newton, who had died in Deadwood, when his corpse passed through the post during shipment back East for burial. McGillycuddy "found it not well embalmed so did what he could to preserve it longer."[61]

Along with ordering and keeping on hand supplies for the post, medical officers prepared medicines for field commands. In the fall of 1876 the post surgeon arranged and packed supplies for two battalions numbering eight hundred men. Like the quartermaster and commissary officer, he sent requisitions for medical stores to department headquarters in Omaha.

As previously discussed, a post hospital was not included in the initial buildings of Camp Robinson. Construction of a permanent, twelve-bed hospital began in July 1875 and was finished by November 8 of that year. Relieved at finally moving his hospital from tents, the surgeon praised Quartermaster Lee for expediting the work. He also expressed appreciation to Captain Jordan, who had "directed the building of the hospital to proceed *pari passu* with other important work."[62]

The post surgeon also treated dependents and other nonmilitary patients and made calls to the Indian camps at Red Cloud Agency. Months after being shot in battle, a recently surrendered Cheyenne warrior received care for the wound from post surgeon Curtis E. Munn. In April 1877 Arapaho leaders Friday and Washington were treated for infirmities. As John Bourke noted, some agency Indians "placed great reliance in our 'medicine' man who possesses considerable influence over them."[63]

Army officers at Camp Robinson also formed strong opinions on Indians and especially Indian bureau policy. In their view the idea of forcing white civilization on the Indian all at once seemed preposterous; change could not come until the Indian himself was ready. The peace policy had failed, and the only way to control agencies such as Red Cloud was through the military. Considering the problems the Red Cloud agent encountered, the need for strict control became apparent for conducting agency business. Luther Bradley, who commanded the post in 1877, wrote of Indian bureau management:

> I wish some man of brains with just a little sensibility could be in charge of the Indians for a year or two with power to use the money appropriated by Congress for the best good of the government and the Indian. Such a man might save thousands of lives and millions of money, in preventing the outbreaks that occur almost every year. And he might so very easily put the Indians in the way of becoming self supporting, and thereby saving the large appropriation of Congress for their support.[64]

Bradley possessed experience in dealing with the Plains Indian and the confidence that he could do the job more successfully than the current crop of incompetent agents. He also felt that with the prevailing "fight and feed" policy, neither Indian nor white benefited, but army officers represented the government and only enforced policy made by others.

John Bourke, aide to General Crook, held similar views, adding that the government should keep its agreements with the Indians. He philosophized on this theme in 1877, writing "[O]ur own faith is worse than Punic, yet we always prattle about Indian treachery." Bourke, as did many frontier officers, developed a growing affection for the people he had been called upon to fight. On leaving Camp Robinson he wrote, "That post has for me a great number of very pleasant reminiscences and not the least pleasant are the Indians."[65]

The Articles of War are a compilation of laws approved by Congress to govern all U.S. soldiers, officers and enlisted men alike. At Camp Robinson the 1863 articles were enforced until December 1875, when a revised version became the law of the post. The most common offenses ruled by the articles included desertion, insubordination, neglect of duty, and drunkenness. Although the articles were very specific in the definition of violations, the army added the sixty-second article, which conveniently covered a multitude of vague offenses that could be considered prejudicial to good order and military discipline.[66]

The Articles of War required the confinement of the accused until verdict and sentence were reached and approved. Soldiers could be placed in the guardhouse overnight but had to be released at guard mount unless written charges were preferred. Trials for violations of military law were by garrison or general court-martial. Garrison courts, composed of three officers, dealt with lesser offenses, with sentences limited to a maximum of thirty days confinement and forfeiture of pay for the same period. Serious crimes, such as desertion or striking an officer, required a general court-martial. More officers were needed to hear this court and were called in from other posts. Emmet Crawford, for example, was ordered from Camp Sheridan to serve on a post general court-martial that was "trying some of the worst scoundrels that wore the uniform of U.S. Soldiers."[67] When found guilty by this court, soldiers were sent to the military prison at Fort Leavenworth, Kansas, to serve their sentences.

The punishments issued for violations of the Articles of War at Camp Robinson resembled those meted out at other posts. Conduct prejudicial to good order brought sentences varying from a two-dollar fine to, in the case of one unfortunate sergeant, reduction in rank to private, thirty days hard labor, and forfeiture of one month's pay. Being found drunk on duty could result in as much as a twenty-five-dollar fine. In 1877 the large concentration of troops at Camp Robinson saw an increase in the number of article violations.

Retribution for army transgressors could be swift and severe. Although fear of punishment went far to discourage bad behavior, standard punishment often gave way to harsher measures. Errant soldiers might also be forced to carry a twenty-five-pound log from reveille to retreat on alternating days, or spend a portion of their sentence standing on a wooden barrel. One soldier, convicted of disobedience and absence from duty, forfeited one month's pay and was confined under the camp guard for thirty days, twelve of which he had to stand seven hours a day on a barrel; the remainder of his time was spent at hard labor.[68]

Desertion remained the most serious military crime during the nineteenth century. A third of the men who enlisted between 1867 and 1891 deserted, this high rate attributed to several factors. The haphazard recruiting system used by the army made it a "dumping ground" for undesirable and totally unfit enlistees. After getting their feet wet, many recruits found the poor food, low pay, and monotony of garrison duty enough of an impetus to leave before an enlistment's expiration. Camp Robinson's desertion rate, though lower than at other, less isolated military stations, saw its worst month in May 1874, when twenty-seven men gave the army "the grand bounce." Between 1874 and 1879, including the period of large troop concentrations in the spring of 1877, desertion averaged 2.9 occurrences a month. Excluding that four-month period, the rate decreased to a respectable average of less than 1.5.[69]

Whenever possible detachments such as those led by the relentless Lieutenant Crawford tracked down and apprehended deserters. Officers believed the quick retrieval and punishment of deserters served as a warning to others considering it. Rewards also helped. In August and October 1874, a total of $120, "incidental" expenses from the post quartermaster's fund, was paid out for the capture of four deserters.

Drinking cursed the lives of countless enlisted men and officers of the frontier army, once so much so that at Camp Robinson the wife of Post Surgeon McGillycuddy simply noted in her diary, "Outfit all drunk."[70] Since the camp's first days, commanding officers had realized the dangers of intoxicants and attempted to halt the illegal liquor trade. The soldiers lived in the midst of a potentially volatile situation, and prohibition became the order of the day. In addition to prohibiting all members of the Sioux Expedition from bringing in liquor, Colonel Smith ordered his officers in charge of the supply trains leaving Fort Laramie to halt wagons after crossing the North Platte and search for contraband liquor. Illegal liquor was destroyed, and the teamsters hauling it arrested. In 1875 the Camp Robinson post commander was authorized to search all wagons or pack trains nearing the military reservation and arrest any parties trying to bring in liquor. Citizens who illegally sold whiskey or other intoxicants to the soldiers were arrested. Enlisted men who were found drunk away from the post were restricted to the post. Officers were even allowed to examine packages arriving by mail for the enlisted men.[71]

Nevertheless, soldiers managed to find something to drink. While accompanying a detachment scouting the Black Hills, Dr. McGillycuddy discovered a box of brandy missing from his medicinal stores. Blame for the missing bottles, justifiable or not, was placed on the soldiers.[72]

At this particular time in its history, the U.S. Army was not entirely "prohibition" minded, but it did want to control liquor availability and hopefully reduce drunkenness. Authorized post traders could sell liquor in their stores, the legal outlet for those wanting to drink and one that military authorities could control. Post trader liquor sales were eventually permitted to all officers, enlisted men, and military employees at the camp, but by 1876 it was necessary to restrict trader store consumption more stringently. The men were permitted no more than two drinks a day, not less than three hours apart, with the bartender required to keep a record of his customers. No Sunday sales were allowed, and no liquor was sold to intoxicated enlisted men. With the best interests of the garrison at heart, the orders stipulated, "The Post Trader will only sell *good* liquors."[73]

Regardless of these attempts to regulate consumption, numerous court-martials were convened to prosecute drunkenness at the post. Sentences for casual drunkenness usually amounted to a fine of several dollars. Being caught drunk on duty was an entirely different matter and warranted harsher punishment. In 1877 Pvt. John Cunningham was tried for drunkenness on duty and sleeping on guard; he was fined ten dollars and spent ten days carrying a thirty-five-pound log from reveille to retreat, with only half an hour off for the noon meal. Another soldier got off with a literally lighter sentence for his on-the-job indulgence. Pvt. Samuel Wynkoop, on extra duty in the quartermaster area, "did become so much under the influence of intoxicating liquor to be totally unfit to perform his duties." He spent seven days in the guardhouse, received a fine of one dollar, and did not have to carry the log.[74]

Drinking by officers was seen in a different light. With the clear-cut division between the classes officer overindulgence enjoyed greater tolerance. Mrs. McGillycuddy's remarks illustrated a less harsh attitude toward officer drinking:

> Major & Mr. [Lieutenant] Simpson returned in high glee a
> little worse for whiskey. But it is all right—Army Officers.[75]

Occasionally, officers found themselves in trouble. When the Big Horn and Yellowstone Expedition returned to Camp Robinson in October 1876, most of the officers, joyous over their return to civilization, indulged in great bouts of drinking. One of the officers broke his abstinence pledge and went on a binge. His regimental commander reminded him of the pledge, court-martialed him, and dismissed him from the army, another casualty of the 1876 campaigns.[76]

Desertion and drinking, however, did not occupy all the time of the garrison courts, which heard cases regarding all types of violations, including the ill treatment of privates by their noncommissioned officers. One particular violator, 1st Sgt. James Sullivan, Company I, Ninth Infantry, was tried in November 1875 for "conduct prejudicial to good order and military discipline." One of the specified charges against Sullivan was striking a soldier, but the other specification reveals more about his abusive nature: "[O]therwise maltreating [Private Smith] by calling him a son of a bitch and saying that he would name him shit and compel him to answer to the same name." Sergeant Sullivan was found guilty of both specifications and reprimanded by the post commanding officer. Striking Smith was justified only "when it becomes necessary to use [force] in enforcing obedience in the part of a private soldier who violently resists such noncommissioned officer in the execution of his duty." Two months later the ill-tempered Sullivan was court-martialed for "catching Pvt. Sheehan by the blouse with one hand and holding the other doubled up in a threatening position." This time he was sentenced to one month in confinement and a ten-dollar fine.[77]

When charges were brought, the accused could end up spending more time in the guardhouse awaiting sentence than serving the actual sentence. One private accused of theft spent thirty days in confinement before receiving a sentence of twenty days for his crime! At other times military justice applied a degree of leniency. One private who failed to make a company formation was court-martialed and sentenced to a fine and five days at hard labor, but had the sentence remitted, "owing to the unanimous recommendation of the court on account of his previous character."[78]

Additional restrictions were placed on the enlisted men to maintain discipline and security. For example, in March 1875 the men were forbidden to leave their barracks after taps, primarily for their own protection, and the guard was ordered to report all violators. For five months in 1876 the enlisted men were prohibited from leaving the military reservation, except on duty. Likewise, the post commander had the authority to restrict civilian movement on the post reservation. All civilians could be excluded from the reservation without written permission, and certain undesirables were specifically barred from the post.[79]

In a more dramatic attempt to purge itself of undesirables, the army command issued orders to list soldiers who could be discharged for "worthlessness." In September 1874 Captain Jordan submitted the names of eighteen men the army could live without, describing the candidates in such glowing terms as "chronic drunkard," "generally worthless," and simply "idiotic." Within a couple of months they were gone.[80]

The army hoped to have well-kept and healthy garrisons in every one of its military stations. This goal was, of course, impossible to attain, with climate, environment, and human inclinations working against it.

A key element for the long-term success of a military post was water, and Camp Robinson proved fortunate in this regard. With the flowing White River, Soldier Creek, and a number of springs located nearby, water was always available, but not taken for granted. Concern about cleanliness of water near the post brought orders that prohibited bathing or watering of post animals in Soldier Creek or above the saw mill. The post surgeons recommended that drinking water be hauled from a large spring located several hundred yards northeast of the post area. In fact the first surgeon argued that a better location for the camp would have been right at the spring, where the agency would have been in full view. Too little level land at the spring site quashed this idea.[81]

Maintaining an adequate, healthful food supply for the camp was a problem at times. For some months in 1876 one contractor consistently furnished poor quality beef for the command. Officers complained, claiming the contractor furnished mostly old work oxen, "very unwholesome as an article of food."[82] His contract was canceled, forcing the post commissary to purchase cattle on the open market. Fearing sickness, especially scurvy, the post commander requested in August 1876 a large amount of potatoes and onions: "[A]s the men will have to work very hard it is particularly important that they be well fed."[83] At least three tons of onions were shipped in before winter to help in the prevention of scurvy.

At the post commissary the garrison could purchase a variety of items besides staples. Delicacies such as pickles, oysters, canned salmon, sardines, jellies, bottled olives, and canned fruits and vegetables were stocked. Officers were not allowed rations, but could purchase food at cost at the commissary. Companies also bought foodstuffs to supplement their regular, monotonous mess hall fare.

Post surgeons, responsible for camp sanitation, filed reports and recommendations to the post commander. Surgeons were continually preoccupied with the removal and proper disposal of the considerable amount of garbage that accumulated, and became particularly annoyed by the lack of sanitary practices among the enlisted men. In January 1876 a disgusted Surgeon R. W. Reynolds recommended:

> [T]he urinating troughs be used by the men for the purpose
> of micturition, instead of the sides of the sink-building. In
> passing some of these, on a warm day, the stench is intoler-
> able.[84]

Although complete medical records are unavailable, Camp Robinson appears to have been a relatively healthy garrison with few serious problems from disease or sickness. As one obvious measure to reduce sickness the soldiers were ordered to dress according to the season. As winter approached, the men were ordered to wear overcoats and any wrappings they might have for the head and hands for all outside activities. Preventative measures could not always be implemented before problems appeared. In August 1876 the garrison suffered an epidemic of whooping cough among its children. Its introduction was blamed on the Indians, who had suffered severely from the disease that summer. The surgeon reported that in one village of two hundred lodges, thirteen children had died in one month. He vaccinated all the post children, but three died before the sickness passed.[85]

The first recorded death at Camp Robinson was that of Pvt. James Brogan, who died on July 2, 1875, fifteen months after the soldiers arrived. Brogan's cause of death was reported as congestion of the brain, supposedly from alcohol. He was buried the next day, the first interment in the post cemetery. Most of the deaths at Camp Robinson were health-related, with causes listed as pulmonary congestion, apoplexy, remittent fever, chronic bronchitis, or inflammation of the lungs. By January 1879 the cemetery contained twenty-five graves, six attributed to soldier- or civilian-inflicted gunshot wounds; thirteen of the twenty-five were soldiers, the rest their dependents or other civilians.[86]

Off duty diversions and entertainment for both officers and enlisted men at Camp Robinson were limited. They lived in a small, self-contained world, with socializing largely restricted to other soldiers at the post. The daily routine was both monotonous and strict. There was no place to go, even if it had not been Indian country. Prior to the Black Hills gold rush the nearest towns were Sidney, 120 miles south, and Cheyenne, even farther to the southwest.

The types of off duty activities for the soldiers matched those found at other isolated frontier stations. Dances, holiday observances, and visits to the post trader's store were common pastimes. Although the enlisted men had few opportunities for interaction with the local Indians, officers assigned to the post commonly visited their camps and entertained their leaders.

The main on-post entertainment center for officers and enlisted men was the trader's store. Post traders were granted exclusive rights to trade on a particular post. Soon after the Sioux Expedition arrived at the agencies, Colonel Smith authorized John S. Collins, the appointed post trader at Fort Laramie, to "suttle" to the troops at Red Cloud.[87] While the post was being constructed, the trader built his store some four hundred feet west of the end of officers' row. The store was a long, log building with an enclosed back area and outbuildings on the north side. Food, drink, clothing, guns, and small tools and trinkets were available at prices regulated by the post council of administration. Post traders extended reasonable credit and frequently entertained the officers and their wives. Other than employees of the quartermaster department, he was the only civilian allowed to live on the military reservation.

The store had segregated saloon facilities for officers and enlisted men, where cards and billiards were played—except on Sundays. On that day of rest, officers frequently patronized the billiard room at Dear's trading store at the agency. A store clerk recalled one lively time:

> One Sunday evening while Lt. [Stanton A.] Mason & Lt. [Joseph H.] Dorst were playing billiards, a drunken bull wacker by the name of Paddy Simmons came into the room and wanted to go into the store. I told him it was closed but he insisted on staying. So I and Lt. Dorst got ahold of his arm and led him to the door and put him out. Short time later he came back with a six shooter and wanted to know who put him out and wanted revenge. I happened to be near the door . . . and grabbed the gun and twisted it out of his hands and the Lieutenant hit him over the head with a billiard cue and layed him out and called for the sergeant of the guard and put him in the caliboose for the night.[88]

Sporting events were always popular with the garrison, and many took part. Horse racing was a favorite pastime, particularly when the post had large numbers of cavalrymen stationed there. Races varied in distance from four hundred to one thousand yards, often witnessed by hundreds of spectators, including Indians, who greatly enjoyed the sport. In an 1876 contest two officers bet two hundred dollars on which of their regiments had the better horse; the Fifth Cavalry horse won, making 2nd Lt. Homer W. Wheeler rich, at least for the day. Baseball became popular in 1876–77 and wagering could be high. One game between cavalry and infantry teams saw two hundred dollars bet on the side, with the cavalry taking the pot. One match had to be canceled in May 1877 when the wind blew so hard that play was halted.[89]

Major holidays and national celebrations were duly observed at Camp Robinson. Christmas usually saw all labor suspended for the day. On New Year's Eve in 1874, work was suspended at recall from fatigue and not resumed until fatigue call on January 2, 1875. Washington's Birthday and the Fourth of July saw similar suspension of duties, except for the post guard. The Fourth of July in 1877 was climaxed by a display of fireworks, courtesy of the post trader, on the hill behind the post after tattoo.[90]

The enlisted men held dances and invited the officers and their ladies. Although enlisted men's wives and the laundresses provided welcome dancing partners, a perennial shortage of females plagued the frontier. At times the restrictions on enlisted men leaving the military reservation were lifted, and the men went to agency dances, held there in a large, log cabin hall with an attached gambling house, the latter reportedly well patronized.[91]

Army officers curious about the Indians attended dances and ceremonies in the nearby villages. As a rule, enlisted men were prohibited from visiting Indian camps except while in the line of duty, but officers regularly witnessed ration distributions and councils, most notably those talks held in the spring of 1877 to persuade agency Indians to enlist to fight the northern warriors. Lieutenant Bourke recalled that a hazard of any visit to the camps was the Indians' dogs; they constantly barked and bit at the horses' heels as the officers rode past.[92]

Their Indian masters showed considerably more hospitality to visitors. Bourke reluctantly had to decline an invitation to attend a dog feast and regretted missing the opportunity to taste this native delicacy, or so he said. Officers were invited to watch some Indian ceremonies. Lieutenant Colonel Bradley attended the 1877 Sun Dance and had an interesting observation about the dancers, many of whom were "the very ones who annihilated the command of Custer on the Little [Big] Horn last summer."[93]

Army officers returned the favor and invited chiefs from the agencies, including Spotted Tail and occasionally Red Cloud, to dine with them on post. These cordial gatherings, though, belied the underlying tension that always characterized Indian–military relations. In late May 1877 Crazy Horse came to the post and paid a visit to Bradley; one hundred days later, they were at the post again, but under much different circumstances, and the ultimate result was the death of the Oglala leader. After the northern Cheyennes surrendered in 1877, Chief Dull Knife and his daughters were entertained at a Camp Robinson dinner. Fifteen months later they too would be at the post under far less cordial circumstances, confined in a cavalry barracks prison.[94]

Indians came onto the post and put on dances for the officers, particularly if a special VIP was present. The performers formed a large circle, open on the side nearest the front porch of one of the officers' quarters. On the porch the officers and their wives and visitors gathered to watch. Bourke described one so-called "squaw dance" that had embarrassing moments for one of the officers:

One old gal acted as mistress of ceremonies; after the dance had proceeded for an hour or so, she came forward and told General Mackenzie they would like to have some of the "nice young men" standing on the porch, join them.

They begged off saying they did not dance, but a group of half a dozen seized Capt. Clarence Mauck, Fourth Cavalry.

Poor Mauck struggled hard for freedom and what with begging, twisting, pleading, kicking, and squirming managed to escape from their clutches.

To conciliate the squaws, we made up a purse and presented it to the dancers who greeted the gift with loud applause.[95]

To have more tangible reminders of their experiences among the "red men," officers often collected Indian artifacts for themselves or to send back East to relatives and friends. Even by the mid-to-late 1870s, bows and arrows were becoming scarce; one officer had both agency traders looking for a set. Another officer found a pair of baby moccasins and sent them home as a gift. First Lt. William P. Clark displayed in his bachelor's quarters a Cheyenne pipe picked up after the November 1876 Red Fork fight. Cheyenne Chief Standing Elk came into Clark's quarters one day for a visit and spotted the pipe. He told Clark that the pipe had belonged to him, but the lieutenant could keep it, with the stipulation that Clark was always to have tobacco on hand. Standing Elk wanted to smoke the pipe whenever he came to call on Clark.[96]

Diversions could take a more feminine form. Washerwomen were an important part of military life until the position was phased out by the army in the late 1870s, and the first white females to arrive at the post were the company laundresses. Two or three laundresses washed the dirty laundry of each company. The soldiers were charged each month for this service at rates set by the council of administration. The laundresses were usually married to enlisted men and entitled to shelter, one daily ration, and medical attention from the post surgeon. By the end of 1874 fifteen laundresses and their families lived at Camp Robinson.

One laundress at the post hired an Indian girl to help her, but soon learned that the girl had the bad habit of appropriating things. The girl went too far when she tried to abduct the washerwoman's six-month-old son.[97]

The wives of the officers added to the female presence at the post, but their arrival was delayed for two reasons, security and housing. The first wives to arrive were probably Mrs. Jordan and Mrs. Lee, who left Fort Russell in November 1874. By then at least one set of quarters had been completed, and it was only natural for the post commander and quartermaster to have first pick. By the summer of 1875 other officers' wives had taken up residence.[98]

Furniture and other possessions of the officers were low priority items for army shipments. After their arrival the women often waited for weeks before moving into their assigned quarters. During this annoying period they stayed with other established families on the row, anxiously awaiting the arrival of supply trains carrying their goods. The wife of one post surgeon had to wait nearly a month for her household goods to reach Camp Robinson. Nevertheless by 1876 the female presence for both officers and enlisted men was well established.

Generally officers and their wives employed servants to keep house, but in the post's early years officers' quarters did not provide domestic housing. The post's remoteness made it virtually impossible to obtain any servants. By January 1876 only two officers were reported as having female servants; the others had either "exhausted" their efforts or "had made all due efforts" to hire civilians. Because of the shortage, officers paid soldiers to help part-time with domestic chores. These soldiers, called "strikers" or "dogrobbers," were excused from fatigue and roll call but were nevertheless required to be fully armed and equipped and ready for instant service when needed.[99]

Leisure-time diversions for the wives were somewhat limited at Camp Robinson. Disappointment with the surroundings usually followed one's arrival. After she arrived, Mrs. McGillycuddy succinctly recorded in her diary, "Commenced enjoying the camp. Finished."[100] Following established social etiquette, the women made calls, held and attended dinners, organized hops, and played games, including croquet, euchre, casino, and chess. Horseback riding—with male escorts—to the nearby buttes and the Indian camps was a popular pastime. After a visit to Red Cloud's camp, Angeline Johnson, the wife of Lt. Charles Johnson, wrote home how

> Mrs. Brown, Mrs. Yates and I "called" on Mrs. Red Cloud the day before he [Red Cloud] left. It was the first time I have been in a teepee. It was just like the one at the [Philadelphia] Centennial, only made of canvas instead of buffalo skin.[101]

Mrs. Johnson also spent Thanksgiving Day of 1876 watching a beef issue at the agency. Fortunately her party left before the warriors started shooting the beeves for slaughter, since she feared,

> They might accidentally shoot over our way. I breathed a great deal freer when we were clear of the pack.[102]

Once in 1876 seven officer wives came up from Fort Laramie for what turned into a prolonged stay. Their husbands had been stationed at the post temporarily, and they decided to visit them and the camp. The women spent an entire month socializing with the post officers and wives before returning to their families at Fort Laramie.[103]

The establishment of the army camps had provoked more thought to finding a shorter supply route than the trail from Cheyenne. One beef contractor suggested that Indian and military freight be shipped directly north from the railroad town of Sidney, Nebraska. He spoke from experience having moved cattle north on this route and finding it considerably shorter. The distance from Sidney to Red Cloud, he explained, was 115 to 120 miles, compared to 165 miles from Cheyenne.[104] To the Indian bureau the Sidney route not only saved miles of wagon travel but also one hundred miles of railroad shipment, a tremendous financial savings. General Ord foresaw a like savings in shipping military supplies by the Sidney route.[105]

In the summer of 1874 Ord sent a detachment to scout the country north from Sidney for a possible road. In late July Company A, Third Cavalry, under command of 1st Lt. Joseph Lawson, left the army's Sidney Barracks to blaze a trail north. The troops arrived at Camp Robinson on August 8, successfully completing their assignment. Chief Red Cloud and other leaders enthusiastically supported this new, economical road to haul their rations and annuity goods. After discussing Lawson's route, two Oglalas, Fire Lightning and Two Lances, even agreed to guide the troops back to Sidney. Under their guidance the soldiers found an even better, shorter trail to use. Upon his arrival at Sidney, Lawson filed a quick report about the proposed trail, which was well watered and had a good crossing of the North Platte River. Two Lances expressed the Oglalas' general satisfaction with the shorter and more passable road,

> We are anxious to have you do it [establish a new route]. Cheyenne is bad, our goods get lost and grow small coming round that way.

Maj. Nathan A. M. Dudley, commanding officer of Sidney Barracks, paid the Sioux guides fifteen dollars for their services.[106]

By summer's end government freighters were on the Sidney Trail. The first haulers made the trip north from the railroad in six days and experienced no difficulty in crossing the river. The Indian bureau soon arranged for all supplies to Red Cloud and Spotted Tail agencies to go via the new route.

In 1875 Cornelius Ferris contracted to carry military freight from Sidney to the northern army camps. His rate for hauling between May and November was $1.08 per one hundred pounds. In the winter months the rate increased to $1.20 per hundred to Camp Robinson and $1.40 to Camp Sheridan.[107] A Sidney newspaper gave some idea of the vast amount of military supplies that moved north by wagon:

> During the fiscal year 76–77 there have been forwarded from this military post to Red Cloud and Spotted Tail agencies [specifically the military posts] the following amounts of supplies: Subsistence 1,745,637, Quartermaster stores 4,543,707, Ordnance 121,635, Medical 19,945, Misc. 322,254, for a total of 6,753,197 [*sic*] pounds.[108]

This amounted to approximately 3,400 tons of military supplies shipped to the agency posts during the height of the Great Sioux War.

One additional bit of official business needed attention, the creation of a military reservation. Military reservations provided a buffer zone free of civilian encroachment and prevented undesirable civilians or their businesses near the soldiers. Reservation lands were removed from the public domain by executive order and reserved solely for army use.

General Ord had instructed Colonel Smith that it was not necessary for the soldier camps to be placed right at the agencies. They could be a short distance away, surrounded by a square mile under exclusive military control. At Camp Robinson Smith actually wanted more land, and in July he recommended a reservation of three square miles. The first declaration of a reservation area for the post came in September 1874, when post general orders defined the bounds of the military land as one square mile, with the center of the parade ground being the center point. The first Camp Robinson reservation was on land reserved for the military, but not set aside by presidential decree.[109]

In 1876 a larger reservation of nine sections was recommended, and a survey of the proposed reserve was made. The engineers took care that the new reservation would not include farms or permanent Indian encampments. The new area ran along the top of the north buttes and included most of the area west of the post and up Soldier Creek for several miles. The post cemetery, brick yard, and gardens south of the camp were included. The expanded reservation gave the army control of well-watered ground with good grass for its herds. On November 14, 1876, a presidential order filed with the General Land Office officially set aside the military reservation of Camp Robinson.[110]

Red Cloud Agency, 1876: (center) **issue bastion;** (right) **Frank Yates's trading post.**

Dr. John J. Saville, agent at Red Cloud Agency, 1873–75.

Frank Appleton, agency clerk and Saville's nephew, who was killed at the agency on February 9, 1874.

Red Cloud, the powerful leader of the Oglala Lakota.
Courtesy W. H. Over Museum, Stanley J. Morrow Collection.

Col. John E. Smith (seated, center), Fourteenth Infantry, commander of the 1874 Sioux Expedition to the White River agencies.

Lt. William H. Carter's sketch of the first Camp Robinson.

Capt. William H. Jordan, Ninth Infantry, builder of Camp Robinson and post commander, 1874–76.

Lt. Jesse M. Lee, Ninth Infantry, post quartermaster during Camp Robinson's initial construction. He later served as acting agent at **Spotted Tail Agency.** Courtesy Fort Laramie National Historic Site.

Camp Sheridan, Robinson's counterpart near Spotted Tail Agency.

Earliest known photograph of Camp Robinson (1875).
Protective cordwood barricade surrounded the buildings.
Six duplex officers' quarters survive today.

The west barracks, built in 1874 to house two infantry
companies, in an 1890s view.

Capt. Emmet Crawford, Third Cavalry, noted Camp Robinson officer and namesake of the nearby town of Crawford.

Red Dog's village one mile south of the agency. In the early years soldiers were restricted from unauthorized visits to nearby Indian camps.

Post trader's store at Camp Robinson, 1875, and a section of the cordwood barricade.

Rufus Zogbaum's drawing of Guy V. Henry's command struggling through a blizzard on its 1875 return from the Black Hills to Camp Robinson. *Harper's Weekly,* July 27, 1895.

Col. Ranald S. Mackenzie, Fourth Cavalry, who commanded the District of the Black Hills during the 1876–77 Sioux War.

Left: **Gen. George Crook,** commander of the Department of the Platte.

Temporary camp of Company E, Ninth Infantry, south of the main post.

Camp Custer, one of the temporary Sioux War cantonments, with the main post beyond.

General Crook proclaimed Spotted Tail as head chief of the Sioux on October 24, 1876. Both are in the crowd at Red Cloud Agency.

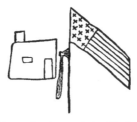

Lakota historians recorded important events in tribal and Fort Robinson history: the Appleton shooting, the flagpole incident, and the killing of Crazy Horse.

Arapaho leaders at Red Cloud Agency, 1877: (front row, left to right) **Friday, Six Feathers, Black Horse, Sharp Nose;** (back row, left to right) **unknown, Dr. Valentine T. McGillycuddy, White Horse,** unknown, and **Old Eagle,** also known as **Washington.**

The Crazy Horse band came to Camp Robinson to surrender in May. *Frank Leslie's Illustrated Newspaper,* June 9, 1877.

Artist Jules Tavernier based his illustration of a Lakota Sun Dance on his 1874 observations near Camp Robinson.

Little Big Man, one-time friend of Crazy Horse, who vied for power at Red Cloud Agency in 1877.

Left: Touch the Clouds, the towering Minneconjou leader who comforted Crazy Horse at his death.

Chapter 4

The Great Sioux War

By the summer of 1875 it was clear that white miners could not be kept out of the Black Hills. As the pressure for entry into the Hills grew, the government changed its policy on this thorny issue with the Lakota. Chief Red Cloud may have provided an expedient solution when he suggested that the whites reach a settlement with the Sioux to purchase the Black Hills. Commissioner of Indian Affairs Edward Smith responded and formed a special committee, the Allison Commission, to "treat with the Sioux for the relinquishment of the Black Hills."[1] He hoped the Sioux would also give up their coveted hunting rights in the Big Horn country in Wyoming.

Senator William B. Allison chaired the commission, which included Brig. Gen. Alfred H. Terry, Samuel D. Hinman, long-time missionary to the Sioux, and trader Geminien P. Beauvais among its members. By September the commissioners had gathered at Red Cloud Agency ready to negotiate. Cavalry companies under command of Capt. James Egan and Lt. Emmet Crawford along with fifteen infantrymen were detailed from Camp Robinson to serve as escorts and guards for the councils. The Oglala and Brulé Sioux of the agency, who had earlier received word about the commission, joined the northern Indians to witness the proceedings. The first days were spent arguing over a location for the council, but finally the parties agreed on a site. A large tent was pitched under a lone cottonwood tree that stood some six miles downriver from Red Cloud (and which subsequently survived as a landmark for several decades).[2]

The council opened on September 20, 1875, with the commissioners offering a price of six million dollars for the Black Hills and a request for the Sioux to cede their hunting rights on nonreservation lands. The

Indians quarreled among themselves over the proposal for several days. The majority apparently wanted to sell for a much higher price, but many northern Indians opposed relinquishing the Hills or their hunting lands at any price. Allison calculated the attendance at 4,500, although neither Crazy Horse's nor Sitting Bull's bands were present.

Finally, on September 23 the council resumed. During the discussion a large mass of mounted warriors broke into the proceedings. A northern warrior named Little Big Man declared he would shoot the white men who were trying to take his land. Confusion reigned as Egan and his troops prepared to defend the commissioners. Coming to their rescue, many Oglala men under Young Man Afraid of His Horses moved between the soldiers and their angry Sioux kinsmen and coolly broke up the council. Although the soldiers were badly outnumbered, fellow officer John Bourke credited Egan and Crawford for their control, "Had it not been for the [ir] coolness and good judgement . . . , there would have been a fearful scene of bloodshed."[3]

Talks continued for four days, along with heated discussions in the camps. The commissioners reasonably concluded that an agreement was impossible for now. As long as the northern, nontreaty Sioux opposed it, the purchase of the Hills was impossible. The commissioners left to take the Sioux response back to Washington.

After the Allison Commission's failure the Indian bureau sent Erwin C. Watkins, a special investigator, to study the situation and make recommendations. On November 9 he made his report, emphasizing that as long as Indians were away from the agencies the "civilizing" work would never occur. Indians who remained away would influence the agency young men to join them to become a formidable fighting force. Finally, Watkins proposed that the army be called on to force the nontreaty Indians to the agencies. Before his report became public, though, one newspaper editor foresaw the bleak future about to unfold:

> The roving tribes and those who are known as wild Indians will probably be given over entirely to the military until they are subdued enough to remain on their reservations and adopt civilized modes of life.[4]

The peace policy approach had failed in its dealings with the Plains warriors. As with the army intervention at Red Cloud nearly two years before, military force was seen, even trumpeted, as a solution where the civil administration had fallen short.

On November 29, 1875, Interior Secretary Zachariah Chandler directed

Commissioner Smith to notify the nonagency Indians to return to their respective agencies by January 31, 1876; all Indians not on the reservation by that date would be subject to military action. Notifying the Indians of this ultimatum by the deadline proved unrealistic. To think that the scattered camps of northern Indians could be found and persuaded to return to their agencies in the dead of winter was sheer folly! Secretary of War William Belknap was nevertheless requested to prepare for military action. In no apparent hurry, Smith waited a week before informing his agents to transmit the message.[5]

Meanwhile military preparations began. In December Sheridan informed Generals Crook and Terry to plan for field operations. On January 3, he reported to Sherman that his generals were ready for "decisive" winter actions. The Indian bureau ultimatum probably failed to impress the nonagency Sioux, and apparently the agency messengers never reached many camps. Some Indains did straggle in by the deadline. On February 24, Agent Hastings reported to the commissioner that "over one thousand" northern Indians had arrived at Red Cloud "in obedience to your request." He added optimistically, "More are expected daily."[6]

In fact, the reverse held true. Events at the agencies influenced many Indians to leave for the northern camps. On January 18, an embargo on the sale of arms and ammunition by agency traders angered many warriors. The halting of arms sales "produced uneasiness and distrust among all the Indians, hence some of the young men left the agencies."[7] In March the agency Indians were prohibited from hunting south of the North Platte River, until then an important right guaranteed by treaty. After March 11, army commanders at posts along the Union Pacific Railroad were to consider hostile any groups of Indians found south of the river and to attack them. An acute shortage of rations further aggravated the Red Cloud and Spotted Tail agency Indians during the winter of 1875–76. Disillusioned with agency life and feeling betrayed by the government, they began to defect.[8]

The army quickly struck the northern holdouts. In early March a large expedition directed by General Crook left Fort Fetterman, Wyoming Territory, to move against northern camps in the Powder River country. On March 17 a force under Col. Joseph J. Reynolds, attacked a mixed village of Cheyennes and Minneconjou Lakotas on the lower Powder. In a sharp engagement the soldiers captured the village and its sizable horse herd; after destroying the lodges and contents the soldiers withdrew. The enraged warriors, however, regrouped and recaptured most of their horses. Crook, infuriated at Reynolds for the loss of the Indian horses, gave up the campaign and returned to Fort Fetterman. Many Indians saw

Crook's winter campaign and the Reynolds fight as a failure, causing "a tendency to awaken the old feeling of superiority" among the young warriors at the agency. Restlessness and defiance grew among the agency people.[9]

In May 1876 Captain Egan, then assigned to Fort Laramie and on a scout, reported his detachment had spotted seven to eight hundred warriors moving north from Red Cloud. By early June Lt. Col. Wesley Merritt, whom Sheridan had sent to survey the situation at Red Cloud, estimated that two thousand Indians had left since May 10; no more than five hundred warriors remained at the agency.

As the discontented left the agency, area depredations mounted dramatically. On April 26 the cattle corral, slaughterhouse, and scales within half a mile of the agency were burned. In mid-May government stock was run off, which occurred four miles from the agency. About this time a party of raiders attempted to run off horses and mules within three hundred yards of the post. Agency traders also became a target. A train of supplies for Frank Yates's store was attacked, the wagons riddled with bullets, and stock animals killed.[10]

Fear again gripped the imperiled agency employees. An anonymous correspondent from Red Cloud, his courage bucked up, wrote, "Men now there [at the agency] do not know when they will be called upon to die, but go about well armed, asking only for a chance to die game."[11] After the arson of the agency scales and slaughterhouse, Agent James Hastings ordered Yates to send his wife to Camp Robinson for protection. The Sidney newspaper further reported that Indians had purportedly shot up the agency storehouse and ransacked the place.[12]

Carrying the mail to the agency posts became extremely hazardous. On May 16 Charles Clarke, the mail carrier between Fort Laramie and Camp Robinson, was killed. Clarke was traveling by wagon about ten miles west of the camp when four warriors attacked and shot him six times. The Indians took the team but did not bother the mail. J. W. Dear and a group of twenty Indian allies unsuccessfully pursued the raiders. Second Lt. Thomas S. McCaleb and ten infantrymen recovered the body and the mail. After the killing the mail contractor for the route between the post and Sidney quit; he had already had Indians steal four of his horses and shoot one out from under a carrier. The post quartermaster blandly informed department headquarters that it "will be difficult to engage any person for this service during the prevalence of Indian depredations."[13]

Attacks on freighters increased along the Sidney road. On May 27, 1876, Indians attacked the train of "Arkansas John" Seckler ten miles north of the North Platte River bridge, near present Bridgeport, Nebraska. The raiders killed two mules and one horse and put an awful scare into Seckler's freighters, who foolishly possessed only two guns among ten men to protect themselves. At the same time two other freighting outfits were attacked on the trail between Red Cloud and the Platte bridge. Travelers were warned that the trail was unsafe and were encouraged to travel in large, well-armed parties.[14]

During the May attacks the Camp Robinson garrison numbered fewer than two hundred men. Agent Hastings criticized the four infantry companies and their inability to deter anything. Captain Jordan was well aware of his insufficient troops and the need for cavalry. Company K, Third Cavalry, was quickly ordered from Camp Sheridan to the post, but a good reason explained the absence of cavalry. It had been diverted to the Big Horn and Yellowstone Expedition, launched by General Crook at Fort Fetterman, 130 miles to the west. This expedition was one of the three columns that moved into Sioux country that fateful summer to punish the nonagency Indians. Crook's operation depleted troop strength throughout the Department of the Platte. Reinforcements came from posts outside the Platte, including the Fifth Cavalry, brought up from the Department of the Missouri to protect the Black Hills road north of Cheyenne.[15]

As a result of the May depredations cavalry companies patrolled the Sidney road. Company K, under the command of Capt. Gerald Russell, set off south from Red Cloud toward Henry T. Clarke's bridge, commonly called the "Sidney" bridge; another Third Cavalry company, commanded by Capt. Henry W. Wessells, Jr., came north from Fort McPherson. Wessells's troops were based at the bridge and monitored the road northward. A blockhouse was hurriedly thrown up on the bridge's north end and a detachment of infantrymen from Sidney Barracks detailed as guards.[16]

Patrolling the trail involved long hours in the saddle with few tangible results. On one trip Company K moved south to the Snake River crossing. There on July 10 the company made camp while the first sergeant and ten men scouted westward for signs of Indians. A number of friendly Indians were camped nearby along the Niobrara River valley. At 1:00 A.M. two of the Indian men came to the cavalry camp and reported the presence of a war party twelve miles to the east. The soldiers quickly readied themselves and headed off to investigate. On the way they ran into another party of friendly Indians, who had surrounded what they thought was the war party. Before shots were fired, everyone discovered that the "hostiles" were four agency Indians who had come from the agency to herd horses.

This particular patrol covered 130 miles. Captain Russell reported that they had met many trains on the road, none of which had thus far been attacked. If nothing else travelers, especially vulnerable freighters, felt reassured by the sight of the troops.[17]

On another patrol Wessells's company watched for cattle raiders and escorted a large ox train through Red Willow Canyon and the "Sand Hills" near Snake Creek, "the most dangerous places on the road."[18] Surveillance by cavalry companies on the Sidney road continued throughout the summer.

Mail carrier Clarke's death illustrated the dangers of the road to Fort Laramie. In June Company D, Ninth Infantry, established a temporary camp on the Niobrara crossing of the Fort Laramie road. Several days later the bulk of the company moved back to the White River and established a new camp about fourteen miles west of Camp Robinson. One sergeant and six privates remained behind to guard the Niobrara crossing, and it was there on June 29 that Sgt. Frank Owens accidentally shot and killed Pvt. Eugene Carlton. The next day Carlton's body was brought to the post for burial; he was the only Camp Robinson casualty during the summer of 1876.[19] Company D withdrew from the protective camp on White River on July 20. By that time were enough troops to make the Fort Laramie trail secure. New calamities concerned the army command.

On July 8, thirteen days after it occurred, Camp Robinson and the Red Cloud Indians heard "the dreadful news of the appalling disaster to General Custer and command."[20] Captain Jordan quickly ordered Russell's company back from road patrol to reinforce his depleted garrison. He feared the news of the great defeat at the Little Bighorn might motivate the agency Indians to hostilities, along with increased restlessness because of the Indian bureau's failure to deliver beef to the hungry Sioux. With no beef issue for some time, the agency people were reduced to receiving only corn and flour. Jordan, who had only received secondhand information on the course of the war, demanded to know what was happening. Department headquarters ordered Lt. Col. Luther Bradley at Fort Laramie to inform Jordan of any relevant news.[21]

Jordan would soon provide his own news. By June eight companies of the Fifth Cavalry, under the command of Eugene A. Carr, its able lieutenant colonel, were congregated at Fort Laramie for field assignment. Later that month the "Dandy Fifth" was deployed north and east along the main Indian trail between the agencies and the Powder River country, its assignment to search for hostile bands and raiders. Accompanying the command was the regiment's old friend and trusted scout, William F. "Buffalo Bill" Cody.[22]

Cody, already a living legend, had scouted for the Fifth several years before when it was headquartered at Fort McPherson. By 1876 he was more often in the East, a budding showman with a stage act billed as the "Buffalo Bill Combination." Carr, a long-time friend, had written Sheridan specifically requesting Cody's services. Cody, who realized the value of such publicity to his stage career, "heeded the beckoning" and joined the Fifth at Fort Laramie. After his arrival one officer's wife recalled, "I remember his fine figure . . . straight and slender, with his scarlet shirt belted in, and his long hair distinguishing him as the well known character."[23]

For several weeks the Fifth rode the trail, now joined by Wesley Merritt, its new colonel, who was recently promoted into the regiment. On July 12 Merritt's command was ordered back to Fort Laramie to refit and to join Crook's main column then in camp at the base of the Big Horn Mountains. The next day, one day's march out of Laramie, word came that the Cheyennes at Red Cloud were planning to leave the agency for the north country. Deciding that the interception of this potentially hostile force was of more immediate importance, Merritt immediately turned his command and marched north again toward the Powder River trail. He also sent Maj. Thaddeus H. Stanton to hurry to Red Cloud and investigate. On July 15 Merritt received word from Stanton that some Cheyennes were in fact leaving. Stanton suggested that Merritt move his men to a location northwest of the agency to intercept the party.

On the morning of July 16 the Fifth Cavalry reached the Sage Creek post, a small station manned by infantry on the Cheyenne–Deadwood Trail. Merritt planned to be in position some place east of Sage Creek toward the Powder River trail. That evening the hard-riding cavalrymen camped on Warbonnet Creek, north of the present Nebraska town of Harrison, where the trail crossed. All told, Merritt's command had marched eighty-five miles in thirty-one hours.[24]

In the early morning of July 17, pickets on two conical hills just above the camp detected Indians moving from the southeast toward the Warbonnet crossing. It was a Cheyenne band under Chief Little Wolf, the same group Stanton had reported leaving the agency. The soldier camp was alerted, and Merritt sent 1st Lt. Charles King to the picket post to signal when the Indian party neared the soldiers' concealed position.

What the pickets saw was a small party of warriors advancing ahead of the main body. They had been sent out to attack two couriers whom the Cheyennes had spotted riding in from the west toward the undetected soldier camp. The warriors closed in on the couriers, completely unaware of the large cavalry force prepared to attack.

As Cody and a handful of soldiers waited ahead of the main body, King watched as the Cheyenne vanguard entered a small ravine that opened into Warbonnet Creek. When the Indians were within a hundred yards, King shouted, "Now, lads, in with you!"[25] As the advance soldiers rushed out, Cody got off a quick rifle shot and killed a warrior named Yellow Hair, which prompted the rest of the forward Cheyenne party to scatter. In what became a celebrated *coup de grace*, Cody then scalped Yellow Hair, apparently the only casualty of the brief skirmish. The cavalry charged out of the creek bottom in hot pursuit of Little Wolf's band, which turned and fled back to the agency, some twenty miles distant. Oddly enough, later that day near Red Cloud Agency, some of these same Cheyennes visited politely with these same Fifth cavalrymen.

After its success on the Warbonnet the Fifth Cavalry moved north to join Crook's column and served throughout the rest of the summer campaign. Cody scouted with the soldiers for several weeks before returning to the stage, touting before eager crowds how he took the "first scalp for Custer." Minor as it was, the Warbonnet skirmish was the first victory for the army in an otherwise dismal summer campaign.[26]

Government officials evidently believed such firm measures were needed to maintain the agency system. On May 29 Sheridan had urged that control of the agency Indians, together with the off-agency roamers, be turned over to the army; several weeks later (after the Custer defeat) he repeated the request. On July 22 he received approval, and on the same day Commissioner Smith telegraphed Hastings to turn over the Red Cloud Agency to the commanding officer at Camp Robinson.[27] According to the law, army officers who served as agents had to surrender their commissions. To circumvent this requirement, officers were appointed on a temporary basis, with control eventually reverting back to civilian agents.

Sheridan wasted no time. On July 26 he issued instructions for the army agents: Make an accurate census of Indians at the agencies and issue supplies only to those enumerated; prevent Indians from leaving the agencies; and allow Indians to return only upon "the unconditional surrender of their persons, ponies, guns and ammunition."[28] The last instruction reflected Sheridan's successful policy earlier in the Red River War against the Southern Cheyenne, Comanche, and Kiowa. He believed hostilities with the Sioux and Northern Cheyenne would end only after they had surrendered their arms and ponies.[29] Sheridan wanted this accomplished immediately with all the Sioux at Red Cloud; however, Captain Jordan had only four companies, three of infantry and one of cavalry. He was allowed to delay the disarming until the arrival of reinforcements.

By August civilian Hastings was still in charge, although Jordan had designated 1st Lt. Oscar Elting, Third Cavalry, to become the new agent. On August 10, Elting belatedly assumed the agent's duties, and Hastings departed. Elting took a thorough census and counted only 4,817 Indians at Red Cloud, considerably fewer than the 13,027 that Hastings had reported in April.[30]

Also in August six companies of the Fourth Cavalry, under command of Col. Ranald S. Mackenzie, arrived from Fort Sill, Indian Territory. Mackenzie commanded the District of the Black Hills and on August 13 established his headquarters at Camp Robinson. The district, a regional administrative unit, consisted of adjoining sections of Wyoming, Nebraska, and Dakota with its headquarters normally at Fort Laramie and existed only during these critical years. By the end of the summer, Camp Robinson ranked as the most important post in the Department of the Platte and the headquarters for operations against the Northern Cheyenne and Oglala Sioux tribes.

Mackenzie, though a competent officer, sometimes appeared excessively irritable, high-strung, and worried. Others described him as an abrupt, brusque man with "dash and vim." He fully realized his complicated task after assuming command at Camp Robinson and wrote General Sheridan, "I will endeavor to act as well as I can, and do right in such way that no honorable man can fail to support me; but my position is, as I say, a very trying one."[31]

Sheridan wanted to gather a large force at Camp Robinson before attempting to disarm the Oglalas, and all through August additional troops strengthened the post. Besides Mackenzie's Fourth Cavalry, companies of the Fifth Cavalry, Fourteenth Infantry, and Fourth Artillery marched in. By month's end 650 more soldiers bolstered the regular two-hundred-man garrison, together a stabilizing influence on the remaining agency Indians. The growing military presence depressed the Indians, who feared they would be massacred as soon as enough soldiers arrived. At daybreak on August 31, a cavalry battalion surrounded an Indian camp to arrest a certain troublemaker. In the process the Oglala leader American Horse, who accompanied the soldiers, shot another warrior named "Sioux Jim." The next day, this particular camp of about fifty lodges broke and stampeded from the agency. After several days the residents returned, and things quieted down. Mackenzie explained to the agency chiefs that in the future they must turn over to Captain Jordan any troublemakers before it became necessary to send troops.[32]

The new companies established several semipermanent camps along the White River between the post and agency. Immediately east of the main post was the camp of the first cavalry battalion, composed of two companies each of the Fourth and Fifth regiments. On August 27 their camp was named "Camp Custer" in honor of the recently slain hero.[33] The second battalion, four companies of Mackenzie's Fourth Cavalry, made its camp half a mile northeast of the post along the river. The Fourth Artillery battalion, formerly stationed at San Francisco, established "Camp Canby," named for a general killed by Indians in California, just west and opposite of Red Cloud in the river bottom. A two-company battalion of the Fourteenth Infantry set up camp at the agency.[34]

A winter's station for most of the troops seemed probable, so work immediately began to build temporary quarters. An allowance of $20,000 was allotted to build shelter and stables with $3,000 designated for extra duty pay. In scope the building of the 1876 temporary cantonments rivaled the 1874 construction of the post itself. Two more sawmills arrived to cut almost two thousand feet of lumber a day; two shingle machines and a planer were kept humming. Men constantly went out to cut wood, causing the quartermaster in charge to proclaim, "This is the first time I have ever been where everybody can have all the lumber they want."[35] The work continued through early fall and into winter.

Camp Custer consisted of over thirty small huts and half a dozen larger cabins to house the men. The huts accommodated twelve men each and were board and batten structures with board floors. Along the slope of the river terrace the bank was excavated for long stables partially dug into the earth. Each stable was 220 feet long and could protect one hundred horses and eighteen mules. The camps had similar huts, a kitchen, storehouse, and stables for the cavalry units. At Camp Canby log structures were built around an open square, with three sets of officers' quarters filling one side and long barracks facing on the other three. After moving in, one officer's wife dutifully wrote home, "The house isn't very large, but we are very comfortably fixed." Attempting to reassure her eastern relatives, she added, "There are sentries out all night, and one walks up and down past the house, so there isn't any danger here."[36]

Although the number of soldiers at the post had grown dramatically, some officers remained apprehensive. First Lt. Henry W. Lawton wrote,

> The Indians are *all well* armed and are good shots. I have not seen an Indian that did not have a repeating rifle.[37]

By now General Crook's summer expedition had run its course with decidedly mixed results. Crook hurried south from the Black Hills to Fort Laramie for a council of war, where he met General Sheridan and Colonel

Mackenzie to plan further, and hopefully more successful operations.[38]

While the soldiers at Camp Robinson occupied themselves building winter quarters, receiving drafts of recruits, and preparing for future field operations, three unlikely visitors rode into the post. In mid-September, M. Notu, the commander-in-chief of the Royal Army of Japan, and two of his top generals visited the post. The Japanese officers, members of a commission inspecting the American military, wanted to observe methods of Indian warfare. The officers, none of whom spoke English, spent several days visiting Camp Robinson before leaving for Fort Laramie on September 20. What they learned remains unknown.[39]

In October Crook and Mackenzie finalized plans for a winter invasion of the Powder River country to find the Indian camps. All the assembled troops, including the regular garrison of Camp Robinson, were designated part of the "Powder River Expedition." In the same month seven more infantry companies and three of cavalry, along with over two hundred recruits and vast amounts of supplies, arrived to form a new garrison for the post. The constant arrival and departure of men during October was fittingly described as "altogether extraordinary."[40]

Adding to this mass of men and materiel was the arrival of the main body of troops from the Big Horn and Yellowstone Expedition. After nearly five months of hard, constant field service the exhausted expeditionary force was finally to be disbanded. Forty men required hospital care, which severely taxed both the facility and the staff. But a surgeon with the expedition noted with satisfaction that in two hours after their arrival, "[A]ll were washed, cleanly clad and in bed, and had beef tea given them."[41]

Second Lt. Eben Swift recalled the scene when the officers "taxed" the sutler's store:

> Never will I forget the evening and the night of the first day at Camp Robinson. The enlisted men found plenty of "speak easies" around, I suppose. There was no room for them at the sutlers store. It was taken over by the officers for themselves, hundreds of them, I should say, a howling mob. Among other performances was Hoel Bishop (2nd Lt. Co. G, 5th Cav) riding his horse into the billiard room and trying to get him to jump over the billiard table.[42]

For several days there were nearly three thousand soldiers in the immediate vicinity of Camp Robinson. On October 24 the expedition was officially disbanded, and the next day the weary, but relieved troops began to return to their regular stations.

Meanwhile relations with the agency Indians worsened. On September 6 a new Indian commission had arrived at Red Cloud. Headed by George W. Manypenny, the commission's object was to force the Sioux to relinquish any claim to nonreservation lands and the Black Hills. If they did not comply with the ultimatum, subsistence appropriations would be cut off. The commissioners lectured the assembled Sioux and laid out these harsh terms; the Indians dispersed to discuss the issue among themselves. After days of argument and confusion the commission secured the reluctant signatures of the Indian chiefs and two headmen from each of the agency bands. Needless to say, few fully understood the agreement they had been forced to accept; many were angered. At one meeting Sitting Bull the Oglala, infuriated over the commissioners' claims that the agreement would benefit the Indians, drove away his fellow tribesmen with the same war club he had used during the 1874 flagpole incident. By the end of September the commissioners returned to Washington, satisified with having secured dubious title to the Black Hills.[43]

Meeting with the commissioners only intensified the Oglalas' defiance. Mackenzie complained to headquarters, "They are treating with utter contempt my authority as the chief representative of the government."[44] In October two camps under Red Cloud and Red Leaf showed their disgust, left the agency, and moved to Chadron Creek, some thirty miles northeast. There they intended to stay, and there they wanted their rations delivered instead of retrieving them at the agency. In mid-October Crook arrived at Camp Robinson and was apprised of the situation, which he concluded was unacceptable. The Indians must remain at their agency, even if military action was needed to force their return.

Crook planned to surround and capture the camps, but feared they might escape to the north. He hoped to postpone the operation until the arrival in camp of the Big Horn and Yellowstone troops. Those troops could block any Indians fleeing in that direction, but realizing that the bands could bolt at any time, he decided to proceed regardless.

During the night of October 22, eight companies of cavalry commanded by Colonel Mackenzie marched on Chadron Creek; accompanying the troops were forty Pawnee Scouts recently mobilized for field service. At dawn of October 23 the Pawnees captured the horse herds, while the Fifth Cavalry battalion surrounded Red Cloud's camp and the Fourth Cavalry battalion encircled Red Leaf's camp. Both camps surrendered to the soldiers without the firing of a shot, and the firearms of 150 warriors were confiscated along with over seven hundred horses. The dejected Indians prepared for the return to the agency, with the women permitted to use horses to haul camp equipment and enable older, feeble Indians to ride. The warriors had to walk back. Crook dashed off a note to Sheridan, "This is the first gleam of daylight we have had in this business."[45]

On November 1 the troops assigned to the Powder River Expedition left the post for Fort Fetterman. Included in the command were Jordan's Ninth Infantry companies, the same troops who had built Camp Robinson two years before.

Maj. Julius W. Mason, the new post commander at Camp Robinson, continued the disarmament begun with the Red Cloud and Red Leaf camps. By December he reported the agency Indians had begun turning over their guns and ponies; he had so far collected nearly three hundred horses after allowing each lodge to retain two mounts to haul issue rations. One hundred and ninety of the horses were herded to Cheyenne Depot and the rest to Sidney to be auctioned off. Mason foresaw no further problems because the Indians were rendered "harmless by want of arms and ponies and disposed to do what is right."[46]

As the 1876–77 winter campaign progressed, so did Camp Robinson's growth. A new cavalry stable and corral area sprang up next to the existing stable. An ordnance storehouse, magazine, granary, and extensions that doubled the size of the quartermaster and commissary storehouses were added. The officers' row now took on a more permanent appearance with new picket fences, boardwalks, cow sheds, and chicken coops.

Mackenzie's and Crook's expedition meanwhile moved into the Powder River country, marching through severe winter weather for several weeks before its Indian scouts found a village. A large camp of over 170 lodges sat in the Big Horn Mountains on the Red Fork of the Powder River. In a well-coordinated attack on November 25 the soldiers drove Chief Dull Knife's Northern Cheyennes from their village and completely destroyed it, forcing the eventual return to the agency of hundreds of Cheyennes.

The expedition continued another month, led by the persistent Crook, who searched through northeastern Wyoming for the elusive Crazy Horse. Failing to find him, the Powder River Expedition broke up in early January. On January 9 Mackenzie and six companies of the Fourth Cavalry marched back to their temporary cantonments at Camp Robinson, where the troops settled in for winter.[47] In January and February 1877 northern warriors and their families trickled into the Nebraska agencies. Gradually the overall army strategy of the Sioux War and the hard campaigns of commanders Crook and Nelson Miles showed results.

Over the winter 1st Lt. William P. Clark busily enlisted the former warriors as Indian scouts. It was naturally assumed that military campaigning would resume in the spring to force the return of more nonagency Indians, including Crazy Horse. Clark interviewed the warriors of each small group that surrendered, but he found most reluctant to talk. For example, none of the eighteen men of one small party would admit to having participated in any of the 1876 fighting. As groups surrendered, their guns and horses were taken, the latter frequently turned over to Indian allies who had served as "peace-talkers" to the northern camps. The vanquished warriors and their families were fed, issued necessities, and assigned to certain camps around the agency.

Nevertheless Sioux raids and depredations increased in the northern Black Hills area. One reason was that with the Black Hills officially opened there were more white targets to be attacked. Troops at Camp Robinson, the nearest army post to the Hills, were called on to provide protection to the settlers. Thus the little known 1877 "Deadwood Expedition" came into existence.[48]

During the second week of February 1877, a lightning series of raids erupted in the northern Black Hills. Minneconjou raiders from the Yellowstone camps ran off large numbers of cattle and horses with at least two white men killed and several wounded. On February 15 the Deadwood mayor frantically telegraphed Sheridan at Chicago and Crook at Fort Laramie asking for military protection. The next morning 2nd Lt. Joseph F. Cummings and sixty-one men of Company C, Third Cavalry, left Camp Robinson to "[p]rotect the citizens in the vicinity of Deadwood from hostile Indians."[49] On February 17 Crook received another plea for troops from the mayor and ordered two additional cavalry companies and a supply train sent north as soon as possible.

On February 21 Cummings's command arrived in Deadwood. The next day the extra cavalry companies and wagons left Camp Robinson under the command of Capt. Peter D. Vroom. That same day, after gauging the situation, Cummings marched north eighteen miles to the Boughton Ranch at the mouth of False Bottom Creek. On the morning of February 23 Company C, accompanied by eight civilian volunteers, moved south along the False Bottom searching for the raiders' trail. After marching fifteen miles up the valley, one of the civilian scouts rode up and reported an Indian camp six miles to the west. The command quickly moved overland, through rough, timbered hills, until they spotted a dozen warriors in camp on Crow Creek. The soldiers prepared to attack.[50]

Cummings advanced with fifteen men to surprise the camp, but had difficulty descending to and crossing the creek. Meanwhile the Indians sighted Cummings's party and rapidly fled west. The soldiers pursued them some distance, but gave up and returned to the camp and the rest of the company. The soldiers found the camp somewhat large for the dozen Indians spotted there. Along with ten lodges the Indians left behind all their equipment and provisions and fourteen horses.

At dusk eleven warriors approached the captured camp from the south. Leaving his first sergeant in charge, Lieutenant Cummings led fourteen men in pursuit for some seven miles. In "a lively brush" with the fleeing tribesmen, Cummings thought perhaps his men hit one or two with carbine fire. After chasing away the Indians, the soldiers recaptured the stock the raiders were driving to their camp; the plunder included seven cattle, two horses, and six hundred sheep! While Cummings's detachment was engaged, another, larger hostile party attacked the soldiers remaining in the camp. First Sgt. William Riley, who had been left in command, ordered out skirmishers and repulsed the attack with one Indian reported killed.[51]

At 4:30 the next morning (February 24) the camp again came under attack, but the assailants were driven off in short order. Later that morning Cummings and a strong detachment set out on the trail of several hundred cattle that raiders had run off toward the Bear Lodge Range, about fifty miles northwest of Deadwood. His pursuit was cut short when the soldiers noticed what they thought were signal fires. Fearing attack if they continued, Cummings decided to return to the Crow Creek camp. By now the soldiers' horses were worn out, and the men were out of rations, subsisting only on meat captured in the Indian camp. On February 26 the cavalrymen and the recovered civilian stock reached the small settlement of Spearfish. Here they received a wagonload of provisions and grain donated by the grateful residents of Deadwood.[52]

The local ranchers and settlers, who were in Cummings's words "very enthusiastic over what little I have done," treated the young lieutenant as a conquering hero. Crook later concurred and issued orders complimenting the conduct of Cummings and his command during the operation.[53] The Crow Creek Fight was the only officially listed battle of the Indian Wars credited to a force composed solely of soldiers from Camp Robinson. It was also the only pursuit from the post that met with a major success—the capture of a hostile camp and recovery of stolen stock.[54]

On March 6 Company C joined Captain Vroom's battalion, which had finally arrived near Deadwood. The combined command then scouted the northern and eastern Hills for other roving bands. In mid-March Crook warned Vroom that his troops might encounter friendly Brulés under Chief Spotted Tail and wanted to avoid any mistaken attack on the party. These Indians had been sent out to find the Crazy Horse camp and to convince its residents to return to the agencies. Vroom's command remained in camp and refrained from pursuing any Indian bands reported, unless, of course, actual depredations were committed. Although snow and inclement weather hampered Third Cavalry operations, the troops investigated several reported depredations near Spearfish and Crook City. Vroom opined that the citizens should be able to protect themselves; their practice of allowing stock to run ten or twelve miles from the settlements only invited raiders.[55]

After several weeks of inactivity, snowstorms, and false sightings, the Deadwood Expedition was ordered back to Camp Robinson. Although the settlers and miners in the northern Hills petitioned to have Vroom's troops permanently stationed at Crook City, his command returned to Camp Robinson on April 17 and 19. It had sustained only the loss of eighteen mules stolen "by the people in the Black Hills whom he had been sent to protect."[56]

As winter turned into spring, the number of surrenders increased weekly. Some returning Indians said they had been advised to surrender to the soldiers on the Yellowstone River (Miles's command) and not at Red Cloud. Returning Cheyennes confirmed they were told that General Crook would treat them badly if they went to Red Cloud Agency; they had been encouraged to give up to Colonel Miles. Many Cheyennes, however, ignored such propaganda and returned to their agency on White River.[57]

Specifically noted were the army carbines, probably the spoils of war from the Custer fight, some Indians surrendered. Other relics of the Little Bighorn were discovered among the returnees. Lieutenant Clark obtained a gold ring containing a bloodstone engraved into a griffin's head he presumed was from the Custer battle. Later Clark discovered that the ring belonged to 2nd Lt. William Van W. Reily, Company E, Seventh Cavalry, who died at the "Last Stand."[58]

Lieutenant Clark, known as "Nobby" to his fellow officers and "White Hat" by the Sioux, played a significant role in the close of the Sioux War at Camp Robinson. After graduation from West Point in 1868, he soon became regimental adjutant for the Second Cavalry. In the late summer of 1876 he became a personal aide to General Crook and led the Indian scouts in the successful attack on Dull Knife's village. Later that fall he was sent to Robinson to serve as Crook's "eyes and ears," monitoring all Indian activity at the northern Nebraska agencies. In this important and sensitive assignment, Crook reported that Clark "virtually controlled the Indians at Spotted Tail and Red Cloud agencies, rendering valuable services to the government in that campaign."[59]

Troop levels at Camp Robinson remained high that spring to oversee the growing numbers of Sioux and Cheyennes. Counting Mackenzie's six companies and the regular garrison, over one thousand soldiers lived at the post. The army realized that with the Crazy Horse and Sitting Bull bands still loose the war was not over. Clark continued to actively recruit Indian scouts, 120 from the Sioux, Cheyenne, and Arapaho camps, who were issued arms and horses and received pay for their services. Peace emissaries—leaders Red Cloud and Spotted Tail included—went forth to find Crazy Horse and to convince him to come in. By mid-April parties from the Crazy Horse village arrived, saying that his band was anxious to make peace, with Crazy Horse himself yielding to the pressure of a long winter of pursuit.[60]

At one surrender on March 14, nineteen lodges of 130 Sioux came to Red Cloud Agency. In February and March similar-sized groups of Minneconjous and Sans Arcs surrendered at Spotted Tail Agency. The Indians, already aware that they had to give up their firearms, faced Clark and his scouts, who sometimes met groups beforehand to prevent the caching of weapons.

The largest surrender to date came when the Northern Cheyennes under Dull Knife arrived. On the morning of April 21 over five hundred Cheyennes approached the agency from the north, singing songs and discharging their rifles. The warriors were divided into four groups, with the lead group carrying a white flag. They were led in by Lieutenant Clark and interpreter William Rowland, followed by Dull Knife, Standing Elk, and other leaders. As the mile-long, irregular cavalcade reached the White River bottoms, the women broke off to set up camp. The 120 or so warriors rode to the agency, where General Crook and his staff stood waiting, and surrendered. Maj. George A. Forsyth, an eyewitness, wrote to Sheridan:

> There was no nonsense about it and the Indians all under-
> stood that it was a clear case of unconditional surrender. The
> chiefs gave their guns into Gen. Crook's hands personally.
> Said they wanted to bury the hatchet and be at peace with
> the whites and would do as he directed.[61]

The Cheyennes were then counted and issued rations. The next day the chiefs and headmen councilled with Crook and Mackenzie at the post. Dull Knife's people had suffered considerably with the loss of their village to Mackenzie in November, and many still needed basic camp equipage. The destitute Indians were given blankets and tents with the understand-ing it was solely on account of their "wretched and forlorn condition" and not as a reward for surrendering. The war was over for Dull Knife's people.[62]

Some of the surrendering Cheyennes complained to Bourke of the unfriendly treatment they had received from the Crazy Horse band. After their village was destroyed, they had marched through bitter winter conditions to his camp on the lower Tongue River, where they expected to find help and sympathy. The Crazy Horse band undoubtedly assisted the suffering tribesmen all they could, but some Cheyennes apparently thought their presence "was only tolerated and not desired." This treatment helped them decide to return to Red Cloud Agency. Now many warriors wanted to enlist as scouts to find and fight Crazy Horse and the northern Indians.[63]

The real prize came in May with the surrender of Crazy Horse and his band of nontreaty followers. The winter campaigns had also taken their toll on the northern Indians, including this Oglala band that had never seen its agency. On April 27 word reached Camp Robinson that Crazy Horse's people would reach the agency in eight or nine days. Second Lt. J. Wesley Rosenquest and fifty Indian scouts were promptly dispatched to meet them with wagons of rations and a beef herd. The two groups met near Hat Creek Station on the Cheyenne–Deadwood trail. After the Indians ate and rested, they began their final march to Red Cloud.[64]

On May 6 Lieutenant Clark rode out and met the Indian column five miles west of the agency along Soldier Creek. Crazy Horse shook hands with Clark and said through an interpreter that he wanted peace. Accompanying Clark was Chief Red Cloud, who was partially responsible for convincing Crazy Horse to come in, and several other agency leaders. He Dog then presented Clark with his war bonnet, shirt, and war horse, this last gift from one of Crazy Horse's lieutenants interpreted as signifying his absence of ill-feeling. The procession then moved on to the agency with Clark, Red Cloud, and the agency Indians in the lead; next came Crazy Horse, Little Big Man, He Dog, and other leaders followed by the rest of the camp. Altogether the train stretched for two miles.

About 2:00 P.M. they entered the camps along White River chanting songs. The women set up the tipis, which numbered 145, in a large crescent. The ponies of the band were given up, seven hundred horses turned over to Red Cloud for his part in the surrender (coincidentally this equaled the number taken from Red Cloud in October). The remainder of the 2,200 horses surrendered by Crazy Horse were distributed among the agency Indians. The warriors then assembled to turn in their firearms. They first surrendered only seventy-six guns. Clark insisted that more existed and searched each tent. Eventually 117 guns were collected, including three Winchesters from Crazy Horse and two from Little Hawk, another lieutenant.

Throughout this procedure soldiers were absent. Mackenzie trusted the details to Clark and kept his soldiers at the post. Red Cloud had explained the situation earlier to Crazy Horse, and the result was order and no apparent bad feeling. However, Clark came prepared for trouble. A company of Cheyenne scouts waited in readiness under the cover of the hill that commanded the village. They quietly watched the progress of the surrender, ready to ride forward and aid Clark if needed.

The count of the Crazy Horse band that surrendered that day numbered 889 men, women, and children, of whom 217 were considered warriors. All told, including advance parties and later stragglers, more than 1,100 northern Indians led by Crazy Horse gave up. A newspaper correspondent summed up the spring surrenders at Camp Robinson:

> This makes a total of nearly 4,000 Indians who have surrendered at Red Cloud and Spotted Tail agencies during the past ten weeks. That they have been influenced almost wholly by the efforts of military in this department under the direction of such field officers as Gen. McKenzie [*sic*], and by Gen. Crook's fine manipulation of the leading warriors, is a fact beyond question.[65]

Because few of the Crazy Horse people had experienced agency life, before, one of the post's civilian employees was detailed to teach the Indian women how to make bread from issue flour. On that domestic note and for all practical purposes, the Great Sioux War of 1876–77 was over.

Chapter 5

The Final Days of Crazy Horse . . . and Camp Robinson

In the spring of 1877 the situation at Red Cloud Agency had greatly improved in the army's view. The Indians seemed content, with adequate food and other annuities arriving regularly. The northern Indians, subdued by military actions, appeared peaceful and cooperative. General Crook boasted to Sheridan,

> The transition here since last October has been almost like magic. You could scarcely recognize these Indians now as being the same people who last spring had such contempt for our government.[1]

The army was also greatly relieved with the surrender of the Crazy Horse band and considered that his capitulation eliminated a threat of continued war. One band of Minneconjous still worried army officials; it remained away from its agency, occasionally raiding in the northern Black Hills country. Nor had Sitting Bull surrendered, but his activities were farther north and a problem for the commander of the Department of Dakota, not for Crook.

Peace at Red Cloud led to a troop reduction at Camp Robinson. It had become exceedingly difficult to maintain the horse herds of the large cavalry force at the post. The agency traders, both of whom had hay contracts for the large number of army horses, had failed to deliver. Trader J. W. Dear could furnish only thirty-eight of the three hundred tons for which he had contracted, and Yates, his counterpart, was short over two hundred tons. Rather than incurring the expense of shipping hay from Cheyenne, a troop reduction was ordered. On May 26, 1877, less than three weeks after Crazy Horse's arrival, Mackenzie's Fourth Cavalry battalion—five hundred enlisted men and officers—departed for its former stations in the Department of the Missouri. The next day Lt. Col. Luther Bradley arrived from Omaha Barracks to assume command of the District of the Black Hills and the post. By summer Camp Robinson's garrison numbered about four hundred men, comprising three companies of infantry and four of cavalry.[2]

Luther Prentice Bradley began his military career late in 1861 as the lieutenant colonel of the Fifty-first Illinois Infantry. He later commanded the regiment through the Chickamauga–Chattanooga campaigns and then on to Atlanta. In July 1864 he was promoted to brigadier general of volunteers, a rank he held until the end of the war. Due to his success as a commander, he was appointed lieutenant colonel of the new Twenty-seventh Infantry under the regular army's postwar reorganization. In1867 he commanded the Bozeman Trail post of Fort C. F. Smith when his regiment was assigned duty there during Red Cloud's War. Bradley later transferred to the Ninth infantry and was stationed with that regiment at Fort Laramie. After he arrived at Robinson, Bradley observed a marked change in the disposition of the Red Cloud Indians. Early in June he wrote that the subdued Indians were "generally quiet & friendly, a marked contrast in their conduct now & in former years." He added, "I hope it is the beginning of a new era."[3]

Reduced troop strength meant that parts of the temporary cantonments built the previous fall became surplus. The unused structures were demolished for their lumber. Also available, sitting unused, was quartermaster and ordnance equipment from the fall troop buildup, such as harness, tools, and stoves. The department chief quartermaster decided to dispose of everything and printed and distributed notices of the impending surplus sale around the area, some sent as far as Sidney and North Platte.[4]

Agency relocation became a pressing issue that spring for both agency Indians and the new northern arrivals. Some months previous Sheridan had suggested to Crook the moving of the Indians to new agencies on the Tongue River and in the Yellowstone country. Although he initially opposed this idea, by 1877 Crook became one of its strongest proponents. He believed agencies in the Yellowstone country had several benefits, including good bottom land for agriculture, a navigable river for supply, and one of the better remaining hunting ranges. More important the Indians would be far from the Black Hills miners and settlers. Crook envisioned a large reservation for the Sioux, Arapaho, and Cheyenne, bounded on the west by the Big Horn Mountains, on the north by the

Yellowstone River, and extending to the east beyond the mouth of the Powder River. Although the Crow tribe, longtime enemies of these three tribes, lived due west, the newly established military posts bordering the region could keep the peace.[5]

Crook and his subordinates thought this an excellent way to keep faith with the agency peoples. Soldier and Indian alike thought the newly elected "Great Father," Rutherford B. Hayes, would "do more for the Indians than any who had proceeded him" and might support the move. The entrenched Indian bureau, however, would find it too difficult to depart from its established policy.[6]

Crazy Horse joined the main agency leaders in their desire for an agency in the north. On the day his band surrendered, Crazy Horse said he wanted a new agency east of the White (Big Horn) Mountains or along Beaver Creek in the Powder River country. He reasoned that Beaver Creek was in the middle of "Sioux Country," and Red Cloud Agency was on its edge. At some time Red Cloud had misleadingly told Crazy Horse that his band would be allowed to settle anywhere it chose, "if you will go to Washington and make your peace with [the Great Father]."[7] As a result, Crazy Horse set his mind to secure a northern agency for his people, which he stubbornly pursued during his entire, tenuous stay at Red Cloud Agency.

On May 25 Crook held a council with the Indians of the northern Nebraska agencies. Beforehand Lieutenant Clark presented his scouts for Crook's review. At noon several hundred mounted scouts massed east of the agency stockade, and afterwards the chiefs formed in line, dismounted, and shook hands with Crook, who for some had only recently been their main adversary. It was here that Crazy Horse first met Crook.[8]

During the council the Indians spoke in friendly terms and expressed their desire for a northern agency, not one along the Missouri River. Some favored a site north of the Black Hills near Bear Butte. Crazy Horse, who told Crook he was happy to meet him, gave his preference, adding that "there is plenty of game in that country." Crook then cautioned the assembly that although he favored the northern agencies, he could not make the decision for the government, only make a recommendation. He discussed the formation of a delegation to Washington to settle the issue. To this the chiefs responded favorably, but firmly reiterated their opposition to any Missouri River location. The meeting then adjourned.[9]

At the council Crook had made much of the fact that the new Great Father, of whom Crook was personally acquainted, wanted to meet them. With the general's support and political connections the agency chiefs held high hopes for the forming of a beneficial, conciliatory policy with the new president. Nevertheless they returned to their camps, awaiting their still uncertain future.

The review of Clark's Indian scouts symbolized one of Crook's key strategies of the Great Sioux War. A master in the use of Indians as scouts and auxiliaries, Crook believed such employment would "reconstruct all hostiles who come in that it will be almost an impossibility to force them on the war path again." In addition to field scouting, the army used enlisted scouts as agency police. Under Clark's close supervision the scouts preserved order in the camps and assisted agency employees with ration and annuity issues. They disarmed and dismounted Indian bands coming from the north to surrender, helped keep the peace between the whites and the agency young men, and protected the camps from white horse thieves.[10]

During the summer of 1877 Clark's scouts saw field service, sometimes accompanying army units from Camp Robinson. Post officers reported the scouts used good judgement while on field operations and were "efficient and obedient."[11] With such traditional activities as warfare and buffalo hunting no longer available, service as army scouts provided a useful outlet and an opportunity to garner power and prestige. Many young men, including recently surrendered northern warriors, saw this and readily enlisted, including Crazy Horse and many of his followers. Although several interpreters strongly opposed his enlistment and saw it as a "dangerous experiment," Crazy Horse and twenty-five of his tribesmen enlisted on May 17.[12] As with other scouts, they were issued Sharps carbines, Colt revolvers, ammunition, and horses. A visiting newspaper correspondent reported the enlistment of the recently subdued warriors:

> A remarkable scene occurred when these Red Soldiers were sworn into Uncle Sam's service. They swore with up-lifted hands to be true and faithful to the white man's government.[13]

Adding the new recruits Clark organized his scouts into five companies of fifty men, each commanded by reliable chiefs. Among others, the Arapaho Sharp Nose, and Sioux chiefs Red Cloud, Little Wound, and Spotted Tail were ranked as company first sergeants. After his enlistment Crazy Horse was appointed as a first sergeant and placed in command of Company C. He was assisted by his headmen Little Big Man, He Dog, and others as sergeants and corporals.[14]

The army, especially Lieutenant Clark, discovered another use for his scouts, espionage, which was thought to make impossible any conspiracy by the northern Indians. Scouts slipped into camps and gathered information, which Clark then funneled to Crook. In August Clark confidently reported to his general that he was "keeping a sharp watch, through some of the scouts I can fully trust on both agencies, and they keep one pretty well posted."[15] By this means power was gained over the Indians at the agencies. As later learned, factors other than loyalty to the army could color any intelligence these spies reported.

The spring brought an additional improvement to the post, a telegraph line. In 1874 General Ord had requested a telegraph line to Camp Robinson from Fort Laramie, but the secretary of war vetoed his proposal, stating that none could be built without a specific congressional appropriation. The Sioux war clearly demonstrated the need for rapid communications, and the matter was reconsidered. On March 15, 1877, a detail went to build the line. As the wire gradually moved east from the main line at Hat Creek, an operator kept his office in a tent at its terminus to expedite telegraphic communications. On April 22 the telegraph line became operational, eliminating the slow, horseback courier.[16]

The spring surrenders prompted decisions regarding the relocation of the various tribes at the Nebraska agencies. Regardless of Crook's suggestions and the desires of the Indians themselves, the Indian bureau never wavered. It still planned to move the Sioux to new agency sites along the Missouri River as dictated by the 1868 treaty. Others called for removing all the defeated Sioux south to faraway Indian Territory. Although Phil Sheridan opposed a Sioux move to Indian Territory, he supported moving the Northern Cheyenne tribe there. Sheridan respected the fighting abilities of the Cheyennes, realized their major role in Custer's 1876 defeat, and feared the impact of their independent spirit on the other northern tribes. At his insistence Crook and Mackenzie urged the Northern Cheyennes to join their southern cousins on the Indian Territory reservation.[17]

Several weeks prior to Crazy Horse's surrender, Crook and Mackenzie met with Cheyenne leaders to convince them. Thinking that he would speak against removal, the Cheyenne leaders selected Standing Elk, a major chief, as their council spokesman. To their dismay he agreed that the south would be a better place to live. When the news broke, many Cheyennes became angry over the planned move. They had quit fighting and given up their arms with the expectation they would remain along the White River; now they had to move. Eventually Standing Elk's decision won out, and the Cheyennes obligingly, but grudgingly consented to relocation. They would try life in Indian Territory and later argue for change if it proved unsatisfactory.[18]

On May 18 the adjutant general of the army informed Sheridan that the commissioner of Indian affairs had approved the move. Two days later

Crook was notified of this approval, and plans for removal quickly commenced. Lt. Henry W. Lawton, who had built the temporary canton-ments, was placed in charge of moving the tribe south and immediately gathered supplies needed to feed the Indians *en route*. An Omaha newspaper reported that the Cheyennes "were very bitter against the Sioux," and "didn't want to live near them any longer," and added they would leave Red Cloud about May 28.[19] On that day Lawton and a small, Fourth Cavalry escort left with nearly one thousand Cheyennes for the Cheyenne–Arapaho Agency near Fort Reno, Indian Territory. About 130 Cheyennes remained at Red Cloud after formally requesting their transfer to Arapaho and Sioux bands there.

Emigration to the southern reservation was also being proposed for the agency Arapahos, who for some years held a tenuous affiliation with the Oglala agency. After warring with the whites in the 1860s, some fifteen hundred Northern Arapahos under leaders Friday, Sharp Nose, and Black Coal, had been allowed to settle with the Sioux at Red Cloud Agency on the North Platte River. They had frequently clashed with the dominant Oglalas, who tried to intimidate them. While these leaders attempted to maintain peace with the whites, more belligerent Arapaho warriors raided freighters and miners in Wyoming's Sweetwater country and fought with the Shoshone tribe. After suffering a July 4, 1874, defeat by the army, the so-called Bates Battle in the Wind River country of Wyoming, the entire tribe moved to White River to draw rations and live in peace. Soon thereafter about a third of the northern bands moved south to join the Southern Arapahos in Indian Territory. The remainder settled into camp on the river valley several miles above Camp Robinson.[20]

Faced with an uncertain future at Red Cloud Agency, the Arapahos readily enlisted in 1876 to serve in the Sioux war. A total of 155 Arapaho men scouted for the army and fought alongside their former white and Shoshone enemies against the Sioux and Cheyenne. By becoming allies they hoped to gain Crook's favor—and a northern reservation. Crook promised them a reservation along the Yellowstone River, a promise he could not fulfill.[21]

Subsequently, in March 1877 the Arapaho had asked Colonel Mackenzie to write the secretary of Interior requesting permission to go west and join their new Shoshone allies in central Wyoming. Mackenzie, like Crook, was sympathetic to their desires, noting "The Arapahoes are thoroughly obedient, they have been entirely loyal to the Government through all the existing troubles with the Sioux and Cheyennes."[22] On the other hand Sheridan was "out and out opposed" to allowing them to move to Shoshone country; he was suspicious of the reported peace between the two traditional enemies. Sheridan wanted them to join the Southern Arapahos, "to whom they originally belonged." Furthermore, the northern people's subsistence and annuity goods had always been appropriated with those for the Southern Arapaho.[23]

Until a decision on their future was made, the Arapahos tranquilly remained in their White River camp, racing horses and hosting officers from the post. Lieutenant Bourke spent many hours in their hospitable lodges, learning their history and vocabulary. Of his visits with Friday he recalled, "I used to talk to him by the hour, and never failed to extract pages of most interesting information concerning savage ideas, manners, and customs."[24]

With relatively quiet agencies and with the departure of the first Indians, the Indian bureau pushed for the return to authority of their civilian agents. In February 1877 the commissioner of Indian affairs had wanted civilians to control all of the agencies except the troublesome northern Nebraska agencies. General Sherman, in turn, wanted to be consulted before any agencies returned to civil control. On March 15 division headquarters ordered the civilian takeover, stating, "[T]he above regulation will take effect at the Spotted Tail and Red Cloud agencies as soon as civil agents have been appointed hereto."[25] Earlier in the month Dr. James Irwin, the agent at the Shoshone and Bannock Agency in Wyoming Territory, was appointed as the new Red Cloud agent. Although he accepted on March 14, there was a delay of several months before he started the new assignment. By the summer of 1877 the army was more than ready to exit the agency business. Lt. Charles Johnson, the last of five officers from Camp Robinson to serve as acting agent, passed the mantle to Irwin on July 1.

Midsummer brought resumed raiding to the northern Black Hills country. Although no settlements came under direct attack, travelers were harassed and livestock taken from ranches in the foothills. It was believed that small groups of agency holdouts, moving between the Yellowstone River country and the agencies, carried out the raids. In July Gov. John L. Pennington of Dakota Territory telegraphed Crook for soldiers.[26]

The trouble in the Hills came at a time of other distractions. July riots in Chicago forced all available troops stationed along the railroad to be sent there to keep order. Hard-pressed to send troops to the Black Hills, the secretary of war was nevertheless later able to report, "[B]y rapid movement, all that could be was done to have them at all points when needed."[27]

Captain Wessells's company scouted in the Spearfish Canyon area.

The press failed to soothe the panicky settlers; one newspaper reported that "at least twenty murders have been reported. . . . Nearly every ranch along the Redwater and in Spearfish valley have [*sic*] been devastated."[28] Another cavalry company sent from Camp Robinson to scout east of the Hills took along ten of Lieutenant Clark's Indian scouts, but returned without seeing any raiders or trails. Units from Fort Laramie also patrolled the Hills. Crook thought that sending out company-sized units was adequate. He was also very skeptical of the newspaper accounts and the exaggerated reports of the settlers. "[S]ome of those frontiersmen are addicted to lying."[29] As it turned out, the raids were the work of small parties of warriors not from the Nebraska agencies.

Sheridan had long favored the establishment of a military post near the Black Hills to ease the burden of sending troops from Fort Laramie and Camp Robinson. In late summer of 1878 a new post near Bear Butte was built to provide permanent security for settlers. The post, eventually to become Fort Meade, was established by Maj. Henry M. Lazelle, First Infantry, the same officer who had served in the army's early days at Red Cloud Agency.

In September 1877 the last group of northern Indians came to the Nebraska agencies to surrender. This was the Lame Deer band of Minneconjous, thought responsible for most of the summer raiding. On May 7 Col. Nelson Miles had finally caught up with and surrounded this village of over fifty lodges in the Yellowstone country. In the ensuing fight Chief Lame Deer and thirteen of his warriors died. Afterwards, scattered remnants of the village surrendered at Red Cloud Agency, where Bradley assured them that regardless of the depredations they had committed, they would be well treated. Finally, on September 11 the main body surrendered at Spotted Tail Agency.[30]

After Crazy Horse surrendered in May, his people settled into the routine of agency life. What army officers saw as the "beginning of a new era" with peace and order at the White River agencies turned into a summer of intrigue, mistrust, jealousy, and deceit.

For Crazy Horse and most of his followers encamped north of the White River several miles northeast of Red Cloud Agency, this was their first time at an agency. The free-roaming days of hunting and war were over; they were now dependent on the agency system for their daily existence. The army itself learned how highly regarded in Lakota camp circles the warrior–chieftain was. Many agency Indians commented on his courage and generosity. The latter trait earned him much of his popularity; some said he kept nothing for himself. Lieutenant Bourke once reported, "I have never heard an Indian mention his name save in terms of respect."[31]

Accompanied by Frank Grouard, the well-known guide and interpreter of Polynesian descent, Bourke went to Crazy Horse's camp the evening following his surrender. When they reached his lodge, they found Crazy Horse seated on the ground. Sorrel Horse, who also accompanied Bourke, told Crazy Horse that Bourke was one of the officers of "Three Stars." Bourke recounted, [Crazy Horse] "leaned forward, grasped my hand warmly and grunted 'How.' This was the extent of our conversation."[32] Bourke further noted Crazy Horse's countenance, "His face is quiet rather morose, dogged, tenacious and resolute. His expression is rather melancholy." Grouard then escorted Crazy Horse to his cabin for supper.

Phil Sheridan voiced his concern about keeping Crazy Horse and other war leaders at the Nebraska agencies. He wrote Sherman, "A sufficient number of the hostile Indians have now surrendered to permit us to take up the question of punishing the leaders with the view of preventing any further trouble."[33] In a continuation of the policy adopted after the Red River War of exiling southern Plains leaders, Sheridan evidently sought Sherman's views on sending Crazy Horse and others to Fort Marion at St. Augustine, Florida. However, the commissioner of Indian affairs believed these Indians had surrendered in good faith as prisoners of war and were not necessarily criminals (unless so proven). Sherman somewhat reluctantly agreed, adding "to send them to St. Augustine they would be simply petted at the expense to the U. S. Better to remove all to a safe place and then reduce them to a helpless condition."[34] The Indian leaders of the Great Sioux War who surrendered at the Nebraska agencies would remain there until the agencies were moved.

In the meantime Crazy Horse became somewhat of a celebrity.[35] There was great interest in his role in Custer's defeat at the Little Bighorn. A reporter from the *Chicago Times* came in late June to interview him about the battle. Lieutenant Clark arranged the interview, with Baptiste "Little Bat" Garnier interpreting, while Horned Horse acted as a spokesman for Crazy Horse. "Horned Horse told the story readily (after some hesitation), which met with the approval of Crazy Horse."[36]

White visitors to his summer camp became a fairly common occurrence. One correspondent remarked that his village presented a better appearance than any other seen; also Crazy Horse had presented him with a pair of his moccasins.[37] After Colonel Bradley arrived at Camp Robinson, the Sioux chiefs, including Crazy Horse, came to the post to meet him. When Bradley was introduced and shook hands with the warrior–chieftain, he found Crazy Horse "a young slender and mild mannered fellow."[38] During these pleasant days Clark, another frequent visitor, tried to cultivate his friendship. Clark thought he had somewhat succeeded and reported to Crook that he was on "excellent dog eating terms" with Crazy Horse.[39] Not all looked favorably on Crazy Horse's new status. Some Indian leaders believed Crazy Horse was receiving special favors. Resentment and jealousy began to appear around some of the campfires.

Shortly after his initial council with Crook, Crazy Horse watched the Cheyennes depart for the southern reservations. He was also hearing the talk of moving the Sioux to the Missouri River. By midsummer his suspicions of the Indian bureau had grown. On the other hand, the Cheyenne departure removed a large body of potential army allies. Due to their supposed ill treatment at Crazy Horse's camp after the Red Fork fight, Lieutenant Bourke believed many Cheyennes remained bitter toward Crazy Horse. He also thought Crazy Horse grew more insolent to the army after the Cheyennes departed.[40]

Crook had promised the agency Indians in the spring that they could go on an organized buffalo hunt in the north, where sizable herds still remained, but only after the last northern bands (meaning Lame Deer's Minneconjous) surrendered. He intended to let the Crazy Horse band participate.[41] Although by summer the Lame Deer band was still out, the agency Indians wanted to depart sometime in July. But Crook held firm: the hunt could not commence until the last northern group surrendered. The army received word in midsummer that the band was coming in, and it appeared that the promise would be kept.

On July 27 a council was held at Red Cloud Agency to discuss preparations. About seventy agency Sioux attended, including Red Cloud, Crazy Horse, Little Big Man, and Young Man Afraid of His Horses. Lieutenant Clark read a message from Crook, who told them that everyone who wanted to go should plan on being gone about forty days. They were to conduct themselves peacefully, and had to return on the date specified. Crook would also allow the agency traders to sell ammunition for hunting. All the Indians present expressed their satisfaction.

As was customary for such councils, a feast was proposed. Agent Irwin would provide three head of beef, coffee, and other essentials after the assembled Sioux decided in whose camp to hold it. Young Man Afraid proposed Crazy Horse's camp. Upon hearing this, Red Cloud and several other leaders immediately arose and walked out.[42]

That night Irwin and Benjamin R. Shopp, a special inspector for the Indian bureau visiting the agency, were informed some Indians wanted to see the agent. Ignoring the late hour, Irwin agreed to meet the persistent visitors, who turned out to be representatives of Red Cloud's and other bands. They told Shopp and Irwin there would be great dissatisfaction if the feast was held at Crazy Horse's camp. Crazy Horse had only recently joined the agency, and "he should come to them." They explained that holding the feast at his village would demonstrate the government's disposition to conciliate him at the expense of the friendly, reliable agency leadership. The delegation also let it be known that Crazy Horse was "tricky and unfaithful to others and very selfish as to the personal interests of his own band." If Crazy Horse left on the hunt, he and his band would return to the warpath. The night visitors only reinforced doubts about Crazy Horse held by Irwin, who had always opposed the hunt.[43]

Crook lifted the prohibition of the sale of ammunition to the Indians the next day. Irwin and others at the agency thought it unwise. One officer's wife at Camp Robinson voiced concern over any renewal of ammunition sales, "[I]n one day they could get enough to help their northern friends ever so much in their war with the whites."[44] Apparently Irwin was able to halt the sales at his agency.

Not all Indians favored this hunt. Spotted Tail in particular opposed the plan and spoke against it to Lt. Jesse Lee, the acting agent at his agency. Along with Capt. Daniel W. Burke, Camp Sheridan's post commander, Lee thought a crisis was at hand. If the Indians at Spotted Tail—Brulés and recently arrived northern Indians—went on a hunt "with all the wild Indians from Red Cloud, trouble might ensue and many would slip away and join Sitting Bull, who had gone north of the line."[45]

Another item on the agenda at the July 27 council was the formation of a Washington delegation. Crook's message announced the Interior secretary's permission for representatives to come East and present their views on moving the agencies to the Missouri. The proposed delegation would leave in September, and Crook advised the council members to pick their best men to protect their interests.

Earlier in the spring Clark had told Red Cloud that he and others would make a trip to Washington to discuss agency relocation. Clark also told the chief that Crazy Horse, after he came in, would accompany any delegation. Red Cloud later informed Crazy Horse of this: "The army wants you to go to the Great White Father," in addition to telling him he would be permitted to select an agency in the north.[46]

Crazy Horse wanted to go to Washington, provided the government let him have a northern agency before his departure. As he remarked to one of his headmen, "When I pick out a land I will pick one right near the Black Hills." He understood the purpose of the Washington trip was to make peace and to select a favorable agency site for his people.[47]

The army was keenly interested in having Crazy Horse join the delegation. Several days after the council Colonel Bradley called both Crazy Horse and Little Big Man to the post and told them the Great Father wanted to see them. Little Big Man agreed to go, but Crazy Horse gave no definite reply, although by this time he was openly telling his followers he would go to Washington only after the agency site was selected. Bradley, though, firmly told him he must go to Washington first.[48]

Jealousy by the agency Indian leaders grew daily, some because white people came to see Crazy Horse and, it was rumored, brought him money.[49] Others feared that if Crazy Horse went to Washington, he would be made chief of all the Sioux.[50] Apparently those agency leaders who had long supported the government now believed they were secondary in stature to Crazy Horse. They feared his popularity would prove a threat to their power and political status.[51] As this jealousy permeated the camps, tension grew and factions among the Oglalas at Red Cloud began to form.

Factions developed in Crazy Horse's own band and damaged old loyalties. For example, an open rift developed between Crazy Horse and He Dog, a shrewd fighter and loyal friend, who moved his camp and switched his allegiance to Red Cloud.[52] Little Big Man, once Crazy Horse's trusted lieutenant, drifted away from his influence, and some thought Little Big Man entertained aspirations of becoming a great Sioux chief. In two years he had converted from the fierce warrior who had broken up the Allison Commission to a willing follower of the whites. With defections in the northern ranks, Bourke rightly observed, "[T]he weakness of faction had been made to replace the solidity of harmony."[53] Within weeks only about half of the band that surrendered in May remained in Crazy Horse's camp.

However, Crazy Horse had one formidable ally. Touch the Clouds, the towering Minneconjou leader, apparently grew sympathetic to his cause. Standing "six foot five in his moccasins," his band was among the 1,300 Minneconjous and Sans Arcs who had surrendered at Spotted Tail Agency in April. As the summer progressed, Touch the Clouds became a power behind the northern Indians there, as well as an ardent backer of Crazy Horse in his growing conflict with the Indian bureau and the army.[54]

The divisiveness in Crazy Horse's camp did not go unnoticed by Philo Clark, who turned to his scouts and informants for intelligence. Spies saturated the camp, all eager to report anything of interest to Clark, true or fabricated. Several scouts, including Lone Bear and his brother, Woman's Dress, spent increasing time lounging outside Crazy Horse's lodge, listening and watching.[55] Throughout Crazy Horse's stay at the agency, "Clark had detectives with ears quick to catch every word that might fall from Crazy Horse's lips, and eyes keen to note his every movement."[56] Many Indians concluded the stories the spies told were the cause for the ill feeling and mistrust that characterized that summer.

Crazy Horse's attitude turned noticeably unfriendly toward both agency Indians and the whites. Shopp reported he was discontented and "seemed to be chafing under restraint." He also became recalcitrant toward his fellow tribesmen.[57] By the end of July Irwin found Crazy Horse acting similarly to his employees, but the army was unconcerned about the agent's assertions. Earlier Bradley had boasted to Crook, "[W]e are quiet here as a Yankee village on a Sunday."[58] Clark, the military's chief contact with Crazy Horse, still had amicable meetings with him. As the army soon learned, "Concealed beneath the apparent calm, however, was a growing turbulence among the various camps and their chiefs."[59]

Later on an issue day Crazy Horse refused to sign receipts for his issue items and made "demonstrations" about the agency. When Irwin reported this to Bradley, he discovered that "it was hardly credited as the military still had faith in Crazy Horse."[60] Continuing this pattern of behavior, Crazy Horse refused his pay at the regular muster of Clark's Indian scouts. When Irwin pressed American Horse to help secure better cooperation with Crazy Horse, American Horse told Irwin flatly that he and other leaders could do nothing with him.[61]

In early August Crook pushed his officers at Camp Robinson to convince Crazy Horse to join the upcoming Washington delegation, but Crazy Horse was less willing to go than ever. Rumors sprang up in the camps that Crazy Horse would be imprisoned or killed if he went with the delegation.[62] By August 15 Crazy Horse had told Bradley he would not go. Two days later Crook sent a telegram urging Crazy Horse to make the trip. To sweeten the deal, Irwin gave Crazy Horse two cattle, and Clark bought items at the commissary for a feast. When Clark approached him about a decision, Crazy Horse replied he would not go, but wanted his selected headmen to go in his place and to replace Red Cloud, Spotted Tail, and other friendly Oglala leaders. Clark tried to explain that headmen from all the bands must go, not just his.[63] This final demand gave Clark the impression that Crazy Horse intended to dictate policy to the government. On the other hand, it seems reasonable that Crazy Horse would not trust the agency leadership, fearing they would consent to an unfavorable agency move as had the Cheyennes.

Rumors of outbreak and renewed war circulated around Red Cloud Agency, heard as early as the end of June during the Sun Dance in Crazy Horse's village. One newspaper warily reported, "Private correspondence from Red Cloud Agency gives information that since the Sun Dance . . . a large number of young bucks have gone back north."[64] Agency employees heard warriors were secretly trading for guns with freighters and other nonagency types. Shopp noted, "[The Indians] seem determined to secure arms at all hazards and will exchange property of great value for them."[65] Clark's spies brought word that Crazy Horse's men were buying and concealing arms in their camp. One informant saw an Indian exchange four ponies for a rifle.[66]

While all this information swirled about, the proposed buffalo hunt was canceled. After the July 27 council, rumors abounded that the northern Indians would use the hunt as a means to break away.[67] With the friendly chiefs and Agent Irwin lined up in opposition from the idea's inception, Crook finally relented. On August 4 ammunition sales were officially halted, and the next day the hunt was postponed. As word of its cancellation passed through the camps, Bradley informed department headquarters, "I think there will be no trouble about postponing the hunt."[68] With no hunt and little word about a northern agency, Crazy Horse and his still-loyal followers grew even more suspicious.

After Crazy Horse's refusal to join the delegation, Clark lost faith in the Oglala leader. Clark learned that some of Crazy Horse's supporters had secretly gone to Spotted Tail Agency to induce the northern Indians to move to his camp. After digesting the rumors, the reports of his spies, and the counsel of the friendly chiefs, Clark became convinced that to preserve order at the agencies Crazy Horse's power must be broken. On August 18 he wrote Crook in frustration, "I am very reluctantly forced to this conclusion because I have claimed and felt all along that any Indian could be 'worked' by other means, but absolute force is the only thing for him."[69]

Crook and some of his subordinates, however, still believed Crazy Horse had good intentions. That summer Crook sent Capt. George M. Randall, his chief of scouts during the Sioux war, to Camp Robinson to observe the agency. Randall believed Crazy Horse wanted to do right but needed time to become more conciliatory toward the whites. Randall told Lieutenant Lee at Spotted Tail Agency that Crazy Horse was "buzzed too much" by prominent Oglalas at the agency.[70]

As these events transpired at Red Cloud, Crook had other distractions. After leaving Camp Robinson in late May, he spent much of July touring the Big Horn and Yellowstone country with generals Sherman and

Sheridan. Both senior generals were anxious to see the Sioux War country, and Sheridan wished to visit the Custer battlefield. As the tour neared its completion, railroad strikes broke out in Chicago; federal troops were called to restore order. On July 27 Sheridan, accompanied by Crook, quickly returned to Chicago to take stock of the situation.[71]

As this urban problem died down, another crisis was brewing on the frontier. The Nez Perce tribe, headed by Chief Joseph, had begun its epic outbreak in the Northwest. The month of August saw the fugitive Nez Perce nearing the borders of the Department of the Platte, which naturally concerned Crook. On August 23 reports came in that Joseph had entered Yellowstone Park in his department. Although it was not known where the Nez Perce would go next, Crook was ordered to prepare an expedition to head them off. To supplement his troops in the field, he mobilized the Sioux scouts at the Nebraska agencies. At Camp Robinson Lieutenant Clark had to organize at least one hundred scouts for field service. Outside events had always affected matters at the agency and the army camp, and now the stage was set for the final chapter in the Crazy Horse saga.[72]

On the evening of August 30 Clark held a council with the agency leaders, including Crazy Horse and Touch the Clouds, to explain Crook's need for scouts and to ask their cooperation. Many of those present were willing to join the fight against the Nez Perce. The northern Indians and Crazy Horse, however, were receiving contradictory messages; they had surrendered and had been asked to make peace, and now they were being asked to make war.

The next day Crazy Horse spoke and expressed his displeasure that the hunt had been canceled, but he added that he and his men would join the soldiers against Joseph. In his interpreting, Frank Grouard garbled the translation and made a grave mistake. He rendered Crazy Horse's reply as saying, in effect, that Crazy Horse would fight until no white men were left, when he probably meant "until there is not a Nez Perce" was left.[73] Louis Bordeaux, another interpreter, noticed the slip and immediately pointed out the error to Grouard, who abruptly left the council. Clark had the reliable Billy Garnett finish the interpreting, but the damage had been done. To Clark it appeared Crazy Horse was threatening war.

Before the council broke up, Crazy Horse told Clark that he would leave with the scouts, but he wanted to bring his whole camp along and do some hunting. Clark would have nothing to do with this proposal, which effectively ended their discussion.[74]

Crazy Horse's misinterpreted statement at the council only reinforced the outbreak rumors Clark had heard. It was also reported—and feared— that Crazy Horse would persuade others, including enlisted scouts, to join his departure. The army estimated that if Crazy Horse left, some two thousand northern Indians at the agencies would accompany him.[75]

Some have argued that the possibility of Crazy Horse and his followers breaking away was highly unlikely.[76] After their surrender, they had lost most of their horses and arms, but the rumors of illicit firearm sales persisted, and some warriors enlisted as government scouts had actually rearmed. Neither the Indian bureau nor the U.S. Army wanted to risk renewed conflict. Crazy Horse could easily create trouble, "and he gave every evidence that he intended to do it."[77]

Sheridan, advised of Crazy Horse's growing defiance, was now keenly aware that a dangerous situation was germinating at the agencies. As he awaited developments in his Chicago headquarters, Crook headed west by rail to direct operations against the Nez Perce. Sheridan hoped the scouts would go as soon as possible to augment the planned expedition against Joseph. By August 31 Bradley had the scout detachment, including scores of new, eager volunteers, ready to move out when an explosive complication to their deployment arose.

Several days earlier word had filtered out that Sitting Bull's band had left Canada to help Chief Joseph fight the whites.[78] Many in the agency camps presumed that the scouts were to be sent out against Sitting Bull instead of Joseph. Also on August 31 Crazy Horse and Touch the Clouds allegedly told Clark that they were no longer going to stay at the agencies; they were leaving with their people for the north. This rumor created considerable excitement among the agency Indians.[79] Bradley quickly telegraphed his superiors, "I think the departure of the scouts will bring on a collision here." He also requested Crook's presence at the agency, "[I]f anyone can influence this Indian [Crazy Horse] he can."[80]

Sheridan quickly responded and ordered Bradley to delay deploying the scouts. He telegraphed Crook, still on board the train heading toward the Wind River country in Wyoming, to go to Red Cloud instead. Sheridan was convinced the growing crisis required Crook's personal attention. Crook, on the other hand, did not initially concur. But Sheridan now made it clear, "The surrender or capture of Joseph . . . is but a small matter compared with what might happen to the frontier from a disturbance at Red Cloud."[81] The time had come, Crook realized, to break up the Crazy Horse band and remove its leader from the agency.

From an eastern Nebraska railroad stop, Crook sent word to Bradley to surround and capture the camps of Crazy Horse at Red Cloud and of Touch the Clouds at Spotted Tail. He cautioned, "Delay is very dangerous in this business."[82] Meanwhile Bradley had quietly called in reinforcements; within two days, four additional Third Cavalry companies rode in from Hat Creek and Fort Laramie. While Crook detrained at Sidney and headed north, the agency chiefs reassured Irwin and Clark that they would side with the government in case trouble erupted.[83]

Clark warned Lieutenant Lee at Spotted Tail to beware of treachery by Touch the Clouds and advised Captain Burke that the capture of both camps was planned. This came as a surprise to Lee and Burke, who had always found the tall Minneconjou extremely cooperative and thought it highly unlikely he could be instigating problems at Red Cloud. Burke immediately called in Touch the Clouds for a council to confirm his loyalty. Touch the Clouds denied threatening war and explained the misinterpretation when Crazy Horse was asked to scout against the Nez Perce. Convinced of Touch the Clouds's good intentions, Lee hurried to Camp Robinson to explain his side of the story to Clark. When he arrived at the post on September 2, Crook was already there, planning the capture of the two belligerent camps that same night.[84]

Crook wanted Spotted Tail's followers to ride with the troops from Camp Sheridan to surround Touch the Clouds's camp, while Red Cloud Indians assisted the Third Cavalry against the Crazy Horse band. To insure success, the chiefs were told to select only their best men for the operation.[85] But often the best laid plans go awry. Later that day word came of the approach of the Lame Deer band, and Crook immediately delayed the action.[86]

In hopes of giving Crazy Horse "one last chance for self-vindication," Crook called him to a council on the morning of September 3.[87] While Crook rode with Clark in an army ambulance to the meeting, the Indian scout Woman's Dress suddenly rode up and warned the general of an assassination plot. While eavesdropping outside Crazy Horse's lodge the night before, the scout claimed to have heard Crazy Horse tell his men he would kill Crook at their meeting. This revelation prompted Crook and Clark to hurry back to Camp Robinson and safety.[88]

Subsequent evidence indicates that Woman's Dress and other enemies of Crazy Horse fabricated the assassination story. One contemporary labeled this conspiracy, "a shrewd plan, skillfully worked and shamefully successful."[89] Billy Garnett for one, a reliable source, claimed that it was all a lie. Garnett said he was present at an 1889 confrontation with Woman's Dress where the plot was exposed as a frame-up against Crazy Horse by jealous rivals.[90] Unfortunately Crook "gave full credit to his story."[91] True or not, Woman's Dress's tale forced the army's hand: Crazy Horse must be removed.

When Crook returned to the post, he ordered Bradley to capture Crazy Horse's village the next morning, even with the Lame Deer band still some distance away. Crook no longer considered Touch the Clouds a threat, and directed his attentions to the capture of Crazy Horse.

According to some accounts, Crook and Clark held a secret meeting at Camp Robinson that afternoon with certain chiefs considered reliable, including Red Cloud, Young Man Afraid, American Horse, and No Water, the latter an avowed enemy of Crazy Horse. Crook told them Crazy Horse was leading their people astray and they must help the army arrest him. The Indians purportedly proposed to kill Crazy Horse, an idea Crook immediately vetoed. He told them that if they and their followers helped in his capture, it would prove they "were not in sympathy with the non-progressive element of their tribe." The agency leaders readily agreed to march with the soldiers the next morning.[92]

Early on the morning of September 4, confident that the situation at Red Cloud was well in hand, Crook turned his attention to the Nez Perce and departed for Cheyenne to resume his trip to Camp Brown, Wyoming Territory. Several hours earlier an anxious Lee rushed back to Spotted Tail Agency to prepare for any collateral trouble that might erupt. At nine o'clock four hundred cavalrymen, three hundred Sioux, and one hundred Arapahos rode to the Crazy Horse camp. Before reaching their destination, some of the Indians unwisely fired at a coyote running along the river bank.[93] The brief fusillade alarmed nearby camps, who believed the soldiers were attacking Crazy Horse. When the large contingent reached the camp, the soldiers found it nearly deserted. Their Indian allies pursued and captured most of the fleeing inhabitants, who were to be redistributed among other bands, where "the people will be subjected to better influences."[94]

Much to their chagrin, Bradley and Clark discovered Crazy Horse had fled the camp before daybreak. Taking his wife, and possibly accompanied by several others, he had departed for Touch the Clouds's camp. As Bradley contacted department headquarters with news of this setback, Clark quickly dispatched twenty of his Indian scouts under No Water to overtake Crazy Horse and dashed off a message to Lieutenant Lee to arrest Crazy Horse if he arrived at Spotted Tail Agency. Clark also warned Lee to keep matters quiet at his agency and to intercept any Crazy Horse followers that might show up.[95]

At four o'clock that afternoon a great commotion broke out in Touch the Clouds's camp when a courier dashed in and reported fighting at Red Cloud Agency; soldiers were on the way. As order was restored, Lee received the startling news that Crazy Horse was in the camp. About this time the scouts sent to pursue Crazy Horse rode in, adding to the chaos. Major Burke and Lieutenant Lee immediately set out for Touch the

Clouds's camp, three miles north of Camp Sheridan. They were met by several hundred northern warriors escorting Crazy Horse to the camp.[96]

After they reached the post, Crazy Horse told Burke and Lee that he had left Red Cloud to get away from the troubles there. Meanwhile Spotted Tail and three hundred of his followers arrived at Camp Sheridan, adding to the gathering throng. The powerful Brulé chief tersely informed his fugitive nephew that this was *his* agency and ominously added, "I do not want anything bad to happen to you here." Desiring a more quiet place to talk, the officers took Crazy Horse into Burke's quarters, where Crazy Horse told them he wanted no trouble and wished to be transferred to the Brulé agency.

> They gave me no rest at Red Cloud. I was talked to night and day and my brain is in a whirl.

He added, "I want to do what is right."[97]

The officers explained that they had no objection to his transfer if what he said was true. Burke and Lee then advised him to return with Lee to Camp Robinson, where "his good words would be told there, that he could tell them himself," to smooth over his difficulties. They reassured him this was his best and only course. Crazy Horse agreed and went back to the Minneconjou village with Touch the Clouds, who assured Burke that Crazy Horse would not escape during the night. After the Indians left, Lee sent a courier to inform Clark that he would bring Crazy Horse to Camp Robinson the next day.[98]

As Wednesday, the fifth of September, dawned, Crazy Horse developed second thoughts. About 9 A.M. he went to Lee and stated that he feared trouble at Red Cloud and that he had changed his mind about returning. The persistent officers bluntly told him to go quietly to Camp Robinson and explain matters there—it was the only thing to do.

Right after this meeting, Crazy Horse and a small party left Spotted Tail Agency for the forty-mile trip to Camp Robinson. Lieutenant Lee, the interpreter Bordeaux, and several Indians, including Touch the Clouds, rode in an army ambulance; according to his wishes, Crazy Horse traveled by horseback.[99] Several other reliable agency Indians rode along. As the curious entourage made its way westward, it was gradually joined by small groups of mounted Indians. Eventually fifty of Spotted Tail's warriors escorted Crazy Horse.[100]

Clark received Lee's message early that morning and sent word to Crook at Cheyenne that Crazy Horse was coming in. Upon Crazy Horse's arrival he would be held under guard in the post guardhouse until nightfall, then whisked off to Fort Laramie. Clark suggested sending several of his followers along to assure Crazy Horse's people of his safe passage. He added optimistically, "Everything quiet and working first rate."[101]

On receiving these recommendations, Crook ordered Bradley to send Crazy Horse with several of his men under strong escort to Laramie and then on to Omaha. Next he telegraphed the good news to Sheridan, requesting, "I wish you would send him off where he can be out of harm's way."[102] Confident and relieved that the crisis was over, Crook further remarked, "[T]he successful breaking-up of Crazy Horses band has removed a heavy weight off my mind and I leave feeling perfectly easy." Sheridan replied, "I wish you to send Crazy Horse under proper guard to these headquarters," meaning, of course, to Chicago.[103]

Between five and six o'clock that evening, Crazy Horse, the ambulance carrying his friends, and the Indian scout–guards reached Camp Robinson. Lee had been informed beforehand to take Crazy Horse to the adjutant's office. The party rode in as the evening parade concluded, and most of the soldiers returned to their barracks.[104] At headquarters Crazy Horse was met by 2nd Lt. Frederic S. Calhoun, post adjutant, whose late brother James was a brother-in-law of George Custer, both killed at the Little Bighorn, possibly by warriors led by Crazy Horse.[105] Lieutenant Calhoun directed that Crazy Horse be turned over to Capt. James Kennington, the officer of the day. Lee had Crazy Horse and the other Indians, including Touch the Clouds, go inside the office while he conferred with Colonel Bradley at his quarters.

Before leaving Spotted Tail Agency, Lee had assured Crazy Horse he would be permitted to have a few words with the post commander.[106] The well-intentioned Lee was obviously unaware of what was in store for Crazy Horse at Camp Robinson; his request for an interview was denied. Increasingly apprehensive Lee returned to the headquarters office to tell the companions of Crazy Horse that he would remain at the post under guard until the following morning.[107]

By now any proposed meeting of reconciliation or explanation between Crazy Horse and Bradley, or any post officer for that matter, was out of the question. Crook's plan was to place Crazy Horse under arrest immediately and have one of the cavalry companies rush him and several of his men to Fort Laramie that night.[108] Several officers later deduced that he was to be imprisoned at Fort Jefferson in the Dry Tortugas off the Florida coast. If Sheridan had exile in mind, he would not have sent Crazy Horse there—the fort had been abandoned for two years. A more likely destination was Fort Marion at St. Augustine, Florida, where southern

Plains leaders had been earlier imprisoned. Nonetheless Crazy Horse and his influence would be effectively excised from the northern Sioux agencies.[109]

A crowd of several hundred agency Sioux, Indian scouts, Arapahos, and northern Indians, including Crazy Horse followers, had assembled on the south side of the parade ground. Red Cloud and his men stood by on one side of the adjutant's office, while American Horse and his warriors waited on the other.[110] Captain Kennington, accompanied by Crazy Horse's one-time close associate Little Big Man, entered the office and escorted Crazy Horse to the guardhouse, some sixty feet to the west. Infantrymen of the post guard followed and attempted to keep outsiders from crowding in. As they neared the guardhouse door, some northerners in the crowd protested Crazy Horse's impending confinement, while other Indians "insisted on non-interference."[111] Once inside, Little Big Man "now became his chief's worst enemy."[112]

The building they entered consisted of two rooms. The main entrance opened into the guardroom, and to the right was the separate prison room where several military prisoners were confined. According to Lee, it was the sight of those prisoners that panicked Crazy Horse.

Crazy Horse, who was still armed with a pistol and knife, drew the latter and struck out wildly at his captors. This unexpected outburst created instant confusion among the soldiers and scouts standing inside the guardroom. Little Big Man immediately seized Crazy Horse's arms from behind in an attempt to control him. Both wrestled their way out the door. In the ensuing struggle the knife slashed Little Big Man's wrist or lower arm, he released his grip, and Crazy Horse broke free. In the next instant, as the noise of the disorderly crowd rose to a din, one of the guards stabbed Crazy Horse in the right side with his bayonet. Seriously wounded, the stricken war leader crumpled to the ground.[113]

The crowd massed before the guardhouse. As the now alerted garrison stood ready, some warriors and agency leaders stepped forward and tried to calm the enraged northern Indians. They largely succeeded. Their quick actions undoubtedly prevented further bloodshed, when "one shot would have been sufficient to start a fight."[114]

At this critical juncture, instead of taking the wounded Crazy Horse back into the guardhouse, he was carried into the more neutral adjutant's office. Assistant post surgeon Valentine T. McGillycuddy stepped forward to lend whatever medical aid was possible. While the assemblage of agency Indians and confused and angered followers of Crazy Horse gradually broke up and returned to the camps, Touch the Clouds and Worm, Crazy Horse's father, were allowed inside to comfort him. Lieutenant Clark telegraphed Crook that Crazy Horse had been stabbed during the attempt to place him in the guardhouse. Because of the wound it would be impossible to move him that night.

Contradictory versions of how the stabbing occurred were already circulating. Some thought the wound was definitely caused by a guard's bayonet (Which guard is still debated). Others insisted Crazy Horse had been stabbed with his own knife during the struggle with Little Big Man. Clark voiced the latter, hoping this scenario would convince the agency Indians that the army had not deliberately intended to harm him.[115]

In the adjutant's office Doctor McGillycuddy, Touch the Clouds, Worm, and others kept vigil. McGillycuddy immediately realized the wound was fatal and gave Crazy Horse some medication to relieve the pain. Near midnight, he died. Then his friend Touch the Clouds reportedly said, "It is good, he has looked for death and it has come."[116] When the still-mourning Fred Calhoun heard of Crazy Horse's death in his office, he exclaimed rather triumphantly, "He was forgiven for murder, but killed for impudence."[117]

Fearing acts of vengeance, the garrison remained under arms, set out pickets, and patrolled the road toward the agency camps throughout the night. At the agency itself the employees and mixed-bloods were brought within the protective stockade. Although considerable excitement and numerous false alarms followed, no hostile forays against the post or agency were ever made.[118]

The next morning Crazy Horse's grieving father took his son's body back to Spotted Tail Agency, where Lee returned to prepare for any ramifications from the killing. For several days turmoil and unrest prevailed, especially among the northern bands, who made open threats against army officers, including Clark and Burke. At Red Cloud rumors turned to panic when residents heard that soldiers and Pawnee scouts would surround the northern camps.[119] Over one thousand northern people stampeded from Red Cloud Agency to the more amiable atmosphere of the Spotted Tail camps. The chiefs supportive of the government, including the controversial schemer Little Big Man, sought to restore order and quiet in the camps. Little Wound, who stood with the army against Crazy Horse, echoed the opinion of the agency chiefs when he declared, "We had a fire brand among us, and we've got rid of it."[120]

On September 9 Clark reported that the excitement had subsided, adding self-servingly, "Crazy Horse had a wonderful influence and if he had lived it would have been war for sure."[121] Many in the army shared this view, confident that the Great Sioux War was now over. In making his final commentary on the episode, Lieutenant Bourke wrote, "As the grave of

Custer marked [the] high-water mark of Sioux supremacy in the trans-Missouri region, so the grave of Crazy Horse, a plain fence of pine slabs, marked the ebb."[122] Years later when asked about the death of Crazy Horse, one Sioux elder replied,

> That affair was a disgrace, and a dirty shame. We killed our own man.[123]

After the threat of outbreak by Crazy Horse's followers and the northern Indians lessened, the Indian bureau proceeded with its removal program. With all the Oglalas gathered and subjugated by coercion and decisive military action, the time seemed right to move them to the long-planned Missouri River agencies. And the Arapaho question remained to be settled. A week after Crazy Horse's death plans were finalized for the agency leaders to confer about the move with the president and department underlings in Washington. The official delegation from the Nebraska agencies consisted of twenty-three representatives of the Oglala, Brulé, northern Indians (Minneconjou and Sans Arc), and Arapaho tribes. The entourage included dependents, interpreters, and government officials and numbered over ninety people. Lieutenant Clark and former agents Howard and Daniels also traveled with the delegation.[124]

The federal government was not the only government entity that wanted to remove the Sioux from the White River agencies; the state of Nebraska expressed the same desire. When the northern boundary of Nebraska was surveyed in 1874, the fact was verified that neither the Red Cloud nor the Spotted Tail agencies sat on previously designated reservation lands. Agitation began in the Nebraska legislature for removal. The Nebraskans claimed they had never agreed to the Indian hunting rights or to restrictions of white travel or settlement in the portions of their state that were specified by the Fort Laramie Treaty of 1868. The presence of "a horde of lawless savages" in the northwest corner of the state stifled its settlement and development.[125] The legislature resolved:

> That we call upon the general government and demand that it shall immediately remove from within the boundaries of the State of Nebraska, the Indian agencies of Red Cloud and Spotted Tail, and the Indians who have been brought into our state and located at and about said agencies without the consent of the state.[126]

The army concurred for its own reasons. Sherman saw the economic and logistic advantages of the agencies along the Missouri River near Fort Randall, where "one dollar will go further toward feeding them than four dollars will at the agencies."[127] Crook and Sheridan favored sites in the Yellowstone country near the mouths of the Powder or Tongue rivers. There the Sioux could live in lands now considered undesirable for white settlement; their supplies could still come by riverboat. Both believed the Indians could be easily convinced to move north.

The Sioux relocation issue was settled in Washington. With the idea of relocation in Indian Territory out of the question, the Indian bureau applied pressure to force the Indians' move to locations on the Missouri River. In councils with President Hayes and Secretary of the Interior Carl Schurz the delegates opposed the move, but compromised and agreed to winter on the river; in the spring the Sioux could choose to return inland. Actually the Red Cloud and Spotted Tail Indians had little room to negotiate. Once they agreed to move, the shipment of supplies to the old agencies ceased. Their food and other necessities were shipped to Missouri River sites proposed by visiting commissioners several months before. Dwindling supplies at the Nebraska agencies would soon be exhausted, and the Indians would have to move posthaste or face starvation.[128]

After the delegation's return on October 11, the leaders held councils to inform their followers of the decision. The agency Indians opposed the move, but Crook told them they had to go. After one council, commander Bradley reported that although a number of objections were raised, he thought the Indians would go quietly. He recorded the Indian preparation for the move and his own thoughts:

> I have had a lot of Indians after me all the morning with various wants. Some for letters showing I think them good men. Some for my picture and some to say goodbye. All in preparation for their move. I am sorry for the poor fellows. They are children in our hands and we ought to care for them a little better.[129]

Years of wishes notwithstanding, the expeditious nature of the decision caught the Indian bureau wholly unprepared to shift thousands of Indians and their possessions several hundred miles. The army was called on to assist once again, and it gathered as many teams and wagons as it could spare. Companies E and L, Third Cavalry, escorted the Oglalas to their new agency; Company H, Third Cavalry, was sent with Spotted Tail's

Brulés. Crook joined the chorus of critics when he harped, "Owing to the lateness of the season, this march was attended with much suffering, and the removal itself was the source of great dissatisfaction to the people of these tribes."[130]

Regardless of such protestations, the Red Cloud Indians left for their new agency on the Missouri on October 25, 1877. The column numbered about eight thousand Oglalas and northern Indians and stretched eight miles when on the march. A large beef herd followed. Due to inclement weather the progress was difficult and slow. As the Indians left the White River, Bradley confided in his diary, "I bid them God-speed, and am glad to get them off my hands."[131]

That fall the Indian bureau decided to grant the Arapahos their wish to live in Shoshone country. In September the president had told the Arapaho chiefs that if they would subsist for themselves over the winter and move near Shoshone lands "without expense to the government," he would create a permanent reservation for them there. Another stipulation was that they must "enter upon permanent friendly relations with the Shoshones."[132]

Plans called for the tribe to move part way and winter in the Sage Creek area near old Fort Caspar. Agent Irwin, who opposed a winter move for the Arapahos, nevertheless recommended that issue items, such as blankets and cotton duck for tipi coverings, be forwarded to Fort Fetterman to await their arrival. On October 27 he wrote the commissioner of Indian affairs to hurry the shipment of Arapaho goods. "I can't urge too strongly the necessity of early attention to these Indians as they will undoubtedly suffer."[133]

The Arapahos, relieved that they did not have to relocate to Indian Territory, quickly prepared for the move. Before they left, Lieutenant Johnson issued beef and such supplies that remained at Red Cloud to the nine hundred men, women, and children. On November 5 2nd Lt. Henry R. Lemly and fourteen enlisted men of Company F, Third Cavalry, left the post as an escort to the Arapahos, who had actually departed on November 1.[134]

The Nebraska press lauded General Crook for his role in ridding the state of Indians:

> General Crook has met with wonderful success in the removal of the Indians, having exerted a powerful influence among them. Their peaceful removal was entirely owing to his efforts, and he is entitled to the greatest credit for the success of the undertaking, which was one of considerable magnitude and beset with many difficulties. The Indians have learned to respect him as a man and a peace maker as well as a warrior.[135]

For the first time in four turbulent years the White River Valley was empty of Indian people.

With them went the main mission of Camp Robinson. The garrisons at both agency posts could be substantially reduced, and as early as October the reduction began. On the first of the month over six hundred soldiers were stationed at Camp Robinson. During October most of the two, Third Cavalry battalions left; two companies escorted Red Cloud's people, one company went with the Brulés, and one moved to Fort Laramie. By mid-November the three infantry companies had left, and the three remaining cavalry companies departed for Fort Laramie, Camp Sheridan, and Hat Creek Station. By November 30, the garrison of Camp Robinson consisted only of Company C, Third Cavalry, leaving the post with a total strength of two officers and sixty-nine enlisted men.[136]

A new mission soon arose. Although Red Cloud Agency was gone, the post still resided near the Great Sioux Reservation, and thus fit into the army's post-Sioux war strategy. The army wanted to restrict the Indians to their reservation and surround it with a ring of military posts. As a result, several new forts were built in what had been the very heart of Sioux country, and existing posts were maintained at strategic points. The Indians would always know the soldiers were nearby.[137]

Camp Robinson continued to occupy a key location on the Sidney–Black Hills Trail, still the major route for Black Hills travelers. By 1877 the gold rush had ended, but the large population in the Hills provided an economic boost to the region. Freighters hauled daily shipments of freight, from foodstuffs to massive stamp mills to process gold ore. In 1877 Black Hills trade over the Sidney trail totaled four million pounds; in 1878 the figure rose to between twenty-two and twenty-five million pounds, half of the total Black Hills imports for the year. The continued military presence at Camp Robinson, however small, was seen as an asset to the Sidney road.[138]

In the late 1870s a few venturesome ranchers started cattle herds along the Niobrara and White River valleys. Troops at Camp Robinson provided these pioneers with a sense of security; however, the removal of the agency and the corresponding troop reduction brought rumors of the post's abandonment. One concerned rancher, Edgar Beecher Bronson, who operated a ranch five miles south of the post on Deadman's Creek, heard of the possibility of Camp Robinson's abandonment in the autumn of 1878. He wrote department headquarters and asked for verification. Somewhat reassuringly, the adjutant general replied that the Omaha headquarters knew of no such plan, hinting that the army would continue to use the post.[139]

The Indian bureau's goal of settling the Red Cloud Indians along the Missouri River was never achieved. When the Oglala column reached the forks of the White River about eighty miles west of their proposed agency, many of the former followers of Crazy Horse and the nonagency faction broke away and headed north. Red Cloud decided he would go no farther east; his people would winter on the White River. After it became evident an agency in the Yellowstone and Powder country was out of the question, the agency leadership, including Red Cloud, favored a site at the White River forks. In fact, Agent Irwin had recommended this alternative to the commissioner of Indian affairs back in July. "I could promise to take them there willingly and indeed gladly."[140] The army firmly opposed Red Cloud's decision, but the bureaucrats relented. Subsequently the bureau permitted Red Cloud and his people to locate even farther from the Missouri River. In the fall of 1878 the Oglalas relocated on White Clay Creek, nearly two hundred miles southwest of the ill-fated Missouri River agency site. Here the last agency for Red Cloud's Oglalas was built and given a new name—Pine Ridge Agency.[141]

During most of 1878 the cavalry company at Camp Robinson performed routine garrison duties and various detached services for the Indian bureau. Small details escorted wagon trains of supplies that were moved from the old agency sites. The several officers at the post often inspected stores at the old agencies prior to shipment. In February several officers formed a board of survey to examine damaged subsistence stores and, if condemnation was necessary, to determine the best method of their disposal. In July Lieutenant Simpson inventoried government property at the old Spotted Tail Agency; the next month 2nd Lt. Frederick H. French inspected and condemned supplies at the same location. Once, troops from the post searched for cattle missing from an Indian bureau herd being moved to the new agencies.[142]

During the summer and fall of 1878 Lieutenant Johnson, formerly an acting agent for the Indian bureau, oversaw the breakup of the old Brulé agency. His detachment removed buildings and shipped the salvageable lumber to the new Pine Ridge Agency. Johnson also received beef cattle for government issue to the Oglalas.[143]

Also in 1878 decisions were made that again proved critical to Camp Robinson's future. Although the agencies were out of Nebraska, they were not as distant as had been anticipated. Crook proposed changes for the former agency post and in April wrote Sheridan:

> As we shall probably have to keep for a long time a post in the country now protected by the small garrisons at Camp

Robinson and Sheridan, I would recommend that these two garrisons be consolidated at the latter point which, in my judgement is the better of the two for military and strategic purposes: if this suggestion meets with your approval, I will cause the concentration to be effected without delay.[144]

Although Camp Sheridan was actually closer to the new Dakota agencies, Crook's recommendation was not followed, and Camp Robinson's life was fortunately extended.

Camp Robinson was advantageously located for strategic and logistic reasons. The post was close to the Black Hills and the Powder River country, two areas that could still lure raider forays. It was relatively close to the railroad and on the Sidney–Black Hills road. All in all, it was easier to move troops and supplies to and fro than at Camp Sheridan's more isolated site. Robinson also possessed a superior location. Camp Sheridan sat in a low creek bottom prone to flooding. Such was never the problem at Camp Robinson, located on a broad plain above the White River.

In August 1878 Crook informed Sheridan that if the post was to be retained, it needed a larger military reservation. He proposed expanding the reservation boundaries farther to the east and south, "in order that grog shops and other disreputable places may be removed from the vicinity of the post." Sheridan agreed and later authorized an enlarged reservation that was four miles square with the post flagstaff at its center.[145]

The outbreak of the Northern Cheyennes from their Indian Territory reservation that fall enhanced the value of the post. Field operations against the Cheyennes validated Sheridan's decision to retain Camp Robinson as a military station: an army post in northwestern Nebraska was still needed.

On November 8 an order came down from the adjutant general's office in Washington concerning the official designation of posts in the military divisions. The order stated that all posts to be permanently occupied by troops be designated "forts." Temporary posts were to remain "camps." This order gave division commanders, including Sheridan, authority to make name changes, and it can be considered the first public confirmation of the retention of Camp Robinson as a permanent military post.[146] On December 30, 1878, Sheridan issued General Orders that officially re-named the post "Fort Robinson."[147]

On the next day a board of survey convened to deal with the last remnants of the old Red Cloud Agency. The board inspected the agency buildings and grounds to determine the value of the remaining lumber prior to its disposal, a quiet end to such a tumultuous place. In only four years the post's role had changed from filling an immediate, temporary need of protecting lives at the agency to becoming a strategically located, permanent post. Ironically, Camp Robinson had outlived the agency it was established to protect. The first phase of its history over, the fort now entered another.[148]

Chapter 6

The Cheyenne Outbreak

The epic flight of the Northern Cheyennes under Little Wolf and Dull Knife in 1878 had its origins early in 1874. The troubles at Red Cloud Agency prompted the Indian bureau decision to move the Northern Cheyenne people eventually to a reservation in Indian Territory. The government wanted to separate the Cheyennes from their Sioux allies, fearing the latter would poison Cheyenne relations with the whites. That year Cheyenne representatives were taken to Washington and told they would live with their Southern Cheyenne kinsmen.[1]

In September 1874 Commissioner Edward Smith informed Agent J. J. Saville to make the transfer as soon as possible because supplies for the Cheyennes at Red Cloud would be withheld. On November 12, chiefs and headmen of the Northern Cheyenne, including Little Wolf and Standing Elk, and the Arapaho tribes signed an agreement at Red Cloud Agency "to go to the southern reservation whenever the President of the United States may so direct." However, they were allowed to remain at Red Cloud until that time arrived.[2]

During the turbulent summer and fall of the Great Sioux War, most Northern Cheyennes fled the agency for the northern camps. When the Sioux Commission arrived at the agency in fall 1876, the remaining Cheyennes, along with the Arapahos, told the commissioners they wanted to remain with the Sioux. The Red Cloud Indians did agree to send a delegation, which included the Cheyenne leaders Calfskin Shirt and Standing Elk, to Indian Territory to inspect the conditions.

After the capture of Dull Knife's village and subsequent military campaigns, many Northern Cheyennes returned to Red Cloud Agency. In May 1877 a conference was held to decide the tribe's ultimate fate. General Crook and Colonel Mackenzie met with Wild Hog, Dull Knife,

Little Wolf, Standing Elk, and other headmen to persuade them to move south. Personal jealousy and bickering destroyed the united front of the Cheyenne leaders. Standing Elk was chosen finally to speak for the tribe, and to the apparent surprise of the others, agreed to move to an Indian Territory reservation. Some thought Mackenzie had misled Standing Elk and the other leaders through his interpreter; however, if they were dissatisfied with Indian Territory, they could return north. Satisfied that a consensus for the move had been achieved—and unconcerned about how it had been reached—the Indian bureau quickly made arrangements for the transfer.[3]

On May 29, 1877, nearly one thousand Northern Cheyennes began their long march. Lt. Henry W. Lawton, Third Cavalry, accompanied by five soldiers, some civilian packers, and interpreters, supervised the group. Before departure the Cheyennes were given back their horses and firearms, ostensibly to use for hunting during the journey, a controversial decision to which the military and civilian officials in the south later strongly objected.[4] The Cheyennes arrived at Fort Reno on August 5. Two days later they were enrolled at the nearby Darlington Cheyenne–Arapaho Agency.

Their acceptance by their long-separated southern tribesmen was partially achieved. About two-thirds of the northern peoples became affiliated with the southern Indians. But the bands of Dull Knife, Wild Hog, and Little Wolf claimed the Southern Cheyenne made no friendly overtures to them. Their bands withdrew from the others and camped by themselves four or five miles away from the agency. White employees feared bickering between the Cheyenne groups would lead to trouble. More ominously, Dull Knife and the others refused to sign the September 1876 treaty because of its language regarding relocation to Indian Territory. They repeatedly told Agent John D. Miles that they had come south only conditionally and then only under great pressure.[5]

This northern group quickly grew dissatisfied with life in Indian Territory. The government had failed to provide adequate subsistence goods for the new arrivals. Lieutenant Lawton reported insufficient rations of poor quality, often three-fourths of the amount guaranteed by treaty. When rations were short, it was hoped that allowing the Cheyennes to go on hunting trips could make up deficiencies; however, the fall hunts found no game. Tribal members also learned that agency officials expected them to take up farming, a lifestyle totally unacceptable to the former hunters and warriors. Agent Miles frequently withheld rations to force compliance, and when distributed the procedure itself led to further difficulties. Miles gave out rations individually to family groups rather than through the band chiefs, the norm at Red Cloud Agency. This seemingly minor change undercut the leaders' power and subsequently disrupted tribal social organization.[6]

Sickness also plagued the northern Indians, who were used to living at a higher elevation and in a less humid climate. Many came down with chills and malaria. Medical supplies at the agency ran short and were soon exhausted. In many cases death followed. Nearly sixty persons died during the first year. Wild Hog later stated the Indians fled the southern reservation "because of starvation and sickness, and all the children were dying off there."[7]

The bands of Dull Knife, Little Wolf, and Wild Hog saw nothing ahead but shortages of food, sickness, and unfriendly neighbors. During the summer of 1878 their talk turned to returning north, a decision they knew would undoubtedly incur the wrath of the government. Regardless of risk, "It was better to die on the way home" than on this hated reservation.[8]

On September 5 Cheyenne informers confirmed the rumors that some northerners were preparing to leave. Also a number of horses reportedly were taken from southern Cheyenne and Arapaho herds. Maj. John K. Mizner, post commander at Fort Reno, quickly relayed to his department headquarters his fears of an outbreak. He then ordered Capt. Joseph Rendlebrock with two Fourth Cavalry companies to camp near the Cheyennes and observe any suspicious movement. Extra cavalry troops came to Reno from Fort Sill. Rendlebrock's camp of observation sat about four miles from Dull Knife's village.[9]

On September 7 Miles asked the Cheyennes to come to the agency to be counted, but this had to be delayed because some members were absent hunting. With the threat of outbreak by some of the Northern Cheyennes imminent, military commanders in the departments likely to be crossed by any northern movement were alerted. Plans were quickly made to intercept Cheyennes if they crossed the Arkansas River north of the reservation as well as at backup points, one along the Kansas Pacific Railroad in central Kansas and the other along the Union Pacific in Nebraska.[10]

On September 9 Little Wolf, Wild Hog, and Old Crow conferred with Miles and Mizner. Miles wanted them to select ten Cheyennes to be held hostage to take the place of three who had fled north. Little Wolf not only refused to provide any hostages, he also told Miles he was going north. If it came to a fight, the soldiers should move from the agency, for in his words, "I do not wish the ground about this agency to be made bloody."[11]

The Indians returned to camp to prepare for a quick departure. At 10:00 P.M. that night they quietly slipped away. The group numbered 92 men, 120 women, 69 boys, and 72 girls. At 3:00 A.M. the next morning the chief of Indian police awoke Miles and told him of the flight. Captain Rendlebrock and his two companies immediately broke camp in pursuit.[12]

As news of the Cheyenne flight reached the outside world, rumors soon spread of uprisings and revolts among their Sioux allies to the north, including raids by Sitting Bull from Canada. Division of the Missouri commanding general Phil Sheridan realized the gravity of the situation. He feared that if the soldiers failed to stop the Cheyennes, other desperate tribes would view it as a sign of army weakness. Such a weakness could place both frontier security and the whole reservation system at risk.[13]

After three days of hot pursuit the Cheyennes abruptly doubled back on their trail to strike at Rendlebrock's command. Near Turkey Springs, Indian Territory, the soldiers attempted to parley with the Cheyennes, but skirmishing broke out. As fighting became general, the soldiers dug in, while the Cheyennes unsuccessfully tried to surround their positions. Although the warriors withdrew at dusk, they later returned and attempted to burn out the entrenched soldiers . The next day Rendlebrock sent a party to reconnoiter, which was promptly attacked and driven back. Heavy skirmishing continued before the soldiers withdrew to Camp Supply, Indian Territory. In the engagements the soldiers lost three men killed and three wounded; the Cheyennes, winners of this first round, moved on.[14]

Meanwhile two infantry companies were hurried from Omaha Barracks and Fort D. A. Russell to Sidney Barracks along the Union Pacific, one of the planned points of interception. When a reporter asked him about the outbreak, Department of the Missouri commanding general John Pope expressed doubt that any serious fighting would develop because the Indians had their families and were "not in fighting trim."[15] He thought they would be stopped before crossing the Kansas Pacific line.

Elsewhere Capt. William C. Hemphill and a Fourth Cavalry company had marched east from Camp Supply to meet Rendlebrock's command. Hemphill followed the Cheyenne trail, and on September 18 attempted to draw them from their strong positions along the Sand Creek breaks in southern Kansas. After a brief skirmish the outnumbered soldiers withdrew to Fort Dodge. Several days later a joint force of 150 soldiers and fifty civilian volunteers under Rendlebrock's command skirmished for two days against the Cheyennes on Sand Creek. On September 23 the Cheyennes successfully crossed the Arkansas River in central Kansas. That same day Lt. Col. William H. Lewis arrived to take command of the pursuing troops.

On Famished Woman's Fork of the Smoky Hill River on September 27,

Lewis found the Cheyennes strongly entrenched and awaiting the soldiers. Lewis, a capable officer, nearly succeeded in surrounding them in the trap they had laid for the soldiers. Before the soldiers could fully engage, however, a Cheyenne bullet severely wounded Lewis in the leg, and his soldiers withdrew. Lewis died of the wound the next day, and Capt. Clarence Mauck, Fourth Cavalry, assumed command of the pursuing force. The Cheyennes crossed the Kansas Pacific Railroad on September 28 and subsequently escaped the troops of the Department of the Missouri by traveling without rest for the next three days.

As the Cheyennes moved north, they raided for fresh horses, and cattle for food. They killed several whites in the process, but the settlers in Decatur and Rawlins counties, northwestern Kansas, suffered the full brunt of the Cheyenne rampage. In all, at least forty Kansas whites died at Cheyenne hands, with the attacks along Sappa and Beaver valleys between September 29 and October 1 being particularly vicious.

For months afterwards western newspapers carried stories of the "most terrible calamity that has ever befallen [*sic*] the citizens of the valleys of the Beaver and the Sappa . . . in the late raid, and massacre by the Cheyenne Indians."[16] One survivor recalled how at one pillaged homestead:

> The Indians tore up and destroyed everything in the house. Cows were shot full of arrows and pigs and chickens killed. Feather beds were ripped open. . . . One tick was opened and shook into the well. After destroying everything in sight except a team of horses, which they took with them, the Indians moved on.[17]

Writers have suggested that the Cheyenne violence was their form of revenge or retaliation for an 1875 army attack on a Southern Cheyenne village on Sappa Creek. It seems unlikely however, that the Northern Cheyennes were, as one scholar stated, "in the mood to revenge tragedies experienced by the southern Cheyennes." The terrible raids on the Sappa and Beaver were simply "random reprisals against any and all manifestations of white culture" in the most settled area through which the Cheyennes passed.[18]

Preparations for intercepting the Cheyennes when they reached the Department of the Platte began three days after the reported break. By September 13 several infantry companies and a cavalry company under the command of Maj. Thomas T. Thornburgh, Fourth Infantry, had been ordered to Sidney Barracks. Cavalry horses to mount the infantrymen came by rail from Fort McPherson, 140 miles east. Department commander Crook telegraphed Thornburgh, "No effort must be spared to either capture or destroy [the Cheyennes]." A special train with its steam up was kept ready at the Sidney rail yard to move at any time.[19]

While the troops gathered at Sidney, 182 armed and mounted Cheyennes under Little Chief unexpectedly appeared from the north! Escorted by a company of Seventh cavalrymen, these Cheyennes, ironically, were on the way *to* Indian Territory. Fearful that Little Chief's party would learn of their kinsmen's outbreak, the soldiers and Cheyennes camped a mile east of the post. On September 22 Crook arrived to confer with the party's leaders and "gave them opportunity to manifest their wishes." The Cheyennes expressed their regret for the outbreak and reassured Crook, who returned to his Omaha headquarters.[20]

Until this dramatic series of events fully evolved later that fall, Fort Robinson did not seem destined to play a key role in the Cheyenne saga. Quiet after Red Cloud Agency was moved, by October 1878 the post housed only a single Third Cavalry company commanded by Lt. Charles A. Johnson, who had remained after his detached service with the Indian bureau. By now the army was convinced the Cheyennes were heading toward the new agency for Red Cloud's Oglalas and not to the old site. If so, the isolated post would merely serve as a temporary base of operations for any army units searching to the east for the fleeing Indians. After the Cheyennes were captured, the army intended to move them back to their reservation in Oklahoma immediately, and that would be the end of it.

With Thornburgh's force ready at Sidney, Maj. Caleb H. Carlton and five companies of the Third Cavalry moved to Camp Robinson. In addition Merritt's regiment of Fifth Cavalry was sent from Fort Russell to Fort Laramie as a reserve force.

For several weeks Thornburgh sent out small detachments to scout along the South Platte River south and east of Sidney. On October 3 one detachment along Frenchman Creek, a fork of the Republican River, caught sight of Indians moving to the northwest. This intelligence led Thornburgh to believe the Cheyennes would cross the rail line west of Sidney. However, reports of the same day indicated the main party was still ahead of Mauck's pursuing cavalry, some seventy-five miles south of Ogallala and heading north. Thornburgh was now advised the fugitives would probably cross the railroad east of Sidney, between Ogallala and Julesburg, sometime during the night of October 5. Thornburgh quickly ordered wagons, ammunition, and subsistence supplies loaded aboard the train waiting in the rail yard. Each of his men was to carry one hundred rounds of ammunition and five days' rations. That same day (October 3) Major Carlton's command backtracked from Camp Robinson toward

Henry T. Clarke's bridge on the North Platte, where Thornburgh would send word as soon as he knew details of the crossing.[21]

At 11:00 A.M. on October 4 Thornburgh learned the Cheyennes had crossed the railroad six miles *east* of Ogallala near Alkali Station. Section workers, who quickly telegraphed the alarm, had spotted them. Delays in loading men, materiel, and horses delayed the train's departure from Sidney until 12:30 P.M. It pulled into Ogallala at 4:00. Within half an hour Thornburgh had unloaded his command, hired two civilian guides, and headed north in pursuit. By dusk the mounted troops reached the North Platte River and made camp. His accompanying supply wagons experienced great difficulty in crossing the Platte River divide and did not reach camp until 11:00 P.M. Captain Mauck's cavalrymen entered Ogallala a few hours after the Thornburgh command and camped there before resuming their long pursuit.[22]

After crossing the North Platte, the Cheyenne band divided, probably on October 4 or 5 at Whitetail Creek in present Keith County. Dull Knife reasoned that because his people were back in their territory, they would be safe from pursuers. He wanted to head directly for the White River and Red Cloud Agency. Little Wolf firmly opposed this course of action, telling Dull Knife, "You can go that way if you wish but I intend to work my way up to the Powder River country. I think it will be better for us all if the party is not divided."[23] Nevertheless Dull Knife and 148 others turned toward White River, unaware the agency had been moved to Dakota Territory.

The next morning Thornburgh, realizing the nearness of the fleeing Cheyennes, sent the slow-moving wagons and most of his infantry back to Ogallala. He set out into a fog "[s]o dense that it obscured objects twenty yards away."[24] His civilian guides were utterly useless, so he sent them back, too. The pursuing soldiers discovered butchered cattle carcasses and a recently vacated Cheyenne campsite, then came across jettisoned Cheyenne horses still wet with sweat and carrying packs, in all twenty-seven head, but no Cheyennes.

The Indians' trail began to break up, indicating they had scattered into small bands. Thornburgh's men rode north, then west, then southwest, covering sixty miles in the vastness of the Nebraska Sand Hills before halting for the night. The next day the troops tried to follow a trail of twenty to thirty ponies that soon spread out in every direction. Men and horses began to suffer from lack of water.[25]

On October 7 Thornburgh lost the trail and decided to head north toward Camp Sheridan. On October 8 he discovered Carlton's trail and sent couriers for rations. Two days later his force marched to the Niobrara River, where it united with the Third Cavalry column. Capt. John Bourke, who rode with the Thornburgh expedition, observed that the Cheyennes knew the soldiers were in hot pursuit and purposefully scattered in all directions. He added, "The Sandhills form certainly the worst country I have ever seen—they are worse that the worst of Arizona."[26] Later one of Dull Knife's Cheyennes told the soldiers that he saw Little Wolf's people abandoning baggage and camp equipment in order to escape the troops. He took it for granted that the soldiers had overtaken and captured or killed Little Wolf's band.[27]

Carlton's movements had been no less circuitous. His cavalry left Camp Robinson at 9:45 P.M. on October 3 for a possible intercept. The next day, while on Snake Creek south of Fort Robinson, he received word of the railroad crossing. The army feared the Cheyennes intended to go to the new agency for Red Cloud's Oglalas, northeast from its old White River location. Mindful of this, Carlton's command marched straight east, then northeast to Snake River, leaving rear parties at ten and fifteen mile intervals to gather and forward information. At one point Carlton saw heavy smoke to the northwest and feared it was caused by Sioux raiders, who had purportedly broken away from their reservation. Carlton then turned northward to the Niobrara to investigate and not surprisingly found no evidence of depredations. On October 9 he received Thornburgh's couriers requesting water and rations. Exhausted and low on supplies, both commands marched to Camp Sheridan to await further developments.[28]

To the south Mauck's weary troops followed Thornburgh's column for several days, then returned to Sidney, ending hundreds of miles of fruitless pursuit. His next assignment was to escort the Little Chief band to Fort Reno.

The press was not kind to the army's conduct of the Cheyenne pursuit in general and to the Thornburgh expedition in particular. One editor proclaimed,

> The Department of the Platte was out[-]generaled. The savages baffled the troops at every point, and led them into the Sand Hills, from which they might never have emerged.[29]

Despite the military's advantages, specifically the telegraph and the railroad, the Cheyennes had slipped through. Heavy criticism also fell on Commanding General William Sherman, who was either "too indolent or too stupid to provide for such an emergency."[30]

To the contrary the army was trying to prevent further outbreaks. Rumors frequently had the Brulés leaving their agency and the Northern

Arapaho exiting their Wind River reservation. Several months before, some three hundred Sioux had been transferred from Red Cloud Agency to the Brulé agency. After difficulties there with Chief Spotted Tail, they returned en masse for Red Cloud. Add to this the movement of Oglalas to White Clay, and it is little wonder Sheridan feared a general outbreak, particularly if the Northern Cheyennes joined the dissatisfied Sioux.[31]

Seven companies of the Seventh Cavalry and several infantry companies were dispatched from Camp Ruhlen (eventually to become Fort Meade) near Bear Butte to the vicinity of the new agency on White Clay Creek. The extra troops kept the Indians under observation while anticipating the need to help capture the Cheyennes.[32]

The rapid deployment of large numbers of soldiers made the Oglalas nervous. To allay their fears, Thornburgh and Carlton invited Red Cloud and a number of his headmen to Camp Sheridan for a conference. Thornburgh told the Sioux leaders the soldiers were only looking for the Cheyennes who had fled from Indian Territory. He warned that the Cheyennes might appear and stir them up; it was best for the Sioux to turn over any Cheyenne fugitives to the soldiers. Red Cloud agreed to this demand, an empty gesture because he believed that by now the Cheyennes were north of the Black Hills. He also added his apologies to the whites who thought the Sioux were on the warpath, when all they were doing was merely moving to their new home.[33]

A shortage of rations at Camp Sheridan prompted Thornburgh and Carlton to move their commands to Fort Robinson. A third Department of the Platte command of 120 mounted Twenty-third infantrymen under Maj. Alexander J. Dallas, which had belatedly followed the Thornburgh expedition to Camp Sheridan, was sent back to Ogallala. On October 15 Thornburgh's troops were back at Camp Robinson, eventually to return to Sidney; Carlton's cavalrymen remained at Robinson to await further developments in the Cheyenne search.

Just before Carlton's troops arrived, Lieutenant Johnson reported that Indians had run off stock near the post. The same day the commanding officer at Sidney Barracks reported the capture of two Cheyennes by a party of cowboys on Snake Creek. The prisoners stated their fleeing comrades wanted to reach their fellow tribesmen who were still near Fort Keogh on the Yellowstone. If not allowed to remain there, they planned never to surrender but to push on to join Sitting Bull in Canada. The prisoners also told Ben Clark, the agency interpreter who had accompanied the troops from Indian Territory, that fifteen Cheyennes had been killed in the various fights after the flight from Fort Reno.[34]

On October 18 the acting agent at the new Oglala agency reported that his Indians had captured a party of ten Cheyennes. Several days later American Horse, the Oglala leader, told Carlton that two parties of Cheyennes had evaded the soldiers after crossing the North Platte and that one remained in the Sand Hills. He added that the agency Indians wanted to help the soldiers catch the Cheyennes—if they could keep any captured horses or arms.[35]

On October 21 Carlton's battalion again sallied forth from Fort Robinson to continue the search. It marched to Chadron Creek and made camp. The next day Capt. John B. Johnson and two companies moved up Chadron Creek six miles and again made camp. On October 23 Johnson's men crossed the rough divide and struck southeast to the Niobrara River. About eighteen miles from the main battalion camp and in a driving snowstorm, the soldiers stumbled into Dull Knife's band. Forty-four days and 750 miles from their Indian Territory reservation the Northern Cheyennes had been found.

The soldiers could see that the Cheyennes did not want to fight, but to talk. Johnson convinced Dull Knife, Old Crow, and Wild Hog to follow him to the battalion camp, and he sent a detail to a nearby ranch to buy beef to feed the hungry Cheyennes. The combined column arrived just before dark, and the Indians went into camp in a thicket near the soldiers' tents. Guards were posted under orders to avoid an engagement if possible, but under no circumstances to allow any to escape.[36]

The next morning Johnson decided to disarm and dismount the Cheyennes. After several hours of tense negotiations in a snowstorm, the Cheyennes gave up 131 horses and nine mules, a dozen rifles and pistols, and about twenty sets of bows and arrows. Johnson had 2nd Lt. George F. Chase drive the surrendered stock to Camp Robinson; due to their poor condition, fourteen horses had to be shot along the way. During the arms surrender Johnson noticed displays of temper among the warriors but ordered no individual searches. Dull Knife actively restrained his young warriors from making trouble during the disarming.[37]

Major Carlton, who had been at Camp Sheridan to confer with Maj. Joseph G. Tilford, the commander of a battalion of the Seventh Cavalry, arrived at the battalion camp at 4:00 P.M. and immediately proposed that Johnson's men tie up the Cheyenne men before heading to Camp Robinson, a measure Johnson considered unnecessary. Some of the officers, uneasy over the disarming, believed the number of arms surrendered disproportionate to those seen with the Indians when first encountered. Carlton then met with the Cheyenne leaders and informed them of the move to Camp Robinson. They refused, declaring they "would die where they were in preference to returning to Indian Territory and seemed to think Camp Robinson a step in that direction." Carlton's offer to take them to Camp Sheridan was also refused. The Cheyennes returned to their camp and ominously began digging rifle pits and making other preparations for a fight.[38]

All day on October 25 the tense stalemate continued. Although Carlton wanted to avoid a fight, he determined that more soldiers were needed to coax the Cheyennes from the thicket. After delivering the surrendered horses to Camp Robinson, Lieutenant Chase's company was quickly recalled to the Chadron Creek camp. It arrived that night, reinforced by two Seventh Cavalry companies Tilford sent from Camp Sheridan. They brought along two artillery pieces if greater "persuasion" became necessary.

The arriving Seventh cavalrymen found themselves faced with what might seem an excellent opportunity for revenge. They now confronted some of the same Cheyenne warriors who had defeated them and killed their comrades two years before at the Little Bighorn. Nearly half of the Seventh Cavalrymen present along Chadron Creek were veterans of that fateful day when the Sioux and Cheyenne destroyed Custer and five companies of the regiment. But nothing happened, no retribution, no slaughter, nothing that could tarnish the Seventh Cavalry, as did the 1890 confrontation at Wounded Knee Creek, South Dakota. If feelings of revenge truly permeated the Seventh Cavalry—as some modern writers claim for 1890—the survivors curiously did nothing to assuage them in 1878.

On the morning of October 26 the Cheyennes awoke to find their camp surrounded, and Carlton called another conference with the leaders. Yesterday he had given them a choice of destinations; today they must go to Camp Robinson. At this point a friendly Sioux, name unknown, joined the council and told the Cheyennes the same thing. Without a shot being fired, the dejected Cheyennes submitted. Their women and children rode in wagons, and the column arrived at the post about 10:00 p.m. All moved into the unoccupied, single-company barracks at the southeast corner of the parade ground. The only troops garrisoning the post lived in the double-company barracks flanking the parade ground. That night the Cheyennes pried up floor boards and hid the weapons they were able to conceal after surrendering on Chadron Creek.[39]

Crook, relieved that part of the Cheyennes had finally been captured, telegraphed Sheridan for further orders, who, in turn, contacted the Indian bureau for instructions on what to do with the Dull Knife Indians. The army had partially fulfilled its assignment. It remained for the Indian bureau to make the final decision on returning the errant Cheyennes to the south. Sheridan wanted the Cheyennes returned to Indian Territory immediately, with outbreak ringleaders exiled to Florida. In November he wrote the adjutant general in Washington:

> "[U]nless these Indians are sent back, the reservation system will receive a shock which will endanger its stability. If Indians can leave without punishment, they will not stay on reservations.

Crook was ordered to keep a strong force at Camp Robinson while the Cheyennes were there. To prevent other Cheyennes at Fort Reno from fleeing, extra troops arrived from the Department of the Missouri. As the Washington bureaucrats mulled, Dull Knife's band awaited an uncertain future at Camp Robinson.[40]

Lieutenant Chase took charge of the Cheyennes after their arrival. In the first two days he made additional searches for firearms, netting six long arms and several pistols. Two noncommissioned officers and nine privates guarded the barracks; two enlisted men cooked for the captives. Chase kept two sentries inside the building at all times to watch for arms, which paid off when a sergeant saw a pistol drop to the floor from under a woman's dress. Dull Knife surrendered the weapon, and Chase ordered that no unauthorized visitors enter the barracks.[41]

Other Cheyenne possessions caught their captors' attention. One officer reported seeing bedspreads, children's clothing, and "fancy" pictures; others noticed engraved silver napkin rings, silver tableware, a parasol, and other items not normally associated with a rapidly moving Indian band, but believed taken from white settlers during the Kansas raids. Several Dull Knife Cheyennes told Chase that members of Little Wolf's band had killed the owners; these items had come into their hands afterwards. However, Wild Hog, Old Crow, and Left Hand later confided that at least fifteen young men in the barracks had "engaged in the massacres."[42]

During the ensuing weeks, army officers and civilian interpreters periodically questioned the band regarding the Kansas raids. Hideous details of the raids along the Beaver and Sappa Creeks flowed daily from Kansas and Nebraska newspapers. The Cheyennes' former Sioux allies joined the chorus, admitting the Cheyennes had "behaved very badly coming up."[43] Understandably the captives remained reticent on the subject. When they did respond, they collectively placed the blame on Dull Knife, Wild Hog, or the young men. At the same time all were steadfast in their refusal to return south. The Cheyennes frequently reiterated their contention that they could not live in Indian Territory, that they had been sick and had starved there. Officers heard that some young men feared being hanged for the Kansas raids; others said they would rather die than return south.[44]

While held at Fort Robinson the Cheyennes were generally free to move around the post and vicinity, as long as everyone returned by supper. One man, though, decided to visit his wife at Pine Ridge Agency. After his absence was discovered, the Cheyenne men were restricted to quarters.[45] Even so, occasionally several men were allowed out under guard to gather kinnikinick, a mixture of plants the Indians smoked. The women were under fewer restrictions and frequently worked for the soldiers unloading grain and policing the post grounds, ostensibly for exercise. In the barracks the Cheyenne men sat in groups smoking and playing cards, while the women did beadwork and made moccasins.[46]

All the Cheyennes received the same daily ration allowed the soldiers as well as beef bones for Chase's cooks to prepare soup, and corn meal from the commissary for mush. Each morning the post surgeon toured the barracks attending the sick. Although many suffered from chills and fever thought to be brought from the south, the surgeon found them in generally good health.[47]

The Indians held dances in the barracks, often attended by soldiers, who gave presents of money to girls who danced with them. The Cheyenne men received gifts of tobacco and cigars. Occasionally, the Cheyennes received Sioux visitors, who once brought 104 pairs of moccasins. All in all, most of the Cheyennes appeared perfectly contented with their treatment—"they had a good time, plenty to eat and nothing to fear"—with the exception of a few who "seemed to be always dissatisfied."[48]

After Dull Knife's capture Carlton's Third cavalrymen did not remain idle. Little Wolf still evaded the soldiers, and detachments continued to search for his band. While at Robinson Carlton's command occupied Mackenzie's old 1876–77 cantonment, a short distance below the main post. Throughout November and December units scouted the area for the missing tribesmen, and occasionally some of the Dull Knife Cheyennes rode along as scouts.[49]

Sheridan grew impatient over the Indian bureau's indecision and delay over the Cheyenne issue. The scuttlebutt in army circles was that the captives would be turned over to civil authorities in Kansas and Nebraska to be tried for their depredations.[50] Talk became action on November 11 when Kansas Governor George T. Anthony wrote Secretary of War George W. McCrary that "an Indian invasion so revolting in its fiendish details demands the adoption of extreme measures to prevent reoccurrence."[51]

He demanded that Dull Knife, Old Crow, Wild Hog, and other leaders be turned over to him to stand trial for the killings and "outrages." The die was cast. On November 22 Secretary of the Interior Carl Schurz recommended that Dull Knife's band be taken to some Kansas post where those accused of the atrocities could be identified and tried, the remainder to be shipped back to the reservation. In mid-December Crook was ordered to send the Cheyennes under guard to Fort Leavenworth. In addition to Generals Crook and Sheridan, only the adjutant general, the governor, and General Pope of the Department of the Missouri were privy to the plan.[52]

Meanwhile on December 4 Capt. Henry W. Wessells, Jr., soon to be a key figure in the Cheyenne saga, assumed command of Camp Robinson. Wessells, the son of a Civil War general, had actually attended the Naval Academy prior to enlisting in the army. In 1865 he was promoted from the ranks and in 1870 transferred to the Third Cavalry. By the winter of 1878 he was an experienced plainsman. He continued the established procedures for guarding the prisoners, but discouraged Sioux visitors and personally inspected the barracks.[53]

Plans to transfer the Cheyennes to Kansas moved apace. On December 20 Crook advised Sheridan that the Cheyennes needed adequate winter clothing before the overland march to the Sidney railhead. On December 23 Pope inquired when the Cheyennes would arrive at Fort Leavenworth because raid witnesses needed to be summoned to make identifications. The next day Crook asked division headquarters to postpone any movement because of the extreme cold reported at Camp Robinson and also repeated his request for clothing, a purchase for which the Indian bureau was responsible. Sheridan immediately telegraphed Crook to make the move as soon as possible.[54]

Although the extra clothing had not arrived, in early January Wessells was ordered to move the Cheyennes to Sidney. On January 3, 1879, he held a conference with Wild Hog, Old Crow, Dull Knife, Tangle Hair, and Left Hand and told them the Cheyennes were returning to Indian Territory. Wessells reported,

> Dull Knife got up first and said that this was the home of the Northern Cheyennes, their fathers buried and their children raised here. They left their agency to come to this place and here they wanted to remain.

Wild Hog then spoke and repeated Dull Knife's wish. Wessells explained to them that he was only following orders, the move could not be avoided, and he hoped they would "go quietly and without trouble." While the leaders returned to the barracks to tell the others, Wessells wisely ordered his two sentries out of the building.[55]

The next afternoon Wessells called in Wild Hog and asked his intentions. Wild Hog said the Cheyennes would do anything but go south; they would die before moving. With this refusal, the captain took drastic measures. He announced that to secure compliance, all food and fuel for the inmates would be withheld after the evening meal on January 4.[56]

After delivering his ultimatum Wessells reported his actions to Crook as "the last and only alternative." The Cheyennes fully understood the cruel demand but kept their resolve. Ultimately, cutting off food only made the Cheyennes more desperate.[57]

As the suffering in the barracks grew worse each day, the young men exerted more control over the band. They had little to say to the older leaders, who grew afraid of them. Their resistance to the removal demand increased. According to an army interpreter, "[I]f anyone of them had been secretly willing to go, his pride would have made him die before acknowledging it."[58] Each day the soldiers asked them to let out the children to be fed. When Dull Knife asked the young men to allow this, they responded, "One starve, all starve." After several days some of the women attempted to leave but were stopped. The situation in the barracks turned dire:

> During these days of starvation some of them acted like a lot of drunken people. A young man would say: "I want to jump out now and be killed." Then the others would hold him and not let him do it. Others used to stand up and make speeches, saying: "We might as well be killed outside as starve here in this house."[59]

The women had some corn, gathered while working at the granary, and some tallow, which eased their gnawing hunger. As the days slowly passed, barracks furnishings were broken up for a meager fire.

Frustrated by the whole affair, Crook telegraphed Sheridan on January 6 of Wessells's ultimatum. The Cheyennes should have been moved south immediately after their capture on Chadron Creek. "[I]t is hard to ask the military to perform this disagreeable duty," he wrote, while making a request for the Indian bureau to send someone to superintend the move.[60] The bureau chose to leave the entire matter in military hands.

The terrible ordeal continued for four days. Water had been cut off, reducing the Cheyennes to scraping frost from windowpanes to relieve their thirst. During the night of January 8 Wessells devised a plan to seize certain Cheyenne leaders, hoping that would cause the others to submit. About 11:00 A.M.. on Saturday, January 9, he summoned Wild Hog and Old Crow to his headquarters, where he repeated his ultimatum. After they refused, soldiers burst into the room and seized both men. In the ensuing scuffle Wild Hog managed to stab one of the guards. The pair was taken in irons to the lower cavalry camp, but not before Wild Hog's wife saw the incident and alarmed the others in the barracks. Left Hand left the barracks, gave himself up, and was likewise sent to the lower camp.[61]

Pandemonium now reigned in the barracks. Several young men came out on the front porch, and fearing an escape, Wessells ordered Companies C and H to take positions in front of and to the east of the building. Inside the frantic Cheyennes believed the soldiers would shoot them through the windows, which they covered with blankets. They tore up floor boards to retrieve their secreted weapons and to dig rifle pits for protection. Angeline Johnson, wife of Lieutenant Johnson, witnessed the turmoil from her quarters across the parade ground:

> The rest of that day we could hear them tearing up the floor and smashing things generally and occasionally singing their death song, knowing some of them would probably be killed when they made their attempt to escape.[62]

As some Cheyennes readied the concealed firearms, others prepared crude clubs from broken flooring. After the arrest of Wild Hog and Old Crow, one officer likened the "prison" to "a den of rattlesnakes, and any white man who had shown his head in the room would have met with certain death."[63]

As the standoff continued through the afternoon, Wessells ordered Dull Knife out, but the young men now in control forced the old chief to remain inside with his people. By 4:00 P.M. things quieted down, and the troops withdrew. Still fearful of an outbreak, though, the men went to stable call under arms. Wild Hog and Old Crow were allowed to return to the barracks and take out their families. In all, nineteen Cheyennes left the barracks; one hundred and thirty remained prisoners.[64]

That evening Lt. James Simpson, the officer of the day, put more guards on duty. Seven sentries surrounded the barracks, with seven more in the barracks guardroom and additional men in the main guardhouse. He had the door from the cookroom barred and the front barracks doors securely fastened from the outside. Simpson inspected the guard at 9:00 P.M. and found everything quiet. However, one guard noticed that the Cheyennes were "working" at the windows, "loosening them so they could be easily pushed in." He warned his comrades of this suspicious activity.[65]

About 9:45 shots rang out, and bullets hit the two guards stationed on the west side of the barracks. Young warriors sprang through the windows and seized the weapons of the fallen. Other fire disabled or drove off the other guards. The desperate Cheyennes escaped en masse through the windows on the east side and fled south toward White River. Some of the women, unaware of the plan, had to be forced out. One woman survivor later recalled:

> [M]y son smashed a window with the gun I had given him.
> Others broke the other window and tore down the door. We
> all jumped out. My son took the younger of the two daughters
> upon his back. The older daughter and I each carried a little
> pack. It was expected the soldiers would be asleep, except the
> few guards. But bands of them came hurrying to shoot at us.[66]

The young leaders, familiar with the terrain around the post, knew their only hope lay in quickly reaching the high, western bluffs ahead of any mounted pursuit. Some may have intended to go south to Edgar Beecher Bronson's ranch on Deadman Creek to seize horses for their flight, but this hope soon evaporated with the unexpectedly quick and deadly response of the soldiers. The main body ran up White River to the bluffs, where they might, as the army later determined, "sell their lives as dearly as possible."[67]

Behind the barracks, five warriors fought a desperate rearguard action, which bought precious time. "[T]he balls flew pretty thick" among the rallying soldiers, who returned fire from the barracks. Many Cheyenne women and children, fleeing in the moonlit night, were hit by the soldier fire.[68]

At the cavalry camp Capt. Peter D. Vroom hurriedly deployed his men. Two Third Cavalry companies, one dismounted, of the four camped there, rushed to the main post, while another moved east and then south toward the southern bluffs. At the fort proper, commander Wessells tried to organize the soldiers for an effective reaction. Unaware of precisely where the Cheyennes had fled, he sent Simpson's company through the low White River bluffs east toward the old agency site. Lieutenant Chase with Company F swung north along the Sidney–Black Hills Road and then south through the looming north buttes into Soldier Creek valley. Wessells joined the men of C and H as they picked up the main route of flight along White River. Sporadic fighting continued for several hours before Wessells regrouped his scattered command. The next morning Wessells telegraphed news of the outbreak to Crook and then organized his forces to renew the pursuit.

By this time the main Cheyenne remnant, thought to number about fifty persons, was strongly positioned in the upper reaches of Soldier Creek, some fifteen miles west of the post. The soldiers searched the rough, timbered ravines and hills to the west for survivors, who were returned to the post. While one surgeon treated soldier casualties, a second, assisted by soldier volunteers, tended the many wounded non-combatants. Mrs. Johnson took in and cared for a badly wounded infant, but unfortunately the baby died several days later. Lt. Emmet Crawford, at the post on general court-martial duty, saw the effects of the soldiers' devastating counterfire on the fleeing Cheyennes and later sarcastically recalled,

> I never saw so many dead Indians than I did during this affair at Robinson. I had no idea that our men were such good marksmen.[69]

By the end of the first day thirty-five Cheyennes had been recaptured, and twenty-seven dead gathered for burial. Female survivors witnessed the burial and identified their friends and relatives among the dead.[70]

Wessells, unsure if the remaining tribesmen had scattered in several groups, dispatched his troops accordingly. Two companies went north-west up the Soldier Creek drainage; two others searched to the southwest along White River. Wessells sought to prevent any from escaping to the Sioux at Pine Ridge Agency. In the hills south of the post one detachment spotted a faint smoke column and encountered a single warrior hidden in a washout. When called to surrender, he fired in response, killing a private. His position was surrounded, and the determined Cheyenne fought to the end:

> The old Cheyenne kept up his rapid fire as long as he could. Toward the last I plainly saw him fire his carbine three times with his left hand, resting the barrel along the edge of the washout, while his right hand hung helpless beside him. Suddenly I saw him drop down in the bottom of the washout, limp as an empty sack.[71]

In the words of an officer present, "The Indian . . . seemed determined to kill his man and then die himself."[72]

By afternoon the troops moving up Soldier Creek attempted to sur-round the Cheyenne holdouts. In the ensuing fight another soldier lost his life. Unable to dislodge the Cheyennes without further loss, Wessells ordered the troops back to the post. He concluded that this, indeed, was the main party and centered on its capture. Some of Wessells's men grew impatient with his caution. One sergeant recalled, "Each time we had them in a tight place Wessells would spend an hour or two calling on them to surrender and not be killed."[73] Wessells, though, preferred to wait patiently until the Cheyennes left the hills into the open, where he "could overtake them no matter where they went."[74]

On January 11 Wessells led three companies to the Cheyenne stronghold. After hours of skirmishing the soldiers had only advanced within two hundred yards of their quarry and then withdrew back to the post. During the skirmish one of Captain Lawson's troop horses was killed, and he had his men burn its corpse to prevent it from falling into the hungry fugitives' hands. The following morning Lieutenant Simpson and two companies returned and determined the band had moved to a new position six miles farther west. In a fight with a small party of warriors, one corporal was killed, followed by Simpson's men running into the main band. That night soldiers camped nearby.

The next morning, January 13, Wessells arrived with reinforcements and two pieces of artillery. Because of the broken terrain, only one of the guns could be used to shell the Indian position. After firing forty rounds with no apparent effect the soldiers camped for the night. That night the Cheyennes, thought now to number forty-five, escaped again. Instead of leaving the hills as Wessells presumed—and hoped—they would, they stayed in the rough country, moving farther west. The next morning the soldiers discovered their absence. Faced with a lack of supplies the troops retired to Fort Robinson later that day.

Meanwhile General Crook grew increasingly impatient with Wessells's tentative pursuit of the Cheyennes. He ordered the troops at Fort Robinson to stay on the trail until the Indians were finally subdued.[75] Two more Third Cavalry companies were dispatched from Fort Laramie to bolster the effort. Captain Lawson's company, loaded with field supplies for six days, took the Hat Creek Road to locate the Cheyennes anew. Lawson arrived at the site of the January 13 fight and trailed the weary Cheyenne band north and northwest for seven miles before calling a halt for the night.

In the days following the January 9 outbreak, criticism mounted over the military's handling of the situation. Newspaper accounts that described how "the troops are in pursuit of the retreating savages, killing them without mercy," created public outrage.[76] Crook received only scant information from the front, so he sent his aide, 1st Lt. Walter S.

Schuyler, to report on all events. Schuyler's reports were immediately forwarded to Sheridan at division headquarters in Chicago. On January 15 the U.S. Senate passed a resolution requiring a complete report on the Cheyenne escape and "subsequent slaughter by United States forces who were charged with their custody."[77] Army supporters quickly pointed out that soldiers were the first victims of the fighting and the subsequent "slaughter" resulted from efforts to recapture the Indians. One editor warned, "The Senate had better begin by inquiring into the reasons why the Cheyennes left their agency in the Indian Territory."[78]

As the deadly game of cat-and-mouse between soldiers and Cheyennes dragged on, Sheridan's ire mounted. He did not consider the army's operations as particularly "creditable," when such a small band could evade capture. On January 19 he telegraphed General Sherman, "I feel somewhat disgusted at the manner in which the whole Cheyenne business has been conducted at Fort Robinson."[79] Crook reminded Sheridan that the Indian bureau had been requested to take charge of the Cheyennes, with the military performing only a guard role. But Sheridan remained perturbed, blaming the prolonged ordeal on "not providing amply against the outbreak."[80] Nevertheless the fugitives' days were numbered.

In the Hat Creek breaks Wessells's company joined Lawson's troops in trailing the Cheyennes. On January 17 they ran into the band "advantageously fortified on a crag." Wessells sent Sioux scout Woman's Dress and mixed-blood John Shangreau to reconnoiter the position.[81] After a brief assault, with one man killed, Wessells pulled back several miles. Fearing the Cheyennes would raid nearby Bluff Station on the Black Hills stage route for horses, he sent Lawson's company there. The Cheyennes salvaged the dead soldier's arms, ammunition, and clothing and again escaped westward into the night. They now were in cattle country, and the soldiers encountered a wake of slaughtered carcasses.

Meanwhile the Indian bureau had decided to turn over the surviving women and children to Chief Red Cloud at Pine Ridge. Agent James O'Brierne, who arrived at Fort Robinson to supervise the transfer, reported "much grief and exhibitions of almost violent mourning observable" among the Pine Ridge Sioux; many were relatives of Cheyenne casualties.[82]

On January 18 Wessells teamed up with the two companies sent from Fort Laramie, one commanded by Capt. John B. Johnson, who had initially cornered the Dull Knife band in October. The joint command scouted the area for the Indians' trail. The next day the troops massed at Bluff Station as twelve wagons of provisions and forage for the four companies arrived from Fort Robinson. Maj. Andrew W. Evans, Third

Cavalry, arrived by stage from Fort Laramie to assume command of all operations. He immediately sent Lawson's company west to see if the Cheyennes had abandoned the bluffs for the open country to the north. Lawson failed to find a trail by nightfall and ordered his company back to the station.

The following morning, January 20, Wessells's command scouted the lower country west along Hat Creek. After spending the day in a futile probe of the country near the Wyoming border, he went into camp.

However, the other companies made contact with the elusive Cheyenne band. Evans and his two companies found them strongly positioned in the bluffs several miles southeast of where Wessells was scouting. The troops advanced on the entrenched Cheyennes until Evans's horse was shot from under him. He dispatched Shangreau to find Wessells and tell him the Cheyennes' location, but before any union could be made, the Indians slipped off during the night.

On the morning of January 21 Wessells and his three companies backtracked to the east, unsure if the Cheyennes had left the breaks for the open country to the north. After conferring with Shangreau, he moved his men within a couple of miles of where Evans had his fight. While part of the command closed in with Evans's force around the suspected Cheyenne position, other troops under Lieutenant Chase continued their search for any trail leaving the bluff country. Eventually, they located moccasin tracks in a prairie dog town heading northwest into open ground. Although cattle tracks soon obscured this new trail, the soldiers realized that the Cheyennes had finally abandoned their protective bluffs. They had also completely changed direction, perhaps in a desperate hope of reaching the distant Sioux reservation. Wessells's troops halted for the night at the base of the Hat Creek breaks, anxious to close in the next morning.

At daybreak, January 22, 1879, Wessells sent a company to hurry along the supply train and moved northeast with the other three companies. Woman's Dress, John Shangreau, and two soldiers served as advance scouts. After moving through a range of small hills into the Antelope Creek Valley, the group suddenly drew fire. Shangreau narrowly escaped injury, but Woman's Dress and one soldier were wounded, the latter fatally. Wessells rapidly brought up the main column. When Shangreau asked what he was going to do, Wessells replied, "I am going to get them today."[83]

The last, free remnants of Dull Knife's band made their final stand in a washout depression on a low promontory just above the creek bed, about thirty miles northwest of Fort Robinson. For the first time in twelve days the Cheyennes were finally caught in a place deemed by Wessells more "favorable to us" than to them.[84]

Lieutenant Chase moved his company within only twelve yards of the entrenched Cheyennes, then to within five yards, delivering several volleys of carbine fire. The men of the other companies came up, surrounded the Cheyennes, and opened fire. Twice during the fight Wessells ordered his men to cease fire while he called on the determined Cheyennes to surrender. Both times shots came back as the reply, the last time wounding Wessells in the head. Chase led the final advance to the washout's very edge. Sgt. Carter P. Johnson recalled the last of the Cheyennes' resistance:

> Three Indians began to sing a war song, jumped out of the hole and into the ranks of the soldiers, one armed with a knife and the other with a six-shooter and the third one, as far as I can remember, had nothing. He went over the bluff and was shot in the head as he jumped over the bluff. The other two flew in to the ranks of the soldiers.[85]

It was over. As Major Evans later reported, "The Cheyennes fought with extraordinary courage and fierceness, and refused all terms but death."[86] His soldiers surveyed the carnage seeking survivors. Of the thirty-two Cheyennes who had fought to the last, seventeen men, four women, and two children lay dead. Nine persons were found alive, six of them wounded, most of them seriously. As the surgeon treated a mortally wounded warrior, he asked if he could do anything further for him. The Cheyenne replied that he just wanted to die and be thrown in the pit where the others had died, and this was where the Cheyenne dead were buried. Three enlisted men were killed and four wounded. Soldiers and survivors returned to Fort Robinson.

A number of loose ends remained in this tragic affair. On January 25 a board of officers convened at Fort Robinson by order of General Crook to "make a through investigation" of the outbreak and to recommend follow-up action. The board ultimately interviewed forty individuals, including nine Cheyenne survivors, who were directly involved in the entire episode. While critical of Carlton's failure to disarm his prisoners completely and of Wessells's inadequate preparations to prevent outbreak, the board declared, "[I]n view of all the circumstances of the unfortunate business . . . no one else, of equal experience or judgement, could have done any better." The board saw the cut in rations as having been the only alternative for convincing the Cheyennes to return south.[87]

The soldiers never caught up with Little Wolf's band. After separating from Dull Knife in October, it wintered in the Sand Hills many miles east of Fort Robinson. Depredations attributed to the band were reported, and in late January Fifth Cavalry companies from Fort D. A. Russell searched for it, but to no avail. For months this group managed to evade detection and capture, and eventually resumed its northern exodus. In late February Little Wolf surrendered his people to Lt. William P. Clark at Fort Keogh, Montana. The Cheyennes were allowed to remain in the Yellowstone country, their promised land.

On January 31, thirty-three women and twenty-two children survivors of Dull Knife's band left Fort Robinson for Pine Ridge Agency. The following fall they were transferred to Fort Keogh to join Little Wolf's band. On the same day Wild Hog, slated to be turned over to Kansas authorities, attempted to stab himself to death. He survived, and on February 4, with six other men and fourteen of their family members, left under escort for Fort Leavenworth to stand trial for the Kansas raids. In October 1879 the case against the Cheyennes was thrown out of court and the defendants returned to Indian Territory. By 1883 all the Cheyennes in Indian Territory who wished to do so were allowed to move to Pine Ridge Agency. In late 1884 President Chester Alan Arthur created the Tongue River Reservation by executive order as a permanent home for the Northern Cheyenne tribe.[88]

After the fight on Antelope Creek, companies B and D, Third Cavalry, the two Fort Laramie units, returned to their proper station. Both companies had seen action in Evans's skirmish near Bluff Station and the last desperate engagement on January 22. In both actions Sgt. William B. Lewis of B Company had displayed "conspicuous bravery and personal gallantry" under fire. Because he was a noncommissioned officer and therefore could not be awarded a certificate of merit, Capt. John B. Johnson requested that he receive the Medal of Honor, which was granted. On April 17 Lewis received the coveted medal before the assembled garrison at Fort Laramie. His was the only medal awarded in the "Cheyenne Outbreak" and the last Medal of Honor ever won in Nebraska.[89]

And what of Dull Knife? After the January 9 breakout he was reported missing and presumedly killed in the pursuit. Immediately after the Cheyennes fled the barracks, however, he and a small party, including several family members, peeled off from the main body and escaped detection. Three weeks later they walked into Pine Ridge Agency and surrendered, weak and emaciated, but alive. The old chief joined the others on Tongue River, where he lived until his death in 1883.

The Cheyenne Outbreak proved to be the bloodiest chapter of the fort's history. Of the 149 Cheyenne men, women, and children held at the post, sixty-four were killed and over twenty wounded. Eleven Third cavalrymen died; ten were wounded. The indomitable resolve of the Cheyennes to resist to the death was echoed by Crook, "[I]n deciding upon their course they knew as well as we the probable result."[90] The determined stand of Dull Knife's band became a tragic yet important part of Fort Robinson history and lore.

Third Cavalry and Fourteenth Infantry officers at Camp Robinson, 1877. Lt. Charles A. Johnson, acting agent at Red Cloud Agency, is seated in the front row next to the Arapaho, Six Feathers. Lt. Frederick S. Calhoun, in whose office Crazy Horse died, stands at the far left. Courtesy The Denver Public Library, Western History Collection.

Colonel Bradley's quarters at Camp Robinson, the last set on the end of officers' row.

Amos Bad Heart Bull, Lakota historian and artist, drew this scene of the Crazy Horse stabbing in the 1890s. From Helen H. Blish, *A Pictographic History of the Oglala Sioux* (University of Nebraska Press, 1967).

Crazy Horse's first grave. This illustration, based on a photograph taken in the fall of 1877 near Camp Sheridan, shows the board fence built by order of Lt. Jesse Lee that surrounded the coffin-scaffold.

Angeline Johnson, an officer's wife, who witnessed the killing of Crazy Horse and the Cheyenne Outbreak.

Right: **Little Wolf** (standing) **and Dull Knife,** who led the Cheyennes on their epic flight north in the fall of 1878.

Fort Robinson as is appeared when it became a permanent military post late in 1878.

"The final fight with the Cheyennes took place on the 22d, fifteen miles from Bluff Station. When the firing ceased the dead bodies of twenty-three Indians were found in the rifle pits occupied by them. This number included seventeen bucks, four squaws, and two papooses. Nine remained, of whom one buck and five squaws were more or less wounded, and three squaws were unhurt." —Dispatch from Fort Robinson, Neb., to N. Y. Herald.

Left: **"The Latest Illustration of Our Humane Indian Policy,"** *Frank Leslie's Illustrated Newspaper,* Feb. 8, 1879.

Cheyenne warriors tore up the floor and dug rifle pits prior to their January 9 breakout. *Frank Leslie's Illustrated Newspaper,* Feb. 15, 1879.

Frederic Remington drew this version of the aftermath of the Antelope Creek fight of January 22, 1879, based on the recollections of one soldier participant. *Harper's New Monthly Magazine,* Aug. 1897.

A Fremont, Elkhorn and Missouri Valley mixed freight unloads at the Fort Robinson depot. Post noncommissioned officers' quarters are in the right background.

The new officers' row during its construction, fall 1887.
Courtesy Jack Ringwalt.

Interior of an 1887 enlisted men's barracks.

Field ordnance at Fort Robinson, about 1887: (left to right) two .50-cal. Gatling guns, a Hotchkiss mountain gun, and a one-inch Gatling gun, all guarded by an ancient ordnance **sergeant.** Courtesy Jack Ringwalt.

John H. Alexander (Class of 1887) **and Charles Young** (Class of 1889), **the second and third black graduates of West Point. Both served with the Ninth Cavalry at Fort Robinson.**

Right: **Col. Edward Hatch, Ninth Cavalry, post commander during the 1887 expansion.**
Courtesy Massachusetts Commandery, Military Order of the Loyal Legion, and the U.S. Army Military History Institute.

Troop K, Ninth Cavalry, during the 1890–91 Pine Ridge Campaign.

Portraits of Fort Robinson soldiers, names unknown.

Ninth Cavalry noncommissioned officers at Fort Robinson.
From the Special Collections, United States Military
Academy Library. Courtesy West Point Museum.

**Squadron of the Ninth Cavalry on the drill field west of the
main post, about 1893.**

"The Pursuit" by visitor Frederic Remington captured a Ninth
Cavalry charge near the Red Cloud Buttes of Fort Robinson.
Harper's New Monthly Magazine, Apr. 1898.

A Fort Robinson guard and his two prisoners from the Sixth
Cavalry on work detail, about 1897.

View of the main post, 1893. Buildings on the left include the 1893 Post Chapel–Schoolhouse and the 1892 Guard-house. Courtesy Montana Historical Society.

The old buildings on the south side of the original parade ground awaited demolition at century's end: (left to right) **1883 Barracks, 1874 Cavalry Barracks, 1874 Adjutant's Office, 1884 Guardhouse, and 1874 Guardhouse.**

Chapter 7

The 1880s Expansion

The decade of the 1880s proved pivotal in the history of Fort Robinson, the period when the U.S. Army decided to retain the fort as an active army post. It was no coincidence that the railroad arrived and ushered in a new mission for the fort. The decade also saw the construction of a new, adjoining post, with a building layout that Fort Robinson was to forever maintain.

Between 1880 and 1889 Fort Robinson's garrisons gradually increased and reflected the fort's continuing strategic importance in the post-Sioux war years. But the decade began humbly. In January 1880, Company C, Third Cavalry—only sixty-five men—made up the garrison. By December 1889 the post was regimental headquarters for the Ninth Cavalry with the band and four troops of that regiment, plus four companies of the Eighth Infantry, a total of nearly five hundred officers and enlisted men in addition to scores of dependents. The 1880s may best be remembered as the initial appearance of the "buffalo soldiers," when the famed black cavalry regiments of the Indian wars first garrisoned Fort Robinson.

Improvement of post facilities in the 1880s began with the building of new telegraph lines. By mid-1881 work commenced on an important line that connected the post with Pine Ridge Agency, sixty-five miles away. During this period the post lines were haphazard affairs. Inferior poles were used and spaced seventy yards apart, a combination that meant frequently downed lines, and troops were constantly repairing them. One observer sarcastically commented, "Getting a dispatch to and from Robinson is as uncertain as an Ohio majority in an October election."[1] Communications were later improved when the army established permanent lines following the railroad's arrival to the area.

In the early 1880s new buildings replaced some of Jordan's log, "temporary" structures. Work began in 1882 on a new administration building to replace the cramped log headquarters. The new, two-story structure was built by soldier labor just west of officers' row. Besides offices for the adjutant and sergeant major, a spacious room was set aside strictly for a post library and reading room. Formerly the library was kept in the 1874 adjutant's office. Upstairs were quarters for the sergeant major and a clerk.

In 1884 on the south side of the parade ground a new guardhouse was built between the original guardhouse and the adjutant's office, scene of Crazy Horse's last hours. The first guardhouse was aptly described as being "too small for use and too worthless and filthy to replace." The building was "so infested with vermin that it is a punishment for a man to go on guard and it is impossible to remove or kill the animals."[2] The new frame facility contained a guard room, general prison room, and three small isolation cells. Although it was immediately criticized for being too small, the guards and prisoners found it a marked improvement.

In 1883 additional barracks accommodated the men. A new log barracks for Troop F, Fifth Cavalry, was built just south of the east double barracks. The new barracks, longer and with its mess hall and kitchen located in an "L" addition, was far more comfortable than the existing log quarters. One proud correspondent from the post boasted in print that it was "not too much to say that the quarters are the finest and most complete of their kind in the country."[3] Nor were the cavalrymen's mounts overlooked; to the south, a new frame stable was built for Troop F horses.

It was said that Fort Robinson had the best furnished hospital in the Department of the Platte. Unfortunately fire destroyed it in September 1883, and a temporary replacement fashioned of slab boards was hurriedly put up. In October 1884 construction began on a new post hospital built of concrete that initially suffered structural problems when the contractor poured the walls in cold weather. Repairs were made, and the twelve-bed facility was completed in July 1885. The building sported a mansard roof, an elegant architectural feature of the day that hearkened back to the French Second Empire. It equaled an impressive two-story house built in 1884 for the post commanding officer on the west end of officers' row.

The new hospital's most famous resident was Capt. Walter Reed, who served as post surgeon from 1884, when he transferred from Fort Sidney, until his 1887 departure to Mount Vernon Barracks, Alabama. Reed was popular with both garrison and local residents, and his farewell prompted the local newspaper to note, "We doubt if Fort Robinson will ever contain a physician as affable and accommodating as the out-going doctor has been, not only to the soldiers but settlers as well." Later remembered as one of the conquerors of yellow fever, Reed's term at Robinson, however, was merely a brief, nondramatic episode in his army service. While at the post he was concerned with treating catarrh, typhoid, and other common soldier ailments and with keeping the ever-present problem of poor sanitation under control. Reed's most famous civilian patient was "Old Jules" Sandoz, the father of writer Mari Sandoz and inspiration for her book *Old Jules*. Sandoz, an irascible Swiss immigrant, had homesteaded along the Niobrara River some fifty miles southeast of Fort Robinson and received a severe compound fracture while digging a well. He was brought to the post by several soldiers, who found him near death on the prairie. He was confined to the post hospital from November 1884 to April 1885 in recovery.[4]

The grounds were beautified as well as the post buildings. Soldier Creek was dammed west of the fort, and irrigation ditches criss-crossed the building area. With an ample, reliable water source now available, the soldiers planted "trees without number."[5] This activity joined the usual post routine because soldier details regularly planted additional or replacement trees and trimmed established trees.

A water distribution system gradually developed at the post. At the main springs northeast of the buildings a windmill pumped water to a large, wooden water tank, the water then hauled throughout the post by water wagon. A small steam engine supplemented the windmill when there was no wind. As the decade passed, appropriations enabled the post to construct a permanent water tower and to pipe water directly to post buildings. By 1889 all of the barracks and quarters had running water; indeed many had flush toilets.

The abandonment of Camp Sheridan, decided in 1878, came about in 1881. It disturbed Dr. Valentine McGillycuddy, no longer a contract army surgeon but now the Indian agent at Pine Ridge, because "the close proximity of that post . . . has a decidedly restraining effect on such turbulent spirits there may be among us."[6] Fortunately the completion of the telegraph line from the agency to Fort Robinson brought him some reassurance and peace of mind.

In May Camp Sheridan's last two companies were transferred to Fort Robinson. Although the army salvaged most of the camp's usable buildings, in August a number of log structures, lumber, and thirty-five tons of hay were auctioned. All that remained was the small post cemetery. In March 1882 the graves of two soldiers and two wives of soldiers were exhumed and moved to the Fort Robinson cemetery, which may have prompted construction of a new fence around the often neglected, but growing graveyard.[7]

In 1879 the army decided the post military reservation needed to be enlarged. The new reservation, declared by executive order on June 28, covered twenty square miles. The enlargement gave the army a larger buffer zone to protect the post from civilian encroachment, and also to secure control of good grazing land. To ensure an adequate supply of wood for fuel and building materials, a wood and timber reserve was declared in November. The sixteen-section wood reserve was located five miles west of the post up Soldier Creek.[8]

As a result of reservation expansion, several civilians found themselves residing on military lands. Expansion forced the closing of J. W. Dear's store at the old agency site. In 1880 Dear, then trading at Pine Ridge, unsuccessfully applied for compensation for the business loss of his store and nearby stage station. After his death the Dear estate again attempted in 1883 to receive compensation. Because Dear had allowed his trader's license to expire in 1879, the army judge advocate ruled that from the time of expiration he had no valid claim for any reimbursement from the government.[9]

Just east of the post one encountered the cabin of "Arkansas John" Seckler, a freighter on the Sidney–Deadwood road. Seckler, a frontiersman who was married to a Cheyenne woman, built his log home in the mid-1870s just off the original, one-square-mile military reservation. Although Seckler was well respected, the expanded reservation found his home on military land, and the army asked him to move. In 1887 a board of officers met to fix a price of compensation for his buildings and other improvements.[10]

Arkansas John was the last "squatter" who remained on post lands. The only individuals allowed to reside off post on the military reservation were army guides, Indian scouts, and some married enlisted men. For a number of years the famed guide Baptiste "Little Bat" Garnier lived in the old Seckler cabin. In addition to potential squatters post orders prohibited outside merchants on the reservation from selling their products, although this ban did not include farmers or "producers of vegetables, fruits, or poultry."[11]

Duties of Fort Robinson troops reflected the drastically reduced number of armed conflicts on the northern Plains. Most of the soldiers' time was spent in garrison duties, involving the endless routine of fatigue and drill. Only occasionally were the troops called out for field service. As an epilogue to the disastrous Cheyenne Outbreak, a group of Cheyennes, some of whom had survived the 1879 outbreak, were permitted to move from Indian Territory to the Pine Ridge Reservation. In August 1883 the fort's Troop H, Fifth Cavalry, escorted the group from Sidney north to Pine Ridge.[12]

Although the Sioux were confined to their Dakota reservation, rumors of outbreak arose periodically in the late 1880s, particularly after vast tracts of reservation lands were opened for white settlement. In late 1886 word was received at Fort Robinson of Sioux raids and depredations in Dakota and Wyoming territories. The basis of the alarm was probably the movement of a party of Oglalas under American Horse that had left the reservation with permission to visit the Wind River Reservation of the Shoshone tribe in central Wyoming. The post commander reported no trace of Indians "committing depredations along the northern frontier." In 1887 rumors circulated of threatened trouble with the Northern Cheyennes living on Pine Ridge, all apparently unfounded.[13]

As Congress reduced reservation lands, some whites became concerned that the Sioux might actively resist encroachment. In May 1888 rumors of Indian trouble centered around Oelrichs, some forty miles northeast of Fort Robinson. An alarmed settler reported that an Indian had told him the Sioux were preparing to rise against the white settlers and soldiers. As a result of such talk, some settlers in the Hat Creek region fled to the post for protection. In response, Troops I and F, Ninth Cavalry, went to the area to restore confidence among the remaining whites. Finding no actual danger there, the troops soon returned to post.[14]

In February 1889 Sioux Indians under Young Man Afraid of His Horses and Red Shirt came to the fort to confer with post commander Col. Edward Hatch. In a fitting turnabout, they came to complain about whites. The Oglala leaders were alarmed over the growing number of whites encroaching on their lands. Later that spring they returned to the post and asked for soldiers to aid them in driving away squatters on the reservation. In response Lt. Col. James S. Brisbin periodically sent out scouts and officers to report on reservation trespassers.[15]

While most of the officers and enlisted men scoffed at the idea of renewed hostilities with the reservation Sioux, others took the rumored threats more seriously. In the summer of 1888 a correspondent named "Rex" wrote from Fort Robinson, "While a brush with the Sioux may not be imminent, the youngsters would like to see some practical test of the long hours spent on the target range and a chance, perhaps, to make a file or two." Interaction between soldier and brave, though, was usually more cordial. In July 1889 many Oglalas came to the post for a gala Fourth of July celebration. For several days they held dances and horse races at Fort Robinson.[16]

153

During this period of relative peace on the rapidly closing frontier and of readily available railroad transportation the U.S. Army had its first opportunity to gather its widespread units and study conventional war. In this innovative training procedure, "camps of instruction" came into vogue for departmental commands across the country. At the camps, usually held in early fall, hundreds of soldiers from scattered garrisons massed for field training and large-scale maneuvers.

The Department of the Platte held such annual encampments in the 1880s. In fall of 1885 it held the first and smallest, "Camp O. O. Howard," near Pine Bluffs, Wyoming, along the Union Pacific Railroad, which involved only eight companies of infantry. Company C, Fourth Infantry, was the only unit to represent Fort Robinson.

In August 1888 "Camp Brooke," named for Brig. Gen. John R. Brooke, the department commander, was held about six miles east of Chadron. Although the site was poorly selected with little water and no open area adequate for battalion drill, all the Eighth Infantry and Ninth Cavalry units at Forts Robinson and Niobrara participated. This camp was the first time since 1871 that the entire Eighth Regiment had been together. For four weeks the men worked with reconnaissance, entrenchment, small unit tactics, and map-reading exercises. Although most participants publicly expressed pleasure at the opportunity of large-scale training, one officer privately complained. Capt. Augustus W. Corliss, Eighth Infantry, a noted prude, found the weather too hot and too windy, and September 15 proved to be:

> A day of drunkenness among the men. This camp is a failure.
> I never saw men run down in discipline as fast as they have
> since these troops came here. Instead of being called a
> "camp of instruction" it ought to be "camp of destruction."[17]

The next camp of instruction, "Camp George Crook," in August and September 1889, occurred on the level ground along Soldier Creek, immediately west of Fort Robinson. Touted as "the largest camp of regular troops assembled together since the close of the war," about 2,500 enlisted men and officers from one cavalry and six infantry regiments participated.[18] Enough soldiers were present to hold brigade drills, the first witnessed by many officers since the Civil War.

The troops were sent on short marches, where they trained in the use of outposts in front of advances and of rear guards behind retreats. A several-days march through the rough hills along the Soldier Creek drainage culminated in a sham battle involving the entire camp. On

September 18 a grand review was held of all the troops, which a number of civilian spectators viewed. One of the problems the massive encampment created was grass fires from its numerous kitchen fires, and soldiers turned out to extinguish flames with gunnysacks and willow boughs. High winds required quick work to save tents and equipment.[19]

On August 30 Brig. Gen. George Crook, the camp's namesake, reviewed the troops. But to some observers the day of mass formations was over, having "almost disappeared from modern tactics, shot to pieces by the long range rifle and improved artillery."[20] Whether this type of gathering truly signalled an end of an era is debatable, but Crook's presence definitely did. This was probably the old soldier's last visit to Fort Robinson; he died in Chicago on March 31, 1890.

The 1880s also brought the army's increased interest in target practice and marksmanship. The days of ten-shots-per-month rifle practice for Fort Robinson garrisons were over. Troops now spent long hours on the ranges, sometimes commencing in the early morning to avoid high winds that affected accuracy during long-range firing. One correspondent reported that target practice was vigorously pursued from "early morn till dewy eve, and the crash of the rifle and carbine awake the echoes of old Crow Buttes."[21]

By 1885 four, six-hundred-yard ranges, two with separate target pits and two with one large pit, and a thousand-yard range, were in use. All the ranges used Laidley revolving targets, then in vogue. Stop butts sat behind the target pits to catch spent bullets. Exercises were also held in sighting and range estimation, all with the idea of improving army marksmanship after its dismal showing of the 1870s. Indoor gallery practice was available in winter months. Troops eagerly sought the newly authorized marksman buttons and pins and vied for slots in the departmental rifle competition held at Bellevue, Nebraska, just south of Omaha.

Increased target practice brought a rash of accidents, some with fatal results. For example, in September 1884 Pvt. Henry Chambers was accidentally shot while on duty scoring targets. A ricochet rifle bullet fired at a distance of three hundred yards struck Chambers in the chest; he died on September 23. Post Surgeon Walter Reed performed an autopsy and dutifully forwarded "a portion of the third and fourth ribs, showing wound entrance, together with bullet and fragments of clothing found in wound" to Washington's Army Medical Museum.[22]

Sometimes the troops drew on all their training and assisted in emergencies and special escorts. In July 1889 a cloudburst resulted in disastrous flooding on White River. Above the post the Duncan family was caught in the torrent, which drowned the father and three children. For several days soldiers from the post searched through piles of debris for the bodies. Eventually they recovered all the victims and buried them in the post cemetery. The garrison donated food, clothing, and two hundred dollars to the widow and her surviving children.[23]

In July 1882 a party of paleontology students from Princeton University arrived at the post. Led by Professor William B. Scott, the fossil hunters were on an expedition to the badlands west of Pine Ridge Agency. While at Robinson, Scott and his students lived in a vacant set of officers' quarters and even made an excursion to some fossil beds north of the fort. When the expedition departed, post commander Maj. Edwin V. Sumner provided them with an army wagon and an escort of two noncommissioned officers and four privates of Company G, Eighth Infantry. Woman's Dress, then employed as an Indian scout, was ordered off furlough on the reservation to accompany the party. After a month of successful collecting, the students and infantry escort returned to Fort Robinson and were surprised by the news of their massacre while on the Sioux reservation! Major Sumner prevailed on the still-alive-and-kicking geologist to present a lecture to the garrison on his findings. After a shave, haircut, and enough loaned "civilian garments to make a respectful ensemble," Scott made his presentation to several hundred soldiers, family members, servants, and civilian employees, all assembled about the post schoolhouse. The student–paleontologists then returned to the East, and the post returned to the even tenor of garrison life.[24]

Off-duty diversions for the soldiers of Fort Robinson in the 1880s mirrored those of other western posts, with baseball and horse racing the perennial favorites. Late in the decade ball games were played against teams from Forts Laramie and Niobrara, and horse racing had become a more organized spectator sport. For the 1888 Fourth of July race a judge's stand and a regulation mile track were constructed, with two grandstands covered with canvas for spectator comfort. One enthusiastic racing fan predicted (incorrectly) that the new track "in the near future will be the best west of Omaha."[25]

In an effort to improve recreational opportunities for the enlisted men garrison commanders established additional post institutions. Many enlisted men and their officers enjoyed the post library, stocked with books and magazines purchased from post funds and free government publications. By 1883 the post library boasted seven hundred volumes, plus a variety of newspapers and periodicals. Soldier–readers always appreciated the arrival of new books:

> We remember yet the looks of pleased anticipation that sat
> on the countenances of the eager readers one night in the
> post library as the librarian cheerfully announced the arrival
> of "new books," and producing a bulky package proceeded
> amid silent interest to undo it. Many were the surmises
> indulged in: was it Zola's latest or Haggard's; or perhaps, one
> of Captain King's delightful stories of frontier life. No, it was
> none of these, and as the librarian silently drew forth and
> held up "Series 1, Vol. 17, Part 2nd. Correspondence, etc. [of the
> interminable, multi-volume *War of the Rebellion* series]" there
> was silence that could be felt, "only that and nothing more."[26]

In 1886 soldiers built of adobe brick a post amusement hall just
beyond the east end of officers' row. After its completion the 30 x 80 foot
hall replaced the barracks as the site for dances and other social gatherings. In addition a "gymnasium" for the enlisted men was set up in the
recently vacated west log barracks. This was the forerunner of the
permanent exercise and recreation facility that was built at Fort Robinson
after the turn of the century.[27]

Perhaps the most appreciated improvement to the life of the enlisted
man came in 1888 when Colonel Hatch approved a post canteen, a
feature successfully introduced in the British Army and transplanted to
American posts. The canteen offered food, beer, and light wines at prices
below those in the post trader's store or in town. This practice encouraged
the enlisted men to spend their leisure time on post, and furthermore the
profits stayed with the troop units. Although the men were the canteen's
most enthusiastic supporters, Captain Corliss again sniffed, "Gen. Hatch
is starting a canteen or post beer-house which I predict will be a dammed
nuisance in every way and work a deal of mischief to the men of the
garrison."[28]

Unfortunately the canteen idea was a bit advanced for its time. Protests
came from a curious coalition—off-post liquor merchants, post traders,
and temperance advocates. In late October 1888 Brig. Gen. Richard C.
Drum, the adjutant general, issued orders effectively closing all canteen
operations across the country. One sympathetic Fort Robinson officer
strongly objected to the closing:

> Breaking up the canteen has sent the garrison back to the old
> pay day times, filling the guard house to its utmost capacity.
> The men will drink, and now must go off to get it.

He also claimed that fights and drunkenness had increased and desertions doubled since the closure.[29]

Another reason for bemoaning the loss of the post canteen movement was the alternative, the "hog ranch," that seedy, combination bar–gambling den–whorehouse that inevitably mushroomed near a military post. One such establishment, kept by one Octavia Reeves, sat along Soldier Creek just beyond the reservation boundary. No words were minced when it was described as:

> the resort of thieves, pimps, tramps, vagabonds, and white and colored prostitutes. Fights and knock-downs are of daily occurrence, while not infrequently the six-shooter is resorted to. . . . In this vile den of iniquity social equality exists in its broadest terms, in one corner of the dance hall can be seen a wench of the blackest type sitting on the lap of a white man, while near by can be seen a white woman adorning the knee of a colored patriot.[30]

County officials later forced the outfit out "owing to the numerous complaints made by residents of the locality."[31] But by that time, the town of Crawford had been founded and brought civilization and its own worldly delights to post residents.

Feminine companionship, hog ranches notwithstanding, had improved markedly for the enlisted men since the 1870s, and so had company dances as a form of entertainment. Troop members and company officers regularly organized formal dances or balls for the garrison, some sponsored by such enlisted men's social clubs as the Ninth Cavalry band's "Oak and Ivy Dancing Club" or G Troop's "Twelve Brothers."[32] The men routinely invited guests to the amusement hall, and partners included female servants and maids, brought to the post to work for the officers' wives. However, the ratio of females to soldiers was still skewed. Nevertheless one participant described the "grand ball" of Company C in a positive note:

> The capacity of Fort Robinson, in turning out lady partners was well tested. The wives and daughters of several sergeants, the servants and waiting maids from the garrison, and a large contingent from laundry row, made the gathering anything but the stag party that might have been expected.[33]

In 1884 the post commander put a damper on soldier–servant fraternization when he added another guard post behind officers' row to keep "the dudes of the post from going to see the officers servant girls."[34]

Officers enjoyed activities that were often reserved for officers only. In the late 1880s they organized an officers' club and mess, complete with constitution and bylaws. The club met in a small building near the post trader's store. Dances honored visiting dignitaries, such as the grand ball given for Seventh Cavalry officers in August 1887. Card parties and other social gatherings, such as "keno" and "California Jack" parties, were common occurrences along officers' row in addition to the frequent calls that polite society demanded.

Post orders published in 1888 also created an officers' lyceum. Here both officers and noncommissioned officers gathered bi-weekly to hear papers on pertinent military topics, reap the educational benefits, and hopefully advance their professional careers. At one such gathering, Colonel Brisbin presented a paper entitled "Observations on War," while Capt. William S. Worth and Capt. Clarence M. Bailey read "The Army and the People" and "Machine Guns," respectively.[35]

Elsewhere both officer and enlisted veterans of the Union army participated in the 1889 formation of "Fort Robinson Post No. 261" of the Grand Army of the Republic. Several local civilian veterans also joined the post, which later moved to the nearby town of Crawford, which had also formed a Masonic lodge. At least nine officers and enlisted men were Freemasons.[36]

Hunting was a popular—and practical—pastime for the Fort Robinson garrison. Successful hunting parties supplemented barracks tables with wild game, especially for holiday feasts. Sometimes post officers joined private hunting parties to the Big Horn Mountains of Wyoming, and such was the case in December 1887 when General Crook, a noted sportsman, went on a big-game hunt. In September 1889, Webb Hayes, the second son of former President Rutherford B. Hayes, came to Fort Robinson to accompany a Crook foray. The trip was marred when one of the soldier escorts was accidentally shot and killed. In September 1896 Ninth Cavalry officers and civilian scout and noted hunting guide "Little Bat" Garnier escorted a party of eastern millionaires headed by W. K. Vanderbilt to the Big Horns. A veteran of the Great Sioux War, Garnier had remained at Fort Robinson as an employee of the quartermaster department. He accompanied many hunting trips into Wyoming. After one successful hunt one officer remarked of Bat, "His mission in life seemed to be to kill, and probably his aggregate bag would surpass that of any other hunter in this country."[37]

Most officers and enlisted men, though, more often hunted closer to home. Although by the 1880s bison had vanished and large game (deer and antelope) was virtually gone from the region, grouse, ducks, and rabbits were still plentiful. In December 1887 the correspondent "Africus" reported:

> Hunting parties have been organized and our ambitious marksmen, of whom we boast a goodly proportion, are scouring the adjacent country in search of game. In view of the large amount of game expected the boys were liberally provided with ammunition and transportation wherewith to haul the trophies of their prowess.[38]

In one local hunting trip an Eighth Infantry private was accidently shot and killed while hunting with other soldiers near the post.[39]

The 1880s brought a new period of consolidation to the army on the Plains. With the removal and restriction of the Plains Indians to reservations, the army redeployed its forces. Larger, more modern posts were planned and constructed, while selected existing posts were greatly expanded; more isolated posts fell to abandonment. Another reason for this consolidation and troop redistribution was the rapidly expanding network of railroads, which expedited troop and supply movements.

By the 1880s Fort Robinson's original log and adobe buildings, merely a decade old, began to require considerable maintenance. Post commander Maj. Louis H. Carpenter commented in April 1884, "Very extensive repairs are now necessary to place the barracks in proper condition, and the old and decaying walls do not seem to be worth the labor and expense which will have to be expended upon them." Summing up the state of affairs of post facilities, Carpenter went on, "If the post is to be retained, it will certainly be economy and good policy to expend a sufficient sum at Fort Robinson to place it in good condition, instead of patching up old and worthless log buildings, which have now lasted as long as could be expected."[40]

By 1882 a route for a new railroad had been surveyed past Fort Robinson and into Wyoming, and by 1883 the Fremont, Elkhorn and Missouri Valley Railroad had extended its tracks to Fort Niobrara in north-central Nebraska. The builders had envisioned a route from Fremont to the Black Hills, but before this could be accomplished, the Chicago and North Western purchased the Elkhorn line. The C&NW proceeded with the plan to build into the Dakota Territory and also to extend a proposed line to the west via the White River Valley. This new route would put Fort Robinson directly on a railroad line.[41]

In his annual report for 1884, Department of the Platte commander Col. John Gibbon urged a larger garrison for both Forts Niobrara and Robinson. The primary basis for his recommendation was the location of each relative to the Sioux reservation: "Forts Robinson and Niobrara are well located as picket posts for the close observation of the most powerful and warlike tribe of Indians on the continent. . . . [W]ise policy would therefore seem to indicate these two posts should be enlarged."[42] With expansion proposed for Fort Robinson the question of Fort Laramie's abandonment resurfaced. That year the post commander there wrote, "It seems to me probable that the new line of railroad ascending the Niobrara reopens the question as to the need of retaining this as a permanent post."[43]

Sparked by rumors of railroad expansion, advertisements promoted the availability of grazing and agricultural lands in the White River Valley for homesteads. In the spring of 1885 settlers began to stream into the region, drawn by the promise of railroad service and available land. Close proximity to the Sioux reservation would be offset by the protection of the Fort Robinson garrison.

By 1885 the decision had been made to expand Fort Robinson. A larger post would have many benefits—increased economy of supply, better discipline of troops, greater proficiency in drill, and improved comfort of officers and enlisted men. In addition, columns of troops for field service could be speedily organized and transported. In his 1884 report Maj. Gen. John A. Schofield, Division of the Missouri commander, stated the stations to be occupied should be permanent (rather than temporary) posts with comfortable barracks and quarters. This included Fort Robinson.[44]

The Fremont, Elkhorn and Missouri Valley Railroad line reached Fort Robinson on May 11, 1886. The town of Crawford, platted just off the east border of the military reservation, was established the same year. The new town was named in honor of Capt. Emmet Crawford, the brave cavalry officer who had served at the post in 1874–75 and who had been killed in Mexico while pursuing Apaches in 1885. Two months after its creation, Crawford contained fifty buildings, its residents optimistic that "the proximity of this town to Fort Robinson . . . will help Crawford wonderfully."[45] The post and town began many years of peaceful coexistence, occasionally marred by ugly incidents typically found in civil-military communities.

If the arrival of the railroad indicated prosperity for northwest Nebraska and continued use for Fort Robinson, it also spelled the end for Fort Laramie. Schofield noted:

> Even if another railroad should hereafter be extended along
> the valley of the North Platte to and beyond Fort Laramie,
> Fort Robinson would still remain much the most important
> station because of its closer proximity to the Sioux Reserva-
> tion. Hence I suggest the construction of additional barracks
> and quarters at Robinson and a corresponding reduction of
> garrison at Fort Laramie.[46]

The War Department proposed to station ten companies, five of
cavalry and five of infantry, at Fort Robinson. In February 1886 construction estimates from Department of the Platte headquarters were forwarded to the adjutant general's office. They recommended building
seven new barracks, three sets of officers' quarters, two storehouses, and
one stable, at a cost of $70,000. An additional appropriation of $12,000
was requested to make "necessary repairs to post." It became evident a
larger parade ground would be required for more troops. But before construction could begin, funding had to be secured from Congress.

It was only natural that a proposed military construction project would
attract the interest of Nebraska politicians. In March 1886 a Nebraska
delegation consisting of Senator Charles F. Manderson and Representatives Archibald J. Weaver and George W. E. Dorsey called on Secretary of
War William E. Endicott.[47] The purpose of the meeting was to urge the
enlargement of Fort Robinson. Manderson, a member of the Committee
on Military Affairs, had taken great interest in the project after hearing
rumors of the post's abandonment late in 1885. A bill for building
additional quarters costing $52,000 was then pending. After the meeting
Dorsey stated, "This is a very important measure for the people of that part
of the state."[48]

Meanwhile the local press reacted to the news from Washington. After
learning of the project and realizing its importance to the region, the
neighboring *Chadron Democrat*, which had reported Dorsey's statement,
stressed the potential danger in case of an Indian outbreak:

> The handful of troops now at Robinson would be of little
> avail. . . . If troops are necessary at all they are necessary
> within reach of the Sioux and Fort Robinson is one of the
> places at which they should be quartered.

However, not all newspaper editors favored expanding the post. The
Sidney Telegraph, more interested in improvements to Fort Sidney, was
hardly sympathetic. "The *Journal* would have us believe the Sioux at Pine

Ridge are a very bad set of Indians liable to break out at any moment and that large numbers of troops are necessary in that neighborhood." Such protests were ignored as the Fort Robinson project moved forward.[49]

In May 1886 the Senate Committee on Military Affairs released its report to accompany S.1935. The bill's supporters sought to enlarge, repair, and complete military quarters and barracks at Forts D. A. Russell, Niobrara, and Robinson. The bill proposed an appropriation of $200,000 to complete this work. Senator Manderson, a member of the committee, staunchly supported the bill, and the report recommended its passage in purple prose calculated to raise the specter of Indian attacks on defenseless settlements:

> The primary object of stationing troops at Fort Robinson and at Fort Niobrara is to hold in check 28,000 savage Sioux on the Sioux Reservation in Dakota, on the confines of Northern Nebraska. This tribe of hostiles is armed with the deadly Winchester rifle, and its warlike disposition had repeatedly left desolation and massacre in the track and trouble therefrom may be again apprehended in spite of the civilizing influences at work to temper its ferocity.[50]

The report also pointed out that there was an influx of population near the threshold of the Sioux reservation, "relying upon government protection ... liable at any moment to experience all the horrors of Indian warfare." The committee's report added that the existing buildings at Fort Robinson were temporary in nature and almost uninhabitable. It went on to stress the importance of consolidation and the potential threat of

> these Indians, many of them were in the Custer massacre, and are among the worst of their species, and have had a taste of white man's blood. . . . Give Robinson a garrison of sufficient size to cow down the savages by certain and immediate punishment.[51]

Congress soon provided funds for additional quarters at Fort Robinson. Part of the funding had been secured in August 1886. A sundry civil bill granted $225,000 for construction and enlargement at posts as determined by the secretary of war. Of this amount $20,000 was earmarked for Fort Robinson. The main funding bill was passed on January 29, 1887, and appropriated $55,000 "to complete barracks and quarters at Fort Robinson for *ten* companies." The secretary of war combined both amounts for a total of $75,000 to be expended for improvements in 1887.[52] A decision then had to be made regarding how many buildings—barracks and officers' quarters—should be built.

Lt. Col. James S. Brisbin, the commanding officer at Fort Robinson, believed the old log barracks could be repaired and remodeled to adequately house five of the ten proposed companies. The bulk of the appropriation was to be expended on new quarters for the other companies. Brisbin also suggested the new post headquarters building be converted into a field grade officers' quarters.[53]

In December Brigadier General Crook, and Maj. George B. Dandy, chief quartermaster for the department, made the first of several visits to Fort Robinson. This visit affected the future design of the post. At least five additional sets of officers' quarters would be required for the larger garrison. Building style and construction material to be used for the officers' quarters had to be determined.

After Dandy's December visit Brisbin was ordered to prepare final plans and specifications. He detailed 2nd Lt. Philip A. Bettens, Jr., Troop K, Ninth Cavalry, on special duty to work on this project along with post quartermaster 1st Lt. Henry H. Wright, also of K Troop. In February Brisbin and Wright made a trip to department headquarters in Omaha to confer on the projected work. As was done at Fort Niobrara, it was decided to build the new quarters of adobe brick. The officers' quarters and the barracks also basically followed the same design used at Fort Niobrara.[54]

Crook and Dandy returned to the post on March 18, 1887. On this visit it was decided to locate the new post just northwest of the existing installation.[55] Fort Robinson's original post area was large enough for five companies, but inadequate for the larger garrison. The broad plain above and west of the old post afforded an excellent site for the new buildings. An officers' row was laid out on the north side of the new parade ground. On the south side would be the barracks and behind them an area for stables. The new layout would be retained through the remainder of the post's military use.

Brisbin realized additional troops would soon arrive. To eliminate household disruptions he requested that new units be put up in tents until their quarters were completed. In May 1887 the headquarters staff and band of the Ninth Cavalry arrived from Fort McKinney, Wyoming, making Fort Robinson a regimental headquarters post. On May 11 Col. Edward Hatch replaced Brisbin as post commander. Besides acting as commanding officer of the regiment Hatch also had to oversee the post enlargement project and soon became a moving force in this endeavor. First Lt. Charles W. Taylor, Ninth Cavalry regimental quartermaster, arrived several days later to replace Lieutenant Wright as the quartermaster officer in immediate charge of expansion operations.[56]

Actual preparations for construction began in late spring. The previous February Brisbin had prepared and submitted final estimates for materials and other contingencies. Beginning in May raw materials for construction work were procured and stockpiled at the post. A steam sawmill was sent over from Fort Niobrara and set up on the wood reserve. Stone was located, quarried, and hauled in for building foundations. Limestone was burnt in temporary kilns for lime to be mixed with sand for mortar. Hundreds of thousands of adobe bricks had to be manufactured. From locations about four miles away clay was plowed and scraped to be hauled to ten adobe mills for forming brick.

With soldiers from the garrison detailed to process building materials Hatch became concerned about the large number of men required to perform this work, plus regular garrison duties and normal training activities. The construction project would require "many and large details to accomplish such portion of the work that the appropriation may be used economically."[57] He recommended that the reinforcing units soon to arrive be ordered to assist in the construction of the quarters they were to occupy. Later he asked that prisoners held in the post guardhouse, sentenced to hard labor at the Leavenworth prison, be retained to augment the labor force at the post. Hatch also requested that other prisoners held at hard labor be sent to Fort Robinson to work.[58]

Reminiscent of 1874, logistical problems continually plagued the construction project. From the onset shipment of building materials from Omaha met with delays. On May 23 Hatch urgently requested that articles needed for the renovation of the existing quarters be hurried, adding, "The necessity is so great they should be forwarded at once."[59] Besides supply problems, there was a serious lack of transportation available at Fort Robinson to haul building materials. When construction began, there were only four, six-mule teams at the post, three of them under orders to accompany a detail to Cheyenne. Hatch realized it would reduce costs if the government provided draft animals and wagons to move materials rather than contracting for this service.[60] He was aware of the fine line between available funding and the number of buildings projected to be built.

On May 23 Hatch asked permission to advertise in the newspapers for bid proposals. The next week he telegraphed Omaha headquarters requesting bid proposal forms. By the middle of June bidders had gathered at the post, anxious to submit proposals for the work, but the forms still had not been received. With potential contractors cooling their heels, Hatch was understandably irritated by the delay.

At about the same time concern arose over availability of timber. It was planned to use wood from the post reserve for the project, but the supply was questionable. To eliminate a possible shortage, Hatch wrote department headquarters, suggesting the addition of eight sections of available land to the wood reserve. The land was well-timbered and was closer to the post. This recommendation, like many that Hatch would submit, was not implemented, and the post reserve continued to supply wood for construction.[61]

On June 15 ground was broken at the new post site for the building foundations. On June 20 all bids were submitted to Department Quartermaster Dandy and the successful ones accepted. Most of the contractors for the masonry and carpentry work came from the Chadron area: Banning and McFarland, Rothwell Brothers, and Benjamin Cooley, who soon proceeded with their work. Much of the foundation and adobe work was to be done by mason Tom Madden, also from Chadron.[62]

The sawmill from Fort Niobrara proved to be the weak link in furnishing the new post with lumber. Post officers described it as worthless and urged its replacement. A new portable sawmill was requested, to be obtained through emergency purchase, so that it would not be charged against the appropriation. However, the old mill continued to be used after replacement parts and new shafting were delivered.

The lack of adequate transportation remained a potential problem as summer began and construction commenced in earnest. A concerned Hatch informed department headquarters that Dandy had assured former Post Quartermaster Wright that enough teams and wagons would be provided for moving materials. At the time there was barely enough transportation at the post for garrison use. Hatch itemized the number of teams and wagons he thought necessary for various tasks in connection with the construction and computed that 254 additional mules were needed. But he then backed down substantially and stated, "There is a bare possibility of completing the work by the addition of 48 mules."[63] At the same time, requisitions were forwarded for six new army wagons and twenty additional front wheels for timber and stone wagons. To help remedy the situation, Dandy transferred teams from Fort Duchesne, Utah, and Fort Bridger, Wyoming.

As the summer progressed, hardware supplies from Omaha were late and caused construction delays. Besides barracks, quarters, and stables, Hatch and Lieutenant Taylor planned to build a new bakery to replace the 1875 structure. By the middle of July they had not received word from Dandy to proceed with its construction. Hatch was impatient with the chief quartermaster's delay and ordered adobes manufactured for the building, trusting that other incidental bills incurred during its construction would be honored.

Just before construction began on the officers' quarters, Hatch attempted to change both their design and the material from which they would be built. He favored the two-story brick quarters similar to those recently built at Fort Russell. In a letter to department headquarters he argued that it was really more economical to use brick instead of adobe. Breakage and loss by rains would be much higher with adobe (about thirty percent), and the contractors could lay up a wall easier and faster with brick than with adobe. He stressed that adobe was not well adapted to the northern climate, and builders in Chadron and Crawford were using brick for fine buildings. This was just another Hatch recommendation ignored by department headquarters that summer.[64]

By August construction at Fort Robinson was in full swing. On August 11 General Crook made a quick inspection visit and found work well underway on five duplex officers' quarters. Each unit contained a parlor, library, main bedroom, and bathroom in the main part, with dining room, kitchen, and maid's room in the rear wing. Each half had about 1,750 square feet of living space, or over twice that of the earlier 1874–75 quarters. Long porches on the front and back sides were added to protect the adobe from the elements; wood siding was later installed on the exposed ends for further protection.

On the south side of the parade ground five barracks were taking shape. Each was built to house a company of men with a main living area 30 x 169 feet and a kitchen and a dining room wing 30 x 70 feet. Like the officers' quarters the barracks were constructed of adobe brick. Behind the barracks three frame troop stables were built. Each stable had a capacity of sixty-six animals and contained a saddle room and granary.[65]

The weather occasionally slowed the work, and soldiers detailed for extra duty on the project sometimes caused problems. On August 24 Pvt. Henry Royster of Troop F, Ninth Cavalry, was charged with driving a six-mule team while intoxicated. For this transgression a garrison court found him guilty and fined him $10. In another case Pvt. Thomas Powell of Company I, Eighth Infantry, was charged with desertion of his post. Powell, assigned to watch over the sawmill, was discovered absent from his post for seventeen hours, endangering the property in his charge. For this offense he was fined $10.50.[66]

More new quarters were required if the fort was to house ten companies. In September it was decided to add barracks for one more cavalry troop and an additional set of officers' quarters. Considerable repair work was done on the old barracks. Earlier that summer two companies of the Eighth Infantry arrived from Fort Bridger, and a troop of the Ninth Cavalry transferred from Fort Niobrara. The new units were housed in tents until adequate barracks housing was completed. The arrival of additional soldiers brought a corresponding increase to the officer staff. By August twenty-three officers were at the fort, half of them awaiting completion of houses on the officers' row. The garrison strength of ten companies, though, was never achieved during Fort Robinson's remaining years as a troop station; no more than eight-company garrisons would ever be stationed there.[67]

On September 18 two of the new barracks were finished and occupied by Companies D and K of the Eighth Infantry. In October three more of the barracks were occupied and most of the officers' quarters completed with the "remainder of those projected being rapidly pushed forward."[68] The following month all the new buildings were finished. On November 2 Senator Manderson arrived as the guest of Colonel Hatch to inspect the newly completed post. Although dwarfed by modern military construction, the expenditures in 1887 were impressive nevertheless. Each barracks cost $6,017.65; the officers' quarters, $6,150.80; and the stables, $1,086.95. Enough was squeezed out of the $75,000 appropriation to also construct the bakery and two small houses for noncommissioned staff officers. Outhouses for all quarters, fencing and boardwalks for the officers' houses, and an icehouse completed Hatch's project.[69] When it was all totaled, there was a slight cost overrun of $1,271.77. This deficit was made up from another sundry civil bill that had been passed March 3, 1887. The new construction at Fort Robinson accounted for twenty percent of the Department of the Platte quartermaster expenditures for 1887–88. What must have been a trying season for commander Hatch was over.

With the enlargement of Fort Robinson, Fort Laramie's days were numbered. On August 31, 1889, General Order No. 69 announced its abandonment. In March 1890 the last garrison marched out and headed for Fort Logan, Colorado, one of the new consolidation posts. The next month Lieutenant Taylor and fourteen men of the Ninth Cavalry went to handle the auction of the abandoned fort. The first soldiers at Fort Robinson originated from Fort Laramie; ironically the last soldiers at Fort Laramie came from Fort Robinson.[70]

Chapter 8

The Buffalo Soldiers

The 1880s began many years of "buffalo soldier" garrisons in Nebraska, and the Ninth Cavalry, one of the two famed black cavalry regiments, made Fort Robinson its home through most of the 1890s. African Americans, though, had played an important role in our nation's military history dating back to the Revolutionary War. This role increased dramatically during the Civil War, when nearly 180,000 blacks fought for the North, but this service was in volunteer units and not in the regular army. When the war ended, advocates moved for the enlistment of black citizens in the regular army. Although faced with considerable opposition, Congress passed "An Act to Increase and Fix the Military Peace Establishment of the United States" on July 28, 1866, which for a brief time increased the size of the army. More important it created new regimental organizations, including four new cavalry regiments, two of which were to be composed of black enlisted men. Thus came about the Ninth and Tenth Regiments, United States Cavalry, as well as four black infantry regiments, which were reduced by two in 1869.[1]

In 1866–67 the organization of the Ninth Cavalry began in New Orleans, its leader Col. Edward Hatch, a volunteer officer in the Civil War who had risen to the rank of major general and had commanded a cavalry division. Hatch, described as a "man full of energy and enthusiasm," immediately went to work to prove "the wisdom of the experiment of colored soldiers."[2] By April 1867 the regiment was enlisted to strength and moved to Texas, where it prepared for field service. For the next eight years the black troopers protected stage routes, scouted for and pursued marauding Indian bands, and brought law and order to West Texas and the Rio Grande country.

In 1875 the regiment was transferred to New Mexico, where the soldiers performed the same type of duties and fought well in the Apache wars. In 1881 the Ninth moved from New Mexico to the Department of the Missouri and served at scattered stations in Kansas and Indian Territory. There the troopers spent their time on patrol removing illegal white intruders on Indian lands. Before they left the Southwest they had already received their famous nickname, "buffalo soldiers," from the Indians, who saw a similarity between the black troopers' hair and that of the American buffalo.

A change of scenery came for the regiment again in the summer of 1885 when the Ninth shifted north into the sprawling Department of the Platte. To the men and officers coming off hard service in the Southwest and southern Plains, duty in the Platte was justifiably seen as "a well-earned rest after the many scouts and campaigns of the preceding eighteen years."[3] The troops soon took station at Forts McKinney and Washakie in Wyoming, Duchesne in Utah, and Niobrara and Robinson in Nebraska. On August 10, troops C, F, and K of the Ninth replaced three troops of the Fifth Cavalry, which left Fort Robinson for Fort Riley.[4]

Two years later in May 1887, the field staff and band of the Ninth arrived from Fort McKinney, making Fort Robinson the Ninth Cavalry regimental headquarters. During the 1880s and 1890s all twelve troops of the regiment eventually served at Robinson at one time or another. Until mobilization for the Spanish-American War in 1898, Ninth Cavalry soldiers were the primary occupants of Fort Robinson.

By the century's last decade the Ninth was considered a veteran cavalry regiment. Many of its noncommissioned officers and enlisted men boasted of long years of duty, as did its officers. By 1890 its officer corps averaged eleven years with the regiment. Some of the troop captains stationed at Fort Robinson, including Patrick Cusack, Eugene D. Dimmick, John S. Loud, and Francis Moore, had served with the Ninth since its inception. Additionally, Colonel Hatch, who had guided the regiment through the blistering deserts of the Southwest to the frigid northern Plains, still served as its commander.[5]

With but a handful of noteworthy exceptions, all of the officers who served in the Ninth Cavalry were white. In the late 1880s, however, two black officers graduated from West Point and were assigned to the regiment. In October 1887 2nd Lt. John H. Alexander, the second black graduate of the United States Military Academy, arrived for duty. One officer described Alexander, an Ohio native, as "quite small but very bright and pleasant."[6] While at Fort Robinson he served with several troops before being assigned as a military science instructor at Ohio's Wilberforce University in 1894. In 1889 Charles Young graduated from the academy and was assigned to the Ninth at Fort Robinson. Until the late

1930s these men were the only black graduates of the United States Military Academy.

Some white officers of the regiment, who protested the assignment of both Alexander and Young to the Ninth Cavalry, believed that with two black officers, other white officers would never choose to transfer into the regiment. One anonymous correspondent urged that either Young or Alexander should be reassigned to the Tenth Regiment, because "no one regiment should be required to labor under those supposed disadvantages." Another took the opposite side, stating that objecting officers "cannot be permitted . . . to dictate, even by implication, as to what officers shall be assigned to the regiment of which he is a member." The black lieutenants remained with the Ninth.[7]

The years after the Great Sioux War saw the function of the U.S. Army in the West change from an Indian-fighting army to a domestic police force. Still a deterrent to recalcitrant warriors, the army played an ever-increasing role in preserving civil law and order. For example, after they arrived in northwestern Nebraska, the first real field service for the Ninth cavalrymen came with the robbery of the Chadron to Fort Robinson stage in January 1886. A lone man with a shotgun had reportedly held up the stage and taken the army payroll of between six and seven thousand dollars. A detachment from Troop F quickly reached the scene to begin tracking the desperado, but no sign was found, and suspicions fell on the driver, the only person with the stagecoach. Thereafter troops escorted the stages hauling their payroll.[8]

In 1887 President Grover Cleveland's order to remove all illegal fencing from public lands sparked heated debate in Wyoming Territory. Troops were called in "to protect the men engaged in the work from interference of cowboys." On May 23 Troop K left Fort Robinson for Cheyenne for related duty. Wyoming citizens became incensed when they heard soldiers, especially black ones, were coming; most residents had never seen blacks in uniform. The black troops, who never cut a fence while in Wyoming in the ensuing months, eventually won the grudging respect of the locals. The troops returned to Fort Robinson later that fall.[9]

In the last months of the 1880s an era ended for the Ninth Cavalry at Fort Robinson with the unexpected passing of its longtime commander, Colonel Hatch. After his successful supervision of the fort's milestone expansion in 1887, Hatch and his men had settled into the regular routine of garrison duty. With the reputation of being an excellent horseman, Hatch enjoyed driving a carriage with his splendid "four in hand" team and giving rides to the ladies of the garrison. In March 1889 while returning from a drive to a nearby railroad construction camp, a whiffletree broke on the lead team. Hatch tried to maintain control, while the ladies abandoned the carriage, but it suddenly overturned, pitched out the occupants, and pinned the unfortunate officer underneath. The lady passengers received a few bumps and bruises, but the colonel suffered a broken right leg six inches above the knee. With Hatch confined to quarters, the regiment's second in command, Lt. Col. James Brisbin, was summoned from Fort Niobrara to assume command of the post and regiment.[10]

For several days the ailing colonel appeared well on the road to complete recovery. At 5:00 A.M. on April 11, however, Hatch awoke and requested a glass of milk, which he drank. Then quite unexpectedly he "called for the nurse in a loud voice, and placing his hand on the back of his head, said 'Oh! Oh!' and, turning very pale, died." His death shocked the garrison. After briefly lying in state at department headquarters in Omaha, his body was taken to Fort Leavenworth's cemetery for burial, escorted by eight veteran NCOs and a number of regimental officers from Robinson and Niobrara. The officers and men of the Ninth contributed $700 for the monument that was erected over Hatch's grave in June 1890.[11] Hatch's death meant that Lt. Col. Joseph G. Tilford, Seventh Cavalry, received the colonelcy of the Ninth by promotion. Tilford arrived on May 8, 1890, to assume command from Brisbin, in time to lead the Ninth Cavalry during the last tragic chapter of the Indian wars on the northern Plains.

The despair and hopelessness felt by the Sioux and other Plains tribes due to reductions in reservation lands, continual white encroachment, and shortages of government rations reached its pinnacle in 1890. The buffalo soldiers at Fort Robinson were again called on to return wandering bands of Indians to the reservation and restore a feeling of security to area whites. In April some Northern Cheyennes under old Tangle Hair, who lived on the Pine Ridge Reservation, left without permission and headed toward the Tongue River Reservation in Montana to join their Cheyenne kinsmen. Cavalrymen from the post intercepted the stray Cheyennes and took them back to Pine Ridge, a portent of future troubles.[12]

In June Troop F rode to the Beaver Valley area east of Chadron to investigate rumors of Indian depredations and to calm nearby settlers, panicked by the perceived "threatening attitude assumed by Indians in the neighborhood."[13] After several days of investigation Capt. Clarence A. Stedman found all reports false and returned his troop to the post.

In July reports were received that Chief Red Cloud and many followers had left Pine Ridge without permission, heading toward the Shoshone reservation on Wind River. Troop I was quickly dispatched north toward Hat Creek to intercept them, but the Indians made it only as far as Oelrichs, South Dakota, before turning back to their reservation.[14]

As summer turned to fall, fear and apprehension grew among the whites bordering the reservation. Army authorities anticipated that sizeable forces might be needed quickly. The soldiers at Fort Robinson were prepared for field service. "Alert training" had been initiated earlier in 1889, and periodically all the men fell out and camped just outside the post "to test their readiness for field service." Through such exercises the Ninth Cavalry and Eighth Infantry units at the post readied themselves for rapid mobilization.[15]

Meanwhile on the Pine Ridge Reservation a promise of hope and renewal had come to the demoralized and destitute Lakotas in the form of a vision of a promised Messiah. This new movement, the Ghost Dance religion, spread like wildfire among the western tribes, especially through the Dakota reservations. Its followers foretold the disappearance of all whites and nonbelievers and the return of the old way of life. Believers engaged in a singular ritual, the Ghost Dance, where participants danced until they fell into a trance. Arising from this semiconscious state, adherents told of communing with the spirits of their deceased relatives and friends. An estimated third of the Lakotas actively took part in the Ghost Dance movement. Wary whites living near the reservations, however, became convinced that the dance was a prelude to an outbreak and general Indian war.[16]

The growing fears of the citizenry, though, did not stem the normal range of activities involving the garrison. In August 1890 Medals of Honor were ceremoniously presented to the Ninth Cavalry's 1st Lt. Matthias W. Day, regimental quartermaster, and 1st Sgt. George Jordan for heroism during engagements in the Southwest. Lieutenant Colonel Tilford further praised the men: "Such public recognition of valuable service on the part of officers and men of his regiment is very gratifying to the regimental commander and an honor to the regiment."[17]

In August 1890 another expedition arrived from Princeton intending to explore the Dakota Badlands. Its indefatigable, fossil-hunting party of students was again led by Professor William Scott, who was greatly impressed with the improvements at the post since his first visit eight years before. While at the fort he examined a nearby fossil bed and stayed as the house guest of Tilford. The commander provided an escort of Ninth cavalrymen and the services of Asst. Surg. Jefferson R. Kean, one of the post surgeons. After a month of fossil hunting along the Cheyenne River, the party returned, whereupon Dr. Kean treated the appreciative Scott to a hot bath and clean clothes. Well satisfied with the results of their western adventures, the students returned to the East.[18]

The next month all troops at the post were marched into Crawford to participate in the annual meeting of the Northwestern Nebraska Veterans Association.[19] Yet in the midst of these activities Fort Robinson soldiers continued their preparations. In late August all cavalry and infantry companies at the post made a long practice march that included sham battles fought along the Niobrara River.

Even with an impending crisis on the horizon, the army reorganization continued, and two companies in each infantry regiment and two troops in each cavalry regiment were eliminated. In September, following War Department orders, Companies I and K of the Eighth Infantry at Fort Robinson were skeletonized, their men transferred to units of the regiment at Fort Niobrara. The decision, coming at such an uncertain period, was regretted locally.[20] Troops L and M of the Ninth were stationed elsewhere, and the garrison apparently felt no effects of their disbanding.

In October things heated up. The army became concerned with the growing Indian militancy, a feature it perceived as associated with the Sioux Ghost Dance. On October 24 1st Lt. John F. Guilfoyle and ten men escorted Maj. Gen. Nelson Miles, the division commander, to Pine Ridge. For several days Miles conferred with Indian leaders and encouraged them to persuade their followers to give up the dance. But by that time hundreds of Lakotas had left their cabins and farms for the dance camps. It was reported, correctly or not, that Indians were stocking up on arms and ammunition. Nonbeliever Indians abandoned their homes and property to raiders and congregated at Pine Ridge Agency, considered a safe haven. Agent Daniel F. Royer, a political appointee who had only been on the job for a few weeks, had become firmly convinced that he and his agency needed military protection. As the dance fever spread, nervous white employees and mixed-bloods also moved to the agency from outlying districts.[21]

On November 16, after receiving alarming reports from officers and agents in the field, President Benjamin Harrison ordered troops readied for field service. Agent Royer panicked and sent frantic telegrams to his superiors demanding soldiers. After receiving approval from Washington, Miles ordered troops to the Pine Ridge and Rosebud agencies on November 17, and the rapid deployment of soldiers in the Department of the Platte began. By the morning of November 19, Fort Robinson soldiers boarded trains at the post depot. The battalion, under command of Capt.

Augustus Corliss, numbered over two hundred men from Troops F, I, and L, Ninth Cavalry, and Company C, Eighth Infantry. After field equipment, supplies, wagons, mules, and one ambulance were loaded, the troops departed for Rushville, Nebraska, a border town due south of the agency. There they met a strong infantry battalion arriving from Fort Omaha. The united force, under the command of Brig. Gen. John Brooke, department commander, wasted no time marching overland to Pine Ridge. Fort Niobrara troops duplicated the same maneuver at Rosebud Agency, home of the Brulés of the long-deceased Spotted Tail. Upon arrival the troops immediately went into camp and awaited further orders. Several days later Guy V. Henry, now a major in the Ninth Cavalry, and Troop D arrived from Fort McKinney to join the regiment.

Government employees and property were now secure, due in no small part to the abrupt departure of hundreds of Indians that matched the unexpected arrival of so many troops. Ghost Dancers fled to the Stronghold, a natural Badlands fortress on Cuny Table, forty miles northwest of Pine Ridge. In the ensuing weeks hundreds of soldiers from other posts encircled the reservation as the army sought to overawe the more militant Ghost Dance adherents into surrender.

Throughout most of the "Pine Ridge Campaign," troops from Fort Robinson, now virtually depopulated, guarded the agency proper. One distressed correspondent lamented,

> Dinner parties among the ladies are the only dissipation in vogue at the post. During the absence of so many of the garrison everything is dull.[22]

In early December lieutenants Charles Taylor and Alexander W. Perry arrived at the post with a hundred Indian scout recruits to be organized and equipped with uniforms and arms. This auxiliary force consisted mainly of Oglalas, but included several Cheyennes of the Standing Elk band still at Pine Ridge Reservation. Before returning to the "front," the lieutenants assured those dependents left behind that there would be a "favorable adjustment" of the Indian troubles.[23]

Back at Pine Ridge, Corliss and 2nd Lt. Alexander W. Piper kept their infantrymen busy. After establishing a daily routine, Piper reassured his wife back at Fort Robinson that "everything is as quiet as Central Park on a week day." Although the soldiers were plagued with high wind and dust, the company dug rifle pits, practiced skirmish formations, and drilled with the Hotchkiss cannon and Gatling gun brought from the fort. Piper also had his men build a brush windbreak for their horses and mules and a bake oven for the company baker.[24]

Major Henry also kept his men busy and drilled his Ninth Cavalry squadron with whistle blasts, a novel idea in the frontier army and one that caught the fancy of civilian observers. He thought the use of whistles expedient because the high winds interfered with his vocal orders. At one blast skirmishers moved out from a moving column to form a square of protective fire around the main body; at the second whistle they returned to their column positions.[25]

As Henry filled their days with drill, the black cavalrymen waited for something to happen. A chance for action finally came in early December when General Brooke sought to use his cavalry, including the Ninth, to surround the Cuny Table Stronghold and to ease the Ghost Dancers south to Pine Ridge. Before his plan could be carried out, however, the Hunkpapa leader Sitting Bull was killed on his Standing Rock Reservation on December 15, which disrupted events at Pine Ridge. Although many dancers had drifted back to Pine Ridge—and to government authority— the army feared bands of Standing Rock Ghost Dancers would complicate matters with the holdouts still at the Stronghold.[26]

On December 23 army officials received word that 350 Minneconjous under Chief Big Foot and remnant Hunkpapa followers of Sitting Bull had left their northern reservations for the south. General Miles, in overall command of army operations, was convinced their destination was the Stronghold. On the afternoon of Christmas Eve he ordered the Ninth Cavalry northwest of the agency to intercept them. Henry's battalion saddled up, loaded supplies on wagons and mules, and rode out of the agency that evening, "buoyed on by the hearty cheers and 'A Merry Christmas' given by the comrades we were leaving behind."[27]

The four-troop battalion of 229 officers and enlisted men with fifty pack mules and thirty wagons reached the vicinity of the Stronghold on Christmas morning. On the march one troop covered fifty-five miles in twenty-four hours. The soldiers established camp and spent the next few days covering the approaches to the Stronghold. Coincidentally while on this march, Henry passed through some of the same country he had seen—or squinted at—on his memorable, yet ill-fated "ride" to the Black Hills in 1874–75. Sixteen years later Henry's "brunettes" performed similar "rough work" in the bitterly cold weather. One veteran later recalled,

> [Y]ou laid out in the cold like a dog, often not in a tent. . . . It was so cold the [tobacco] spit froze when it left your mouth.[28]

On December 28 Henry's men entered the Stronghold and found it empty. The last dancers had departed and were returning to the agency. More ominously, they did not find Big Foot's people, who had unexpectedly changed course for the agency and the protection of Chief Red Cloud. Brooke sent other cavalry units from Pine Ridge in hopes of intercepting them—which the Seventh Cavalry accomplished.

The Seventh cavalrymen took their prisoners to Wounded Knee Creek and made camp, some fifteen miles northeast of Pine Ridge Agency. Strengthened during the night by additional troops from Pine Ridge, the officers gave orders the next morning, December 29, to disarm Big Foot's band. Gunfire broke out, and violence erupted. The result, and wholesale killing, was the infamous Wounded Knee Massacre.

Although the Ninth Cavalry buffalo soldiers were not involved at Wounded Knee, two of their officers were. Along with Seventh Cavalry reinforcements, thirty Oglala scouts commanded by Lieutenant Taylor arrived there on the night of December 28. Just prior to the fatal confrontation Taylor and his scouts formed a line several hundred yards south of Big Foot's tipi camp. Taylor's assistant, 2nd Lt. Guy H. Preston, stood in the middle of the camp, helping gather surrendered arms from the tribesmen. During the fighting the scouts captured the Indians' horse herd, then followed the fear-stricken Minneconjou survivors and coaxed them to surrender. Preston survived wild firing and with one enlisted man and one Oglala scout carried the first news of the fight to General Brooke at Pine Ridge Agency.[29]

After a long, quiet day of scouting, Henry's battalion made camp on the evening of December 29th, forty-four miles northwest of the agency. Just as his men were bedding down, a courier brought startling news of the Wounded Knee fight. The men must return to Pine Ridge now. Leaving Capt. John S. Loud's Troop D to escort the wagons, Henry and three troops made a forced march to the agency. Henry broke camp at 9:45 P.M. and reached the agency by 6:00 A.M. Including the distance covered while on the December 29 scout, the troopers covered eighty-four miles in twenty-four hours, no mean feat.[30]

As the tired cavalrymen went into camp and the comfort of a well-deserved rest, Cpl. William O. Wilson, one of Loud's troopers, galloped in to say that the wagons were under attack. About two miles north of the agency, a large band of warriors attacked the train and killed one of the column's advance guard. The wagons circled quickly, and a sharp skirmish followed. Henry's men remounted, some of them bareback, and rode to the scene. They chased off the attackers and escorted the wagons to the battalion camp.[31]

Again the black troopers relaxed, and again word came of more fighting. Lakota warriors, enraged over the massacre at Wounded Knee, had set fire to a cabin near the Drexel Mission, a Catholic sanctuary four miles north of the agency. This time Seventh Cavalry troops went forth to investigate, while Henry's exhausted command was allowed to rest. About a mile north of the mission the Seventh came under heavy fire from Indians holding commanding hills on both sides of the regiment's position. A plea came for Henry's battalion to help extricate the white troopers from their predicament.

At noon Henry's battalion "moved at once to the sound of the guns." Reaching the mission, the battalion divided and swept the warriors off the hills above the imperiled Seventh Cavalry. After the fighting had ceased, comrades of both regiments embraced one another openly on the field; as one veteran recalled with considerable understatement, "We were indeed glad to see Col. Henry and the Ninth Cavalry reinforce us during that fight." Both commands returned to Pine Ridge. The fight at Drexel Mission was the last major engagement between the Sioux nation and the United States Army.[32]

What was undoubtedly "the longest day" in Ninth Cavalry history was over. The march of the buffalo soldiers on December 29–30 has gone down in history as "Henry's Ride" with the troopers credited as logging 102 miles in thirty hours. This was in addition to relieving the wagon train and joining in the Drexel fight, all over rough country in extreme winter conditions. One historian later labeled this celebrated ride as "probably the most famous ride ever performed by troops in the United States."[33]

As Henry's battalion made its remarkable ride, the troops at Pine Ridge Agency stood ready to repel any hostile attack. Angry warriors gathered in groups on the hills around the soldier camps, and shots rang out near Captain Corliss's company. The infantrymen took cover as heavy rifle fire rained among the camps. After several minutes the firing ceased, but Corliss ordered his men to remain under arms for an hour and a half. Just as the men were permitted to stack their arms, firing resumed, and the soldiers went back on the alert. The tense situation continued through the next day. Although several enlisted men in the agency camps suffered wounds, none of the Fort Robinson infantry was injured. Nevertheless Corliss and Piper sent daily telegraph messages of reassurance to their families.[34]

The first, sketchy word of the Wounded Knee disaster reached Fort Robinson and cast a gloom over family members, "filled with anxiety and suspense, not knowing what day may bring the news that their own loved ones are among the wounded."[35] At Pine Ridge General Miles personally visited the Ninth Cavalry camp and complimented the men on their extraordinary actions. As tensions eased, the buffalo soldiers were assigned easier duty and scouted west and south of Pine Ridge.

On January 16, 1891, the last of the agency defectors surrendered, nearly five thousand people all told, and the Ghost Dance "uprising" effectively ended. On January 18 Miles officially announced the end of the Pine Ridge Campaign, the largest single military operation in the United States since the Civil War. By February the large army of 3,500 had begun to break up and to return to stations. Because Fort Robinson was the military post nearest the reservation, Major Henry and his Ninth cavalrymen were ordered to remain as watchmen at the agency until spring.

For the buffalo soldiers remaining in tents at Pine Ridge, the brutal winter of 1891 was a trying experience. The troops endured twelve snowstorms in thirty days. One soldier wrote from the agency, "Horses do not complain, for they can't, and men do not, for it would make no difference." Another, Pvt. W. H. Prather of Troop I composed "some lively rhymes of the Sioux War" that expressed the bitterness of those remaining in the field:

> The rest have gone home,
> And to meet the blizzard's wintry blast,
> The Ninth, the willing Ninth,
> Is camped here till the last.
>
> We were the first to come,
> Will be the last to leave,
> Why are we compelled to stay,
> Why this reward receive?[36]

The regiment was not forgotten. In March the editor of the *Army and Navy Journal*, a national weekly newspaper, presented Major Henry and his battalion officers with engraved silver whistles to commemorate the Ninth's notable march. Eventually on March 24, the Ninth Cavalry was relieved of agency duty, and Henry and his troops started back to Fort Robinson. Bitter coincidence struck again. Reminiscent of Henry's 1875 return march from the Black Hills, the battalion was caught in a severe winter storm that again taxed man and beast. Upon reaching Chadron Henry rented a skating rink to house his unlucky command. The next day the troops reached Fort Robinson, but many suffered from snow blindness, frostbite, and the flu. For the buffalo soldiers the Pine Ridge campaign was finally over, and to celebrate this gala occasion the men staged a ball with eighteen dances that "could hardly have been equaled by the celebrated Delmonico."[37]

In May 1891 one of the Ninth's troops received a plum assignment, transfer from Fort Robinson to Fort Myer, Virginia, just across the Potomac from Washington, D.C. Earlier in January, Major Henry had offered his black troops for Fort Myer duty, and Commanding Gen. John M. Schofield later concurred with his adjutant general that a representative troop come from Henry's remarkable battalion. In March Henry was directed to choose which troop would receive the coveted appointment. At Fort Robinson the cavalrymen anxiously awaited the decision, reassured that "who ever they are we know they will keep the reputation of the 9th Horse." Troop K, which boasted of three Medal of Honor men, was tapped for the honor, and left with Major Henry on May 22. The troop stayed at Fort Myer for three and a half years before returning to Robinson. Until the Spanish-American War, this was the only black unit of the regular army to be stationed east of the Mississippi River.[38] Incidentally Troop K was stationed at Fort Robinson for nearly ten years, longer than any other single troop or company.

Corporal Wilson, the trooper who had brought word of the attack on Loud's wagons, became a historical footnote himself. His bravery was rewarded with the Medal of Honor, and he remained at Fort Robinson another two years. Wilson's later years are a bit murky because he unexpectedly deserted from the army and dropped from sight. Only recently was his unmarked grave discovered in a Maryland cemetery.

For the rest of the men, honors came simply with the words of one correspondent who wrote, "The troops have uncomplainingly endured the hardships, and the 9th Cavalry is happy in the reflection that it has done its part nobly."[39]

After the Pine Ridge Campaign the army of the 1890s, along with its Fort Robinson detachment, found itself frequently called on to perform a variety of tasks, some quite enjoyable. In 1892 two buffalo soldier troops left Fort Robinson on a different sort of exercise. The U.S. Army wished to have a large representation at the opening of the World's Columbian Exposition in Chicago. Select cavalry, infantry, and artillery units and regimental bands from department posts, including Fort Robinson, were slated to attend. Troops A and F of the Ninth, with their horses, of course, left the post October 13 to take part in the elaborate dedication. Traveling east by rail, they accompanied the all-Indian Troop L of the Sixth Cavalry, which came from Fort Meade. The western contingent arrived in Chicago on October 17 and went into camp with other units for more days of preparation.

October 21 became "Dedication Day" when the massed cavalry units led by General Miles escorted a "procession of guests" to the exposition grounds. There a formal opening of the "World's Fair" buildings was held. The program concluded the next day with joint military maneuvers involving state and federal troops which gave the public "a chance to see the boys in blue." Soon thereafter the military encampment broke up. Before the Fort Robinson troops departed, Gen. Eugene A Carr, in command of all participating units, issued orders expressing his appreciation to all soldiers for their "handsome performance of all duties and their general good conduct and gentlemanly behavior."[40]

More often major deployments involved those to "ensure domestic tranquility." In fact, between 1886 and 1895 soldiers of the U.S. Army were called out to quell 328 civil disturbances across the United States. One controversial, and less pleasant, episode took place in the aftermath of Wyoming's infamous Johnson County War in 1892. Soldiers moved into the new state to restore order after the range war between the large cattle barons and the small ranchers. On June 7 six troops of the Ninth Cavalry under Maj. Charles S. Ilsley left by rail for the Burlington Railroad crossing of the Powder River some forty miles northeast of Buffalo. After reaching their destination, the Ninth cavalrymen established "Camp Bettens" (named after a recently deceased, former officer of the regiment), four miles south of a rough, end-of-tracks town at the crossing named Suggs. Their assignment was to prevent any further civil disorder; instead the peace-keepers found themselves the target of racial prejudice and violence by the townspeople.[41]

The whites in Suggs resented the presence of the blacks and constantly insulted both the officers and the enlisted men. On June 16 a white prostitute from Crawford refused service to a Troop G private and former customer. The soldier and a comrade then entered a saloon where they were denied service and insulted. Threats followed, and someone fired at the black soldiers as they rode off to the safety of their camp. The buffalo soldiers decided to teach the whites a lesson. Several nights later twenty soldiers rode into town, fired a volley in the air, and shot up the buildings. In an exchange of gunfire with white citizens Pvt. Willis Johnson of Troop I was killed and two soldiers wounded. The soldiers retreated to camp under heavy fire from the townspeople. The officers quickly threw out pickets to prevent further violence. The army, embarrassed considerably by the ugly incident, made no effort to protect the soldiers' rights.

Regardless of the bitter feelings shared by Suggs inhabitants and the soldiers, most of the troops remained at Camp Bettens until late September 1892. Troops D and E remained until November 15, when they returned to Robinson.

Two years later Fort Robinson soldiers again saw service on the domestic front, this time as a police force during the Pullman Strike of 1894. President Grover Cleveland directed the army to remove "obstructions" to the mail and to protect the railroads. In western states detachments of soldiers guarded tunnels, bridges, and switchyards. On July 18 Troops A, D, G, and I left the post dismounted by rail for Butte, Montana, to guard railroad facilities. The two Eighth Infantry companies were sent to Evanston and Rawlins, Wyoming, to guard railroad properties. By mid-August the strike had cooled, and the troops returned. In October both of the infantry companies were transferred to Fort Russell, leaving Fort Robinson garrisoned by eight troops, or two squadrons, of the Ninth Cavalry.[42]

Although the successful movement of Fort Robinson troops by rail had been proven repeatedly, the mainstay of 1890s field training remained the annual practice march. Hikes lasted about two weeks and often headed to Hot Springs, South Dakota. While the soldiers encamped, the officers' dependents came by train to visit the camp and to stay at Evans Hotel, a popular tourist attraction. Unfortunately tragedy struck the 1896 camp. During a swim at a nearby spring 1st Lt. James W. Benton's wife, the daughter of Maj. Guy V. Henry, inquired about Benton's whereabouts, and another officer discovered his body at the bottom of the pool. He had apparently suffered a heart attack while swimming and drowned. That was the last Ninth Cavalry march to Hot Springs.[43]

During the buffalo soldiers' tenure at Fort Robinson further expansion came to the post. In 1891–92 a new troop barracks, in addition to the one built in 1889, increased the capacity of the new post to eight full companies, or two squadrons. The two new barracks were built of frame rather than adobe, and two corresponding stables, each with a capacity of sixty-six horses, joined the stable row. After these buildings' completion the last units moved out of the old "east end," or original post, to the new, larger "west end." Also during this period five additional sets of duplex officers' quarters were erected. The new houses were two-story, frame structures, built according to standard quartermaster plans. Each half contained 2,300 square feet of living space, or about four times the space of the original 1874 quarters. On the west end of the new parade ground now sat a single set of the same style quarters for the commanding officer, which replaced his 1884 house on the old parade ground. By 1895 the new parade ground also sported two outdoor, asphalt tennis courts.[44]

In 1891 a new guardhouse was constructed, its location closing in the east end of the upper parade ground. The facility, nearly four times larger than the 1884 structure it replaced, could hold forty prisoners. A number of quartermaster support buildings were added immediately north of the "east end," or original post. Directly behind the guardhouse, a new warehouse area sprang up in 1892, two large L-shaped buildings for quartermaster and commissary supplies. Rail sidings from the main line ran alongside the warehouses for easy unloading and shipping of boxcars. On the hill just north of the warehouses new structures for quartermaster employees and livestock replaced older, deteriorating QM facilities. The new stable was an immense structure, 30 x 380 feet, with seventy-five double stalls for quartermaster animals. Pack train stables, assorted housing for civilian employees, a brick magazine, and a gun shed all appeared between 1892 and 1895. Elsewhere a combination chapel–schoolhouse was built in 1893. By 1895 the post contained over one hundred structures, all necessary to house and support its military activities.

Fort Robinson's improvement did not go unnoticed. Combined with its conspicuous role in the Indian wars of the 1870s and the Ninth Cavalry's recent exploits, the post had been recognized as one of the most notable in the service, enjoying an "enviable reputation" in army circles. Plus it looked good. In 1895 Lieutenant General Schofield, the commanding general of the U.S. Army, honored the post with a visit and inspection. The day began with a dress review of the regiment at 9:15. The officers then retired for a brief reception in 1st Lt. Grote Hutcheson's quarters, while the men changed for a second review in their field uniforms. This review included wagons and pack train, after which the men formed for battle and fired volleys. The general complimented Col. James Biddle for having his men "in a high state of efficiency and prepared for active field service."[45] An 1896 visitor wrote, "There are few army posts that equal and none that excel Ft. Robinson in point of beauty," especially the buttes to the north that had "the appearance of a fortress." Equally impressive was the large parade ground, surrounded with trees irrigated by Soldier Creek water, a scene "quite unusual in this part of the country." Together with a large flagpole displaying the American flag and its buildings all painted quartermaster red, the fort must have made a splendid scene.[46]

Appearances, though, could be deceiving. The pell-mell expansion of the garrison—and that of the associated civilian population—brought increased sanitation problems to the post. The accumulation of horse manure, trash, and kitchen waste was a continual problem at cavalry posts. Nor were nineteenth century hygienic practices always conducive to healthy lifestyles. For example, in 1886 post orders directed the provost sergeant to dump manure around water pipes and hydrants to prevent them from freezing. The main dumping area for manure was unfortunately the area below the "east end" near the cemetery, a site some found offensive.[47] In 1893 the post surgeon, the officer responsible for making recommendations to improve the general sanitation of the garrison, disgustedly wrote of the dump:

> The only object to its location is an aesthetic one. The road to the post cemetery runs through it. If the spirit of the departed attends the corpse to its final resting place as it passes across this expanse of ill looking and foul smelling "rubbish" it may well murmur with additional meaning, "This is the last of earth. I am content."[48]

The tranquil, bucolic setting of Fort Robinson aside, a certain amount of violence always characterized garrison life in the frontier military. With the closeness of barracks life, petty disputes and bad blood in the ranks often escalated to dangerous, sometimes fatal, affairs. In two years there were three unsolved murders of Ninth cavalrymen at Fort Robinson. In September 1886 Pvt. Thomas Menlow, detailed as a gardener, was found in his tent at the gardens south of the post with his throat slit from ear to ear and his face smashed in. No trace of the murderer was ever found. Later in December Pvt. Henry Roberts of Troop F was shot and fatally wounded while absent without leave in a Crawford saloon. Although a soldier suspect was arrested, guilt was not proved, and he was released.[49]

A third, higher profile killing came on Christmas Eve 1887, when Sgt. Emanuel Stance was found dead on the road between Crawford and the fort.[50] Stance had a long, stormy military career during which he was awarded the Medal of Honor in 1870 for actions against Kickapoo Indians in Texas. He was, in fact, the first black soldier to receive the medal for heroism against an Indian enemy. He was also court-martialed and reduced in rank five times. When he arrived at Fort Robinson, Stance was the first sergeant of Troop F, renowned as a strict disciplinarian. One troop member described him as a "dirty man" who beat and terrorized his soldiers and lied about them to the officers.[51] Officers often remained unaware of the problem, and Stance's superiors apparently held him in high esteem.[52] His soldiers, though, occasionally stood up to the abusive sergeant. Once an enlisted man warned Stance that he was "tired of your bulldozing." Another, in response to a Stance upbraiding, had replied, "Anyone who approaches me this morning is tired of living."[53]

At 8 o'clock on Christmas morning Stance's dead body was found; it

contained four gunshot wounds. An investigation was immediately begun to find the guilty party or parties. Some officers thought he had been
killed by members of his own troop. Suspects were brought in for
questioning, but no one would confess or accuse another. After Stance's
death some officers continued to defend his leadership style, "[H]is troop
needed a strong hand, and it took a pretty nervy man to be first sergeant."[54]
This comment reflected a fairly common attitude running through the
frontier army officer corps. Troop F commanding officer Capt. Clarence
Stedman, a seventeen-year veteran with the Ninth, was out of touch with
the enlisted ranks and let his NCOs run the unit. Pvt. Simpson Mann in an
oral interview years later explained,

> The captain didn't know as much of the soldiers as he
> should. Didn't take time to find out for himself, but he
> believed what his non-coms told him.[55]

But many officers were not just unaware of their surroundings; they
were totally absent from their command. A persistent problem was the
absence of too many officers from their regular troop duties. Between
1887 and 1890 an average of thirty percent of the Ninth Cavalry officers
assigned to Fort Robinson were away from post on extended leave or
detached service. One post report grudgingly admitted, "The officering of
the command has been greatly lessened during the past summer by the
usual scarcity of officers."[56] Less oversight meant lagging discipline.
During the Ninth Cavalry stay, there were about four hundred garrison
court martials a year, an indication of the effects of lax officer control
during the decade.

In an effort to stem soldier-on-soldier violence Colonel Hatch prohibited the carrying of firearms in the barracks and followed up with frequent
surprise inspections. Gun control measures were strictly enforced. In
1890 a Troop F corporal on guard duty pulled a revolver and menaced a
private. For this infraction the corporal from this troublesome unit was
reduced in rank, heavily fined, and confined at hard labor for twelve
months, punishment "[s]evere, but just," in the words of one reporter.[57]

Interestingly no serious racial violence ever erupted between the
black cavalrymen and the white infantrymen forming the garrison. At this
time the barracks normally housed single company units, white or black,
but sometimes soldiers of both races were temporarily housed together,
coexistence on a level not generally found then in American society.
There were, of course, recorded incidents of violence between the
soldiers, probably related to duty rather than race. In one instance a black

sergeant on guard duty struck an attacking white infantry prisoner on the head with his carbine. The prisoner, described by Colonel Biddle as "one of the vilest of the vile when using liquor," died as a result of the blow. The sergeant was exonerated and even received Biddle's praise for demonstrating "restraint" and not shooting the prisoner outright. Another time a white prisoner objected to a black sergeant escorting him to the guardhouse. When two troopers came to aid the noncom, the prisoner openly resisted and shouted racial epithets at the guards. He ended up in the guardhouse, with an additional thirty days confinement tacked on for his outbursts.[58]

Discrimination did exist, though, in an institution that was far from colorblind. With white officers aloof at best toward their black counterparts, Lieutenants Alexander and Young were excluded or declined invitations to officer social gatherings. Alexander explained his choice in the matter:

> I have been consistent in drawing the line as closely as those around me might wish it drawn, and I don't want to injure my present pleasant relations with the garrison by giving grounds for criticism which may make matters unpleasant in the future.

Consequently Alexander spent his free time by himself, much the same as he did during his years at West Point.[59] The enlisted men suffered also and voiced their complaints in 1894. They pointed out that the commissary and post exchange clerks were white; there were only white enlisted men on duty in the officers' club, adjutant's office, post library, and pump house. Therefore, men from the *two* Eighth Infantry companies filled these positions, none from the *six* cavalry units at the post. No redress for these affronts came to the black soldier in the 1890s.[60]

The purpose of a military post was to provide shelter for soldiers; housing for dependents was of secondary importance, at least regarding those of the enlisted men. The Ninth Cavalry apparently had more than the usual number of dependents among its enlisted component, possibly because many of its men made the army their career. As a result Fort Robinson suffered a chronic housing shortage for married soldiers. After completion of the new post in 1887, some of the old log barracks were turned over to enlisted families. Although the main dormitory area of the 1874 cavalry barracks served as quartermaster storage, the mess hall and front rooms became apartments. Nicknamed "The Bee Hive," the old barracks housed several families. Separate housing was provided for the staff noncommissioned officers permanently attached to the post. By 1891, 198 dependents, counting all families and servants in the officers' quarters, lived at Fort Robinson, and this in an era when the army openly discouraged soldiers to marry, much less bring their families on post.[61]

Shortages and overcrowding, sometimes marital strife, forced several spouses to find housing in Crawford. Infidelity could cost a soldier wife her right to live on post. For example, in 1894 the wife of Trumpeter Lewis Fort wrote the secretary of war for permission to live on post after Colonel Biddle, the commanding officer, refused her the privilege. Although Mrs. Fort had worked for one of the officers, trouble with another man forced her departure. Now she wanted to move back in with her husband. Biddle responded to the secretary,

> I have used my best judgement in this case. There are too many wives of soldiers on the post now.[62]

Nevertheless the army made an effort to accommodate dependents. Post schools were intended for both enlisted men and children. In 1883 orders had been issued to begin troop schools for noncoms and selected privates on tactics and regulations. By 1885 evening classes in reading and writing were held for Ninth cavalrymen to teach the basic rudiments, first in the old adjutant's office, then in the post chapel after its completion in 1893 and under the supervision of the chaplain.

Teachers for officer children were hired from nearby communities and boarded on officers' row. Select, educated enlisted men were detailed to teach the enlisted men's children. By 1884 all enlisted children were required to attend school from 9:30 to 11:30 A.M. and 1:30 to 2:30 P.M. daily during the winter months. They were given the following rules:

> Before coming to school all children are required to be washed and cleanly dressed. Rewards and punishments but not whipping allowed. Prompt attendance will be required.[63]

Enlisted children's school was held in the amusement hall or in a room partitioned off in one of the log barracks, the latter described as "cold, leaky, and uncomfortable."[64] During the 1890s the post chaplain also supervised this school, but the operation of a post school was extracurricular to regular military activities. By the turn of the century dependent children began attending public school in Crawford.

The relationship of the fort to the town, which ran hot and cold, took other forms. By 1890 the controversial post canteen system returned, and Fort Robinson's opened for business in the old post trader store. The enlisted men welcomed its reestablishment, which thrived financially.[65] Naturally Crawford saloon owners again opposed it. They protested that it operated in violation of Nebraska law, which mandated a saloon license. The army argued that the post was not under state jurisdiction, making a license unnecessary. Furthermore the enlisted men decided to boycott Crawford businesses. This divided the town merchants, most of whom opposed the attack on the canteen. No fools, they realized that Crawford's prosperity largely depended on good relations with Fort Robinson. The boycott apparently proved successful because the saloonmen backed down and soldier patronage of town businesses resumed. The important economic relationship between Crawford and Fort Robinson was maintained.[66]

The only other blip in the canteen's operations came later. By regulation, assigned officers closely oversaw and reviewed its finances. They found the accounts of the officer in charge, 1st Lt. James A. Swift, short some four thousand dollars. Appropriately named, Swift had the reputation of being a "fast" man and was quickly discharged from this duty. Rumor had it he had embezzled the funds to cover gambling debts. On January 9, 1896, the scandal ended abruptly after Lieutenant Swift committed suicide by shooting himself.[67]

A serious rift between the black cavalrymen and white townspeople, far more dangerous than the canteen flap, developed in the spring of 1893. Crawford now harbored an assortment of "toughs, pimps, gamblers and abandoned women of both colors," all of whom preyed on the soldiers.[68] Things came to a head when a discharged soldier named Diggs was accused of shooting at a white gambler. After a brief detention in the town jail Diggs was released only to face a lynch mob. His soldier friends rescued him and hid him for several days at Fort Robinson. Some soldiers blamed Crawford saloon owners for the attempted lynching. Soon a small, printed broadside appeared, sent to persons believed involved with the assault on Diggs. To alarmed officers at the post the flyers were dangerous, even "incendiary" in nature because of the following:

> [W]e give warning now to the town of Crawford that these
> things must cease. You lynch, you torture, and you burn
> Negroes in the South, but we SWEAR BY ALL THAT IS GOOD
> AND HOLY that you shall not outrage us and our people right

here under the shadow of "Old Glory," while we have shot and shell and if you persist, we will repeat the horrors of San Domingo—we will reduce your homes and firesides to ashes and send your guilty souls to—Hell.[69]

To cap it off the warning was signed "500 men with the bullet or torch." A newspaper in nearby Chadron observed, "It would not be surprising if there was a merry time between the nigger soldiers and saloon men and gamblers at Crawford almost anytime."[70]

All soldiers were immediately confined to the post and troop officers required to frequently inspect the barracks at night to count heads. A hurried investigation deduced the leaflets had been printed in Omaha, and Sgt. Barney McKay of Troop G had received and distributed them to the enlisted men. Subsequently the sergeant was confined to the guard-house, charged with "conduct to the prejudice of good order and military discipline," in violation of the sixty-second Article of War.[71]

By the end of May feelings had cooled enough that a Ninth Cavalry detachment participated in Decoration Day ceremonies at Crawford. On June 1 the court-martial of Sergeant McKay began. The prosecution brought in a number of witnesses to connect McKay to the leaflets. On June 21 the court found McKay guilty. He was reduced in rank to a private, forfeited all pay and allowances, and confined at hard labor in the federal penitentiary at Fort Leavenworth. Due to a technicality he was released from jail—also from the service—after serving five months.[72]

Like McKay, Chaplain Henry V. Plummer, the first black regular army chaplain, felt the sting of military justice the next year. Plummer, who had been appointed chaplain of the Ninth Cavalry in 1884, reported for duty at Robinson in 1891. He actively promoted education and temperance among the enlisted men. In accordance with his principles he openly opposed alcoholic sales at the post canteen; he also complained about being assigned quarters in the "lower row" with the noncommissioned officers. By 1894 Plummer, now considered a disturbing element, had run afoul of a succession of post commanders. Some fellow officers even accused him as being the author of the infamous 1893 broadside. However, it was trumped-up charges of intemperance that brought his undoing.

On July 3, 1894, charges of conduct unbecoming an officer and gentleman were brought against Chaplain Plummer. Several black non-commissioned officers alleged he had been drinking liquor with enlisted residents of the lower row, providing additional liquor, and drunkenly "wearing the blouse of Sergeant Major of Cavalry."[73] Although at least one of his accusers held a personal grudge—a fact brought out in the court-martial—Plummer had lost his credibility because of the drinking charges, particularly since he had so openly embraced the cause of temperance.

In late summer Plummer was found guilty of misconduct after an eleven day court-martial trial. The proceedings were reviewed at length, and although efforts were made for acquittal, he was dismissed from the army on November 10. The army replaced him in June 1895 with Chaplain George W. Prioleau, who served with the regiment until 1915. Plummer moved to Kansas, served as a pastor, and died at Kansas City, Missouri, in 1905.

The Ninth Cavalry turned from fighting themselves to face a common enemy. In July 1895, during a summer of rumors of an uprising among the Bannock tribe of Idaho, troops from the fort went into northwest Wyoming to ease the fears of alarmed settlers in the Jackson Hole vicinity. An argument arose when the Bannocks vigorously insisted that treaty rights immunized them to state hunting laws. Wyoming's governor called for federal troops, and on July 25 a Ninth Cavalry battalion departed by rail from Fort Robinson for Market Lake, Idaho. The soldiers spent several months scouting for parties of Bannocks that were supposedly threatening Wyoming settlers, a danger that never materialized. In October the troops were withdrawn. As with the rumored troubles of the late 1880s, the Bannock "uprising" was another example of groundless fears resulting in an excessive military reaction.[74]

In the summer of 1897 more fears arose, this time on the Fort Hall Reservation of the Blackfeet tribe in Idaho. Lt. Col. John M. Hamilton, commander of the regiment, and 240 men with their horses and equipment were loaded on a train as an expeditionary force. Just as they were prepared to pull out, a telegram arrived to stop the train. Department headquarters had decided the reports of a Blackfeet uprising were exaggerated. The cavalrymen detrained, unloaded their gear, and returned to their barracks. This time a long, costly trip had been avoided.[75]

On a lighter note, Fort Robinson received a visit at that time from the renowned artist and illustrator Frederic Remington, who was on assignment for *Harper's New Monthly Magazine*. The artist, who had brought alive the frontier army to thousands of American readers, eagerly observed cavalry training and visited old friends from the Southwest campaigns, including Colonel Hamilton. After participating on night maneuvers, however, Remington was not quite ready for the next day's work:

> In the morning I resisted the Captain's boot, and protested that I must be let alone, which being so, I appeared groomed and breakfasted at a Christian hour, fully persuaded that as

between an Indian and a Ninth Cavalryman I should elect to be an Indian.[76]

Regardless of his feigned reluctance, Remington again rode that day with the buffalo soldiers, who were "doing real work" and "not being stupefied by drill ground routine." While at the post he made a series of soldier sketches that later became magazine illustrations.[77]

As Remington's appearance at Fort Robinson hearkened back to the Indian-fighting cavalry, the appearance of soldiers mounted on bicycles anticipated the day of army mechanization. In July 1897 the army's celebrated bicycle corps of the Twenty-fifth Infantry, another African American regiment, stopped at Crawford for a noon break. The purpose of their trip from Fort Missoula, Montana, to St. Louis, Missouri, was to field test the bicycle for military use. After eating and resting for several hours, the cyclists, consisting of one officer, one surgeon, and twenty-four enlisted men, left town, cheered on by the Ninth Cavalry band and hundreds of spectators. That same year Fort Robinson's own 2nd Lt. Matthew A. Batson, a later Medal of Honor recipient, and two enlisted men on high-wheel Columbian bicycles accompanied a detachment of mounted cavalrymen on a march near the post. They had difficulty keeping up with the horsemen in rough terrain but easily outdistanced them on level ground. Batson later used a bicycle to map parts of the post reservation.[78]

On February 15, 1898, the *U.S.S. Maine* sank in Havana Harbor, and war with Spain looked imminent. At Fort Robinson the flag was lowered to half-staff in memory of the sailors who had lost their lives. Chaplain Prioleau, Plummer's replacement, conducted memorial services, sponsored by the Army and Navy Union, with over four hundred persons in attendance. The Ninth Cavalry and two Sixth Cavalry troops at Robinson had already been preparing for war service. Since December 6, 1897, the troops had made a total of thirty-six practice marches, where men received training in patrol, attack, and screening duties. By March 1898 the troops anxiously awaited the coming order to mobilize.[79]

On March 22, tragedy struck closer to home. After the earlier move of all soldiers to the west end of the post, part of the old log barracks, including the former "Cheyenne Outbreak" barracks, had been turned over to married enlisted men. Seven soldiers and their families, including Sgt. Harry Wallace, his wife, and three children, occupied the subdivided building.

On that day Mrs. Wallace had to leave to make a call and locked two of her daughters, ages two and four, in the rooms the Wallaces occupied. About 3 P.M. smoke was seen coming from the roof; soon afterwards the building was in flames.

> By the time the troops reached the fire it had gained such headway that it was impossible to enter that portion of the building. When the word passed that two babies were in the burning rooms several soldiers made bold but futile efforts to rescue them. After the fire had burned itself out the two babies were found on a bed, burned to a crisp.[80]

Authorities determined that the fire had broken out in the room where the children were found. The girls were buried in the post cemetery, and the families whose quarters were destroyed were housed in the gymnasium hall. An old set of NCO quarters on the east side of the barracks also suffered severe damage and was demolished when the other debris was cleared. The sense of loss produced by the children's pitiful deaths extended beyond the post. "It is one of the saddest affairs that has occurred in this section of the country for many a long time."[81] In the late 1980s Nebraska State Historical Society archaeologists excavated the site of the 1874 barracks. They found broken objects reflecting its former inhabitants—a belt plate from a soldier's uniform, several unfired .45-caliber rounds possibly hidden by a Cheyenne prisoner, and a child's porcelain doll, scorched by fire.

The post was barely over the shock of the fire when mobilization orders came, affecting all Fort Robinson cavalry units. On April 18 Troop I, Eighth Cavalry, arrived from Fort Meade, South Dakota, to man the post. In the early morning of April 20 the Fort Robinson garrison began loading train cars for a trip to Chickamauga Park, Georgia, to mass with other regiments for the invasion of Cuba. The troops departed in five separate trains, the first leaving at 6:30 A.M. and pulling eighteen freight cars of wagons and field equipment. At 7:30 two more trains departed with thirty-six cars containing the horses of both regiments. At 9:45 a train of eight passenger cars containing Ninth cavalrymen left. The last train left at 11:00 with the balance of the Ninth Cavalry, the two Sixth Cavalry troops, and officers of both regiments. Hundreds of citizens gathered to see the men off to war. "The depot platform was crowded with Crawford people to witness their departure for the Cuban war and bid them God speed on their mission to whip the Spaniards." To older spectators in the excited crowd it reminded them of a Civil War scene.[82]

In May the Fort Robinson's Ninth Cavalry units joined others of the regiment from Forts Washakie and Duchesne at Tampa, on the west coast of Florida. On June 8 the regiment, now part of the Fifth Corps, sailed for Cuba's southern coast and the attack on Santiago, seen by army planners as the key to victory. In the subsequent brief, but bitter Santiago Campaign, the regiment saw heavy fighting around San Juan Hill, that immortal site in the Spanish-American War. Its most noted battle casualty was Fort Robinson's former commander, Lieutenant Colonel Hamilton, who was killed on July 1. By the end of July the short-lived war was over, and in August the victorious American forces, though decimated by tropical sicknesses, began their return to the states.[83]

Because of the Ninth's long association with Fort Robinson and northwest Nebraska, the state's citizens followed the newspaper reports in the Cuban war with interest. Already known as a "famous regiment," the press christened it the "Ninth Nebraska." But when this regiment of buffalo soldiers went off to fight the Spaniards, they left Nebraska for good, never to return. New duties beckoned, and thirteen years of Ninth Cavalry garrisons at Fort Robinson had ended.[84]

For months after the war, army garrisons constantly shuffled among the posts in the nation's interior as fresh troops left to relieve those suffering in Cuba. In October 1898 Troop I of the Eighth Cavalry left for Huntsville, Alabama. It was replaced by Troop C, First Cavalry, which had come from Camp Wikoff at Montauk Point, Long Island, New York, the "rest and recuperation" center for troops returning from the Caribbean. In January 1899 Fort Robinson again became a regimental headquarters post when headquarters staff and band and three additional troops of the First Cavalry came north from Fort Riley, Kansas.

Fresh from their imperial adventures, Fort Robinson soldiers in 1899 once again went about settling a civil disturbance. That spring the Western Federation of Miners led a walkout in the Coeur d'Alene mining district in Idaho. The government, to the pleasure of the mine owners, sent in troops on May 19 to preserve order and to protect property. Lt. Col. Charles D. Viele dispatched Troops A and L to Wallace, Idaho, and Camp Wardner.[85] The First Cavalry headquarters and band moved to Fort Meade. The next month Troop B was transferred to Fort D. A. Russell, leaving Troop C once again in sole possession of Fort Robinson.

The two troop units in Idaho spent long months in the mining districts guarding railroad property as well as striker–prisoners detained at Camp Wardner. Unfortunately the contamination of mountain stream water by area mining operations took a fearful toll on their horses. Between July and October, fifty-eight First Cavalry horses died, with most deaths attributed to lead poisoning from drinking contaminated water. Troop A was eventually recalled to Robinson, while Troop L remained in Idaho.[86]

The turn of the century saw the passing of a reminder of Fort Robinson's past, Baptiste "Little Bat" Garnier, the noted mixed-blood scout, guide, and hunter. Garnier, an army scout since 1873, had served as the fort's chief of scouts since 1887. He had earned an illustrious reputation as a fearless and reliable man, who performed valiant and hazardous work for the army during the Ghost Dance troubles and Pine Ridge Campaign of 1890–91.

On the evening of December 15, 1900, Garnier entered George Dietrich's saloon in Crawford, now the downtown corner of Second and Main. As he reached inside his bulky buffalo-hide coat for money to pay for a drink, bar manager James Haguewood, who later claimed Bat was reaching for a gun, pulled a pistol from under the bar and shot Garnier nearly point-blank. The unarmed Little Bat staggered out of the bar into the street and fell mortally wounded. He died at 3:00 A.M. the next day, when the famous scout "breathed his last and passed out to the unexplored plains of the great beyond."[87] Garnier, whose career extended from the earliest days of Red Cloud Agency and Camp Robinson, was buried in the post cemetery alongside three of his children. At his trial Haguewood testified that Garnier had earlier threatened him, an implausible but successful defense because on March 1901 he was found not guilty of murder.[88]

Century's end brought changes to Fort Robinson's appearance. In the winter of 1899–1900, the last original log buildings thrown up in 1874 by Jordan's Ninth infantrymen disappeared. The 1887 expansion had essentially moved the soldiers to the upper parade ground, with the original area now being of secondary importance. The older buildings generally functioned as storage and as married enlisted men's housing or were simply abandoned. During the mid-1890s, however, the old adobe officers' quarters (then housing noncommissioned officers) received attention, their side porches removed and lap-siding installed over the mud brick walls. But the log barracks, stables, and warehouses of the first fort were allowed to deteriorate, ramshackle eyesores when compared to the modern, adjoining post.

In December 1899 post surgeon A. H. Simonton recommended that "[m]any of the oldest buildings are unoccupied, are beyond repairs for use and should be destroyed as they harbor disease germs."[89] Post commander 1st Lt. Edmund S. Wright concurred, and demolition commenced in January 1900. By March sixteen buildings around the 1874 parade ground had been torn down; useful lumber was salvaged and debris piled and burned. In April more structures, including the old trader's store, once the center of social activity at the post, were razed. By May all of the old log and frame buildings were gone, except for the 1883 cavalry barracks, and that lingered only until 1904. Surgeon Simonton was pleased to report, "[T]the grounds have been thoroughly policed, trees well trimmed, Fort Robinson today appears like a well kept park."[90]

Epilogue

Fort Robinson saw dramatic changes in its initial quarter-century as an army post. The old Red Cloud Agency, which Camp Robinson was established to protect, was completely gone—as were the Sioux, Cheyenne, and Arapaho villagers, long since relocated from the White River Valley to South Dakota, Montana, and Wyoming reservations. By the turn of the century the log fort built in 1874 had also disappeared, replaced by better, more substantial facilities. Men who served at Camp Robinson as subalterns and company grade officers were now field commanders or held higher ranks. Arthur MacArthur, who had signed the first post return, now commanded a division in the Philippines as a major general of volunteers.

The town of Crawford, named for the brave officer who rode to the agency during the flagpole crisis, had prospered and expanded. The area's population grew as settlers moved into northwestern Nebraska. With its strategic location on rail and telegraph lines, Fort Robinson became an important troop station after the army in the West was consolidated. Handy rail transportation also brought the garrison into closer contact with life back east, a welcome benefit to its residents.

By 1895 Mrs. Ellen Biddle, wife of post and Ninth Cavalry commanding officer Col. James F. Biddle, expressed satisfaction with life at Fort Robinson. Mrs. Biddle had followed her husband across the western states throughout his career and noted the improved quality of army life at Robinson. She commented on social life at the post, comparing it favorably to that found in eastern cities. She was impressed with the practice of officers making formal evening calls, later writing, "I was a bit surprised at the formality, as I had never seen a visiting card during all the years I had lived on the frontier." She found that "books, magazines and papers were in profusion." As for foodstuffs, "[A] fine market was only twelve hours away." The quarters on officers' row were excellent with "good plumbing," the first she had experienced in the army. All in all, life at Fort Robinson in the "Gay Nineties" was pleasant indeed.[1]

Everyday life for the enlisted men had likewise improved. The barracks on the upper parade ground provided spacious and superior housing in contrast to the crude, log barracks built by Jordan's men in the 1870s. The men enjoyed about twice the amount of air space per man in the newer, well-lighted barrack dormitories, a vast improvement when compared to the dark, crowded structures of old. Opportunities for recreational and social activities had also improved. Participation in fraternal and social organizations was popular, while athletic activities gained official sanction. The post canteen, library, and other amusement facilities had replaced the old trader's store. Even with these changes, though, the army was essentially—eternally—the same. The daily routine of the bugle calls, fatigue and drill, guard mount, parade and retreat continued as the army entered the twentieth century.

In 1897 Sir Rose Price, a baronet and veteran British Army officer, accompanied department commander Brig. Gen. John J. Coppinger on an inspection tour of the latter's posts, including Fort Robinson. Years before, Price had visited Coppinger when the general was but a company-grade captain at Fort Hartsuff, Nebraska. The baronet now came away impressed with the lot of the American army. Price later recalled that he had never seen soldiers as well-fed or housed, or cavalry as well-trained, as he had during that trip. After witnessing several mounted drills, he noted, "I very much doubt if we have a single cavalry regiment in our army which could turn out for inspection and perform all the tricks and maneuvers that I saw at Forts Meade and Robinson." In the waning years of the western frontier, the Englishman found that America had "a rattling good little army."[2]

The days of this good little army abruptly and dramatically ended. War with Spain and a new empire to police no longer limited it to stateside service. By 1900 the bulk of the regular army was deployed overseas in the Caribbean or fighting a strange, new enemy in the Philippines. Surprisingly the military presence at Fort Robinson would continue for nearly fifty years, a survivor of a series of abandonment proposals. Its subsequent continuation brought changes of function that would have been unbelievable to the tense soldiers who marched to the site from Fort Laramie in 1874.

Much of the old fort survives today, not as a military post but as a state park, a museum, and a national historic landmark. Despite all the changes that came to the army and its world, Fort Robinson remained along the White River below the silent buttes, an outpost in the American West.

Appendix A

Commanding Officers at Fort Robinson, 1874–1899,
Compiled from Monthly Post Returns.

Interims in italics

Mar. 7, 1874–Apr. 16, 1874	Capt. James J. Van Horn, Eighth Infantry
Apr. 16, 1874–May 20, 1874	Capt. Arthur MacArthur, Jr., Thirteenth Infantry
May 20, 1874–July 12, 1874	Captain Van Horn
July 12, 1874–Oct. 24, 1876	Capt. William H. Jordan, Ninth Infantry
Aug. 16–31, 1874	*Capt. Deane Monahan, Third Cavalry*
Oct. 24, 1874–Nov. 12, 1874	*Capt. Frederick Mears, Ninth Infantry*
Oct. 24, 1874–Jan. 29, 1877	Maj. Julius W. Mason, Third Cavalry
Jan. 29, 1877–Mar. 14, 1877	Capt. Daniel W. Burke, Fourteenth Infantry
Mar. 14, 1877–May 26, 1877	Col. Ranald Mackenzie, Fourth Cavalry
May 26, 1877–Nov. 5, 1877	Col. Luther P. Bradley, Ninth Infantry
Nov. 5, 1877–Apr. 3, 1878	Capt. Frederick Van Vliet, Third Cavalry
Apr. 3, 1878–Dec. 5, 1878	1st Lt. Charles A. Johnson, Fourteenth Infantry
Dec. 5, 1878–Jan. 22, 1879	Capt. Henry W. Wessells, Jr., Third Cavalry
Jan. 22, 1879–Febr. 3, 1879	*Capt. Peter D. Vroom, Third Cavalry*
Febr. 3, 1879–Mar. 2, 1879	*1st Lt. James F. Simpson, Third Cavalry*
Mar. 2, 1879–May 8, 1880	Captain Van Vliet
June 31, 1879–July 8, 1879	*Captain Wessells*
Aug.15–Oct. 6, 1879	*Captain Wessells*
Jan. 12–28, 1880	*2nd Lt. Joseph F. Cummings, Third Cavalry*
May 21, 1880–Dec. 10, 1880	Maj. Edwin V. Sumner, Fifth Cavalry
Aug. 27–31, 1880	*Capt. Alfred Morton, Ninth Infantry*
Dec. 10, 1880–June 1, 1881	Capt. John M. Hamilton, Fifth Cavalry
Apr. 3–17, 1881	*Captain Morton*
June 1, 1881–Mar. 23, 1883	Major Sumner
Sept. 1–3, 8–10, 21–24 1881	*Captain Hamilton*
Oct. 3–15, 1881	*Captain Hamilton*
Nov. 9, 1881–Dec. 10, 1881	*Capt. John B. Babcock, Fifth Cavalry*
June 13–19, 1882	*Captain Babcock*
Febr. 2–14, 19–27, 1882	*Captain Hamilton*

Apr. 16–May 12, 1882	*Captain Hamilton*
May 20–24, 1882	*Captain Morton.*
Mar. 25–May 6, 1883	Capt. Edwin M. Coates, Fourth Infantry
Apr. 2–12, 1883	*Captain Hamilton*
May 6, 1883–May 27, 1885	Maj. Louis H. Carpenter, Fifth Cavalry
Nov. 15–30, 1883	*Captain Coates*
Febr. 26–Mar. 7, 1884	*Captain Coates*
May 27, 1885–Aug. 10, 1885	Captain Coates
Aug. 10, 1885–Feb. 20, 1886	Maj. Thomas B. Dewees, Ninth Cavalry
Feb. 21, 1886–July 1, 1886	Captain Coates
July 15, 1886–Nov. 26, 1886	Lt. Col. Joshua S. Fletcher, Second Infantry
Nov. 26, 1886–May 12, 1887	Lt. Col. James S. Brisbin, Ninth Cavalry
May 12, 1887–Dec. 11, 1887	Col. Edward Hatch, Ninth Cavalry
Sept. 27, 1887–Oct. 2, 1887	*Maj. Andrew S. Burt, Eighth Infantry*
Oct. 27–31, 1887	*Major Burt*
Nov. 12–23, 1887	*Major Burt*
Dec. 11, 1887–Feb. 12, 1888	Major Burt
Feb. 12, 1888–Mar. 15, 1889	Colonel Hatch (died at Fort Robinson, Apr. 11, 1889)
Aug. 29–Sept. 30, 1888	*Capt. Clarence M. Bailey, Eighth Infantry*
Mar. 16, 1889–May 8, 1889	Lieutenant Colonel Brisbin
May 8, 1889–Dec. 2, 1889	Col. Joseph G. Tilford, Ninth Cavalry
July 20, 1889–Aug. 20, 1889	*Lieutenant Colonel Brisbin (promoted to colonel, First Cavalry)*
Aug. 21, 1889–Sept. 19, 1889	*1st Lt. Edgar Hubert, Eighth Infantry*
Dec. 2, 1889–Apr. 19, 1890	Maj. James F. Randlett, Ninth Cavalry
Apr. 19, 1890–Jan. 18, 1891	Colonel Tilford
Aug. 25, 1890–Sept. 1, 1890	*Captain Bailey*
Jan. 18, 1891–Mar. 28, 1891	Capt. William S. Worth, Eighth Infantry
Mar. 28, 1891–Apr. 12, 1891	Capt. Augustus W. Corliss, Eighth Infantry
Apr. 12, 1891–May 22, 1891	Maj. Guy V. Henry, Ninth Cavalry
May 22, 1891–June 16, 1891	Captain Corliss
June 16, 1891–Aug. 11, 1891	Lt. Col. Alfred T. Smith, Eighth Infantry

Aug. 11, 1891–Dec. 11, 1891	Col. James Biddle, Ninth Cavalry
Aug. 5–18, 1891	*Capt. James A. Hutton, Eighth Infantry*
Nov. 20, 1891–Dec. 1, 1891	*Captain Corliss*
Dec. 12, 1891–June 7, 1892	Lt. Col. George B. Sanford, Ninth Cavalry
Apr. 11–16, 1892	*Maj. Charles S. Ilsley, Ninth Cavalry*
June 7, 1892–Sept. 24, 1892	Captain Corliss
Sept. 27, 1892–Mar. 17, 1893	Colonel Biddle
Mar. 17, 1893–June 6, 1893	Lt. Col. Reuben F. Bernard, Ninth Cavalry
June 6–19, 1893	*Captain Corliss*
June 19, 1893–Oct. 12, 1893	Colonel Biddle
Sept. 24–30, 1893	*Lieutenant Colonel Bernard*
Oct. 12, 1893–Dec. 29, 1893	Lieutenant Colonel Bernard
Oct. 29, 1893–May 14, 1894	Colonel Biddle
May 14, 1894–June 4, 1894	Major Ilsley
June 4, 1894–Dec. 11, 1896	Colonel Biddle (retired Dec. 11, 1896)
Aug. 30, 1894–Sept. 5, 1894	*Lieutenant Colonel Bernard*
Dec. 11, 1896–Jan. 12, 1897	Capt. Eugene D. Dimmock, Ninth Cavalry
Jan. 12, 1897–Oct. 5, 1897	Col. David Perry, Ninth Cavalry
Oct. 5, 1897–Apr. 19, 1898	Lt. Col. John M. Hamilton, Ninth Cavalry
Apr. 19–30, 1898	Capt. Argalus G. Hennisee, Eighth Cavalry
May 1, 1898–July 5, 1898	Major Hennisee, Second Cavalry (promoted May 31, 1898)
July 17, 1898–Sept. 14, 1898	1st Lt. George E. Stockle, Eighth Cavalry
Sept. 14–Oct. 2, 1898	2nd Lt. Albert L. Saxton, Eighth Cavalry
Oct. 2, 1898–Jan. 4, 1899	1st Lt. John D. L. Hartman, First Cavalry
Jan. 4, 1899–Sept. 30, 1899	Lt. Col. Charles D. Viele, First Cavalry
Febr. 16, 1899–Mar. 1, 1899	*Capt. Frank A. Edwards, First Cavalry*
Sept. 30, 1899–Nov. 24, 1899	1st Lt. Milton F. Davis, First Cavalry
Nov. 24, 1899–Mar. 8, 1900	1st Lt. Edmund S. Wright, First Cavalry

Appendix B

Units Stationed at Fort Robinson, April 1874–December 1899,
Compiled from Monthly Post Returns

FS&B signifies "Field, Staff, and Band." F&S signifies "Field and Staff."
Other letters are company or troop letters within the regiments.
Number is total monthly aggregate figure reported.

1874

April	F, Eighth Infantry; B, K, Thirteenth Infantry; F, Fourteenth Infantry; G, Third Cavalry	343
May	F, Eighth Infantry; B, F, K, Thirteenth Infantry; F, Fourteenth Infantry; G, Third Cavalry	379
June	F, Eighth Infantry; B, F, Thirteenth Infantry; F, Fourteenth Infantry; G, Third Cavalry	300
July	A, I, Ninth Infantry; B, F, Thirteenth Infantry; G, Third Cavalry	288
August	A, I, Ninth Infantry; B, F, Thirteenth Infantry; G, Third Cavalry	277
September	A, I, Ninth Infantry; B, F, Thirteenth Infantry; G, Third Cavalry	262
October	A, D, G, I, Ninth Infantry; G, Third Cavalry	271
November	A, D, G, I, Ninth Infantry; G, Third Cavalry	260
December	A, D, G, I, Ninth Infantry; D, Third Cavalry	240

1875

January	A, D, G, I, Ninth Infantry; D, Third Cavalry	240
February	A, D, G, I, Ninth Infantry; D, Third Cavalry	236
March	A, D, G, I, Ninth Infantry; D, Third Cavalry	227
April	A, D, G, I, Ninth Infantry; D, Third Cavalry	247
May	A, D, G, I, Ninth Infantry; K, Second Cavalry; D, Third Cavalry	355
June	A, D, G, I, Ninth Infantry; K, Second Cavalry; D, Third Cavalry	358
July	A, D, G, I, Ninth Infantry; K, Second Cavalry; D, Third Cavalry	352
August	A, D, G, I, Ninth Infantry; K, Second Cavalry; D, Third Cavalry	347
September	A, D, G, I, Ninth Infantry; K, Second Cavalry; D, Third Cavalry	345
October	A, D, G, I, Ninth Infantry; D, K, Third Cavalry	341
November	A, D, I, Ninth Infantry; K, Third Cavalry	222
December	A, D, I, Ninth Infantry; K, Third Cavalry	215

1876

January	A, D, I, Ninth Infantry; K, Third Cavalry	218
February	A, D, I, K, Ninth Infantry	181

March	A, D, I, K, Ninth Infantry	180
April	A, D, I, K, Ninth Infantry	194
May	A, D, I, K, Ninth Infantry	190
June	A, D, K, Ninth Infantry; K, Third Cavalry	204
July	A, D, K, Ninth Infantry; K, Third Cavalry	218
August	A, D, K, Ninth Infantry; K, Third Cavalry	215
September	A, D, K, Ninth Infantry; K, Third Cavalry	247
October	D, G, Fourth Infantry; B, C, F, I, Fourteenth Infantry; A, D, G, K, Ninth Infantry; B, C, K, L, Third Cavalry	806
November	D, G, Fourth Infantry; B, C, F, I, Fourteenth Infantry; A, D, G, K, Ninth Infantry; B, C, K, L, Third Cavalry	876
December	D, G, Fourth Infantry; B, C, F, Fourteenth Infantry; A, D, G, K, Ninth Infantry; B, C, K, L, Third Cavalry	819

1877

January	G, Ninth Infantry; B, C, F, Fourteenth Infantry; B, C, L, Third Cavalry; B, D, E, F, I, M, Fourth Cavalry	1,109
February	G, Ninth Infantry; B, C, F, Fourteenth Infantry; B, C, L, Third Cavalry; B, D, E, F, I, M, Fourth Cavalry	1,096
March	G, Ninth Infantry; B, C, F, Fourteenth Infantry; B, C, L, Third Cavalry; B, D, E, F, I, M, Fourth Cavalry	1,059
April	G, Ninth Infantry; B, C, F, Fourteenth Infantry; B, C, L, Third Cavalry; B, D, E, F, I, M, Fourth Cavalry	1,000
May	G, Ninth Infantry; B, C, F, Fourteenth Infantry; B, C, H, L, Third Cavalry	529
June	G, Ninth Infantry; B, F, Fourteenth Infantry; B, C, H, L, Third Cavalry	408
July	G, Ninth Infantry; B, F, Fourteenth Infantry; B, C, H, L, Third Cavalry	400
August	G, Ninth Infantry; B, F, Fourteenth Infantry; B, C, H, L, Third Cavalry	391
September	G, Ninth Infantry; B, F, Fourteenth Infantry; B, C, D, E, F, G, H, L, Third Cavalry	601
October	G, Ninth Infantry; B, F, Fourteenth Infantry; B, C, F, G, Third Cavalry	328
November	C, Third Cavalry	71
December	C, Third Cavalry	70

1878

January	C, Third Cavalry	73

February	C, Third Cavalry	72
March	C, Third Cavalry	71
April	C, Third Cavalry	75
May	C, Third Cavalry	72
June	C, Third Cavalry	71
July	C, Third Cavalry	69
August	C, Third Cavalry	68
September	C, Third Cavalry	69
October	C, Third Cavalry	69
November	C, Third Cavalry	69
December	C, H, Third Cavalry	135
1879		
January	C, H, Third Cavalry	131
February	C, H, Third Cavalry	128
March	C, H, Third Cavalry	124
April	C, H, Third Cavalry	122
May	C, H, Third Cavalry	117
June	A, C, H, I, Third Cavalry	228
July	A, C, H, I, Third Cavalry	222
August	A, C, H, I, Third Cavalry	217
September	A, C, H, I, Third Cavalry	216
October	A, C, H, I, Third Cavalry	214
November	A, C, H, I, Third Cavalry	214
December	C, Third Cavalry	57
1880		
January	C, Third Cavalry	65
February	C, Third Cavalry	67
March	C, Third Cavalry	65
April	C, Third Cavalry	63
May	H, Fifth Cavalry	69
June	H, L, Fifth Cavalry	123
July	G, Ninth Infantry; H, L, Fifth Cavalry	169
August	G, Ninth Infantry; H, L, Fifth Cavalry	163

September	G, Ninth Infantry; H, L, Fifth Cavalry	155
October	G, Ninth Infantry; H, L, Fifth Cavalry	155
November	G, Ninth Infantry; H, L, Fifth Cavalry	155
December	G, Ninth Infantry; H, L, Fifth Cavalry	148
1881		
January	G, Ninth Infantry; H, L, Fifth Cavalry	141
February	G, Ninth Infantry; H, L, Fifth Cavalry	138
March	G, Ninth Infantry; H, L, Fifth Cavalry	137
April	G, Ninth Infantry; H, L, Fifth Cavalry	136
May	E, G, Ninth Infantry; H, L, M, Fifth Cavalry	229
June	G, Ninth Infantry; H, M, Fifth Cavalry	156
July	G, Ninth Infantry; H, M, Fifth Cavalry	154
August	G, Ninth Infantry; H, M, Fifth Cavalry	133
September	G, Ninth Infantry; H, M, Fifth Cavalry	129
October	G, Ninth Infantry; H, M, Fifth Cavalry	124
November	G, Ninth Infantry; H, M, Fifth Cavalry	133
December	G, Ninth Infantry; H, M, Fifth Cavalry	136
1882		
January	G, Ninth Infantry; H, M, Fifth Cavalry	140
February	G, Ninth Infantry; H, M, Fifth Cavalry	149
March	G, Ninth Infantry; H, M, Fifth Cavalry	151
April	G, Ninth Infantry; H, M, Fifth Cavalry	144
May	G, Ninth Infantry; H, M, Fifth Cavalry	134
June	G, Ninth Infantry; H, M, Fifth Cavalry	129
July	G, Ninth Infantry; H, M, Fifth Cavalry	125
August	G, Ninth Infantry; H, M, Fifth Cavalry	140
September	G, Ninth Infantry; H, M, Fifth Cavalry	142
October	C, Fourth Infantry; H, M, Fifth Cavalry	136
November	C, Fourth Infantry; H, M, Fifth Cavalry	138
December	C, Fourth Infantry; H, M, Fifth Cavalry	150
1883		
January	C, Fourth Infantry; H, M, Fifth Cavalry	154
February	C, Fourth Infantry; H, M, Fifth Cavalry	165
March	C, Fourth Infantry; H, M, Fifth Cavalry	148

April	C, Fourth Infantry; H, M, Fifth Cavalry	134
May	C, Fourth Infantry; H, M, Fifth Cavalry	134
June	C, Fourth Infantry; H, M, Fifth Cavalry	144
July	C, Fourth Infantry; F, H, M, Fifth Cavalry	206
August	C, Fourth Infantry; F, H, M, Fifth Cavalry	221
September	C, Fourth Infantry; F, H, M, Fifth Cavalry	214
October	C, Fourth Infantry; F, H, M, Fifth Cavalry	251
November	C, Fourth Infantry; F, H, M, Fifth Cavalry	240
December	C, Fourth Infantry; F, H, M, Fifth Cavalry	245

1884

January	C, Fourth Infantry; F, H, M, Fifth Cavalry	246
February	C, Fourth Infantry; F, H, M, Fifth Cavalry	250
March	C, Fourth Infantry; F, H, M, Fifth Cavalry	246
April	C, Fourth Infantry; F, H, M, Fifth Cavalry	241
May	C, Fourth Infantry; F, H, M, Fifth Cavalry	232
June	C, Fourth Infantry; F, H, M, Fifth Cavalry	231
July	C, Fourth Infantry; F, H, M, Fifth Cavalry	222
August	C, Fourth Infantry; F, H, M, Fifth Cavalry	226
September	C, Fourth Infantry; F, H, M, Fifth Cavalry	225
October	C, Fourth Infantry; F, H, M, Fifth Cavalry	222
November	C, Fourth Infantry; F, H, M, Fifth Cavalry	222
December	C, Fourth Infantry; F, H, M, Fifth Cavalry	217

1885

January	C, Fourth Infantry; F, H, M, Fifth Cavalry	216
February	C, Fourth Infantry; F, H, M, Fifth Cavalry	218
March	C, Fourth Infantry; F, H, M, Fifth Cavalry	215
April	C, Fourth Infantry; F, H, M, Fifth Cavalry	212
May	C, Fourth Infantry	42
June	C, Fourth Infantry	54
July	C, Fourth Infantry	53
August	C, Fourth Infantry; C, F, K, Ninth Cavalry	222
September	C, Fourth Infantry; C, F, K, Ninth Cavalry	221
October	C, Fourth Infantry; C, F, K, Ninth Cavalry	224

November	C, Fourth Infantry; C, F, K, Ninth Cavalry	221
December	C, Fourth Infantry; C, F, K, Ninth Cavalry	220

1886

January	C, Fourth Infantry; C, F, K, Ninth Cavalry	214
February	C, Fourth Infantry; C, F, K, Ninth Cavalry	209
March	C, Fourth Infantry; C, F, K, Ninth Cavalry	211
April	C, Fourth Infantry; C, F, K, Ninth Cavalry	211
May	C, Fourth Infantry; C, F, K, Ninth Cavalry	205
June	C, Fourth Infantry; C, F, K, Ninth Cavalry	202
July	I, Second Infantry; C, F, K, Ninth Cavalry	191
August	I, Second Infantry; C, F, K, Ninth Cavalry	186
September	I, Second Infantry; C, F, K, Ninth Cavalry	182
October	I, Second Infantry; C, F, K, Ninth Cavalry	185
November	C, Eighth Infantry; C, F, K, Ninth Cavalry	184
December	C, I, Eighth Infantry; C, F, K, Ninth Cavalry	248

1887

January	C, I, Eighth Infantry; C, F, K, Ninth Cavalry	247
February	C, I, Eighth Infantry; C, F, K, Ninth Cavalry	258
March	C, I, Eighth Infantry; C, F, K, Ninth Cavalry	284
April	C, I, Eighth Infantry; C, F, K, Ninth Cavalry	279
May	C, I, Eighth Infantry; C, F, K, FS&B, Ninth Cavalry	299
June	C, I, Eighth Infantry; C, F, K, FS&B, Ninth Cavalry	324
July	C, D, I, K, Eighth Infantry; C, F, K, FS&B, Ninth Cavalry	399
August	C, D, I, K, Eighth Infantry; C, F, K, FS&B, Ninth Cavalry	416
September	C, D, I, K, Eighth Infantry; C, F, K, FS&B, Ninth Cavalry	409
October	C, D, I, K, Eighth Infantry; C, F, I, K, FS&B, Ninth Cavalry	463
November	C, D, I, K, Eighth Infantry; C, F, I, K, FS&B, Ninth Cavalry	455
December	C, D, I, K, Eighth Infantry; C, F, I, K, FS&B, Ninth Cavalry	465

1888

January	C, D, I, K, Eighth Infantry; C, F, I, K, FS&B, Ninth Cavalry	467
February	C, D, I, K, Eighth Infantry; C, F, I, K, FS&B, Ninth Cavalry	464
March	C, D, I, K, Eighth Infantry; C, F, I, K, FS&B, Ninth Cavalry	473
April	C, D, I, K, Eighth Infantry; C, F, I, K, FS&B, Ninth Cavalry	473
May	C, D, I, K, Eighth Infantry; C, F, I, K, FS&B, Ninth Cavalry	458

June	C, D, I, K, Eighth Infantry; F, I, K, FS&B, Ninth Cavalry	388
July	C, D, I, K, Eighth Infantry; F, I, K, FS&B, Ninth Cavalry	386
August	C, D, I, K, Eighth Infantry; B, F, I, K, FS&B, Ninth Cavalry	457
September	C, D, I, K, Eighth Infantry; B, F, I, K, FS&B, Ninth Cavalry	454
October	C, D, I, K, Eighth Infantry; B, F, I, K, FS&B, Ninth Cavalry	458
November	C, D, I, K, Eighth Infantry; B, F, I, K, FS&B, Ninth Cavalry	471
December	C, D, I, K, Eighth Infantry; B, F, I, K, FS&B, Ninth Cavalry	480
1889		
January	C, D, I, K, Eighth Infantry; B, F, I, K, FS&B, Ninth Cavalry	501
February	C, D, I, K, Eighth Infantry; B, F, I, K, FS&B, Ninth Cavalry	488
March	C, D, I, K, Eighth Infantry; B, F, I, K, FS&B, Ninth Cavalry	481
April	C, D, I, K, Eighth Infantry; B, F, I, K, FS&B, Ninth Cavalry	492
May	C, D, I, K, Eighth Infantry; B, F, I, K, FS&B, Ninth Cavalry	484
June	C, D, I, K, Eighth Infantry; B, F, I, K, FS&B, Ninth Cavalry	474
July	C, D, I, K, Eighth Infantry; B, F, I, K, FS&B, Ninth Cavalry	473
August	C, D, I, K, Eighth Infantry; B, F, I, K, FS&B, Ninth Cavalry	476
September	C, D, I, K, Eighth Infantry; B, F, I, K, FS&B, Ninth Cavalry	473
October	C, D, I, K, Eighth Infantry; B, F, I, K, FS&B, Ninth Cavalry	473
November	C, D, I, K, Eighth Infantry; B, F, I, K, FS&B, Ninth Cavalry	467
December	C, D, I, K, Eighth Infantry; B, F, I, K, FS&B, Ninth Cavalry	478
1890		
January	C, D, I, K, Eighth Infantry; B, F, I, K, FS&B, Ninth Cavalry	480
February	C, D, I, K, Eighth Infantry; B, F, I, K, FS&B, Ninth Cavalry	481
March	C, D, I, K, Eighth Infantry; B, F, I, K, FS&B, Ninth Cavalry	489
April	C, D, I, K, Eighth Infantry; B, F, I, K, FS&B, Ninth Cavalry	487
May	C, D, I, K, Eighth Infantry; B, F, I, K, FS&B, Ninth Cavalry	484
June	C, D, I, K, Eighth Infantry; B, F, I, K, FS&B, Ninth Cavalry	476
July	C, D, I, K, Eighth Infantry; B, F, I, K, FS&B, Ninth Cavalry	471
August	C, D, I, K, Eighth Infantry; B, F, I, K, FS&B, Ninth Cavalry	462
September	C, D, Eighth Infantry; F, I, K, FS&B, Ninth Cavalry	393
October	C, D, Eighth Infantry; F, I, K, FS&B, Ninth Cavalry	379
November	C, D, Eighth Infantry; F, I, K, FS&B, Ninth Cavalry	371
December	C, D, Eighth Infantry; F, I, K, FS&B, Ninth Cavalry	389

1891

January	C, D, Eighth Infantry; A, D, F, G, I, K, FS&B, Ninth Cavalry	614
February	C, D, Eighth Infantry; A, D, F, G, I, K, FS&B, Ninth Cavalry	603
March	C, D, Eighth Infantry; A, D, F, G, I, K, FS&B, Ninth Cavalry	593
April	C, D, Eighth Infantry; A, D, F, G, I, K, FS&B, Ninth Cavalry	589
May	C, D, Eighth Infantry; A, D, E, F, G, I, FS&B, Ninth Cavalry	506
June	C, D, Eighth Infantry; A, D, E, F, G, I, FS&B, Ninth Cavalry	555
July	C, D, Eighth Infantry; A, D, E, F, G, I, FS&B, Ninth Cavalry	557
August	C, D, Eighth Infantry; A, D, E, F, G, I, FS&B, Ninth Cavalry	547
September	C, D, Eighth Infantry; A, D, E, F, G, I, FS&B, Ninth Cavalry	546
October	C, D, Eighth Infantry; A, D, E, F, G, I, FS&B, Ninth Cavalry	541
November	C, D, Eighth Infantry; A, D, E, F, G, I, FS&B, Ninth Cavalry	530
December	C, D, Eighth Infantry; A, D, E, F, G, I, FS&B, Ninth Cavalry	526

1892

January	C, D, Eighth Infantry; A, D, E, F, G, I, FS&B, Ninth Cavalry	528
February	C, D, Eighth Infantry; A, D, E, F, G, I, FS&B, Ninth Cavalry	530
March	C, D, Eighth Infantry; A, D, E, F, G, I, FS&B, Ninth Cavalry	509
April	C, D, Eighth Infantry; A, D, E, F, G, I, FS&B, Ninth Cavalry	499
May	C, D, Eighth Infantry; A, D, E, F, G, I, FS&B, Ninth Cavalry	484
June	C, D, Eighth Infantry; A, D, E, F, G, I, FS&B, Ninth Cavalry	479
July	C, D, Eighth Infantry; A, D, E, F, G, I, FS&B, Ninth Cavalry	500
August	C, D, Eighth Infantry; A, D, E, F, G, I, FS&B, Ninth Cavalry	516
September	C, D, Eighth Infantry; A, D, E, F, G, I, FS&B, Ninth Cavalry	515
October	C, D, Eighth Infantry; A, D, E, F, G, I, FS&B, Ninth Cavalry	521
November	C, D, Eighth Infantry; A, D, E, F, G, I, FS&B, Ninth Cavalry	518
December	C, D, Eighth Infantry; A, D, E, F, G, I, FS&B, Ninth Cavalry	538

1893

January	C, D, Eighth Infantry; A, D, E, F, G, I, FS&B, Ninth Cavalry	549
February	C, D, Eighth Infantry; A, D, E, F, G, I, FS&B, Ninth Cavalry	583
March	C, D, Eighth Infantry; A, D, E, F, G, I, FS&B, Ninth Cavalry	575
April	C, D, Eighth Infantry; A, D, E, F, G, I, FS&B, Ninth Cavalry	568
May	C, D, Eighth Infantry; A, D, E, F, G, I, FS&B, Ninth Cavalry	558
June	C, D, Eighth Infantry; A, D, E, F, G, I, FS&B, Ninth Cavalry	565
July	C, D, Eighth Infantry; A, D, E, F, G, I, FS&B, Ninth Cavalry	563

August	C, D, Eighth Infantry; A, D, E, F, G, I, FS&B, Ninth Cavalry	559
September	C, D, Eighth Infantry; A, D, E, F, G, I, FS&B, Ninth Cavalry	552
October	C, D, Eighth Infantry; A, D, E, F, G, I, FS&B, Ninth Cavalry	546
November	C, D, Eighth Infantry; A, D, E, F, G, I, FS&B, Ninth Cavalry	533
December	C, D, Eighth Infantry; A, D, E, F, G, I, FS&B, Ninth Cavalry	527

1894

January	C, D, Eighth Infantry; A, D, E, F, G, I, FS&B, Ninth Cavalry	528
February	C, D, Eighth Infantry; A, D, E, F, G, I, FS&B, Ninth Cavalry	541
March	C, D, Eighth Infantry; A, D, E, F, G, I, FS&B, Ninth Cavalry	549
April	C, D, Eighth Infantry; A, D, E, F, G, I, FS&B, Ninth Cavalry	544
May	C, D, Eighth Infantry; A, D, E, G, I, FS&B, Ninth Cavalry	471
June	C, D, Eighth Infantry; A, D, E, G, H, I, FS&B, Ninth Cavalry	533
July	C, D, Eighth Infantry; A, D, E, G, H, I, FS&B, Ninth Cavalry	539
August	C, D, Eighth Infantry; A, D, E, G, H, I, FS&B, Ninth Cavalry	526
September	C, D, Eighth Infantry; A, D, E, G, H, I, FS&B, Ninth Cavalry	523
October	A, D, E, G, H, I, K, FS&B, Ninth Cavalry	463
November	A, C, D, E, G, H, I, K, FS&B, Ninth Cavalry	515
December	A, C, D, E, G, H, I, K, FS&B, Ninth Cavalry	533

1895

January	A, C, D, E, G, H, I, K, FS&B, Ninth Cavalry	543
February	A, C, D, E, G, H, I, K, FS&B, Ninth Cavalry	539
March	A, C, D, E, G, H, I, K, FS&B, Ninth Cavalry	537
April	A, C, D, E, G, H, I, K, FS&B, Ninth Cavalry	530
May	A, C, D, E, G, H, I, K, FS&B, Ninth Cavalry	520
June	A, C, D, E, G, H, I, K, FS&B, Ninth Cavalry	506
July	A, C, D, E, G, H, I, K, FS&B, Ninth Cavalry	507
August	A, C, D, E, G, H, I, K, FS&B, Ninth Cavalry	516
September	A, C, E, G, H, K, FS&B, Ninth Cavalry	398
October	A, C, E, G, H, K, FS&B, Ninth Cavalry	414
November	A, C, E, G, H, K, FS&B, Ninth Cavalry	415
December	A, C, E, G, H, K, FS&B, Ninth Cavalry	411

1896

January	A, C, E, G, H, K, FS&B, Ninth Cavalry	414
February	A, C, E, G, H, K, FS&B, Ninth Cavalry	413

March	A, C, E, G, H, K, FS&B, Ninth Cavalry	411
April	A, C, E, G, H, K, FS&B, Ninth Cavalry	418
May	A, C, E, G, H, K, FS&B, Ninth Cavalry	406
June	A, C, E, G, H, K, FS&B, Ninth Cavalry	400
July	A, C, E, G, H, K, FS&B, Ninth Cavalry	403
August	A, C, E, G, H, K, FS&B, Ninth Cavalry	418
September	A, C, E, G, H, K, FS&B, Ninth Cavalry	423
October	A, C, E, G, H, K, FS&B, Ninth Cavalry	420
November	A, C, E, G, H, K, FS&B, Ninth Cavalry	418
December	A, C, E, G, H, K, FS&B, Ninth Cavalry	416
1897		
January	A, C, E, G, H, K, FS&B, Ninth Cavalry	413
February	A, C, E, G, H, K, FS&B, Ninth Cavalry	410
March	A, C, E, G, H, K, FS&B, Ninth Cavalry	407
April	A, C, E, G, H, K, FS&B, Ninth Cavalry	407
May	A, C, E, G, H, K, FS&B, Ninth Cavalry	408
June	A, C, E, G, H, K, FS&B, Ninth Cavalry	410
July	A, C, E, G, H, K, FS&B, Ninth Cavalry	423
August	D, I, Sixth Cavalry; A, C, E, G, H, K, FS&B, Ninth Cavalry	523
September	D, I, Sixth Cavalry; A, C, E, G, H, K, FS&B, Ninth Cavalry	526
October	D, I, Sixth Cavalry; A, C, E, G, H, K, FS&B, Ninth Cavalry	521
November	D, I, Sixth Cavalry; A, C, E, G, H, K, FS&B, Ninth Cavalry	526
December	D, I, Sixth Cavalry; A, C, E, G, H, K, FS&B, Ninth Cavalry	518
1898		
January	D, I, Sixth Cavalry; A, C, E, G, H, K, FS&B, Ninth Cavalry	522
February	D, I, Sixth Cavalry; A, C, E, G, H, K, FS&B, Ninth Cavalry	526
March	D, I, Sixth Cavalry; A, C, E, G, H, K, FS&B, Ninth Cavalry	524
April	I, Eighth Cavalry	91
May	I, Eighth Cavalry	128
June	I, Eighth Cavalry	123
July	I, Eighth Cavalry	124
August	I, Eighth Cavalry	125
September	I, Eighth Cavalry	133

October	C, First Cavalry	127
November	C, First Cavalry	110
December	C, First Cavalry	116
1899		
January	A, B, C, L, FS&B, First Cavalry	444
February	A, B, C, L, FS&B, First Cavalry	257
March	A, B, C, L, FS&B, First Cavalry	338
April	A, B, C, L, FS&B, First Cavalry	423
May	A, B, C, L, First Cavalry	404
June	A, C, L, First Cavalry	320
July	A, C, L, First Cavalry	310
August	A, C, L, First Cavalry	303
September	A, C, L, First Cavalry	289
October	A, C, L, First Cavalry	301
November	A, C, L, First Cavalry	298
December	A, C, L, First Cavalry	300

Notes

Abbreviations

AAG = assistant adjutant general

AG = adjutant general

ANJ = Army and Navy Journal

DBH = District of the Black Hills

DM = Division of the Missouri

DP = Department of the Platte

FR = Fort Robinson

FRM = Fort Robinson Museum

GO = General Order

GPO = Government Printing Office

LR = Letters Received

MH = Medical History

NA = National Archives

NSHS = Nebraska State Historical Society

PO = Post Order

QM = Office of the Chief Quartermaster

RCA = Red Cloud Agency

RG = Record Group

SDSE = Selected Documents Sioux Expedition

SO = Special Order

1. The Soldiers Come

1. The full text of the 1868 treaty can be found in George P. Sanger, ed., *Statues at Large, Treaties and Proclamations of the United States of America from December 1867 to March 1869* 15 (Boston: Little, Brown & Co., 1869): 635–47.

2. Agencies for Sioux tribes already located on the Missouri River were Standing Rock Agency for the Hunkpapas, Cheyenne River for the Minneconjous and Sans Arcs, White River for the Lower Brulés, and Crow Creek for the Yanktonnais and Two Kettles.

3. The best single source on agency location and the complexities of dealing with the Oglalas remains James C. Olson, *Red Cloud and the Sioux Problem* (Lincoln: University of Nebraska Press, 1965).

4. Robert M. Utley, *Frontier Regulars: The United States Army and the Indian, 1866–1890* (New York: Macmillan Publishing Co., 1973), 191; Francis B. Heitman, *Historical Register and Dictionary of the United States Army* (Washington: Government Printing Office [GPO], 1903), 184.

5. Olson, *Red Cloud*, 104. For more on the peace policy, see Robert M. Utley, *The Indian Frontier of the American West, 1846–1890* (Albuquerque: University of New Mexico Press, 1984), 129–34.

6. George Hyde's classic studies of Oglala and Brulé history adequately portray the difficulties of the agents. See Hyde, *Red Cloud's Folk: A History of the Oglala Sioux Indians* (Norman: University of Oklahoma Press, 1937), and *Spotted Tail's Folk: A History of the Brulé Sioux* (Norman: University of Oklahoma Press, 1961). See also Robert H. Keller, Jr., "Episcopal Reformers and Affairs at Red Cloud Agency, 1870–1876," *Nebraska History* 68 (Fall 1987): 116–26. The most current biography of Chief Red Cloud is Robert W. Larson's *Red Cloud: Warrior–Statesman of the Lakota Sioux* (Norman: University of Oklahoma Press, 1997).

7. Olson, *Red Cloud*, 138.

8. Hyde, *Red Cloud's Folk*, 177.

9. Olson, *Red Cloud*, 158.

10. A. T. Andreas, *History of the State of Nebraska* (Chicago: The Western Historical Company, 1882), 428; H. Dyer to C. Delano, July 7, 1873, Agent Files, Record Group (RG) 48, Office of the Secretary of Interior, National Archives, Washington, D.C.

11. Annual report of Saville, Aug. 31, 1874, *Report of Secretary of the Interior 1874* 1 (Washington: GPO, 1875): 251.

12. Annual report of Daniels, Aug. 17, 1873, *Report of Secretary of Interior 1873* 1 (Washington: GPO, 1874): 243–44; Hyde, *Red Cloud's Folk*, 201.

13. Saville report, 1874, 251.

14. For more on the census difficulties, see Thomas R. Buecker, "The Red Cloud Agency Ledger Book," manuscript at the Fort Robinson Museum (FRM), and Thomas R. Buecker and R. Eli Paul, eds., *The Crazy Horse Surrender Ledger* (Lincoln: Nebraska State Historical Society, 1994).

15. Saville report, 1874, 251.

16. Saville to E. P. Smith, Dec. 11 and 29, 1873, Letters Received (LR), Red Cloud Agency (RCA), RG 75, Records of the Bureau of Indian Affairs, NA.

17. Delano to Smith, Mar. 7, 1874, LR Department of the Platte (DP), RG 393, Records of the United States Army Continental Commands, NA.

18. Olson, *Red Cloud*, 163–64.

19. The witness was William Rowland, the Cheyenne interpreter at the agency. Hyde, *Red Cloud's Folk*, 211–12.

20. Edwin A. Howard to Col. Smith, Febr. 8, 1874, LR DP; *Omaha Weekly Bee*, Febr. 18, 1874.

21. *Sioux City Journal*, Mar. 6, 1874; *Omaha Weekly Bee*, Febr. 25, 1874.

22. Saville had hired his brother-in-law, Amos Appleton, to build the agency. Appleton's two sons, Oliver and Frank, also worked at the agency.

23. The sequence of the Appleton shooting comes from several sources, including the *Sioux City Journal*, Febr. 15, 1874; William H. Carter, *The History of Fort Robinson* (Crawford: Northwest Nebraska News, 1941); Eli S. Ricker interview with William Garnett, Tablet 1, MS 8, Eli S. Ricker Collection, Nebraska State Historical Society Archives (NSHS).

24. *Omaha Weekly Bee*, Febr. 25, 1874. Saville claimed the assailant, Kicking Bear, was killed soon afterward at Spotted Tail; however, Kicking Bear was active in the Ghost Dance troubles in 1890.

25. *Omaha Daily Bee*, Febr. 18, 1874.

26. Saville to E. P. Smith, Febr. 26, 1874, printed in the *Omaha Weekly Bee*, Mar. 4, 1874; Telegram, Saville to Smith, Febr. 9, 1874, LR DP.

27. Col. Smith to asst. adj. gen. (AAG), DP, Febr. 12, 1874, LR DP; Carter, *History of Fort Robinson*, 5–6; B. William Henry, "Fort Robinson Namesake Killed by Indians," *Casper Star–Tribune*, Mar. 31, 1974.

28. General Order (GO) 2, Fort Laramie, Febr. 19, 1874, *Army and Navy Journal* (*ANJ*), Mar. 7, 1874. Mary Robinson's father had also been killed by Indians just after the Civil War in Texas. *ANJ*, Febr. 21, 1874.

29. Henry, "Fort Robinson Namesake."

30. Thomas R. Buecker, "Red Cloud Agency Traders, 1873–1877," *The Museum of the Fur Trade Quarterly* 30 (Fall 1994): 10.

31. J. W. Dear to Oliver Unthank, Febr. 17, 1874, J. W. Dear Correspondence, Fort Laramie National Historic Site, Fort Laramie, Wyo.

32. Oliver Unthank to Addison E. Sheldon, Jan. 7, 1926, Correspondence of the Superintendent, NSHS Archives.

33. Roger T. Grange, "Fort Robinson, Outpost on the Plains," *Nebraska History* 30 (Sept. 1958): 196.

34. Saville to Col. Smith, Febr. 20, 1874; Lt. Col. James W. Forsyth to AAG, Military Division of the Missouri (DM), Mar. 27, 1874, LR, Office of the Adjutant General (AG), 1871–1880, RG 94, Records of the Office of the Adjutant General, NA.

35. *Omaha Weekly Bee*, Febr. 18, 1874.

36. *Yankton Press and Dakotaian*, Febr. 19, 1874.

37. *ANJ*, Febr. 21, 1874.

38. Sheridan to Ord, Febr. 18, 1874, LR DP.

39. "The Views of a Veteran Trapper," *Omaha Daily Bee*, Febr. 25, 1874.

40. Paul A. Hutton, *Phil Sheridan and His Army* (Lincoln: University of Nebraska Press, 1985), 289.

41. *Omaha Weekly Bee*, Febr. 18, 1874.

42. Delano to Belknap, Febr. 26, 1874, LR DP.

43. Smith to AAG, Febr. 12, 1874, LR DP.

44. Ord to Smith, Febr. 19, 1874, Selected Documents Sioux Expedition (SDSE), RG 393.

45. Post Returns, Fort D. A. Russell, Febr. 1874, RG 94.

46. James Fornance letter, Mar. 16, 1874, James Fornance Collection, United States Military Academy Library, West Point, N.Y.

47. Saville to Col. Smith, Febr. 20, 1874; *Sioux City Journal,* Mar. 6, 1874.

48. Special Order (SO) 2, Sioux Expedition, Febr. 28, 1874, SDSE.

49. Col. Smith to Baker, Mar. 1, 1874, SDSE; Ord to Col. Smith, Febr. 19, 1874, SDSE.

50. Olson, *Red Cloud*, 167.

51. Ibid.

52. *Omaha Herald*, Mar. 5, 1874; Smith to Ord, Apr. 6, 1874, SDSE.

53. Fornance letter, Mar. 16, 1874; Col. Smith to AAG, Mar. 12, 1874, LR DP; *Crawford Clipper*, Sept. 5, 1890.

54. *Crawford Clipper*, Sept. 5, 1890; Carter, *History of Fort Robinson*, 7.

55. Forsyth to AAG, Mar. 27, 1874, LR AG.

56. *Cheyenne Leader*, Mar. 9, 1874.

57. Hutton, *Phil Sheridan*, 289.

58. Fornance letter, May 2, 1874.

59. Col. Smith to Van Horn, Mar. 8, 1874, SDSE.

60. Col. Smith to Saville, Mar. 8, 1874, SDSE.

61. Col. Smith to AAG, Mar. 12, 1874, LR DP.

62. *Crawford Clipper*, Sept. 5, 1890. The trenches and earthworks are still evident today at the site, some ten miles northeast of Chadron, Nebraska. For more on the establishment of the Spotted Tail camp, see Thomas R. Buecker, "History of Camp Sheridan, Nebraska," *Periodical: Journal of America's Military Past* 22 (1995): 55-73.

63. Fornance letter, May 2, 1874; Saville to commissioner of Indian affairs, Mar. 5, 1874; *ANJ*, Mar. 14, 1874; Col. Smith to Ord, Apr. 6, 1874, LR DP.

64. Saville report, 1874, 251.

65. Ord to Col. Smith, June 20, 1874, SDSE.

66. Ruggles to Col. Smith, Aug. 29, 1874, SDSE.

67. Col. Smith to Lazelle, May 2, 1874, SDSE.

68. Hyde, *Red Cloud's Folk*, 224; Hyde, *Spotted Tail's Folk*, 200.

2. The Establishment of Camp Robinson

1. Olson, *Red Cloud*, 167; Carter, *History of Fort Robinson*, 7–8.

2. Hyde, *Red Cloud's Folk*, 215.

3. Smith to AAG, Aug. 12, 1874, LR DP.

4. SO 43, Mar. 24, 1874, DP; *ANJ*, Apr. 4, 1874.

5. Post Orders, 1874–1880, Fort Robinson (PO FR), RG 98, Records of United States Army Commands, NA.

6. In 1867 Fort Fetterman, Wyoming, was named in honor of Capt. William Fetterman, who was killed with his entire command on December 21, 1866, near Fort Phil Kearny. After the Battle of Little Bighorn, Forts Custer, Keogh, and Yates were all named for officers who died in that engagement. Robert Frazer, *Forts of the West* (Norman: University of Oklahoma Press, 1980), 79, 82, 116, 181.

7. Heitman, *Historical Register*, 900.

8. Robert A. Murray, *Military Posts in the Powder River Country of Wyoming, 1865–1894* (Lincoln: University of Nebraska Press, 1968), 101.

9. Heitman, *Historical Register*, 652. See also Kenneth Ray Young, *The General's General: The Life and Times of Arthur MacArthur* (Boulder: Westview Press, 1994).

10. Post Returns, Camp Robinson, Apr.–July, 1874, RG 94, NA.

11. SO 32, July 21, 1874, SDSE.

12. Carter, *History of Fort Robinson*, 7–8.

13. Ibid., 8; Forsyth to AAG, Mar. 27, 1874, LR AG.

14. Ray to chief quartermaster, May 30, 1874, LR, Office of the Chief Quartermaster (QM), DP.

15. Smith to AAG, Aug. 12, 1874, LR DP.

16. Fornance letter, May 2, 1874.

17. Sheridan to Sherman, Mar. 31, 1874, LR DP.

18. Ibid.

19. Grange, "Fort Robinson Outpost," 201; Ricker extracts from "Record of Medical History of Post Medical Department," Tablet 31, Ricker Collection.

20. Carter, *History of Fort Robinson*, 9; GO 13, July 16, 1874; GO 14, July 18, 1874, PO FR.

21. *Omaha Daily Herald*, June 17, 1874.

22. GO 13, July 16, 1874 PO FR.

23. GO 37, Dec. 6, 1874 PO FR.

24. AAG to Smith, May 15, 1874, SDSE.

25. Ray to Perry, Apr. 27, 1874, LR QM DP; Perry to AAG, June 16, 1874, LR DP; Auman to Perry, July 27, 1874, LR QM DP.

26. Robert Taft, *Artists and Illustrators of the Old West, 1850–1900* (New York: Charles Scribner's Sons, 1953), 110–11.

27. Carter, *History of Fort Robinson*, 10; Taft, *Artists and Illustrators*, 110.

28. Smith to AAG, June 22, 1874, LR DP; Carter, *History of Fort Robinson*, 8.

29. Carter, *History of Fort Robinson*, 10.

30. *Cheyenne Daily News*, Nov. 28, 30, 1874.

31. John Hunton made the claim about Kenssler leading the February raid. "Early Day Happenings in the Vicinity of Fort Laramie," *Fort Laramie Scout*, July 7, 1927.

32. Copy of letter forwarded to Department of the Platte headquarters, LR DP.

33. Ord to Smith, June 20, 1874, SDSE.

34. *Rocky Mountain News* (Denver), June 26, 1874.

35. Heitman, *Historical Register*, 584.

36. Endorsement to letter of Sept. 5, 1874, LR QM DP.

37. Perry to AAG, July 7, 1874, LR DP.

38. Ibid.

39. Endorsement by Sheridan to building proposals, July 14, 1874, LR QM DP.

40. Meigs found the act appropriating the $30,000 for construction on page 23 of the Sundry Civil Appropriations Act, approved July 23, 1874. Meigs to sec. of war, July 23, 1874, LR QM DP. His comments referring to cutting wood are found in his endorsement on the proposal, dated July 24.

41. Perry to AAG, July 7, 1874, LR DP.

42. Auman to Perry, July 16, 1874, LR QM DP; Perry endorsement on same, dated Aug. 7, 1874.

43. SO 34, Aug. 7, 1874, SDSE; Smith to AAG, Aug. 12, 1874, LR DP.

44. GO 11, July 24, 1874, PO FR.

45. Post commander, Camp Robinson, to post adjutant, Fort Laramie, Aug. 8, 1874, LR DP; Ricker, "Medical History," 11–12.

46. John S. Billings, *A Report on the Hygiene of the United States Army with Descriptions of Military Posts* (Washington: GPO, 1875. Reprint. New York: Sol Lewis, 1974), 366–67.

47. Ricker, "Medical History," 12–13.

48. Post commander to post adjutant, Fort Laramie, Aug. 8, 1874, LR DP; Lee to Perry, Apr. 21, 1875, LR QM DP.

49. Smith to AAG, Aug. 12, 1874, LR DP.

50. Perry to AAG, Aug. 8, 1874, LR DP.

51. Lee to Perry, Sept. 5, 1874, LR QM DP. In the summers of 1987 and 1988, excavation of the cavalry barracks revealed the sill for the original, seventy-five-foot plan and sills for the completed, ninety-foot end.

52. Auman to Perry, Aug. 21, 1874, LR QM DP; Lee to Perry, Oct. 15, 1874, LR QM DP. There is no indication that Lieutenant Lee's request met with success.

53. Lee to Perry, Oct. 15, 1874, LR QM DP.

54. Special Field Order 3, Sept. 10, 1874; SO 7, Oct. 25, 1874, Orders, District of the Black Hills (DBH).

55. Lee to post adjutant, Camp Robinson, Sept. 28, 1874; Perry endorsement of same, dated Oct. 7, 1874, LR QM DP.

56. Lee to Perry, Oct. 15, 1874, LR QM DP.

57. Lt. Col. Cuvier Grover, acting inspector general, to AAG, Oct. 21, 1874, LR DP.

58. Events behind the flagpole incident are compiled from several sources, including: Amos Appleton letter, Oct. 26, 1874, Appleton Family Collection, NSHS; Ricker interview with Garnett; *Report of the Special Commission to Investigate Affairs at the Red Cloud Agency* (Washington: GPO, 1875), 310–12, 317–18, 568–74; Hyde, *Red Cloud's Folk*, 220–23; *Cheyenne Daily News*, Nov. 9, 1874. See also Charles W. Allen, *From Fort Laramie to Wounded Knee: In the West That Was*, ed. Richard E. Jensen (Lincoln: University of Nebraska Press, 1997), 14–25.

59. William Jordan testimony, *Report of the Special Commission*, 311.

60. Emmet Crawford testimony, ibid., 569.

61. Harry H. Anderson, "The War Club of Sitting Bull the Oglala," in *The Nebraska Indian Wars Reader, 1865–1877*, ed. R. Eli Paul (Lincoln: University of Nebraska Press, 1998), 122-23; Appleton letter, Oct. 26, 1874, NSHS.

62. Crawford testimony, *Report of the Special Commission*, 569.

63. Ricker interview with Garnett; Mari Sandoz, *Hostiles and Friendlies: Selected Short Writings of Mari Sandoz* (Lincoln: University of Nebraska Press, 1959), 97–99.

64. *Fourth Annual Report of the Bureau of Ethnology* (Washington: GPO, 1886): 145; "Red Cloud Manuscript," Charles P. Jordan Collection, NSHS; Appleton letter, Oct. 26, 1874, NSHS.

65. Jordan to AAG, Oct. 19, 1874, LR DP.

66. Lee to Perry, Nov. 19, 1874, LR QM DP.

67. Ricker, "Medical History," 16–18.

68. Ibid., 13–14.

69. Ibid., 14–15.

70. Lee to Perry, Nov. 23, 1874, LR QM DP.

71. Jordan to AAG, Dec. 7, 1874, LR DP.

72. Edwin A. Curley, *Guide to the Black Hills* (Mitchell, S.Dak.: Dakota Wesleyan Press, 1973; reprint of 1877 edition), 90–91.

73. Lee to Perry, July 29, 1875, LR QM DP. The sixty-six-foot measurement equals one surveyor's chain length.

74. Lee to Perry, July 29, 1875, LR QM DP; Acting inspector general to AAG, Oct. 21, 1874, LR DP.

75. *Omaha Weekly Bee*, May 5, 1875.

76. Lee to Perry, July 29, 1875, LR QM DP.

77. Ibid., May 24, 1875, LR QM DP; Acting inspector general to AAG, May 4, 1876, LR DP.

3. Life and Death at Camp Robinson

1. Jordan to AAG, June 2, 1876, LR DP.

2. Heitman, *Historical Register*, 523.

3. Ibid., 336; Shelly B. Hatfield, "The Death of Emmet Crawford," *The Journal of Arizona History* 29 (Summer 1988): 131–48.

4. Grange, "Fort Robinson Outpost," 196.

5. Chandler to Belknap, Nov. 29, 1875, LR DP; Jordan to AAG, Nov. 13, 1875, LR DP.

6. Jordan to AAG, Jan. 5, 1876, LR DP.

7. Hastings to Smith, Jan. 8, 1876, LR DP.

8. Endorsement by judge advocate, Department of the Platte, Febr. 5, 1876, LR DP.

9. Endorsement by Sherman and Sheridan to commissioner of Indian affairs letter, May 1, 1876, LR DP.

10. 1st Lt. Charles A. Johnson to post commander, Mar. 12, 1877, LR DP.

11. Watson Parker, "The Majors and the Miners: The Role of the U.S. Army in the Black Hills Gold Rush," *Journal of the West* 2 (Jan. 1972): 99–113.

12. SO 10, Dec. 23, 1874, DBH. For a thorough discussion of Henry's ill-fated march to the Black Hills, see Thomas R. Buecker, "'The Men Behaved Splendidly': Guy V. Henry's Famous Cavalry Rides," *Nebraska History* 78 (Summer 1997): 54–63.

13. Guy V. Henry, "A Winter March to the Black Hills," *Harper's Weekly* 39 (July 27, 1895): 700.

14. The cabin was near the 1871–73 site of Spotted Tail Agency on the White River, west of present Whitney, Nebraska. John H. Bridgeman was married to an Oglala woman and later worked as an assistant farmer at Red Cloud Agency. Buecker, "The Men Behaved Splendidly," 63.

15. Henry, "A Winter March," 700.

16. Ibid.

17. SO 3, Mar. 26 and SO 13, Dec. 31, 1874, DBH; Frank N. Schubert, *Buffalo Soldiers, Braves, and the Brass: The Story of Fort Robinson, Nebraska* (Shippensburg, Penn.: White Mane Publishing Co., 1993), 8–10.

18. Post Returns, Camp Robinson, May, June, Dec., 1875.

19. Simpson to post adjutant, Camp Robinson, Jan. 1, 1877, LR DP.

20. Post Returns, Camp Robinson, Sept. 1876.

21. GO 26, Oct. 5, 1874, PO FR.

22. Jordan to AAG, Oct. 6, 1876, LR DP.

23. SO 6, Oct. 19, 1874, DBH.

24. Post Returns, Camp Robinson, June, Sept. 1876; GO 38, May 15, 1878, PO FR.

25. Post Returns, Camp Robinson, Mar. 1877; SO 75, Sept. 17, 1878, PO FR.

26. SO 9, Nov. 29, 1874, DBH; SO 10, Dec. 23, 1874, DBH.

27. Don Rickey, Jr., *Forty Miles a Day on Beans and Hay: The Enlisted Soldier Fighting the Indian Wars* (Norman: University of Oklahoma Press, 1963), 137.

28. War Department, *Revised United States Army Regulations of 1861* (Philadelphia: George Childs, 1864), 40.

29. Rickey, *Forty Miles a Day*, 90.

30. Lee to Perry, June 21, 1875, LR QM DP.

31. Thomas Wilhelm, *A Military Dictionary and Gazetteer* (Philadelphia: L. R. Hamersly, 1881), 203.

32. GO 36, June 30, 1875, PO FR.

33. War Dept., *Revised U.S. Army Regulations*, 61–65.

34. GO 71, Nov. 21, 1875, PO FR.

35. "Camp Robinson Guard Record Book, 1877–1878," NSHS; Rickey, *Forty Miles a Day*, 91–92.

36. Inspection report, June 16, 1875, LR DP.

37. GO 75, Oct. 21, 1876, PO FR.

38. GO 59, Aug. 6, 1876; GO 68, Sept. 17, 1876, PO FR.

39. GO 54, Oct. 15, 1875, PO FR.

40. John G. Bourke Diaries, 1876–1877, entry for Febr. 7, 1877, United States Military Academy Library.

41. Assistant inspector general's report, Oct. 21, 1874, LR DP.

42. Wilhelm, *Military Dictionary*, 409.

43. GO 13, Mar. 22, 1875, and GO 1, Jan. 7, 1876, PO FR; War Dept., *Revised U.S. Army Regulations*, 50–52.

44. For information on what the soldier wore and carried at this time, see Douglas C. McChristian, *The U.S. Army in the West, 1870–1880: Uniforms, Weapons, and Equipment* (Norman: University of Oklahoma Press, 1995).

45. GO 49, July 3, 1876; GO 41, Aug. 28, 1875; GO 78, Dec. 18, 1875, PO FR.

46. GO 13, Febr. 21, 1876, PO FR.

47. "Consolidated Report of Target Practice at Camp Robinson for the Month of September 1875," LR DP. Posts prepared and submitted standard report forms to department headquarters each month during target season. For more on this subject, see Douglas C. McChristian, *An Army of Marksmen: The Development of United States Army Marksmanship in the 19th Century* (Fort Collins, Colo.: The Old Army Press, 1981).

48. Wilhelm, *Military Dictionary*, 343.

49. GO 33, Oct. 30, 1874; GO 41, Dec. 30, 1874; GO 21, Dec. 31, 1878, PO FR.

50. Bourke diary, Febr. 7, 1877. He refers to Capt. Daniel W. Burke, Fourteenth Infantry, who commanded Camp Robinson in January and February, 1877.

51. Jordan to Crook, Aug. 27, 1875; Russell to AAG, July 12, 1876, LR DP.

52. Smith to Ray, July 17, 1874, SDSE.

53. SO 107, Dec. 11, 1878; SO 30, Apr. 25, 1878; SO 1, Jan. 13, 1877, PO FR.

54. SO 43, Apr. 20, 1877; SO 3, Jan. 13, 1878, PO FR.

55. SO 84, Oct. 20, 1878, PO FR.

56. Information compiled from garrison court-martial findings published in Post General Orders, 1874–78.

57. Post Returns, Camp Robinson, May–June, 1878.

58. SO 21, May 19, 1874, SDSE; Post Returns, Camp Robinson, Oct. 1876–Nov. 1877.

59. Post Returns, Camp Robinson, Aug., Oct. 1876.

60. Paul L. Hedren, "The Sioux War Adventures of Dr. Charles V. Petteys, Acting Assistant Surgeon," *Journal of the West* 32 (Apr. 1993): 31.

61. Fanny McGillycuddy Diary, 1877–1878, typescript, entries for Aug. 13, Oct. 5, 1877, South Dakota Historical Society, Pierre; "Exact copy of a Notebook kept by Dr. V. T. McGillycuddy, M.D., while a Member of the Yellowstone and Big Horn Expedition, May 26–Dec. 13, 1876, and Notes Kept by His Wife Fanny, at Camp Robinson, Dec. 13, 1876–Feb. 22, 1877, and With the Army on Expedition to the Black Hills, Feb. 23–April 11, 1877," typescript, entries for Jan. 15, Febr. 16, 1877, NSHS.

62. Ricker, "Medical History," 35–36.

63. Bourke diary, Apr. 29, 1877.

64. Luther P. Bradley diary, entry for Oct. 8, 1877, Luther P. Bradley Papers, U.S. Army Military History Institute, Carlisle Barracks, Penn.

65. Bourke diary, May 7, 1877.

66. GO 80, Dec. 20, 1875, PO FR; Utley, *Frontier Regulars*, 84. The full text of the revised Articles of War is found in *Revised Statutes of the United States, Passed at the First Session of the Forty-third Congress, 1873–74* (Washington: GPO, 1875): 229–41.

67. Crawford letter, Jan. 8, 1879, Charles Morton Collection, Arizona Historical Society, Tucson.

68. Punishments come from various garrison court-martial findings published in General Orders, 1877.

69. Desertions reported in Post Returns, Apr. 1874–Dec. 1878. See also John D. McDermott, "Were They Really Rogues?: Desertion in the Nineteenth-Century U.S. Army," *Nebraska History* 78 (Winter 1997): 165–74.

70. McGillycuddy notebook, Dec. 28–31, 1876.

71. SO 25, Sept. 29, 1874, PO FR; SO 8, Nov. 4, 1874, DBH; GO 67, Nov. 12, 1875, PO FR.

72. McGillycuddy notebook, Mar. 23, 1877.

73. GO 12, Febr. 19, 1876, PO FR.

74. GO 35, Apr. 12, 1877; GO 17, Apr. 4, 1875, PO FR.

75. McGillycuddy notebook, Apr. 1, 1877.

76. Paul L. Hedren, "Eben Swift's Army Service on the Plains," *Annals of Wyoming* 50 (Spring 1978): 146–47.

77. GO 73, Nov. 24, 1875; GO 4, Jan. 22, 1876, PO FR.

78. GO 31, Apr. 6, 1877, PO FR.

79. GO 13, Mar. 22, 1875; GO 58, Aug. 1, 1876, PO FR.

80. Jordan to AAG, Sept. 21, 1874, LR DP.

81. Ricker, "Medical History," 9, 20; GO 50, July 11, 1876, PO FR.

82. Capt. Michael J. Fitzgerald to post commander, Mar. 31, 1876, LR DP.

83. Mackenzie to AAG, Aug. 23, 1876, LR DP.

84. Ricker, "Medical History," 37.

85. GO 66, Nov. 12, 1875, PO FR; Ricker, "Medical History," 43–44. Vaccination of children in the Indian camps would have been the agency physician's responsibility.

86. Ricker, "Medical History," 28; "Report of Interments in Post Cemetery, Fort Robinson, from Establishment to February 16, 1883," LR DP. For an indication of the prevalence of gunshot fatalities, see James E. Potter, "'He . . . Regretted Having to Die That Way': Firearms Accidents in the Frontier Army, 1806–1891," *Nebraska History* 78 (Winter 1997): 175–86.

87. SO 6, Mar. 17, 1874, SDSE; David M. Delo, *Peddlers and Post Traders: The Army Sutler on the Frontier* (Salt Lake City: University of Utah Press, 1992), 172–73.

88. "Winter of 1876–1877 at Camp Canby," typescript, Fred Bruning Collection, NSHS.

89. Homer Wheeler, *Buffalo Days: Forty Years in the Old West.* New York: A. L. Burt, 1925), 120; Henry W. Lawton scrapbook, letters of Oct. 15, 1876, and May 20, 1877, Newberry Library, Chicago.

90. GO 42, Dec. 31, 1874, PO FR; Fanny McGillycuddy diary, July 4, 1877.

91. Bruning, "Winter of 1876–1877."

92. John G. Bourke, *On the Border With Crook* (New York: Charles Scribner's Sons, 1891), 409.

93. Bourke diary, Apr. 11, 1877; Bradley diary, June 29, 1877.

94. Bradley Papers, letter dated May 26, 1877; Bourke, *On the Border with Crook*, 402.

95. Bourke diary, Apr. 29, 1877.

96. Lawton scrapbook, letter of Oct. 15, 1876; Fornance letter, Oct. 3, 1874; Bourke diary, May 5, 6, 1877.

97. Edward M. Coffman, *The Old Army: A Portrait of the American Army in Peacetime, 1784–1898* (New York: Oxford University Press, 1986), 308; Alice Shields, "Army Life on the Wyoming Frontier," *Annals of Wyoming* 13 (Oct. 1941): 336. For more on army dependents and laundresses, see Patricia Stallard, *Glittering Misery: Dependents of the Indian Fighting Army* (San Rafael, Calif.: Presidio Press and The Old Army Press, 1978).

98. *Cheyenne Leader*, Nov. 11, 1874.

99. Camp Robinson bi-monthly inspection report, Jan. 1876, LR DP.

100. McGillycuddy notebook, Dec. 14, 1876.

101. Phillip G. Twitchell, ed., "Camp Robinson Letters of Angeline Johnson, 1876–1879," *Nebraska History* 77 (Summer 1996): 92.

102. Ibid., 91.

103. Fanny McGillycuddy diary, Sept. 13–Oct. 16, 1877.

104. Forsyth to AAG, Mar. 27, 1874, LR AG.

105. War Dept., *Report of the Secretary of War* 1 (Washington: GPO, 1875): 34.

106. Dudley to AAG, Aug. 14, 1874, LR DP.

107. War Dept., *Report of the Secretary of War* 1 (Washington: GPO, 1876): 275.

108. *Sidney Telegraph*, July 7, 1877.

109. Ord to Smith, June 20, 1874; Smith to AAG, July 21, 1874, SDSE; GO 18, Sept. 4, 1874, PO FR.

110. Secretary of war to president, Nov. 13, 1876, "Compilation of Correspondence and Orders Relative to the Establishment and Boundaries of Military Reservations in the Department, 1859–1895," DP, RG 393.

4. The Great Sioux War

1. Olson, *Red Cloud*, 201.

2. Ibid., 201–4.

3. Bourke diary, May 6, 1877.

4. *Chicago Inter-Ocean*, Nov. 8, 1875, in John S. Gray, *Centennial Campaign: The Sioux War of 1876* (Fort Collins, Colo.: The Old Army Press, 1976), 27.

5. Gray, *Centennial Campaign*, 30–31.

6. Ibid., 32; Harry H. Anderson, "A Challenge to Brown's Sioux Indian Wars Thesis," in *The Great Sioux War, 1876–77: The Best from* Montana The Magazine of Western History, ed. Paul L. Hedren (Helena: Montana Historical Society Press, 1991), 49–50.

7. George Manypenny, *Our Indian Wards* (Cincinnati: Robert Clark & Co., 1880), 308.

8. Headquarters circular, Mar. 11, 1876, LR DP; Gray, *Centennial Campaign*, 33–34.

9. Olson, *Red Cloud*, 217–18. For a thorough discussion of the expedition, see J. W. Vaughn, *The Reynolds Campaign on Powder River* (Norman: University of Oklahoma Press, 1961).

10. AAG to Sheridan, May 30, 1876, LR AG; Merritt to Sheridan, June 6, 1876, LR AG; *Omaha Republican*, May 24, 1876. See also Thomas R. Buecker, "The Long Summer: Red Cloud Agency and Camp Robinson in 1876," *7th Annual Symposium of the Custer Battlefield and Historical Museum Association* (1993): 1–12.

11. *Omaha Republican*, May 24, 1876.

12. *Sidney Telegraph*, June 17, 1876.

13. Jordan to AAG, May 16, 1876, LR DP; *Omaha Republican*, May 24, 1876; Post quartermaster to Perry, June 1, 1876, LR QM DP.

14. *Sidney Telegraph*, May 27, 1876; *ANJ*, May 20, 1876.

15. The best single source on the 1876 summer campaign remains Gray's *Centennial Campaign*. A recent recounting of the Great Sioux War as a whole is Charles M. Robinson, III, *A Good Year to Die: The Story of the Great Sioux War* (New York: Random House, 1995).

16. Post Returns, Camp Robinson, June 1876.

17. Russell to AAG, July 12, 1876, LR DP.

18. Wessells to AAG, Aug. 10, 1876, LR DP.

19. Post Returns, Camp Robinson, June 1876; Ricker, "Medical History," 41–42.

20. Jordan to AAG, July 10, 1876, LR DP.

21. Ibid., July 10, 14, 1876, LR DP.

22. The complete story of the Warbonnet skirmish is covered in Paul L. Hedren, *First Scalp for Custer: The Skirmish at Warbonnet Creek, Nebraska, July 17, 1876, with a Short History of the Warbonnet Battlefield* (Lincoln: University of Nebraska Press, 1987). See also Charles King, *Campaigning with Crook and Stories of Army Life* (New York: Harper Brothers, 1890).

23. Dan L. Thrapp, *Encyclopedia of Frontier Biography* (Lincoln: University of Nebraska Press, 1991), 293–94; Hedren, *First Scalp*, 37.

24. Hedren, *First Scalp*, 61.

25. King, *Campaigning with Crook*, 37. Another King account is found in Harry H. Anderson, ed., *Indian Campaigns: Sketches of Cavalry Service in Arizona and on the Northern Plains* (Fort Collins, Colo.: The Old Army Press, 1984), 56.

26. Hedren, *First Scalp*, 68, 83–84. For Cheyenne accounts, see Jerome A. Greene, *Lakota and Cheyenne: Indian Views of the Great Sioux War, 1876–1877* (Norman: University of Oklahoma Press, 1994), 80–84.

27. Buecker, "Red Cloud Ledger Book," 13.

28. Buecker and Paul, *Crazy Horse Surrender Ledger*, 7.

29. Richmond L. Clow, "General Philip Sheridan's Legacy: The Sioux Pony Campaign of 1876," *Nebraska History* 57 (Winter 1976): 461–77.

30. Buecker and Paul, *Crazy Horse Surrender Ledger*, 7.

31. Paul A. Hutton, ed., *Soldiers West: Biographies from the Military Frontier* (Lincoln: University of Nebraska Press, 1987), 177; *ANJ*, Oct. 14, 1876; Mackenzie to Sheridan, Sept. 2, 1876, RG 393, Records of the Adjutant General's Office, Document File 4163 (Sioux War), NA. For a recent biography of Mackenzie, see Michael D. Pierce, *The Most Promising Young Officer: A Life of Ranald Slidell Mackenzie* (Norman: University of Oklahoma Press, 1993).

32. Mackenzie to AAG, Sept. 2, 1876, LR DP.

33. Post Returns, Camp Robinson, Aug. 1876.

34. Ibid., Aug.–Sept., 1876.

35. Lawton scrapbook, letter of Oct. 15, 1876.

36. Twitchell, "Camp Robinson Letters," 91.

37. Lawton scrapbook, letter of Oct. 15, 1876.

38. For more on Crook's late summer campaign, see Jerome A. Greene, *Slim Buttes, 1876: An Episode of the Great Sioux War* (Norman: University of Oklahoma Press, 1982).

39. Paul L. Hedren, *Fort Laramie in 1876: Chronicle of a Frontier Post at War* (Lincoln: University of Nebraska Press, 1988), 164; Hutton, *Phil Sheridan*, 323; Post Returns, Camp Robinson, Sept. 1876.

40. Ricker, "Medical History," 48.

41. Mary C. Gillett, *The Army Medical Department, 1865–1917* (Washington: Center of Military History, United States Army, 1995), 78.

42. Hedren, "Eben Swift," 146.

43. Olson, *Red Cloud*, 224–28. Anderson, "War Club of Sitting Bull," 123.

44. Mackenzie to AAG, Sept. 30, 1876, LR DP.

45. Hedren, *Fort Laramie in 1876*, 185; Robert Bruce, *The Fighting Norths and Pawnee Scouts: Narratives and Reminiscences of Military Service on the Old Frontier* (Lincoln: Nebraska State Historical Society, 1932), 45; Telegram, Crook to Sheridan, Oct. 24, 1876, LR DM. For more on the Norths and the Pawnees, see Donald F. Danker, ed., *Man of the Plains: Recollections of Luther North, 1856–1882* (Lincoln: University of Nebraska Press, 1961), and Thomas W. Dunlay, *Wolves for the Blue Soldiers: Indian Scouts and Auxiliaries with the United States Army, 1860–90* (Lincoln: University of Nebraska Press, 1982.

46. Mason to AAG, Dec. 3, 1876, LR AGO.

47. For more on the winter Powder River Expedition, see John G. Bourke, *Mackenzie's Last Fight with the Cheyennes: A Winter Campaign in Wyoming and Montana* (Ft. Collins, Colo.: The Old Army Press, 1970; reprint of 1890 edition.).

48. Robert Lee, *Fort Meade and the Black Hills* (Lincoln: University of Nebraska Press, 1991), 10.

49. Post Returns, Camp Robinson, Febr. 1877.

50. Cummings to Bourke, aide-de-camp to General Crook, Febr. 26, 1877, LR DP. This report contains all the details of the Crow Creek fight.

51. Ibid. These sheep were probably a flock owned by a man named Ames, who in the fall of 1876 brought the first flock into the Black Hills. Indian raiders ran off the sheep, and Ames was greatly surprised to see troops returning his stolen animals. Jesse Brown and A. M. Willard, *The Black Hills Trail* (Rapid City, S.Dak.: Rapid City Journal Co., 1924), 483.

52. Cummings to Bourke, Febr. 26, 1877; Thomas R. Buecker, "'Can You Send Us Immediate Relief?': Army Expeditions to the Northern Black Hills, 1876–1878," *South Dakota History* 25 (Summer 1995): 105.

53. Cummings to Bourke, Febr. 26, 1877; *ANJ*, Mar. 31, 1877.

54. Buecker, "Can You Send Relief," 106–7.

55. Vroom to Bourke, Mar. 7, 1877, LR DP.

56. Bourke diary, Apr. 5, 1877.

57. Ibid., Apr. 17, May 4, 1877; Thomas B. Marquis, *A Warrior Who Fought Custer* (Minneapolis: The Midwest Co., 1931), 295.

58. Bourke diary, Apr. 12, 1877; *ANJ*, Apr. 14, 1877.

59. Thomas R. Buecker, "Lt. William Philo Clark's Sioux War Report and Little Big Horn Map," *Greasy Grass* 7 (May 1991): 13; Robert A. Clark, ed., *The Killing of Chief Crazy Horse* (Lincoln: University of Nebraska Press 1988), 138.

60. Oliver Knight, "War or Peace: The Anxious Wait for Crazy Horse," in R. Eli Paul, ed., *The Nebraska Indian Wars Reader, 1865–1877* (Lincoln: University of Nebraska Press, 1998), 161–79; Bourke diary, Apr. 17, 1877. For more on Indian emissaries, see Harry A. Anderson, "Indian Peace-Talkers and the Conclusion of the Sioux War of 1876," *Nebraska History* 44 (Dec. 1963): 233–54, and Kingsley M. Bray, "Crazy Horse and the End of the Great Sioux War," *Nebraska History* 79 (Fall 1998): 94–115.

61. Forsyth to Sheridan, Apr. 22, 1877, LR DM.

62. *New York Tribune*, Apr. 23, 1877; Forsyth to Sheridan, Apr. 22, 1877, Sioux War File.

63. Bourke diary, Aug. 1, 1878 (24:12–14,17). In this twenty-fourth volume, on or about this date, Bourke wrote his narrative of the last days of Crazy Horse and also copied key telegrams and reports sent to Crook in the field.

64. Information on the surrender of Crazy Horse is compiled from several sources, including: *Omaha Weekly Bee*, May 16, 1877; Paul D. Riley, ed., "Oglala Sources on the Life of Crazy Horse: Interviews Given to Eleanor H. Hinman, in Paul, *Nebraska Indian Wars Reader*, 180–216; Bourke, *On the Border with Crook*, 412–14.

65. *Chicago Tribune*, May 8, 1877.

5. The Final Days of Crazy Horse . . . and Camp Robinson

1. Telegram, Crook to Sheridan, Febr. 1, 1877, LR DM.

2. Mackenzie to Bourke, Mar. 14, 1877, LR DP; Post Returns, Camp Robinson, May–June, 1877.

3. Heitman, *Historical Register*, 239; Bradley Papers, diary entry for June 12, 1877.

4. Inspector general's report, Aug. 6, 1877, LR DP; Department quartermaster to post quartermaster, Apr. 5, 1877, LR DP.

5. Crook to Sheridan, Apr. 20, 1877, LR DM.

6. *New York Herald*, Apr. 28, 1877.

7. Riley, "Oglala Sources," 193, 196 (He Dog), 207 (Short Buffalo); Clark, *Killing of Chief Crazy Horse*, 59.

8. *Omaha Daily Bee*, May 29, 1877.

9. Johnson to commissioner of Indian affairs, June 4, 1877, LR RCA; *Omaha Weekly Bee*, June 6, 1877.

10. Telegram, Crook to Sheridan, Febr. 1, 1877, LR DM; Clark to Bourke, Apr. 2, 1877, LR AG.

11. Van Vliet to post adjutant, July 13, 1877, LR DP.

12. Ricker interview of Garnett, Tablet 2.

13. *Omaha Daily Bee*, May 8, 1877.

14. Personal correspondence with Ephriam Dickson, 1995, FRM.

15. Clark to Crook, Aug. 18, 1877, Bourke diary, 24:76.

16. AAG DP to Ord, Dec. 31, 1874, LR DP; Twitchell, "Camp Robinson Letters," 92; Post Returns, Camp Robinson, Mar.–Apr., 1877.

17. Hutton, *Phil Sheridan*, 334–35.

18. Harry H. Anderson, "Cheyennes at the Little Big Horn: A Study of Statistics," *North Dakota Historical Quarterly* 27 (Spring 1960): 91–92.

19. Lawton to AAG, May 25, 1877, LR DP; *Omaha Daily Bee*, May 25, 1877.

20. Loretta Fowler, *Arapahoe Politics, 1851–1978: Symbols in Crises of Authority* (Lincoln: University of Nebraska Press, 1982), 48–52.

21. Ibid., 59, 63; Bourke, *On the Border with Crook*, 391–92. The Bourke diaries for the period contain numerous references to the Arapaho scouts.

22. Mackenzie to secretary of interior, Mar. 17, 1877, LR DM.

23. Sheridan endorsement to ibid., Mar. 27, 1877.

24. Bourke, *On the Border with Crook*, 406.

25. Buecker, "Red Cloud Ledger Book," 20–21.

26. Buecker, "Can You Send Relief," 111–13.

27. *Report of the Secretary of War* 1 (Washington: GPO, 1877): 85.

28. *Omaha Daily Bee*, July 27, 1877.

29. Ibid., Dec. 12, 1877.

30. Jerome A. Greene, *Yellowstone Command: Colonel Nelson A. Miles and the Great Sioux War, 1876–1877* (Lincoln: University of Nebraska Press, 1991), 208–13; *Omaha Daily Bee*, June 4, 1877; Telegram, Bradley to AAG, July 23, 1877, LR AG.

31. Bourke diary, May 6, 1877; Clark, *Killing of Chief Crazy Horse*, 27.

32. Bourke diary, 24:30–31, and May 6, 1877.

33. Telegram, Sheridan to Sherman, May 7, 1877, LR AG.

34. Commissioner of Indian affairs to secretary of interior, May 23, 1877, and endorsement to same by Sherman, LR AG.

35. Bailey Millard, "The Man Who Captured Crazy Horse," *Human Life*, Sept. 1909, 13.

36. "Crazy Horse's Story of Custer Battle," *South Dakota Historical Collections* 6 (1912): 224–28; *Yankton Press and Dakotaian*, June 7, 1877.

37. *Omaha Daily Republican*, July 13, 1877.

38. Bradley Papers, letter to his wife Ione, May 26, 1877.

39. Clark to Crook, Aug. 18, 1877, Bourke diary, 24:72.

40. Clark, *Killing of Chief Crazy Horse*, 28; Bourke diary, 24:12–14, 35.

41. Bourke diary, 24:34; Shopp to commissioner of Indian affairs, Aug. 15, 1877, LR AG.

42. Shopp to commissioner of Indian affairs, Aug. 15, 1877.

43. Ibid.

44. Twitchell, "Camp Robinson Letters," 92.

45. Jesse M. Lee, "The Capture and Death of an Indian Chieftain," *The Journal of the Military Service Institution* 54 (May–June, 1914): 326.

46. Shopp to commissioner of Indian affairs, Aug. 15, 1877; Olson, *Red Cloud*, 238; Clark, *Killing of Chief Crazy Horse*, 59.

47. Riley, "Oglala Sources," 201 (Red Feather).

48. Bourke diary, 24:78; Riley, "Oglala Sources," 196 (He Dog), 207 (Short Buffalo).

49. Riley, "Oglala Sources," 197 (Red Feather).

50. Ibid., 210 (Little Killer).

51. Ibid., 212 (Valentine T. McGillycuddy); Olson, *Red Cloud*, 242; Grange, "Fort Robinson Outpost," 213.

52. *New York Sun*, Sept. 14, 1877; Riley, "Oglala Sources, 193 (He Dog).

53. Ricker interview of A. G. Shaw, Tablet 11; Bourke diary, 24:32.

54. *New York Sun*, Sept. 14, 1877; Telegram, AAG to Crook, Aug. 31, 1877, Bourke diary, 24:55.

55. Bourke, *On the Border with Crook*, 418; Riley, "Oglala Sources," 196 (He Dog), 202 (Red Feather).

56. Lee, "Capture and Death," 331.

57. Shopp to commissioner of Indian affairs, Aug. 15, 1877.

58. Olson, *Red Cloud*, 240.

59. Clark to commissioner of Indian affairs, Sept. 10, 1877, LR DP; Clark, *Killing of Chief Crazy Horse*, 26.

60. Irwin to commissioner of Indian affairs, Aug. 31, 1877, LR RCA.

61. Bourke diary, 24:35: Eloise Holcomb, "Fort Robinson: Its Role in the Subjugation of the Sioux Indians, 1874–1878" (Master's thesis, Chadron State College, Chadron, Nebr., 1966), 28.

62. Clark, *Killing of Chief Crazy Horse*, 60; Riley, "Oglala Sources," 209 (Carrie Slow Bear).

63. Clark to Crook, Aug. 18, 1877, Bourke diary, 24:73–74.

64. *Omaha Daily Bee*, July 20, 1877.

65. Shopp to commissioner of Indian affairs, Aug. 15, 1877.

66. Thomas M. Anderson, "Army Episodes and Anecdotes, or Life at Vancouver Barracks: The Romance and the Reality of the Frontier," 35, 46, William Robertson Coe Collection, Yale University Library, New Haven, Conn.; *Omaha Daily Bee*, July 20, 1877.

67. Shopp to commissioner of Indian affairs, Aug. 15, 1877.

68. Richard G. Hardorff, *The Oglala Lakota Crazy Horse: A Preliminary Genealogical Study and an Annotated Listing of Primary Sources* (Mattituck, N.Y.: J. M. Carroll & Co., 1985), 23; Telegram, Bradley to AAG DP, Aug. 15, 1877, Bourke diary, 24:54.

69. Clark to Crook, Aug. 18, 1877, Bourke diary, 24:75–76.

70. Lee, "Capture and Death," 327.

71. Paul L. Hedren, "'Holy Ground': The United States Army Embraces Custer's Battle-field," in *Legacy: New Perspectives on the Battle of the Little Bighorn*, ed. Charles E. Rankin (Helena: Montana Historical Society Press, 1996), 195–96: Clark, *Killing of Chief Crazy Horse*, 28.

72. Bourke diary, 24:36–37; Telegram, Sheridan to AAG DP, Aug. 28, 1877, LR AG.

73. The council and resulting misinterpretation are mentioned in several sources, including Lee, "Capture and Death," 328–29; Ricker interview of Louis Bordeaux, Tablet 11; Valentine T. McGillycuddy, "Dr. McGillycuddy's Story of Crazy Horse," *Nebraska History* 12 (Jan.–Mar., 1929): 36–38.

74. "Report of William Garnett, Interpreter to General H. L. Scott and Major James McLaughlin," Thomas Wright Collection, NSHS.

75. Bourke diary, 24:33.

76. P. E. Byrne, *Soldiers of the Plains* (New York: Minton, Balch & Co., 1926), 232–33.

77. Olson, *Red Cloud*, 242.

78. Telegram, AAG to Sheridan, Aug. 30, 1877, LR AG; Bradley diary, Aug. 31, 1877.

79. Telegram, AAG DP to Crook, Aug. 31, 1877, Bourke diary, 24:55.

80. Telegram, Bradley to Sheridan, Aug. 31, 1877, LR AG; Telegram, Bradley to AG DP, Aug. 31, 1877, LR AG.

81. Telegram, Sheridan to Crook, Sept. 1, 1877, LR AG; Bourke diary, 24:38–39, 56.

82. Telegram, Crook to Bradley, Sept. 1, 1877, Bourke diary, 24:38, 57.

83. Third Cavalry Regimental Returns, Sept. 1877, RG 94; Irwin to commissioner of Indian affairs, Sept. 1, 1877, LR RCA; Bourke memorandum to telegram, Bradley to AG DP, Aug. 31, 1877, LR DP.

84. Lee, "Capture and Death," 328–30.

85. Telegram, Crook to Bradley, Sept. 1, 1877, Bourke diary, 24:57–58.

86. Bourke diary, 24:40–43.

87. Ibid., 24:43.

88. Ibid., 24:43–44; Clark to commissioner of Indian affairs, Sept. 10, 1877, LR DP; *Omaha Daily Bee*, Sept. 13, 1877; Riley, "Oglala Sources," 198 (Red Feather).

89. Ricker interview of Shaw.

90. Byrne, *Soldiers of the Plains*, 240–42.

91. Bourke diary, 24:44.

92. The several sources on the afternoon meeting include: Bourke diary, 24:81; Riley, "Oglala Sources," 198 (Red Feather); Bourke, *On the Border with Crook*, 420; and "Report of William Garnett."

93. *ANJ*, Sept. 15, 1877; *New York Sun*, Sept. 14, 1877.

94. Telegram, Bradley to Crook, Sept. 4, 1877, LR AG; Clark to commissioner of Indian affairs, Sept. 10, 1877, LR DP.

95. Telegram, Clark to Crook, Sept. 4, 1877, LR AG; Bourke diary, 24:47, 58.

96. Lee, "Capture and Death," 332; Lee to commissioner of Indian affairs, Sept. 30, 1877, LS Spotted Tail Agency, RG 75.

97. Clark, *Killing of Chief Crazy Horse*, 64 (He Dog); Lee to commissioner of Indian affairs, Sept. 30, 1877.

98. Lee to commissioner of Indian affairs, Sept. 30, 1877; *New York Sun*, Sept. 14, 1877.

99. Lee, "Capture and Death," 335; *New York Sun*, Sept. 14, 1877.

100. Ricker interview of Bordeaux; Bradley Papers, letter of Sept. 5, 1877.

101. Telegram, Clark to Crook, Sept. 5, 1877, Bourke diary, 24:61–62.

102. Telegram, Crook to Bradley, Sept. 5, 1877, Ibid., 24:62; Telegram, Crook to Sheridan, Sept. 5, 1877, LR AG.

103. Telegrams, Crook to Sheridan, Sept. 5, 1877, and Sheridan to Crook, Sept. 5, 1877, Bourke diary, 24:63–64.

104. The reported times of his arrival at Camp Robinson vary from 3:00 to 7:00 P.M. Amos Charging First, Crazy Horse Biography File, South Dakota State Historical Society, Pierre; Lee, "Capture and Death," 336.

105. Thomas R. Buecker, "Frederic S. Calhoun: A Little-known Member of the Custer Clique," *Greasy Grass* 10 (May 1994): 16.

106. Lee, "Capture and Death," 336; Bruce R. Liddic and Paul Harbaugh, *Camp on Custer: Transcribing the Custer Myth* (Spokane: The Arthur Clark Co., 1995), 145–46 (Louis Bordeaux). These are two of the numerous references to this conference.

107. Liddic and Harbaugh, *Camp on Custer*, 146.

108. H. R. Lemly, "The Passing of Crazy Horse," *The Journal of the Military Service Institution* 54 (May–June, 1914): 321. Lemly apparently also authored the *New York Sun*, Sept. 14, 1877, article.

109. Early accounts published in newspapers first stated that Crazy Horse was to be taken to the Dry Tortugas, and later writers accepted this. Lemly in the article above later stated it correctly.

110. "Report of William Garnett; "Riley, "Oglala Sources," 193 (He Dog).

111. *New York Sun*, Sept. 14, 1877.

112. Ibid.

113. This version is compiled from a number of primary accounts of the incident. At times modern historians—including this writer—have named Pvt. William Gentles, Company F, Fourteenth Infantry, as the sentry on Post No. 1 who inflicted the fatal thrust. However, Crazy Horse historian Ephriam Dickson presents a strong argument that Crazy Horse died as a result of a guard's bayonet, but his identity remains questionable. Ephriam D. Dickson, III, "Crazy Horse: Who Really Wielded Bayonet that Killed the Oglala Leader?," *Greasy Grass* 12 (May 1996): 2–10.

114. *Omaha Daily Herald*, Oct. 6, 1877 (Edwin D. Woods).

115. Telegram, Clark to Crook, Sept. 5, 1877, Bourke diary, 24:65.

116. Bradley Papers, diary entry for Sept. 5, 1877.

117. Jesse Lee interview, Walter Camp field notes, folder #116, Walter Mason Camp Collection, Harold B. Lee Library, Brigham Young University, Provo, Utah.

118. Clark to commissioner of Indian affairs, Sept. 10, 1877, LR RCA; Twitchell, "Camp Robinson Letters," 93; Charles P. Jordan, "The Death of Crazy Horse," undated newspaper clipping on file at FRM.

119. Clark to Crook, Sept. 9, 1877, LR AG; Bradley Papers, Daniel Burke to Bradley, Sept. 7, 1877.

120. Bradley Papers, Lee to Bradley, Sept. 10, 1877, and diary entry for Sept. 11, 1877; Clark to commissioner of Indian affairs, Sept. 10, 1877, LR DP. For his "assistance" in the Crazy Horse episode, Little Big Man apparently received a silver medal, which has survived. Paul L. Hedren, "The Crazy Horse Medal: An Enigma from the Great Sioux War," *Nebraska History* 75 (Summer 1994): 195-99; Hedren, "Postscript," *Nebraska History* 77 (Summer 1996): 114.

121. Clark to Crook, Sept. 9, 1877, LR AG.

122. Bourke, *On the Border with Crook*, 423.

123. Riley, "Oglala Sources," 185.

124. The composition of the delegation varies according to sources. The account used here reported: (Oglalas) Red Cloud, Little Wound, Young Man Afraid of His Horses, Yellow Bear, American Horse, Three Bears, Little Big Man, Big Road, and He Dog; (Brulé) Spotted Tail, Swift Bear, White Tail, Good Voice, Spotted Tail Jr., Hollow Horn Bear, and Little Hawk; (Minneconjou) Iron Crow and Touch the Clouds; (Sans Arcs) Red Bear; (Arapaho) Black Coal, Sharp Nose, and Friday; (interpreters) Leon Palladay, Antoine Janis, William Hunter (Garnett), and Jose Merrivale. *Chicago Tribune*, Sept. 22, 1877.

125. *Laws, Joint Resolutions and Memorials Passed at the Eleventh Session of the Legislative Assembly of the State of Nebraska* (Omaha: Omaha Daily Republican, 1875), 338–39.

126. Ibid., 338.

127. *ANJ*, Apr. 14, 1877.

128. Olson, *Red Cloud*, 248–53; Hyde, *Red Cloud's Folk*, 299; *New York Sun*, Oct. 3, 1877; *Omaha Daily Bee*, Oct. 2, 1877.

129. Bradley Papers, letter of Oct. 25, 1877.

130. *Report of the Secretary of War* 1 (Washington: GPO, 1878): 89.

131. Bradley diary, Oct. 25, 1877.

132. *Omaha Daily Bee*, Oct. 18, 1877.

133. Irwin to Ezra Hayt, Oct. 27, 1877, LR RCA.

134. SO 34, Oct. 30, 1877, DBH; Post Returns, Camp Robinson, Nov. 1877.

135. *Omaha Daily Bee*, Nov. 1, 1877.

136. Post Returns, Camp Robinson, Oct.–Nov., 1877.

137. Utley, *Frontier Regulars*, 290–91.

138. William E. Lass, *From the Missouri to the Great Salt Lake: An Account of Overland Freighting* (Lincoln: Nebraska State Historical Society, 1972), 201–12.

139. Bronson to AAG, Aug. 6, 1878, LR DP.

140. Irwin to commissioner of Indian affairs, July 26, 1877, LR RCA.

141. Olson, *Red Cloud*, 255, 261–63.

142. SO 8, Febr. 10, 1878; SO 62, July 20, 1878; SO 14, Mar. 2, 1878, PO FR.

143. SO 62, July 20, 1878; SO 72, Sept. 3, 1878; SO 108, Dec. 14, 1878, PO FR.

144. Crook to Sheridan, Apr. 23, 1878, George Crook Letterbook, Rutherford B. Hayes Presidential Center, Fremont, Ohio.

145. Crook to AAG DM, Aug. 14, 1878, "Compilation of Correspondence Relating to the Establishment and Boundaries of Military Reservations," 229, DP, RG 393.

146. Frazer, *Forts of the West*, xxii–xxiii.

147. GO 9, Dec. 30, 1878, DM, "Compilation of Correspondence," 228–29.

148. SO 117, Dec. 31, 1878, PO FR.

6. The Cheyenne Outbreak

1. Ramon S. Powers, "Why the Northern Cheyenne Left Indian Territory in 1878: A Cultural Analysis," *Kansas Quarterly* 3 (Fall 1971): 73.

2. Smith to Saville, Sept. 15, 1874; "Treaty with Northern Cheyenne and Arapahoe Indians, November 12, 1874," LR RCA, NA–Central Plains Region, Kansas City, Mo.

3. Powers, "Why the Northern Cheyenne Left," 74–75; James W. Covington, "Causes of the Dull Knife Raid," *The Chronicles of Oklahoma* 26 (Spring 1948): 15.

4. Thomas R. Buecker and R. Eli Paul, "Cheyenne Outbreak Firearms," *The Museum of the Fur Trade Quarterly* 29 (Summer 1993): 4.

5. Covington, "Causes of the Dull Knife Raid," 15, 19; Powers, "Why the Northern Cheyenne Left," 75.

6. Powers, "Why the Northern Cheyenne Left," 77.

7. Covington, "Causes of the Dull Knife Raid," 18; "Proceedings of a Board of Officers Convened by Virtue of the Following Special Order: Headquarters Department of the Platte, Fort Omaha, Nebraska, January 21, 1879, Special Orders No. 8," in "Papers Relating to Military Operations against the Northern Cheyennes, 1878–79," *National Archives Microfilm Publication M666*, roll 428.

8. Covington, "Causes of the Dull Knife Raid," 19.

9. Peter M. Wright, "The Pursuit of Dull Knife from Fort Reno in 1878–1879," *The Chronicles of Oklahoma* 46 (Summer 1968): 143.

10. Philip H. Sheridan, *Record of Engagements with Hostile Indians Within the Military Division of the Missouri* (Washington: GPO, 1882. Reprint. The Old Army Press, 1969), 79.

11. Wright, "Pursuit of Dull Knife," 144; George B. Grinnell, *The Fighting Cheyennes* (New York: Charles Scribner's Sons, 1915), 388.

12. Wright, "Pursuit of Dull Knife," 144–45.

13. Donald J. Berthrong, *The Cheyenne and Arapaho Ordeal: Reservation and Agency Life in the Indian Territory, 1875–1907* (Norman: University of Oklahoma Press, 1976), 34.

14. Unless otherwise indicated all information on military operations in Oklahoma and Kansas is summarized from Wright, "Pursuit of Dull Knife," and Sheridan, *Record of Engagements*.

15. *Chicago Tribune*, Sept. 16, 1878.

16. Undated Omaha newspaper article, copy on file at FRM. For more on the Kansas raids, see William D. Mather, "The Revolt of Little Wolf's Northern Cheyenne" (Master's thesis, University of Wichita, 1958).

17. "Billy O'Toole's Story of the Raid," *Atchison* (Kans.) *Champion*, July 9, 1881.

18. Powers, "Why the Northern Cheyenne Left," 80; Ramon S. Powers, "The Kansas Indian Claims Commission of 1879," *Kansas History* 7 (Autumn 1984): 210.

19. Telegrams, Crook to Thornburgh, Sept. 13, 19, 1878, Telegrams Received, DP.

20. Sheridan, *Record of Engagements*, 80; *ANJ*, Sept. 28, 1878; *Sidney Telegraph*, Sept. 28, 1878. For more on the movement of the Little Chief band to Indian Territory, see Ricker interview of Heber M. Creel, unnumbered tablet.

21. Thornburgh to AAG, Oct. 19, 1878, LR DP; Telegram, AAG to DM, Oct. 4, 1878; *Chicago Tribune*, Oct. 5, 1878.

22. Thornburgh to AAG, Oct. 19, 1878, LR DP.

23. Grinnell, *The Fighting Cheyennes*, 394–95.

24. *Omaha Weekly Bee*, Oct. 16, 1878.

25. Thornburgh to AAG, Oct. 19, 1878; Bourke to AAG, Oct. 15, 1878, LR DP.

26. Bourke to AAG, Oct. 15, 1878, LR DP.

27. Carlton to AAG, Oct. 29, 1878, LR DP.

28. Ibid., Oct. 16, 1878, LR DP.

29. *Omaha Weekly Bee*, Oct. 16, 1878.

30. *Chicago Tribune*, Oct. 7, 1878.

31. *ANJ*, Oct. 9, 12, 1878; *Chicago Times*, Oct. 7, 1878; Olson, *Red Cloud*, 262.

32. Melbourne C. Chandler, *Of Garryowen in Glory: The History of the 7th U.S. Cavalry* (Annandale, Va.: Melbourne C. Chandler, 1960), 77.

33. Carlton to AAG, Oct. 16, 1878; Thornburgh to AAG, Oct. 19, 1878, LR DP.

34. Sheridan, *Record of Engagements*, 81.

35. Ibid., 82.

36. Johnson to battalion adjutant, Oct. 25, 1878; Endorsements on letter of Frank Price to AAG DM, Jan. 18, 1879, LR DP.

37. "Board of Officers," 26, 52, 60, 63–64.

38. Ibid., 61; Carlton to AAG, Oct. 29, 1878, LR DP.

39. "Board of Officers," 62, 175; Buecker and Paul, "Cheyenne Outbreak Firearms," 8.

40. "Briefs of Dispatches," received at division headquarters and found in "Papers Relating to Military Operations," telegrams of Oct. 28, Nov. 1, 19, 1878.

41. Buecker and Paul, "Cheyenne Outbreak Firearms," 8; "Board of Officers," 30.

42. "Board of Officers," 4, 55–56, 67–68; Telegram, Schuyler to AAG, Jan. 16, 1879, LR AG.

43. "Board of Officers," 106.

44. Ibid., 90, 138, 162.

45. Grinnell, *The Fighting Cheyennes*, 402–3.

46. "Board of Officers," 16–17, 71, 78, 93.

47. Ibid., 30–31, 71, 122, 137.

48. Ibid., 84, 93; Grinnell, *The Fighting Cheyennes*, 402.

49. Grinnell, *The Fighting Cheyennes*, 402.

50. *ANJ*, Nov. 2, 1878.

51. "Briefs," Gov. George T. Anthony to secretary of war, Nov. 11, 1878.

52. "Briefs," Dec. 5, 16, 1878.

53. Heitman, *Historical Register*, 1019; Wessells to AAG, Jan. 12, 1879, LR AG.

54. "Briefs," Dec. 20, 23, 24, 1878.

55. Wessells to AAG, Jan. 12, 1879, LR AG.

56. Ibid.

57. Telegram, Schuyler to Crook, Jan. 15, 1879, "Papers Relating to Military Operations."

58. "Board of Officers," 139.

59. Grinnell, *The Fighting Cheyennes*, 404.

60. "Briefs," Jan. 6, 1879.

61. Wessells to AAG, Jan. 15, 1879, LR DP; "Board of Officers," 6, 72, 94–95.

62. Twitchell, "Camp Robinson Letters," 95.

63. "Board of Officers," 141; Telegram, Schuyler to Crook, Jan. 15, 1879, "Papers Relating to Military Operations."

64. "Board of Officers," 80, 96; "Captain Carter P. Johnson's Statement in Relation to the Cheyenne Outbreak," Ricker Collection.

65. "Board of Officers," 96–97, 167.

66. Thomas B. Marquis, *Cheyenne and Sioux: The Reminiscences of Four Indians and a White Soldier* (Stockton, Calif.: Pacific Center for Western Historical Studies, 1973), 22.

67. Edgar B. Bronson, *Reminiscences of a Ranchman* (New York: The McClure Company, 1908), 177; "Board of Officers," 193. Unless otherwise noted, all subsequent information on the course of the outbreak is reconstructed from Rickey D. Malcolm, "The Cheyenne Outbreak," manuscript, held at FRM. This work is a day-by-day chronology of troop movements compiled from the "Board of Officers" testimony.

68. Twitchell, "Camp Robinson Letters," 95.

69. *Chicago Times*, Jan. 22, 1879; Twitchell, "Camp Robinson Letters," 95; Crawford to Charles Morton, Febr. 26, 1879, Morton Collection.

70. "Board of Officers," 157; *Sidney Telegraph*, Jan. 18, 1879.

71. Bronson, *Reminiscences of a Ranchman*, 191.

72. "Board of Officers," 118.

73. "Interview with Carter P. Johnson," Robert S. Ellison Papers, Western History Collection, Denver Public Library, Denver, Colo.

74. "Board of Officers," 75.

75. "Briefs," Jan. 15, 1879.

76. *Chicago Times*, Jan. 11, 1879.

77. William B. Allison to secretary of war, Jan. 17, 1879, "Papers Relating to Military Operations."

78. *ANJ*, Jan. 18, 1879.

79. "Briefs," Jan. 15, 19, 1879; Telegram, Sheridan to Sherman, Jan. 19, 1879, "Papers Relating to Military Operations."

80. Telegram, Sheridan to Sherman, Jan. 22, 1879, "Papers Relating to Military Operations."

81. The sister of Woman's Dress was one of the captured Cheyennes. Remembering fondly how he had warned Crook of an assassination plot by Crazy Horse back in September 1877, the army made arrangements to have the sister and her daughter and infant turned over to him. Hayt to secretary of interior, Jan. 16, 1879, "Papers Relating to Military Operations."

82. *Sidney Telegraph*, Jan. 18, 1879.

83. Ricker interview with John Shangrau, Tablet 9.

84. "Board of Officers," 77.

85. "Captain Carter P. Johnson Statement."

86. *ANJ*, Febr. 1, 1879.

87. "Board of Officers," 201, 204.

88. Todd D. Epp, "The State of Kansas v. Wild Hog, et al." *Kansas History* 5 (Summer 1982): 139–46.

89. Theophilus F. Rodenbough, ed., *Fighting for Honor: A Record of Heroism* (New York: G. W. Dillingham, 1893), 392–400; James E. Potter, "The Pageant Revisited: Indian Wars Medals of Honor in Nebraska, 1865–1879," in Paul, *Nebraska Indian Wars Reader*, 217–29. A certificate of merit, awarded for heroism in combat, entitled the recipient to receive two extra dollars of pay each month. At that time the law prohibited an NCO from receiving this award. Endorsement of Sherman on Johnson's request for Lewis to receive the MOH, Mar. 1, 1879.

90. *Chicago Times*, Jan. 25, 1879.

7. The 1880s Expansion

1. *Omaha Weekly Bee*, Sept. 26, 1883.

2. Annual Inspection Report, Apr. 20, 1882, LR DP.

3. *Omaha Daily Bee*, Dec. 5, 1883.

4. *Crawford Crescent*, July 14, 1887.

5. *Omaha Weekly Bee*, Sept. 26, 1883.

6. McGillycuddy to Crook, Sept. 1, 1880, LR DP.

7. Buecker, "Camp Sheridan," 70–71.

8. "Compilation of Correspondence," 223–34, 338–40.

9. "For the Relief of the Administrator of the Estate of John W. Dear, Deceased," *Senate Reports*, No. 180, Febr. 15, 1884, 48th U. S. Cong., 1st sess., 1883–1884, Serial 2174.

10. Augustus W. Corliss Diary, May 27, June 22, 1887, Western History Collection, Denver Public Library, Denver, Colo.

11. Orders 202, Dec. 6, 1886, PO FR.

12. Post Returns, Fort Robinson, Aug.–Sept., 1883.

13. *ANJ*, Oct. 17, 1886; Corliss diary, Oct. 31, 1887.

14. Orders 101, May 27, 1888, PO FR; Corliss diary, May 30, 1888; Schubert, *Buffalo Soldiers, Braves, and Brass*, 25.

15. Corliss diary, Febr. 28, 1889; Orders 109, May 10, 1889, and Orders 134, June 8, 1889, PO FR.

16. To "make a file" referred to a promotion within the enlisted ranks. *ANJ*, June 23, 1888. The description of the Fourth of July celebration comes from the Corliss diary, July 8, 1889.

17. Corliss diary, Sept. 15, 1888.

18. *ANJ*, July 27, 1889.

19. Stephen P. Jocelyn, *Mostly Alkali* (Caldwell, Idaho: Caxton Printers, 1953), 327.

20. *Omaha Daily Bee*, Sept. 23, 1889.

21. *ANJ*, Oct. 31, 1886.

22. *Annual Report of the Secretary of War, 1885* (Washington: GPO, 1885): 776.

23. *ANJ*, Aug. 3, 1889; Corliss diary, July 13–14, 1889.

24. Orders 99, July 21, 1882, and Orders 102, July 24, 1882, PO FR; William B. Scott, *Some Memories of a Paleontologist* (Princeton: Princeton University Press, 1939), 154-55, 157-58.

25. *ANJ*, July 21, 1888.

26. Ibid., Dec. 31, 1887.

27. Fort Building File, FRM; see "Manuscript Materials" in the bibliography. *ANJ*, July 30, Dec. 31, 1887, Jan. 21, 1888.

28. Jack D. Foner, *The United States Soldier Between Two Wars: Army Life and Reforms, 1865–1898* (New York: Humanities Press, 1970), 92; Corliss diary, May 1, 1888.

29. Foner, *United States Soldier*, 79; Delo, *Peddlers and Post Traders*, 199; *ANJ*, Dec. 22, 1888.

30. *Sidney Telegraph*, Jan. 9, 1886.

31. *Crawford Crescent*, July 14, 1887.

32. Schubert, *Buffalo Soldiers, Braves, and Brass*, 93.

33. *Omaha Daily Bee*, Sept. 6, 1883.

34. Ibid., Jan. 9, 1884.

35. Orders 15, 1888, PO FR; *ANJ*, Febr. 16, 1889.

36. Corliss diary, Jan. 17, 1889, July 11, 1889.

37. *ANJ*, Dec. 3, 1887; *Crawford Tribune*, Sept. 18, 1896; James Cooper Ayres, "After Big Game with Packs," *The Century Magazine* 58 (June 1899): 225. See also "A Western Hunting Trip, September 1889," *Hayes Historical Journal* 12 (Fall 1992–Winter 1993): 59–64, and Potter, "Firearms Accidents," 179.

38. *ANJ*, Dec. 31, 1887.

39. Corliss diary, Oct. 7, 1889.

40. Maj. Louis H. Carpenter to AAG DP, Apr. 24, 1884, LR QM DP.

41. Thomas R. Buecker, "The Fort and the Railroad: Fort Robinson, Nebraska, on the C&NW," *North Western Lines* 23 (Fall 1996): 23.

42. *Annual Report of the Secretary of War, 1884* 1 (Washington: GPO, 1885): 116.

43. Remi Nadeau, *Fort Laramie and the Sioux Indians* (Englewood Cliffs, N.J.: Prentice Hall, Inc., 1967), 294.

44. *Annual Report of the Secretary of War, 1884* 1:84–85, 103–4.

45. *Omaha Daily Bee*, July 27, 1886.

46. Leroy R. Hafen and Francis M. Young, *Fort Laramie and the Pageant of the West, 1834–1890* (Glendale, Calif.: The Arthur Clark Co., 1938), 390.

47. U.S. Sen. Charles F. Manderson from Omaha served from 1883 to 1895 and was a member of committees on Indian and military affairs. Archibald J. Weaver was the First District Representative from Falls City, Nebraska, from 1883 to 1887. George W. Dorsey was Third District Representative from Fremont, Nebraska, from 1885 to 1891. Dorsey secured appropriations for buildings at Forts Niobrara, Omaha, and Robinson and at the Indian school at Genoa, Nebraska.

48. *Chadron Democrat*, Mar. 18, 1886.

49. Ibid., Febr. 11, 1886; *Sidney Telegraph*, Jan. 30, 1886, referring to the *Dawes County Journal*, another Chadron newspaper.

50. "To Enlarge, Repair, and Complete Certain Military Quarters and Barracks in Wyoming Territory and in the State of Nebraska," *Senate Reports*, No. 930, May 5, 1886, 49th U.S. Cong., 1st sess., 1885–1886, Serial 2360.

51. Ibid., 2-3.

52. *Annual Report of the Secretary of War, 1887* (Washington: GPO, 1888): 430.

53. Lt. Col. James S. Brisbin to AAG DP, Dec. 5, 1886, and Jan. 18, 1887, LS FR, 1884–1900, RG 98.

54. Orders 9, Jan. 18, 1887, PO FR.

55. Corliss diary, Mar. 18, 1887. Dates regarding visits of officers and general construction activity are from the diary.

56. All information regarding garrison strength, troop transfers and duties, and officer transfers and duties are from monthly Post Returns from January to December, 1887.

57. Hatch to AAG DP, May 26, 1887, LS FR.

58. Ibid., June 19, 1887, LS FR.

59. Telegram, Hatch to chief quartermaster DP, May 23, 1887, LS FR.

60. Letter endorsement, May 21, 1887, LS FR.

61. Telegram, Hatch to AAG DP, June 17, 1887; Letter endorsement, Hatch to AAG DP, July 11, 1887, LS FR.

62. Telegram, Hatch to AAG DP, June 29, 1887, LS FR; *Chadron Democrat*, June 30, July 14, 1887; *Crawford Crescent*, July 14, 1887.

63. Hatch to AAG DP, June 13, 1887, LS FR.

64. Ibid., July 12, 1887, LS FR.

65. All information on buildings involved in the 1887 expansion and the later construction mentioned is compiled from materials held in the Fort Building File at the FRM.

66. Orders 177, Sept. 5, 1887, PO FR; Orders 188, Sept. 23, 1887, PO FR.

67. Hatch to AAG DP, Sept. 14, 1887; Telegram, Hatch to AAG DP, July 11, 1887, LS FR.

68. Monthly medical report by Capt. Arthur W. Taylor, post surgeon, Sept.–Oct. 1887. Fort Robinson Medical History (MH FR), RG 98.

69. Fort Robinson completion reports, Oct. 30, Nov. 1, 30, 1887, FR LS.

70. Hafen and Young, *Fort Laramie*, 393–94.

8. The Buffalo Soldiers

1. The standard source on black cavalry in the West remains William H. Leckie, *The Buffalo Soldiers: A Narrative of the Negro Cavalry in the West* (Norman: University of Oklahoma Press, 1967). See also John M. Carroll, ed., *The Black Military Experience in the American West* (New York: Liveright Publishing Company, 1971), and John P. Langellier, *Men A-marching: The African American Soldier in the West, 1866–1896* (Springfield, Penn.: Steven Wright Publishing, 1995). For an in-depth study of all aspects of black enlisted life at Fort Robinson, see Schubert, *Buffalo Soldiers, Braves, and The Brass.*

2. Heitman, *Historical Register*, 510; Grote Hutcheson, "The Ninth Regiment of Cavalry," in Carroll, *Black Military Experience*, 68.

3. Hutcheson, "The Ninth Regiment," 74.

4. Unless otherwise indicated, all information on troop movements in this chapter are from Post Returns, Fort Robinson.

5. Compiled from individual entries in Heitman, *Historical Register.*

6. Corliss diary, Oct 1, 1887; Frank N. Schubert, *On the Trail of the Buffalo Soldier: Biographies of African Americans in the U.S. Army, 1866–1917* (Wilmington, Del.: Scholarly Resources, Inc., 1995), 3–4. For Young see 489–90.

7. *ANJ*, Jan. 18, 1890.

8. *Chadron Democrat*, Jan. 14, 1886; *ANJ*, Mar. 6, 1886.

9. *Cheyenne Leader*, Oct. 20, 1887; Gerald M. Adams, *The Post Near Cheyenne: A History of Fort D. A. Russell, 1867–1930* (Boulder: Pruett Publishing Company, 1989), 95–96.

10. *Army and Navy Register*, Mar. 23, 1889; *ANJ*, Mar. 30, 1889.

11. *ANJ*, Apr. 20, 1889.

12. Orders 88, Apr. 26, 1890, PO FR; Schubert, *Buffalo Soldiers, Braves, and Brass*, 25.

13. Fort Robinson Annual Report, Aug. 21, 1890, LS FR.

14. Orders 154, July 25, 1890, PO FR.

15. Corliss diary, July 30, Dec. 3, 1889.

16. The standard source on the Ghost Dance troubles and the Pine Ridge campaign is Robert M. Utley, *The Last Days of the Sioux Nation* (New Haven: Yale University Press, 1963. Another valuable source is Richard E. Jensen, R. Eli Paul, and John E. Carter, *Eyewitness at Wounded Knee* (Lincoln: University of Nebraska Press, 1991).

17. *ANJ*, Aug. 2, 1890; Schubert, *On the Trail*, 249.

18. Scott, *Some Memories*, 177–79.

19. Corliss diary, Oct. 2, 3, 1890; Post Returns, Aug. 1890.

20. Corliss diary, Sept. 11, 1890.

21. Unless otherwise noted, this narrative is based on Utley, *Last Days*, and Jensen, et al, *Eyewitness*.

22. *ANJ*, Nov. 29, 1890.

23. Charles W. Taylor, "The Surrender of Red Cloud, 1891," in *The Unpublished Papers of the Order of the Indian Wars* 2, ed. John M. Carroll (New Brunswick, N.J.: Privately published, n.d.), 4; *ANJ*, Dec. 9, 1890.

24. John M. Carroll, ed., "Extracts from Letters Written by Lieutenant Alexander R. Piper, 8th Infantry, at Pine Ridge Agency, South Dakota, to His Wife, Marie Cozzens Piper, at Fort Robinson, Nebraska, during the Sioux Campaign, 1890–1891," in *The Unpublished Papers of the Order of Indian Wars* 10 (New Brunswick, N.J.: Privately published, 1977), 1, 2, 4.

25. *ANJ*, Dec. 6, 1890.

26. William Fitch Kelley, *Pine Ridge 1890: An Eye Witness Account of the Events Surrounding the Fighting at Wounded Knee*, eds. Alexander Kelley and Pierre Bovis (San Francisco: Pierre Bovis, 1971), 116–17; Jensen, et al, *Eyewitness*, 32.

27. Guy V. Henry, "A Sioux Episode," *Harper's Weekly* 40 (Dec. 26, 1896): 1273.

28. Ibid., 1274; Leckie, *Buffalo Soldiers*, 255.

29. For an interesting, rarely cited Wounded Knee reminiscence, see John M. Carroll, ed., "Letter from Brigadier General Guy H. Preston," in *The Unpublished Papers of the Order of Indian Wars* 7 (New Brunswick, N.J.: Privately published, 1977), 27–32.

30. Utley, *Last Days*, 235–36; Ninth Cavalry Regimental Returns, Dec. 1890.

31. *ANJ*, Jan. 10, 17, 1891; Preston E. Amos, *Above and Beyond in the West: Black Medal of Honor Winners, 1870–1890* (Washington: Potomac Corral, The Westerners, 1974), 37–38. The Ninth cavalryman killed in the attack was Pvt. Charles Haywood, Troop D. Schubert, *On the Trail*, 197.

32. *Winners of the West*, Apr. 30, 1929, letter from J. B. Hartzog, former member of Light Battery E, 1st Artillery.

33. Lt. Alex W. Perry, "The Ninth Cavalry in the Sioux Campaign of 1890," in Carroll, *Black Military Experience*, 254; Cyrus T. Brady, *Indian Fights and Fighters* (New York: Doubleday, Page & Co., 1913), 354.

34. Carroll, "Extracts from Letters," 6–7.

35. *ANJ*, Jan. 10, 1891.

36. Ibid., Mar. 14, 1891; Foner, *United States Soldier*, 134–35. Other verses appear in James Mooney, *The Ghost-Dance Religion and the Sioux Outbreak of 1890* (Lincoln: University of Nebraska Press, 1991), 883.

37. *ANJ*, Mar. 9, 28, Apr. 4, May 2, 1891.

38. Foner, *United States Soldier*, 143; *ANJ*, May 9, 1891; Coffman, *Old Army*, 371.

39. Wilson's later troubles are noted in Amos, *Above and Beyond*, 38–39; Schubert, *On the Trail*, 480; and Frank N. Schubert, *Black Valor: Buffalo Soldiers and the Medal of Honor, 1870–1898* (Wilmington, Del.: Scholarly Resources, Inc., 1997), 117–32; *ANJ*, Jan. 31, 1891.

40. Oct. 1892, PR FR; *Chicago Tribune*, Oct. 18, 1892; *ANJ*, Oct. 22, 29, 1892.

41. For more on the Suggs affair, see Robert A. Murray, "The United States Army in the Aftermath of the Johnson County Invasion," *Annals of Wyoming* 38 (Apr. 1966): 59–75, and Frank N. Schubert, "The Suggs Affray: The Black Cavalry in the Johnson County War," *Western Historical Quarterly* 4 (Jan. 1973): 57–68. The camp was named in honor of 1st Lt. Philip A. Bettens, Jr., a former Ninth Cavalry officer who died on March 27, 1892.

42. Marvin E. Fletcher, *The Black Soldier and Officer in the United States Army, 1891–1917* (Columbia: University of Missouri Press, 1974), 89.

43. Ellen M. Biddle, *Reminiscences of a Soldier's Wife* (Philadelphia: J. B. Lippincott Company, 1907), 232–33; *ANJ*, Sept. 12, 1896.

44. All information on 1890s construction comes from Fort Building File, FRM.

45. *ANJ*, June 29, 1895.

46. *Nebraska State Journal* (Lincoln), Sept. 27, 1896.

47. Post circular, Oct. 23, 1886, with Orders 177, PO FR.

48. Report on post, June 30, 1893, MH FR, 246–47.

49. *Chadron Democrat*, Sept. 16, 1886; Frank N. Schubert, "The Violent World of Emanuel Stance, Fort Robinson," *Nebraska History* 55 (Summer 1974): 207; Schubert, *On the Trail*, 279, 292, 355.

50. For a complete analysis of the Stance incident, see Schubert, "Violent World."

51. Don Rickey interview of Simpson Mann, Wadsworth Veterans' Hospital, Leavenworth, Kans., 1965, typescript, NSHS Archives.

52. *ANJ*, Dec. 31, 1887.

53. Schubert, *Buffalo Soldiers, Braves, and Brass*, 85.

54. *Army and Navy Register*, Jan. 7, 1888; *ANJ*, Jan. 14, 1888.

55. Schubert, "Violent World," 209; Simpson Mann interview.

56. Fort Robinson Annual Report, Aug. 28, 1891, LS FR.

57. *ANJ*, Jan. 4, 1890.

58. Col. James Biddle to AAG DP, Oct. 15, 16, 19, 1891, LS FR; Schubert, *Buffalo Soldiers, Braves, and Brass*, 81.

59. *Crawford Tribune*, Apr. 6, 1894.

60. Schubert, *Buffalo Soldiers, Braves, and Brass*, 133.

61. Sanitary Report, July 1891, MH FR.

62. Schubert, *On the Trail*, 149; Biddle endorsement on letter from Bertie Fort to secretary of war, July 28, 1894, copy on file at FRM.

63. Orders 191, Dec. 23, 1883, PO FR; Order 6, Jan. 8, 1884, PO FR.

64. Fort Robinson Annual Report, Aug. 28, 1891, LS FR.

65. Ibid.; Foner, *United States Soldier*, 93–94;

66. Coffman, *Old Army*, 361; *ANJ*, Apr. 11, May 9, 1896.

67. Unidentified newspaper clipping found in Augustus Corliss Scrapbook, copy at FRM; *ANJ*, Jan. 28, Febr. 8, 1896.

68. *Chadron Citizen*, May 4, 1893.

69. "Sergeant Barney McKay, Trial by General Court Martial at Fort Robinson, Nebraska, June 1–21, 1893," Exhibit B, RG 153, Records of the Judge Advocate General, NA. The full text of the broadside was also published in the *Chadron Citizen*, May 4, 1893.

70. *Chadron Democrat*, Apr. 28, 1893.

71. *Crawford Tribune*, May 5, 1893. For a thorough study of this event, see Earl F. Stover, "Chaplain Henry V. Plummer, His Ministry and His Court Martial," *Nebraska History* 56 (Spring 1975): 21–50.

72. *Crawford Tribune*, June 2, 1893; Schubert, *Buffalo Soldiers, Braves, and Brass*, 90–91.

73. Stover, "Chaplain Henry V. Plummer," 36.

74. Schubert, *Buffalo Soldiers, Braves, and Brass*, 34.

75. Ibid., 34; *Crawford Tribune*, July 2, 1897.

76. Frederic Remington, "The Essentials at Fort Adobe," *Harper's New Monthly Magazine* 96 (Apr. 1898): 727–35.

77. An exact date for Remington's visit in 1896 or 1897 has not been determined. Peter H. Hassrick and Melissa J. Webster, *Frederic Remington: A Catalogue Raisonné of Paintings, Watercolors and Drawings* 2 (Cody, Wyo.: Buffalo Bill Historical Center, 1996): 598–99.

78. *Crawford Tribune*, July 9, 1897; Grange, "Fort Robinson Outpost," 229.

79. *Crawford Tribune*, Mar. 4, 1898; Post Returns, Fort Robinson, Mar. 1898.

80. *ANJ*, Apr. 2, 1898; Schubert, *On the Trail*, 446.

81. *Crawford Tribune*, Mar. 25, 1898.

82. Ibid., Apr. 22, 1898.

83. Medley & Jensen, *Illustrated Review, Ninth Cavalry, United States Army, Fort D. A. Russell, Wyoming* (Denver: Medley & Jensen, Publishers, 1910), 67. For more on the army in this conflict, see Graham A. Cosmas, *An Army for Empire: The United States Army in the Spanish-American War* (Columbia: University of Missouri Press, 1971).

84. *Afro-American Sentinel* (Omaha), Apr. 16, 1898; *Nebraska State Journal*, July 10, 1898. The other black cavalry regiment, the Tenth Cavalry, garrisoned Fort Robinson from 1902 to 1907.

85. Schubert, *Buffalo Soldiers, Braves, and Brass*, 35, 39.

86. Post Returns, Fort Robinson, July–Oct., 1899.

87. *Crawford Tribune*, Dec. 21, 1900.

88. Betty Loudon, ed., "Pioneer Pharmacist J. Walter Moyer's Notes on Crawford and Fort Robinson in the 1890s," *Nebraska History* 58 (Spring 1977): 115.

89. Sanitary Report, Dec. 1899, MH FR.

90. Ibid., May, 1900, MH FR.

Epilogue

1. Biddle, *Reminiscences of a Soldier's Wife*, 222–24, 227.

2. Price, Sir Rose L., *A Summer in the Rockies* (London: Sampson Low, Marston & Co., 1898), 235, 241.

Bibliography

Manuscript Materials

Arizona Historical Society, Tucson, Ariz.
  Charles Morton Collection.

Brigham Young University, Provo, Utah
  Walter Mason Camp Collection, Harry B. Lee Library.

Denver Public Library, Denver, Colo.
  Augustus Corliss Diary, Western History Collection.

  Robert S. Ellison Papers. Western History Collection.

Fort Laramie National Historic Site, Fort Laramie, Wyo.
  J. W. Dear Correspondence.

Fort Robinson Museum, Crawford, Nebr.
  Fort Building File, information on file collected on each building or structure erected at the fort, 1874–1948.

  Rickey D. Malcolm, "The Cheyenne Outbreak," a daily record of events, transcribed and organized chronologically from "Proceedings of a Board of Officers Investigating the Cheyenne Outbreak."

National Archives and Records Administration, Washington, D.C.
  RG 48, Records of the Office of the Secretary of the Interior: Agent Files

  RG 75, Records of the Bureau of Indian Affairs: Letters Received by the Office of Indian Affairs, Red Cloud Agency, 1871–1880, and Spotted Tail Agency, 1875–1880

  RG 92, Records of the Office of the Quartermaster General

  RG 94, Records of the Office of the Adjutant General: Letters Received, 1871-1880; Post Returns, Fort Robinson, 1874–1899; Returns from Regular Army Cavalry Regiments; Returns from Regular Army Infantry Regiments

  RG 98, Records of the United States Army Commands: Fort Robinson Medical History, 1887–1900; Letters Sent, Fort Robinson, 1884–1900; Post Orders, 1874–1897

  RG 153, Records of the Judge Advocate General: "Sergeant Barney McKay, Trial by General Court Martial at Fort Robinson, Nebraska, June 1–21, 1893"

  RG 393, Records of the United States Army Continental Commands
    Adjutant General's Office: Document File 4163 (Sioux War); Document File 6470 (Cheyenne Indians, 1878–1879).

    Department of the Platte: "Compilation of Correspondence and Orders Relative to the Establishment and Boundaries of Military Reservations in the Department, 1859–1895; Letters Sent and Received, 1874–1879; Chief Quartermaster Letters Sent and Received, 1874–1879.

    District of the Black Hills: General Orders and Special Orders, 1874–1877.

    Military Division of the Missouri: Letters Sent and Received, 1876–1877; Selected Documents Sioux Expedition, 1874.

National Archives and Records Administration, Central Plains Region, Kansas City, Mo.
RG 75, Records of the Bureau of Indian Affairs: Letters Received, Red Cloud Agency, 1874.

Nebraska State Historical Society Archives, Lincoln, Nebr.
Appleton Family Collection: Amos Appleton Letters from Red Cloud Agency.

Fred Bruning Collection: Manuscript, "Winter of 1876–1877 at Camp Canby."

Fort Robinson, Nebraska, Records, 1874–1948: Fort Robinson Guard Book, September 17, 1877 to April 1, 1878.

Charles P. Jordan Collection: "Red Cloud Manuscript."

"Exact Copy of a Notebook kept by Dr. V. T. McGillycuddy, M.D., While a Member of the Yellowstone and Big Horn Expedition, May 26–Dec.13, 1876, and Notes Kept by His Wife, Fanny, at Camp Robinson, Dec.13, 1876–Feb. 22, 1877, and With the Army on an Expedition to the Black Hills, Feb. 23–April 11, 1877."

Eli S. Ricker Collection.

Correspondence of the Superintendent, Nebraska State Historical Society

Thomas Wright Collection: Report of William Garnett, Interpreter, to General H. L. Scott and Major James McLaughlin.

Chris Nelson, Annandale, Va.
Augustus Corliss Scrapbook.

Newberry Library, Chicago, Ill.
Henry W. Lawton Scrapbook, Letters from Camp Robinson, Oct. 15, 1876, and May 20, 1877.

Rutherford B. Hayes Presidential Center, Fremont, Ohio.
George Crook Letterbook.

South Dakota State Historical Society, Pierre, S.Dak.
Crazy Horse Biography File.

Fanny McGillycuddy Diary, 1877–1878.

United States Army Military History Institute, Carlisle Barracks, Penn.
Luther P. Bradley Papers.

United States Military Academy Library, West Point, N.Y.
John G. Bourke Diaries, 1876–1877.

James Fornance Letters from Camp Robinson, Mar. 16–Oct. 10, 1874.

Yale University Library, New Haven, Conn.
Thomas M. Anderson Manuscript, William Robertson Coe Collection.

Unpublished Materials
Buecker, Thomas R. "History of Camp Robinson, Nebraska 1874–1878," Master's thesis, Chadron State College, Chadron, Nebr., 1992.

———. "The Red Cloud Agency Ledger Book." Manuscript. Fort Robinson Museum.

Holcomb, Eloise. "Fort Robinson: Its Role in the Subjugation of the Sioux Indians, 1874–1878." Master's thesis, Chadron State College, Chadron, Nebr., 1966.

Mather, William D. "The Revolt of Little Wolf's Northern Cheyenne." Master's thesis, University of Wichita, Wichita, Kans., 1958.

Government Publications
Annual Reports: Commissioner of Indian Affairs, Secretary of Interior; Secretary of War.

National Archives Microfilm Publications: "Proceedings of a Board of Officers Convened by Virtue of the Following Special Order: Headquarters Department of the Platte, Fort Omaha, Nebraska, January 21, 1879, Special Orders No. 8," in "Papers Relating to Military Operations against the Northern Cheyennes, 1878–79," M666, roll 428; "Returns from Regular Army Infantry Regiments, June 1821–December 1916," M665, rolls 47, 48, 95, 96, 155, 156; "Returns from Regular Army Cavalry Regiments, 1833–1916," M744, rolls 30, 31, 43, 54, 66, 90, 91.

Report of the Special Commission Appointed to Investigate the Affairs of the Red Cloud Agency, July, 1875. Washington: GPO, 1875.

Revised Statutes of the United States, Passed at the First Session of the Forty-third Congress, 1873–74. Washington: GPO, 1875.

Senate Miscellaneous Documents: "Escape of Cheyenne Indians from Fort Robinson," No. 64, 45th U.S. Cong., 3rd sess., 1879.

Senate Reports: "The Removal of the Northern Cheyennes from the Sioux Reservation to the Indian Territory," No. 708, June 8, 1880, 46th U.S. Congress, 2nd sess., 1879–1880, Serial 1899; "For the Relief of the Administrator of the Estate of John W. Dear, Deceased," No. 180, Febr. 15, 1884, 48th U. S. Cong., 1st sess., 1883-1884, Serial 2174; "To Enlarge, Repair, and Complete Certain Military Quarters and Barracks in Wyoming Territory and in the State of Nebraska," No. 930, May 5, 1886, 49th U.S. Cong., 1st sess., 1885–1886, Serial 2360.

Newspapers
Afro-American Sentinel (Omaha)

Army and Navy Journal (New York)

Army and Navy Register (Washington)

Atchison Champion

Casper Star–Tribune

Chadron Citizen

Chadron Democrat

Cheyenne Daily News

Cheyenne Leader

Chicago Tribune

Crawford Clipper

Crawford Crescent

Crawford Tribune

Fort Laramie Scout

Nebraska State Journal (Lincoln)

New York Herald

New York Sun

Northwest Nebraska News (Crawford)

Omaha Daily Bee

Omaha Daily Herald

Omaha Daily Republican

Omaha Herald

Omaha Weekly Bee

Omaha World-Herald

Rocky Mountain News (Denver)

Sidney Telegraph

Sioux City Journal

Winners of the West (St. Joseph)

Yankton Press and Dakotaian

Books
Adams, Gerald M. *The Post Near Cheyenne: A History of Fort D. A. Russell, 1867–1930*. Boulder: Pruett Publishing Co., 1989.

Adjutant General's Office. *Chronological List of Actions &c. with Indians from January 15, 1837 to January, 1891*. Reprint of 1891 edition. Fort Collins, Colo.: The Old Army Press, 1979.

Allen, Charles W. *From Fort Laramie to Wounded Knee: In the West That Was*, ed. Richard E. Jensen. Lincoln: University of Nebraska Press, 1997.

Amos, Preston E. *Above and Beyond: Black Medal of Honor Winners, 1870–1890*. Washington: Potomac Corral, The Westerners, 1974.

Anderson, Harry H., ed. *Indian Campaigns: Sketches of Cavalry Service in Arizona and on the Northern Plains*. Fort Collins, Colo.: The Old Army Press, 1984.

Andreas, A. T., ed. *History of the State of Nebraska*. Chicago: The Western Historical Company, 1882.

Berthrong, Donald J. *The Cheyenne and Arapaho Ordeal: Reservation and Agency Life in the Indian Territory, 1875–1907*. Norman: University of Oklahoma Press, 1976.

Biddle, Ellen M. *Reminiscences of a Soldier's Wife*. Philadelphia: J. B. Lippincott Co., 1907.

Billings, John S. *Circular No. 8: A Report on the Hygiene of the United States Army with Descriptions of Military Posts*. Reprint of 1875 edition. New York: Sol Lewis, 1974.

Blish, Helen H. *A Pictographic History of the Oglala Sioux*. Lincoln: University of Nebraska Press, 1967.

Bourke, John G. *Mackenzie's Last Fight With the Cheyennes: A Winter Campaign in Wyoming and Montana*. Reprint of 1890 edition Fort Collins, Colo.: The Old Army Press, 1970.

————. *On the Border With Crook*. New York: Charles Scribner's Sons, 1891.

Brady, Cyrus T. *Indian Fights and Fighters*. New York: Doubleday, Page & Co., 1913.

Bronson, Edgar B. *Reminiscences of a Ranchman*. New York: The McClure Co., 1908.

Brown, Jesse, and A. M. Willard. *The Black Hills Trail*. Rapid City: Rapid City Journal Co., 1924.

Bruce, Robert. *The Fighting Norths and Pawnee Scouts: Narratives and Reminiscences of Military Service on the Old Frontier*. Lincoln: Nebraska State Historical Society, 1932.

Buecker, Thomas R., and R. Eli Paul, eds. *The Crazy Horse Surrender Ledger*. Lincoln: Nebraska State Historical Society, 1994.

Byrne, P. E. *Soldiers of the Plains*. New York: Minton, Balch & Co., 1926.

Carroll, John M., ed. *The Black Military Experience in the American West*. New York: Liveright Publishing Corp., 1971.

Carter, William H. *The History of Fort Robinson*. Crawford, Nebr.: Northwest Nebraska News, 1941.

Chandler, Melbourne C. *Of Garryowen in Glory: The History of the 7th U.S. Cavalry*. Annandale, Va.: Melbourne C. Chandler, 1960.

Clark, Robert A., ed. *The Killing of Chief Crazy Horse*. Lincoln: University of Nebraska Press, 1988.

Coffman, Edward M. *The Old Army: A Portrait of the American Army in Peacetime, 1784–1898*. New York: Oxford University Press, 1986.

Corbusier, William T. *Verde to San Carlos: Recollections of a Famous Army Surgeon and His Observant Family on the Western Frontier, 1869–1886*. Tucson: Dale S. King, 1968.

Cosmas, Graham A. *An Army for Empire: The United States Army in the Spanish-American War*. Columbia: University of Missouri Press, 1971.

Cox-Paul, Lori A., and James W. Wengert. *A Frontier Army Christmas*. Lincoln: Nebraska State Historical Society, 1996.

Curley, Edwin A. *Guide to the Black Hills*. Reprint of 1877 edition. Mitchell, S.Dak.: Dakota Wesleyan University Press, 1973.

Danker, Donald F., ed. *Man of the Plains: Recollections of Luther North, 1856–1882*. Lincoln: University of Nebraska Press, 1961.

Delo, David M. *Peddlers and Post Traders: The Army Sutler on the Frontier*. Salt Lake City: University of Utah Press, 1992.

Dunlay, Thomas W. *Wolves for the Blue Soldiers: Indian Scouts and Auxiliaries with the United States Army, 1860-90.* Lincoln: University of Nebraska Press, 1982.

Fletcher, Marvin E. *The Black Soldier and Officer in the United States Army, 1891–1917.* Columbia: University of Missouri Press, 1974.

Foner, Jack D. *The United States Soldier Between Two Wars: Army Life and Reforms, 1865–1898.* New York: Humanities Press, 1970.

Fowler, Loretta. *Arapahoe Politics, 1851–1978: Symbols in Crises of Authority.* Lincoln: University of Nebraska Press, 1982.

Frazer, Robert W. *Forts of the West: Military Forts and Presidios and Posts Commonly Called Forts West of the Mississippi River to 1898.* Norman: University of Oklahoma Press, 1980.

Ganoe, William G. *The History of the United States Army.* New York: D. Appleton–Century Co., 1942.

Gillett, Mary C. *The Army Medical Department, 1865–1917.* Washington: Center of Military History, United States Army, 1995.

Gray, John S. *Centennial Campaign: The Sioux War of 1876.* Fort Collins, Colo.: The Old Army Press, 1976.

Greene, Jerome A. *Slim Buttes, 1876: An Episode of the Great Sioux War.* Norman: University of Oklahoma Press, 1982.

———. *Yellowstone Command: Colonel Nelson A. Miles and the Great Sioux War, 1876–1877.* Lincoln: University of Nebraska Press, 1991.

———, ed. *Lakota and Cheyenne: Indian Views of the Great Sioux War, 1876–1877.* Norman: University of Oklahoma Press, 1994.

Grinnell, George B. *The Fighting Cheyennes.* New York: Charles Scribner's Sons, 1915.

Hafen, LeRoy A., and Francis M. Young. *Fort Laramie and the Pageant of the West, 1834–1890.* Glendale, Calif.: The Arthur Clark Co., 1938.

Hardorff, Richard G. *The Oglala Lakota Crazy Horse: A Preliminary Genealogical Study and an Annotated Listing of Primary Sources.* Mattituck, N.Y.: J. M. Carroll & Co., 1985.

Hassrick, Peter H., and Melissa J. Webster. *Frederic Remington: A Catalogue Raisonné of Paintings, Watercolors and Drawings,* 2 vol. Cody, Wyo.: Buffalo Bill Historical Center, 1996.

Hedren, Paul L. *First Scalp For Custer: The Skirmish at Warbonnet Creek, Nebraska, July 17, 1876, with a Short History of the Warbonnet Battlefield.* Lincoln: University of Nebraska Press, 1987.

———. *Fort Laramie in 1876: Chronicle of a Frontier Post at War.* Lincoln: University of Nebraska Press, 1988.

———, ed. *The Great Sioux War, 1876–77: The Best from* Montana The Magazine of Western History. Helena: Montana Historical Society Press, 1991.

———. *Traveler's Guide to the Great Sioux War.* Helena: Montana Historical Society Press, 1996.

Heitman, Francis B. *Historical Register and Dictionary of the United States Army.* Reprint of 1903 edition. Urbana: University of Illinois Press, 1965.

Hutton, Paul A. *Phil Sheridan and His Army.* Lincoln: University of Nebraska Press, 1985.

————, ed. *Soldiers West: Biographies from the Military Frontier.* Lincoln: University of Nebraska Press, 1987.

Hyde, George E. *Red Cloud's Folk: A History of the Oglala Sioux Indians.* Norman: University of Oklahoma Press, 1937.

————. *Spotted Tail's Folk: A History of the Brulé Sioux.* Norman: University of Oklahoma Press, 1961.

Jensen, Richard E., R. Eli Paul, and John E. Carter. *Eyewitness at Wounded Knee.* Lincoln: University of Nebraska Press, 1991.

Jocelyn, Stephen P. *Mostly Alkali.* Caldwell, Idaho: Caxton Printers, 1953.

Kelley, William Fitch. *Pine Ridge 1890: An Eye Witness Account of the Events Surrounding the Fighting at Wounded Knee,* eds. Alexander Kelley and Pierre Bovis. San Francisco: Pierre Bovis, 1971.

King, Charles. *Campaigning With Crook and Stories of Army Life.* New York: Harper & Brothers, 1890.

Langellier, John P. *Men A-marching: The African American Soldier in the West, 1866–1896.* Springfield, Penn.: Steven Wright Publishing, 1995.

Larson, Robert W. *Red Cloud: Warrior–Statesman of the Lakota Sioux.* Norman: University of Oklahoma Press, 1997.

Lass, William E. *From the Missouri to the Great Salt Lake: An Account of Overland Freighting.* Lincoln: Nebraska State Historical Society, 1972.

Laws, Joint Resolutions and Memorials Passed at the Eleventh Session of the Legislative Assembly of the State of Nebraska. Omaha: Omaha Daily Republican, 1875.

Leckie, William H. *The Buffalo Soldiers: A Narrative of the Negro Cavalry in the West.* Norman: University of Oklahoma Press, 1967.

Lee, Robert. *Fort Meade and the Black Hills.* Lincoln: University of Nebraska Press, 1991.

Liddic, Bruce R., and Paul Harbaugh. *Camp On Custer: Transcribing the Custer Myth.* Spokane: The Arthur Clark Co., 1995.

Manypenny, George W. *Our Indian Wards.* Cincinnati: Robert Clark & Co., 1880.

Marquis, Thomas B. *Cheyenne and Sioux: The Reminiscences of Four Indians and a White Soldier.* Stockton, Calif.: Pacific Center for Western Historical Studies, 1973.

————. *A Warrior Who Fought Custer.* Minneapolis: The Midwest Co., 1931.

McChristian, Douglas C. *An Army of Marksmen: The Development of United States Army Marksmanship in the 19th Century.* Fort Collins, Colo.: The Old Army Press, 1981.

————. *The U.S. Army in the West, 1870–1880: Uniforms, Weapons, and Equipment.* Norman: University of Oklahoma Press, 1995.

McGillycuddy, Julia B. *McGillycuddy Agent: A Biography of Dr. Valentine T. McGillycuddy*. Stanford University, Calif.: Stanford University Press, 1941.

Medley and Jensen. *Illustrated Review Ninth Cavalry, United States Army, Fort D. A. Russell, Wyoming*. Denver: Medley & Jensen Publishers, 1910.

Milner, Joe, and Earle R. Forrest. *California Joe: Noted Scout and Indian Fighter*. Caldwell, Idaho: The Caxton Printers, 1935.

Mooney, James. *The Ghost Dance Religion and the Sioux Outbreak of 1890*. Lincoln: University of Nebraska Press, 1991.

Murray, Robert A. *Military Posts in the Powder River of Wyoming, 1865–1894*. Lincoln: University of Nebraska Press, 1968.

Nadeau, Remi. *Fort Laramie and the Sioux Indians*. Englewood Cliffs, N.J.: Prentice-Hall Inc., 1967.

Olson, James C. *Red Cloud and the Sioux Problem*. Lincoln: University of Nebraska Press, 1965.

Paul, R. Eli, ed. *Autobiography of Red Cloud: War Leader of the Oglalas*. Helena: Montana Historical Society Press, 1997.

———, ed. *The Nebraska Indian Wars Reader, 1865–1877*. Lincoln: University of Nebraska Press, 1998.

Pierce, Michael D. *The Most Promising Young Officer: A Life of Ranald Slidell Mackenzie*. Norman: University of Oklahoma Press, 1993.

Price, Sir Rose Lambart. *A Summer in the Rockies*. London: Sampson Low, Marston & Co., 1898.

Rickey, Don, Jr. *Forty Miles a Day on Beans and Hay: The Enlisted Soldier Fighting the Indian Wars*. Norman: University of Oklahoma Press, 1963.

Robinson, Charles M. *A Good Year to Die: The Story of the Great Sioux War*. New York: Random House, 1995.

Rodenbough, Theophilus F., ed. *Fighting for Honor: A Record of Heroism*. New York: G. W. Dillingham, 1893.

Sandoz, Mari. *Hostiles and Friendlies: Selected Short Writings of Mari Sandoz*. Lincoln: University of Nebraska Press, 1959.

Sanger, George P., ed. *The Statutes at Large, Treaties, and Proclamations of the United States of America from December 1867, to March 1869, Vol. 15*. Boston: Little, Brown & Co., 1869.

Schmitt, Martin F., ed. *General George Crook: His Autobiography*. Norman: University of Oklahoma Press, 1946.

Schubert, Frank N. *Black Valor: Buffalo Soldiers and the Medal of Honor, 1870–1898*. Wilmington, Del.: Scholarly Resources, Inc., 1997.

———. *Buffalo Soldiers, Braves, and The Brass: The Story of Fort Robinson, Nebraska*. Shippensburg, Penn.: White Mane Publishing Company, 1993.

———. *On the Trail of the Buffalo Soldier: Biographies of African Americans in the U.S. Army, 1866–1917.* Wilmington, Del.: Scholarly Resources, Inc., 1995.

Scott, William B. *Some Memories of a Paleontologist.* Princeton: Princeton University Press, 1939.

Sheridan, Philip H. *Outline Descriptions of the Posts in the Military Division of the Missouri.* Reprint of 1876 edition. Fort Collins, Colo.: The Old Army Press, 1969.

———. *Record of Engagements with Hostile Indians Within the Military Division of the Missouri.* Reprint of 1882 edition. The Old Army Press, 1969.

Stallard, Patricia Y. *Glittering Misery: Dependents of the Indian Fighting Army.* San Rafael, Calif.: Presidio Press and The Old Army Press, 1978.

Taft, Robert. *Artists and Illustrators of the Old West, 1850–1900.* New York: Charles Scribner's Sons, 1953.

Thrapp, Dan L. *Encyclopedia of Frontier Biography.* Lincoln: University of Nebraska Press, 1991.

Utley, Robert M. *Frontier Regulars: The United States Army and the Indian, 1866–1891.* New York: Macmillan Publishing Co., 1973.

———. *The Indian Frontier of the American West 1846–1890.* Albuquerque: University of New Mexico Press, 1984.

———. *The Last Days of the Sioux Nation.* New Haven: Yale University Press, 1963.

Vaughn, J. W. *The Reynolds Campaign on Powder River.* Norman: University of Oklahoma Press, 1961.

War Department. *Regulations for the Army of the United States, 1889.* Washington: Government Printing Office, 1889.

———. *Revised United States Army Regulations of 1861, With an Appendix Containing the Changes and Laws Affecting Army Regulations and Articles of War to June 25, 1863.* Philadelphia: George W. Childs, 1864.

Wheeler, Homer W. *Buffalo Days: Forty Years in the Old West.* New York: A. L. Burt Publisher, 1925.

Whitman, S. E. *The Troopers: An Informal History of the Plains Cavalry, 1865–1890.* New York: Hastings House Publishers, 1962.

Wilhelm, Thomas. *A Military Dictionary and Gazetteer.* Philadelphia: L. R. Hamersly, 1881.

Articles

Allen, Charles W. "Red Cloud and the U.S. Flag," 113–21, in *The Nebraska Indian Wars Reader, 1865–1877,* ed. R. Eli Paul. Lincoln: University of Nebraska Press, 1998.

Anderson, Harry H. "A Challenge to Brown's Sioux Indian Wars Thesis," 39–52, in *The Great Sioux War, 1876–77: The Best from* Montana The Magazine of Western History, ed. Paul L. Hedren. Helena: Montana Historical Society Press, 1991.

———. "Cheyennes at the Little Big Horn: A Study of Statistics," *North Dakota Historical Quarterly* 27 (Spring 1960): 81–93.

————."Indian Peace-Talkers and the Conclusion of the Sioux War of 1876," *Nebraska History* 44 (Dec. 1963): 233–54.

————."The War Club of Sitting Bull the Oglala," 122–27, in *The Nebraska Indian Wars Reader, 1865–1877*, ed. R. Eli Paul. Lincoln: University of Nebraska Press, 1998.

Ayres, James Cooper."After Big Game with Packs," *The Century Magazine* 58 (June 1899): 221–29.

Bray, Kingsley M."Crazy Horse and the End of the Great Sioux War," *Nebraska History* 79 (Fall 1998): 94–115.

Brininstool, E. A., ed."Chief Crazy Horse, His Career and Death," *Nebraska History* 12 (Jan.–Mar. 1929): 1–78.

Buecker, Thomas R."'Can You Send Us Immediate Relief?': Army Expeditions to the Northern Black Hills, 1877–1878," *South Dakota History* 25 (Summer 1995): 97–115.

————."Crazy Horse: The Search for the Elusive (and Improbable) Photo of Famous Oglala Chief," *Greasy Grass* 14 (May 1998): 27–35.

————."The Crazy Horse Surrender Ledger: A New Source for Red Cloud Agency History," *Nebraska History* 75 (Summer 1994): 191–94.

————."The 1887 Expansion of Fort Robinson," *Nebraska History* 68 (Summer 1987): 83–93.

————."The Fort and the Railroad: Fort Robinson, Nebraska, on the C&NW," *North Western Lines* 23 (Fall 1996): 23–32.

————."Frederic S. Calhoun: A Little Known Member of the Custer Clique," *Greasy Grass* 10 (May 1994): 16–25.

————."History of Camp Sheridan, Nebraska," *Periodical: Journal of America's Military Past* 22 (1995): 55–73.

————."An Indian Department Marked Issue Blanket," *The Museum of the Fur Trade Quarterly* 32 (Summer 1996): 7–11.

————."Lt. William Philo Clark's Sioux War Report and Little Big Horn Map," *Greasy Grass* 7 (May 1991): 11–21.

————."The Long Summer: Red Cloud Agency and Camp Robinson in 1876," *7th Annual Symposium of the Custer Battlefield and Historical Museum Association* (1993): 1–12.

————."'The Men Behaved Splendidly': Guy V. Henry's Famous Cavalry Rides," *Nebraska History* 78 (Summer 1997): 54–63.

————."Red Cloud Agency Traders," *The Museum of the Fur Trade Quarterly* 30 (Fall 1994): 4–14.

————."The Uncertain Surrender: Crazy Horse at Red Cloud Agency," *12th Annual Symposium of the Custer Battlefield and Historical Museum Association* (1998).

———— and R. Eli Paul."Cheyenne Outbreak Firearms," *The Museum of the Fur Trade Quarterly* 29 (Summer 1993): 2–12.

Carroll, John M., ed."Extracts from Letters Written by Lieutenant Alexander R. Piper, 8th

Infantry, at Pine Ridge Agency, South Dakota, to His Wife, Marie Cozzens Piper, at Fort Robinson, Nebraska, during the Sioux Campaign, 1890–1891," in *The Unpublished Papers of the Order of Indian Wars* 10. New Brunswick, N.J.: Privately published, 1977.

———, ed. "Letter from Brigadier General Guy H. Preston," in *The Unpublished Papers of the Order of Indian Wars* 7. New Brunswick, N.J.: Privately published, 1977.

Clow, Richmond L. "General Philip Sheridan's Legacy: The Pony Campaign of 1876," *Nebraska History* 57 (Winter 1976): 461–77.

Covington, James W. "Causes of the Dull Knife Raid," *The Chronicles of Oklahoma* 26 (Spring 1948): 13–22.

"Crazy Horse's Story of Custer Battle," *South Dakota Historical Collections* 6 (1912): 224–28.

Dickson, Ephriam D., III. "Crazy Horse: Who Really Wielded Bayonet that Killed the Oglala Leader?," *Greasy Grass* 12 (May 1996): 2–10.

Epp, Todd D. "The State of Kansas v. Wild Hog, et al," *Kansas History* 5 (Summer 1982): 139–46.

Grange, Roger T. "Fort Robinson, Outpost on the Plains," *Nebraska History* 39 (Sept. 1959): 191–241.

———. "Treating the Wounded at Fort Robinson," *Nebraska History* 45 (Sept. 1964): 273–94.

Guentzel, Richard. "The Department of the Platte and Western Settlement, 1866–1877," *Nebraska History* 56 (Fall 1975): 389–418.

Hatfield, Shelly B. "The Death of Emmet Crawford," *The Journal of Arizona History* 29 (Summer 1988): 131–48.

Hedren, Paul L. "Camp Hat Creek, Wyoming," *Periodical: Journal of the Council of Abandoned Military Posts* 6 (Winter 1974–75): 29–32.

———. "The Crazy Horse Medal: An Enigma from the Great Sioux War," *Nebraska History* 75 (Summer 1994): 195-99; and "Postscript," *Nebraska History* 77 (Summer 1996): 114.

———. "Eben Swift's Army Service on the Plains," *Annals of Wyoming* 50 (Spring 1978): 141–55.

———. "Holy Ground: The United States Army Embraces Custer's Battlefield," in *Legacy: New Perspectives on the Battle of the Little Big Horn*, ed. Charles E. Rankin (Helena: Montana Historical Society Press, 1996): 189–206.

———. "The Sioux War Adventures of Dr. Charles V. Petteys, Acting Assistant Surgeon," *Journal of the West* 32 (Apr. 1993): 29–37.

Henry, Guy V. "A Sioux Episode," *Harper's Weekly* 40 (Dec. 26, 1896): 1273–74.

———. "A Winter March to the Black Hills," *Harper's Weekly* 39 (July 1895): 700.

Hutcheson, Grote. "The Ninth Regiment of Cavalry," 65–75, in *The Black Military Experience in the American West*, ed. John M. Carroll. New York: Liveright Publishing Corp., 1971.

Keller, Robert H., Jr. "Episcopal Reformers and Affairs at Red Cloud Agency, 1870–1876," *Nebraska History* 68 (Fall 1987): 116–26.

Knight, Oliver. "War or Peace: The Anxious Wait for Crazy Horse," 161–79, in *The Nebraska Indian Wars Reader, 1865–1877*, ed. R. Eli Paul. Lincoln: University of Nebraska Press, 1998.

Lee, Jesse M. "The Capture and Death of An Indian Chieftain," *The Journal of the Military Service Institution* 54 (May–June 1914): 323–40.

Lemly, H. R. "The Passing of Crazy Horse," *The Journal of the Military Service Institution* 54 (May–June 1914): 317–22.

Loudon, Betty, ed. "Pioneer Pharmacist J. Walter Moyer's Notes on Crawford and Fort Robinson in the 1890s," *Nebraska History* 58 (Spring 1977): 89–117.

Mahnken, Norbert R., "The Sidney–Black Hills Trail," *Nebraska History* 30 (Sept. 1949): 203-25.

McDermott, John D. "Were They Really Rogues?: Desertion in the Nineteenth-Century U.S. Army," *Nebraska History* 78 (Winter 1997): 165–74.

McGillycuddy, Valentine T. "Dr. McGillycuddy's Story of Crazy Horse," *Nebraska History* 12 (Jan.–Mar. 1929): 35–42.

Millard, Bailey. "The Man Who Captured Crazy Horse," *Human Life*, Sept. 1909.

Murray, Robert A.. "The United States Army in the Aftermath of the Johnson County War," *Annals of Wyoming* 38 (Apr. 1966): 59–75.

Parker, Watson. "The Majors and the Miners: The Role of the U.S. Army in the Black Hills Gold Rush," *Journal of the West* 2 (Jan. 1972): 99–113.

Perry, Alex W. "The Ninth Cavalry in the Sioux Campaign of 1890," 251–54, in *The Black Military Experience in the American West*, ed. John M. Carroll. New York: Liveright Publishing Corp., 1971.

Potter, James E. "'He . . . Regretted Having to Die That Way': Firearms Accidents in the Frontier Army, 1806–1891," *Nebraska History* 78 (Winter 1997): 175–86.

———. "The Pageant Revisited: Indian Wars Medals of Honor in Nebraska, 1865–1879," in R. Eli Paul, ed., *The Nebraska Indian Wars Reader, 1865–1877*. Lincoln: University of Nebraska Press, 1998.

Powers, Ramon S. "The Kansas Indian Claims Commission of 1879," *Kansas History* 7 (Autumn 1984): 199–211.

———. "The Northern Cheyenne Trek Through Western Kansas in 1878: Frontiersmen, Indians and Cultural Conflict," *The Trail Guide* 16 (Sept.–Dec. 1972): 1–35.

———. "Why the Cheyenne Left Indian Territory in 1878: A Cultural Analysis," *Kansas Quarterly* 3 (Fall 1972): 72–81.

Remington, Frederic. "A Sergeant of the Orphan Troop," *Harper's New Monthly Magazine* 95 (Aug. 1897): 441–51.

———. "The Essentials at Fort Adobe," *Harper's New Monthly Magazine* 96 (Apr. 1898): 727–35.

Riley, Paul D., ed. "Oglala Sources on the Life of Crazy Horse: Interviews Given to Eleanor H. Hinman," 180–216, in *The Nebraska Indian Wars Reader, 1865–1877*, ed.

R. Eli Paul. Lincoln: University of Nebraska Press, 1998.

Schubert, Frank N. "The Violent World of Emanuel Stance, Fort Robinson," *Nebraska History* 55 (Summer 1974): 203–19.

————. "The Suggs Affray: The Black Cavalry in the Johnson County War," *Western Historical Quarterly* 4 (Jan. 1973): 57–68.

Shields, Alice. "Army Life on the Wyoming Frontier," *Annals of Wyoming* 13 (Oct. 1941): 332–37.

Stover, Earl F. "Chaplain Henry V. Plummer, His Ministry and His Court-Martial," *Nebraska History* 56 (Spring 1975): 21–50.

Taylor, Charles W. "The Surrender of Red Cloud, 1891," in *The Unpublished Papers of the Order of the Indian Wars* 2, ed. John M. Carroll. New Brunswick, N.J.: Privately published, n.d.

Twitchell, Philip G., ed. "Camp Robinson Letters of Angeline Johnson," *Nebraska History* 77 (Summer 1996): 89–96.

"A Western Hunting Trip, September 1889," *Hayes Historical Journal* 12 (Fall 1992–Winter 1993): 59–64.

Wright, Peter M. "The Pursuit of Dull Knife from Fort Reno in 1878–1879," *The Chronicles of Oklahoma* 46 (Summer 1968): 141–54.

Index